BEACHES
AND COASTS
*

BEACHES
AND COASTS

By

CUCHLAINE A. M. KING, M.A., Ph.D.

Lecturer in Geography
University of Nottingham

LONDON
EDWARD ARNOLD (PUBLISHERS) LTD.

Printed in Great Britain
by W. & J. Mackay & Co Ltd, Chatham

PREFACE

Since D. W. Johnson's book on *Shore Processes and Shoreline Development* was published in 1919 much work has been done on the processes at work on the coast and on the evolution of different coastal areas. A number of books have appeared, such as Shepard's *Submarine Geology*, Steers' *Coastline of England and Wales* and Guilcher's *Morphologie Littorale et Sous-marine*, which deal with coastal features. This work approaches the subject from a rather different aspect, and is an attempt to gather together some of the recent work on coastal problems, especially those associated with the character of the beach.

For most people the seashore is an area for relaxation, but some, such as Civil Engineers concerned with coastal processes, must look more critically at the forces at work on the coast. It is hoped that this book may contain information of use to them and to other workers engaged in research or planning on the beach and coast. Of the forces acting upon the shore, waves are the most important in the development of the beach and coast, but they are also one of the most difficult to analyse, especially near the coast.

My thanks are due to all who have assisted in many ways. I would like to acknowledge gratefully, the help and advice kindly given by Dr. G. E. R. Deacon, F.R.S. and other members of the staff of the National Institute of Oceanography, particularly Mr. Darbyshire, in the preparation of the chapter on waves. However, any errors in this and other chapters are solely my responsibility. Acknowledgement is also made to all who have kindly permitted figures from their published work to be reproduced and especially to the Beach Erosion Board, Washington, whose Technical Memoranda provide a valuable source of data on current research.

The Geography Department,
Nottingham University.
April 1959.

CONTENTS

Chapter 3. WAVES

Chapter 4. MOVEMENT OF MATERIAL ON THE BEACH

CHAPTER 5. BEACH PROFILES—EXPERIMENTAL
RESULTS AND SURVEYING TECHNIQUES

CHAPTER I

THE MAIN FACTORS ON WHICH THE CHARACTER OF THE BEACH DEPENDS

A BEACH is one of the most variable of land forms; it can be there one day and gone the next. This variability provides both opportunity and difficulty for those engaged in a study of beach problems. Opportunity, because beach changes can be measured over an interval of relatively short duration, unlike many other geomorphological processes. The difficulty arises because the observations, under the conditions in which the changes are most rapid, are by no means easy to make. The complexity of the forces causing the beach changes is another major difficulty; it is this that makes the mechanism of the detailed processes causing beach movement so little understood. Knowledge of these forces and their effect on the beach is, however, growing steadily.

A beach is an accumulation of loose material around the limit of wave action. For this book the beach may be taken to extend from the extreme upper limit of wave action to the zone where the waves, approaching from deep water, first cause appreciable movement of the bottom material. The first factor on which the character of the beach depends is the nature of the material of which it is composed; its size, sorting and quantity are all significant factors determining in part its final form. The character of the foundation on which this incoherent beach material rests is also relevant to the study of the beach. Its gradient, height in relation to mean sea level and its permeability are important, while its resistance to erosion is significant in the general rate of development of the coastline. The beach foundation normally has the character of a wave-cut bench; the formation of which has yet to be fully explained, although they occur frequently round the coastline of rocky land masses.

In considering the material of which the beach is formed it is important to differentiate between sand and shingle as the response of the material is different in some very significant respects. The character of the material affects the form of the beach and the way in which the waves break on it, there is, therefore, a somewhat complex inter-relationship between the beach material and the waves working on it.

The waves are the fundamental force operative on the beach. They themselves depend on the winds that generate them in the ocean. The character of wind waves has been studied theoretically by mathematicians, experimentally in model tanks and by direct observation and measurement in the sea; as a result the data on this topic are now numerous. Waves at sea are always complex owing to the variation of the wind and the superposition of numerous wave trains; an analysis of their effect on the beach is inevitably not straightforward. It has, however, been established that particular characteristics of the dominant waves are of great significance in their effect on the beach material. The size of the waves is partly determined by the distance of water over which the wind can blow, known as the fetch of the waves. This factor is closely related to the exposure of the beach; an exposed beach will differ from an otherwise similar one in a sheltered area.

The wind is also important in explaining beach changes; it can work with or against the wave action to produce very different results. The height of the water level can be vitally affected at times by variations in wind and pressure, with which the wind is intimately connected. One of the main causes of the disastrous North Sea flooding in 1953 was the exceptional height to which the water level was raised. Where there is a considerable rise and fall of tide, pressure and wind may cause considerable differences between predicted and actual water levels.

The tide is another important factor affecting beaches, although in the past the importance of tidal currents has tended to be exaggerated; the tide must nevertheless not be ignored. It seems likely that variations in typical beach profiles can be related in some instances to the variations in tidal régime. One beach profile appears to be typical of a tideless sea while another is only found on tidal beaches. Tidal currents may be significant in some areas but their influence in others is doubtful. A good example of this is seen on the north coast of Norfolk where the flood tide current flows east while the direction of movement of beach material is to the west. This is the result of coastal alignment in relation to the direction of approach of the dominant waves and wind from a northerly point.

The main factors affecting the beach may now be summarized; they are:

1. The beach material
2. The waves
3. The wind
4. The tide

Secular changes of sea-level are of significance in the long term, but in the relatively short-term changes they can usually be ignored. Human interference can also have a marked affect on the beach; the building of structures, sea-walls, groynes, harbours and piers all disturb the natural movement of beach material and may cause profound changes in the immediate vicinity and adjoining areas. These may be starved of material or receive an unusually large supply, causing problems of siltation. Bunbury harbour, Western Australia, provides an example of this.[1]

1. BEACH MATERIAL

(a) Character of material

Three aspects of the beach material are important. The first is the grading of the material which is concerned with the distribution of particle size in any one sample. The second is the sorting which considers the variation of particle size from place to place on the beach and the third is the quantity of material. The loose material forming the beach may range from clay-sized particles to large blocks of rock. It is necessary to define the exact limits of the various categories of beach sediment. There are several definitions of beach sediment size, but only three will be mentioned; the one that will be used is that proposed by the British Standard Code of Practice,[2] 1947, issued on behalf of the committee by the British Standards Institution. Table 1 gives the size range of the various groups of sediment in millimetres. Another commonly used classification is based on a geometrical division of the millimetre scale as devised by Wentworth and called after him. This can easily be converted into the third classification as the same divisions are used. Both these are shown on table 2. The third classification was proposed by Inman (1952),[3] it uses ϕ units instead of millimetres, where ϕ is $-\log_2$ of the diameter in millimetres. Although there are minor differences in the ranges covered by the different materials in the first and the last two classifications the range covered by sand is almost the same in each, the differences increase at the extremities of the scales.

TABLE 1

Types		Predominant particle size mm.	Field identification
Stones	boulders	more than 200	Larger than 8 in.
	cobbles	60–200	Mostly between 3 and 8 in.
Gravel	coarse	20–60	Mostly between 7 B.S. sieve and 3 in.
	medium	6–20	
	fine	2–6	
Sand	coarse	0·6–2	Mostly between 7 and 25 B.S.
	medium	0·2–0·6	Mostly between 25 and 72 B.S.
	fine	0·06–0·2	Mostly between 72 and 200 B.S.
Silt	coarse	0·02–0·06	Particles mostly invisible or barely visible to the naked eye. Some plasticity and exhibits dilatancy.
	medium	0·006–0·02	
	fine	0·002–0·006	
Clay		less than 0·002 more than 30%	Smooth to touch, plasticity but no dilatancy.

TABLE 2

Type	φ units	mm. Wentworth
Boulder	more than −8·0	more than 256
Cobble	−8·0 to −6·0	256−64
Pebble	−6·0 to −2·0	64− 4
Granule	−2·0 to −1·0	4− 2
Very coarse sand	−1·0 to 0	2− 1
Coarse sand	0 to 1·0	1− 0·5
Medium sand	1·0 to 2·0	0·5−0·25
Fine sand	2·0 to 3·0	0·25− 0·125
Very fine sand	3·0 to 4·0	0·125− 0·0625
Coarse silt	4·0 to 5·0	0·0625 − 0·0312
Medium silt	5·0 to 6·0	0·0312 − 0·0156
Fine silt	6·0 to 7·0	0·0156 − 0·0078
Very fine silt	7·0 to 8·0	0·0078 − 0·0039
Coarse clay	8·0 to 9·0	0·0039 − 0·00195
Medium clay	9·0 to 10·0	0·00195− 0·00098

The Inman and Wentworth classifications are rather more detailed, having fifteen types of material. The one using φ units is being increasingly used in American work on beach problems, it is, therefore, necessary to be able to compare the two systems. The advantages of the logarithmic scale will be considered when the methods of expressing size characteristics of beach samples are discussed in chapter 4, pp. 158–161.

Sediments in the different size groups possess important and distinctive properties which will be mentioned briefly. The types of material can be divided broadly into two groups; the coarser material, sand and gravel, are non-cohesive especially when they are dry, but the finer materials are cohesive. The non-cohesive materials can be distinguished by the negligible capillary forces in gravel while sand may have appreciable capillarity. Although sand is non-cohesive when dry, when it is damp it can stand at any angle up to vertical (see chapter 9, p. 281 and fig. 9–2); this is not possible in gravel.

The finer materials, silt and clay, possess cohesion; the silts can, however, easily be reduced to powder when they are dry. Clays on the other hand shrink on drying and although they can be broken into lumps when dry they cannot be powdered and are highly cohesive. The term 'dilatancy' is applied to sediments which, when wet and shaken in this state, will exude water. For example, if a pat of silt is shaken and then pressed this water retreats into the silt, leaving a shiny surface because of an increase in volume of pore space. In its dilatant state the deposit is hardened and rendered more resistant to shear. This is the result of the closer packing of the grains rendering the material more resistant but at the same time increasing its capacity to hold water as the volume of the pore spaces increases.

Experiments[4] designed to demonstrate the state of dilatancy in beach material showed that although the physical state was apparently present it did not affect the resistance of the sand under the conditions of the experiment. The material used consisted of very fine sand with 1 – 3 per cent silt and clay, 80 per cent of the material passed a sieve with apertures of 0·12 mm. (100 B.S.). These tests did, however, demonstrate the state of thixotropy which is present in some finer grain beach sediments. This is a state which shows a decrease in viscosity upon agitation or a decreased resistance to shear when the rate of shear increases. Unlike dilatancy, thixotropy in the sediment results in a reduction in resistance with increased rate of shear. The decrease in viscosity ceases as soon as agitation is discontinued. The semi-quicksand character which can be induced in some beach materials is the result of their thixotropic property; this property becomes more effective as the sediment approaches saturation.

The sorting of beach material gives rise to several points of interest, for instance, the sorting of shingle to the top of a beach or the deposition of silt or clay in sheltered runnels on some beaches. There is also the remarkable lateral sorting shown on some shingle beaches of which Chesil beach in Dorset is one of the best known examples. The material ranges in size from pea-sized pebbles at Bridport in the west to cobbles 2–3 in. in diameter at Portland. The sorting is very gradual and uniform and does not show abrupt discontinuities which occur when sand is suddenly replaced by shingle at the top of the beach. Because it is a lateral rather than a perpendicular sorting it is due to a different cause, which will be discussed in chapter 4.

The total thickness of material on the beach is an important factor; the frequency with which the sea can attack the solid rocks of the coast depends to a large extent on this. If the supply of beach material is restricted storm waves can move it entirely from the beach to deeper water, exposing the platform and cliffs to the attack of the waves. If, on the other hand, there is a considerable thickness of beach material it is unlikely that storms will sweep the platform clear and the beach will therefore be an efficient protection to the coast from wave attack. This point is considered in detail in chapter 9.

(b) Source of material

The material on the beach can come from one or more of four sources, the cliffs behind the beach, from the land via the rivers or to a lesser degree as a rule by the wind, from offshore and finally alongshore. The material moving alongshore must itself have been derived originally from one of the first three sources. The relative proportion of material from these sources will vary in different areas. A beach backed by cliffs of glacial sand and gravel, for example parts of Holderness or Norfolk and Suffolk, will derive much material from this source as the cliffs can be easily attacked by the sea. However, not all the material eroded from the cliffs goes to replenish the beaches; Valentin (1954)[5] has shown that only 3 per cent of the material worn from the boulder clay cliffs of Holderness reaches the sandy spit of Spurn Head to the south. On the other hand beaches backed by cliffs of hard rock, as in Cornwall, receive little each year from this source. The evidence of inter-glacial features on such coasts indicates that this source is negligible over a considerable period of time. Clearly, for this source of material to be available the sea must be able to attack the cliffs at intervals at least; it will not be a source of material on those beaches which are so thick and high that they are an effective protection to the cliffs.

Naturally the supply of material reaching the beaches from inland will depend on the nature of the hinterland; its type of rock, stage of erosion, vegetation and climate are all relevant factors in determining the amount and calibre of the load which the rivers carry down to the sea. Observations reported by the Royal Commission on Coast Erosion (1911)[6] show that at the mouth of the Humber the water is much less charged with sediment in suspension than farther up the river, indicating that in this area the finer sediment is derived largely from inland. In areas where there is not drainage to the coast, the wind may be more important in carrying sediment to the sea. In other places material may be brought to the sea by glaciers or fluvio-glacial streams as in south-east Iceland.

The heavy mineral analysis of river sediment has been carried out by Trask (1952)[7] in California to enable its movement along the shore to be traced. The technique of heavy mineral analysis has been used in some areas to trace the source and distribution of marine sediment. A very detailed study of the sediments of the southern North Sea has been made by Baak (1936).[8] He divides the area into different parts each of which has its own characteristic assemblage of heavy minerals. On the eastern side the H group includes the mixed allochthonous sand of the Dutch group, the A group is related to fluvio-glacial and glacial material from Scandinavia. On the English coast an E group rich in garnet and augite is recognized, while the sediment brought down by the Rhine makes up the final North Hinder group. The sand along the coast of north France, Belgium and Holland, from Dielette near Cherbourg in Normandy eastwards, is very similar due to the resorting by waves of vast quantities of glacial detritus brought into the North Sea and washed through the Straits of Dover. This largely belongs to the H group, with some admixture of the North Hinder group. Detailed work on the mineralogy of the sands of the coasts of Picardy and the Flemish coast has been done by Pugh (1953)[9] which also includes some study of the

English coast in the neighbourhood of Worthing and Folkestone. This shows that there is a distinctive sand which is called the Sussex group.

Material from offshore can reach the beach under the influence of wave action, but the depth from which it can be moved is limited. Work done on the beaches of California by Trask (1955)[10] shows that this movement can only take place to an appreciable extent in water which is less than 60 ft. deep, movement in large quantities is probably confined to depths of about 30 ft. or less. The exposure of the beach is one of the limiting factors in this case; where the beach is open to the full effect of ocean waves the depth at which material can be moved on the bottom will be greater than in sheltered areas.

Summary

The character of the beach depends mainly on the beach material, the waves which are associated with the exposure of the beach, the wind and tide. Human interference can also have profound effects.

Beach material can be differentiated according to size; the different size groups have significant variation in their properties. Gravel is non-cohesive in all states while sand has this property when it is dry, but when damp the grains cohere. Silts and clays possess cohesion. The finer sediments can also have thixotropic and dilatant properties. Three schemes for the classification of material include the British Standard Code of Practise, the Wentworth geometrical scale and the log type ϕ unit scale, they vary slightly in the grade divisions, particularly at the limits of the scales. Sorting and volume of beach material are important factors.

Beach material is derived from the cliffs behind the beach, from inland via the rivers or wind, from offshore and alongshore. The latter material must initially have been derived from one of the first sources. Heavy mineral analysis can give valuable information concerning the source of beach material.

2. WAVES

In this section an attempt will be made to enumerate the characteristics of waves which are significant in their effect on the beach and coast. A more detailed discussion of the theoretical, experimental and observational data which is relevant to the topics discussed later will be given in chapter 3. Oscillatory wind waves in the open ocean are formed by the transference of energy from the wind blowing over the ocean to the water itself. The waves and formulae relating to them discussed in this section are the ideal waves of classical hydrodynamic theory. Waves in the open ocean are more complex and will not be considered in detail in this chapter.

(a) Length, velocity and period

The three properties of wave length, velocity and period are closely associated. In deep water the relationship between the three properties is given by $L = C\,T$, where L is the wave length C is the wave velocity and T is the wave period. The length is the distance between two successive crests, C is the speed of movement of the wave form and the period is the time taken for the wave form to move on the distance of one wave length. The water may be defined as deep when the depth is greater than the wave length. For any one velocity in deep water there is only one appropriate wave length and period. If the period, therefore, is measured in deep water, which can be done relatively easily, the wave length and velocity can be obtained from it. The latter two cannot be measured with ease in the open sea. The relationship between the wave length and period may be given by the formula $L = 5 \cdot 12\ T^2$, where L is the length in feet and T is the period in seconds. The velocity and length are related by the formula $C = \sqrt{\dfrac{g\,L}{2\pi}}$ which is derived from the formula $C = \sqrt{\dfrac{gL}{2\pi}} \tanh \dfrac{2\pi d}{L}$ where g is the force of gravity and d the depth of water. In deep water d/L is large and $\tanh \dfrac{2\pi d}{L}$ approaches 1, giving the first formula. If d/L is $0 \cdot 5$ $\tanh \dfrac{2\pi d}{L}$ is $0 \cdot 9963$, for most purposes, therefore, the water may be considered to be deep if the ratio d to L is more than $0 \cdot 5$. The above formulae apply strictly only to waves of very low amplitude, but can in fact be used for waves of finite height without too much error. To a closer order of accuracy $C = \sqrt{\dfrac{gL}{2\pi}\left(1 + \dfrac{\pi^2 H^2}{2L^2}\right)}$ showing that the steeper waves travel rather faster than the flat waves, but at the maximum steepness H/L of $1/7$ the increase is only about 10 per cent according to Stokes' theory.

(b) Height

The height of the wave, measured vertically from trough to crest is an equally important wave characteristic. It is on the relationship between the two fundamental dimensions of the waves, the length and height, that their effect on the beach ultimately depends.

(c) Steepness

The steepness relationship may be stated in the form of a ratio, H/L, the height over the length, which gives the steepness. It has been known for some time that this factor is fundamental in the constructive and destructive effect of the waves on the foreshore. The steepness cannot exceed 1/7 or the wave becomes unstable and breaks, but this value is rarely reached in nature. Another limiting dimension is that the angle at the crest of the wave must not exceed 120 deg. or the wave will become unstable. Waves in the open ocean are often below 0·02 steepness although they may exceptionally attain steepness value of 0·055, which corresponds to a wave 10 ft. high and 6-sec. period and 184 ft. long. The other wave could have a height of 10 ft. and a length of 512 ft. with a 10-sec. period.

(d) Form

Waves in the open sea are more complex in form than the ideal waves which can be treated theoretically. In the open ocean there are nearly always a large number of waves superimposed on each other giving the water surface a confused appearance. This is more marked in the area where the wind is actively generating waves at the time; here there are waves of different lengths superimposed on one another and variations in the direction of the wind cause still greater confusion. The waves in the area in which they are being generated are known as 'sea', but as they move out of this area into one of calm or light winds they become 'swell'. It is here that the wave pattern and form assumes some measure of order; the shorter, slower travelling waves are left behind and the longer ones dominate the system. Where there is only one major set of waves travelling as a swell they are usually long crested. Their crests are continuous over a considerable distance at right-angles to their direction of movement. These waves may be contrasted with the short-crested waves which occur if two wave trains are travelling in different directions so that their respective crests only occasionally coincide to make a particularly high wave, neither set of waves has continuous crests, owing to the interference of the other set. This interaction of the two sets is shown in fig. 1–1.

According to different theories which will be mentioned later (chapter 3, p. 54), the form of an ideal low wave is sinusoidal or trochoidal, a trochoid being the curve swept out by a point within a circle which is rolled along a straight line. The trochoidal wave has a flatter trough and sharper crest than the smooth profile of a sinusoidal wave whose trough and crest are symmetrical. The asymmetry of the trochoidal wave increases and the crest becomes sharper as the wave steepness increases. Waves in the generating area are even more irregular owing to the effect of the wind.

(e) Energy

The energy of the wave is another important characteristic which depends again on its length and height. The energy determines the

amount of work that any wave can do on the beach but it does not determine whether the work done will be destructive or constructive, which
depends primarily on the wave steepness. Waves of great energy can do
very much more work in a given time than low energy waves, hence the
importance of this characteristic. The energy in a wave in deep water
is half potential, due to the height of the wave crest above the still water
level, and half kinetic, due to the velocity of the water particles within
the wave form. The kinetic energy remains stationary but the potential
energy moves at the wave velocity, thus the total energy of a wave train
moves at half the velocity of the wave form. A train of waves of limited

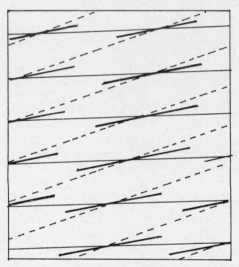

Fig. 1–1. The interference of two wave trains from different directions, giving a short
crested wave pattern.

number travelling through still water appears to move at half the speed
of the individual waves; these appear to travel through the whole train,
forming in the rear and dying out in the front.

The actual amount of energy, E, in ft.-lb. per foot of wave crest per
wave length is given by $E=\dfrac{w\,L\,H^2}{8}$, where w is the weight of 1 cubic
ft. of sea-water (64 lb.). It is clear that the energy depends on the square
of the wave height and one power of the wave length, it increases
rapidly, therefore, as the wave height increases. The formula may be
expressed as $E=0.64\,w\,H^2\,T^2$ or $E=41\,H^2\,T^2$, where T is the wave
period, this enables the wave energy to be calculated from the wave
height and period. These formulae apply strictly only to waves of low
amplitude and sinusoidal form but can in fact be applied to waves of

finite height within the accuracy of observation. The formula for waves of finite height is $E = \dfrac{w\,L\,H^2}{8}\ 1 - 4\cdot93\ \dfrac{H^2}{L^2}.$

(f) Orbital velocity and mass transport

Although the wave form advances with a speed dependent on the length of the wave the actual particles of water normally move at a much lower velocity. At the surface their velocity depends on the wave period and height. They must complete one orbit, whose diameter is equal to the height of the wave during the wave period. Therefore water in high short waves will move more rapidly than that in low, long waves; it is only in breaking waves that the water at the crest of the wave moves more rapidly than the wave form. The movement of the particles on the surface is in very nearly circular orbits, but each time the particle advances slightly in the direction of wave advance, the circles are therefore called open; this slight forward movement of the water is known as the mass transport. The velocity of mass transport is very small compared to the wave velocity and to the orbital velocity of the water especially when the waves are low, it is then almost negligible. It is, however, significant in considering the water movement close inshore, as it involves the movement of considerable volumes of water and affects the velocity of bottom flow.

Beneath the surface the orbits of the particles remain almost circular but they decrease very rapidly in diameter. For every 1/9 of the wave length in depth the orbit is approximately halved; at a depth equal to the wave length the orbit is 1/535 of its surface value and at 1·5 L it is 1/12,400 of its surface value. For most purposes the water can be considered to be still at a depth equal to about one wave length.

(g) Growth

The size of wind waves depends on three factors; these are the wind speed, the wind duration and the fetch. Any one of the three can set a limit to the size of the waves. Thus, however long the wind blew at great speed it could not generate large waves if the fetch, or stretch of open water over which it was blowing, were limited. This limit could be imposed either by the meteorological situation, which determines the distance over which a wind is blowing in a constant direction, or by the configuration of the land which determines the water available for wave generation in some areas. In this way the exposure of a coast is a very significant factor in its characteristic type of beach because it has an effect on the normal size of wave reaching the beach. For example, in a sheltered area, where the fetch is limited long waves will never be generated. The generation of waves is treated more fully in chapter 3.

(h) Decay

When the waves move out of the generating area into an area of calm they change from sea to swell. They cease to grow in size and to gain energy, and may be said to decay. In this process they slowly change form and lose energy. The loss of energy is, however, very slow and swells can be traced for thousands of miles from their generating area. For example waves generated during storms off Cape Horn have been recorded on the Cornish coast after travelling 6,000 miles.

Swells also tend to modify their form slightly as they move through the decay zone. The sharp crests typical of the storm area become rounded and the swell becomes almost sinusoidal. The crests become longer and more uniform. Owing to their great length they may not be very conspicuous especially if smaller local waves are superimposed on them. Such long swells, however, become rejuvenated as they approach a shore and will become the dominant waves on the beach as a result of their great energy due to their considerable length and moderate height.

(i) Changes in shallow water

The rejuvenation of swell as it approaches the coast is due to the changes which the waves undergo as they enter shallow water. All the characteristics of the wave change as they begin to feel the bottom, except the period and initially the energy.

i. LENGTH, PERIOD AND VELOCITY. The velocity of an ideal wave ceases to depend entirely on the wave length; application of the formula $C^2 = \dfrac{gL}{2\pi} \dfrac{\tanh 2\pi d}{L}$ shows that the depth now affects the wave velocity. This leads to a gradual decrease of wave velocity as the water becomes shallow. When the depth of water is less than $0\cdot05$ d/L, $\tanh \dfrac{2\pi d}{L}$ becomes almost $\dfrac{2\pi d}{L}$; the formula now becomes $C^2 = gd$. In very shallow water, therefore, the wave velocity depends only on the depth of water and solitary waves may occur. As the wave velocity decreases so the wave length decreases in proportion. A set of curves shown in fig. 1–2 gives the relationship between wave length, water depth and wave period. From it the length can be read off from the measured period for any required water depth. This technique was used during the 1939–45 war to arrive at a value of the gradient of enemy-held beaches when landings were being planned in Normandy and the Mediterranean (Williams, 1947[11]) (see chapter 5, pp. 194, 195).

ii. HEIGHT. Wave height does not vary with such regularity when the waves enter shallow water. According to Bigelow and Edmonson

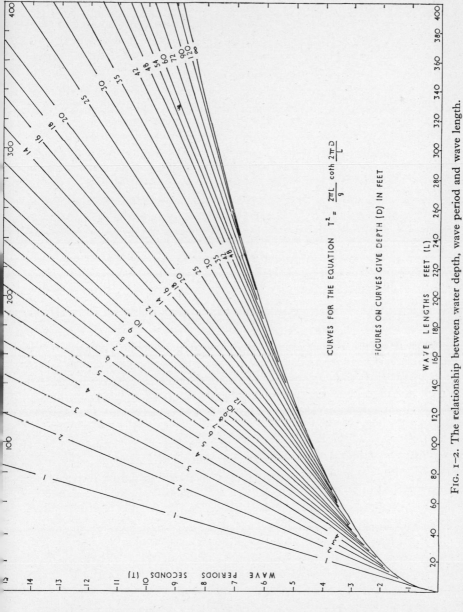

FIG. 1-2. The relationship between water depth, wave period and wave length.

CURVES FOR THE EQUATION $T^2 = \dfrac{2\pi L}{g} \coth \dfrac{2\pi D}{L}$

FIGURES ON CURVES GIVE DEPTH (D) IN FEET

WAVE LENGTHS FEET (L)

WAVE PERIODS SECONDS (T)

(1947)[12] when the ratio d/L falls below 0·5 there is a slight decrease in wave height, which amounts to less than 0·9 H/H_o, the original height is regained when d/L is 0·06 and thereafter there is a rapid increase in height till the break-point is reached, as shown in fig. 1–3. The increase is greater for longer waves than for shorter waves of the same height. Thus a very flat wave may double its deep water height before it breaks, while a very steep wave will only show a small increase.

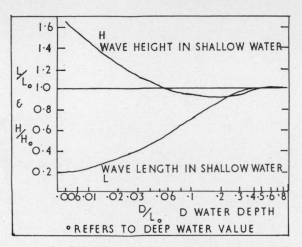

FIG. 1–3. The change of wave length and wave height in relation to the ratio of depth to wave length. (After Russell and Macmillan.)

iii. STEEPNESS. Naturally with the changing wave length and height there is a change in wave steepness; the increase is small at first, because although the waves are becoming shorter their height is not yet increasing. In depths less than $d/L=0.06$, however, the increase is very rapid as the wave length is decreasing while the height is increasing. This increase is rarely sufficient to cause the waves to reach an unstable degree of steepness.

With the change in steepness there is also a change in the form of the wave. The crest of the wave becomes narrower and sharper while the trough becomes longer and flatter. This change in the wave form is most noticeable in long, low swell, in which the smooth sinusoidal crests become sharp and conspicuous.

iv. ENERGY. While the wave length is decreasing and the wave height is increasing the wave energy remains more or less constant, although some energy is lost by contact of the wave with the bottom. The energy, which is uniform along the wave crest in deep water, does not necessarily remain so as the wave enters shallow water. The convergence or divergence of energy in waves in shallow water is the result of wave refraction which will be considered in part 3 of chapter 3, pp. 93–100. It plays an important part in explaining the concentration of wave attack along the coast.

v. ORBITAL VELOCITY. The orbital paths of the water particles within the wave are also modified as the wave enters shallow water. They change from being open circles to become open ellipses, with the longer axis horizontal. The orbital speed of movement no longer remains constant, but as the wave form changes so the orbital velocities change; under the sharp crest of the wave there is a short but rapid landward acceleration, while under the long flat trough there is a much slower seaward movement of water.

The movement along the bottom is particularly significant in shallow water as this exerts a very large influence on the movement of material on the sea bed. Here the water is moving to and fro along the bed approximately horizontally with the acceleration landward under the crest already mentioned and a longer, slower seaward flow under the trough. The increase of wave height with the constant wave period leads to an increase in the orbital velocity of the particles. When the wave gets into shallower water the elliptical orbit is larger than the deep water circular one which also causes an increase in the orbital velocity.

vi. TYPE OF BREAKERS. This increase of the orbital velocity is significant when the breaking of the waves in shallow water is considered. A wave will break when the increasing velocity of the water at the wave crest exceeds the decreasing velocity of the wave form. The water then overtakes the wave form and the wave falls over and breaks. Another factor affecting the breaking of waves relates to the decrease in volume of water within the wave form. As the particle orbits increase in size the water in the wave is reduced by the decrease in wave length so that insufficient water remains to complete the orbit causing the front of the wave to become unsupported. The crest, therefore, collapses into the trough and the wave breaks. Breaking will occur when the depth of water is about 4/3 of the wave height at break-point. A flat wave may break in water which is twice as deep as its deep water height owing to the increase in height from deep water to the break-point.

There are two types of breakers depending largely on the beach gradient and the wave steepness; these are plunging and spilling breakers (see fig. 1–4). The former type, in which the crest of the wave falls into the trough enclosing a pocket of air, normally occurs when a fairly low wave approaches a steep beach; this type of breaker is therefore common on steep shingle beaches. The form of the wave is lost in the process of breaking. A spilling breaker, on the other hand, advances at the correct speed for the depth with a foaming crest; the wave does not loose its identity, but gradually decreases in height until it becomes swash on the beach. Such waves are often fairly steep in deep water and advance over a gently sloping, usually sandy beach. It is these waves that produce several rows of breakers advancing shoreward simultaneously and they may be called surf waves. The two types of breakers grade into each other. In all plunging breakers some part of the front face of the wave must be vertical as they break, which is not necessarily so in spilling breakers.

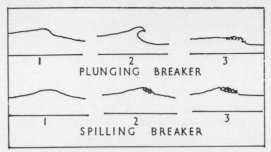

FIG. 1–4. Plunging and spilling breakers.

vii. BREAKING ON WALLS, CLIFFS, ETC. Whenever a wave approaches a beach it almost always breaks but this does not necessarily happen when a wave approaches a vertical cliff or sea-wall extending into relatively deep water. In this case the wave may be reflected without breaking. When this occurs an equal and opposite wave travels seawards from the vertical structure. This, however, is rarely truly vertical and smooth with a sufficient depth of water below it to allow a perfect reflection for which the waves must also approach parallel to the shore. Where a vertical barrier does descend into deep water the reflected wave interacts with the primary wave to form a standing wave or deep water clapotis, as shown in fig. 1–5 (A). The wave crests do not advance under these conditions but the wave troughs and crests rise and fall as shown in the diagram, with nodes occurring every half-wave length. If the incoming wave is not parallel to the structure, they will be reflected at an angle equal to their angle of incidence, a diagonal crest pattern resulting. Such a pattern can rarely be seen well developed in nature but can be generated in a model wave-tank.

A more likely result of waves approaching a sea-wall or cliff is the formation of a shallow water clapotis, which occurs when the depth of water is not sufficient for a perfect reflection (see fig. 1–5 (B)). The reflected wave is not now perfectly formed owing to the loss of energy of the advancing wave over the relatively shallow bed. The retreating wave, of smaller amplitude, can be seen passing through the advancing wave. In both these types the pressures exerted on the cliff or wall is approximately equal to the hydrostatic pressure of the water, if it were still.

If the water is even shallower the returning wave will not be formed as the energy of the wave will be destroyed by breaking. If the wave breaks against the wall, this will be subjected to the force of the moving particles, which will be approximately equal to the wave velocity at that point, but shock pressures will not result (see fig. 1–5 (C)). When, however, the water is sufficiently shallow to allow the breaking wave to trap a pocket of air between the wall and the water as it breaks then shock pressures are likely to be set up leading to damage to the structure or erosion of the cliff. High pressures are set up due to the compression of the air as the wave breaks (see fig. 1–5 (D)). If the water is so shallow that the wave breaks before it reaches the base of the wall, no shock pressures will be experienced and the wave form will be lost (see fig. 1–5 (E)).

viii REFRACTION. While reflection only occurs when waves actu-

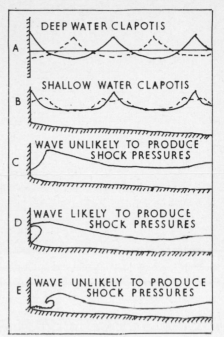

FIG. 1–5. The effect of waves on vertical structures in relation to the depth of water. (After Russell and Macmillan.)

ally reach a steep coast, refraction takes place as soon as the wave begins to feel the bottom. It results from the change of wave length and velocity as the wave enters shallow water. The result is to turn the wave crest to approach the shore more nearly parallel. That part of the wave which is in deeper water moves more rapidly than the part in shallower water which causes the crest to swing round parallel to the bottom contours. As the crests swing round so the distribution of energy along them ceases to be uniformly spaced, as shown by the orthogonals, which are lines drawn everywhere at right angles to the wave crests. There is a concentration of energy on the headlands and a dissipation in the bays if the waves approach the coast at right-angles as shown in the diagram, fig. 1–6. Less obvious, perhaps, but equally significant, is the convergence of orthogonals and wave energy over submarine ridges and the divergence over submarine valleys. This can occur even if the coastline itself is straight. It leads to a variation in the height of the waves along the coast, which reflects the variation of wave energy distribution. The method of construction of wave refraction diagrams will be considered in chapter 3, pp. 93–96

ix. LONGSHORE CURRENTS. Very significant in the action of the waves

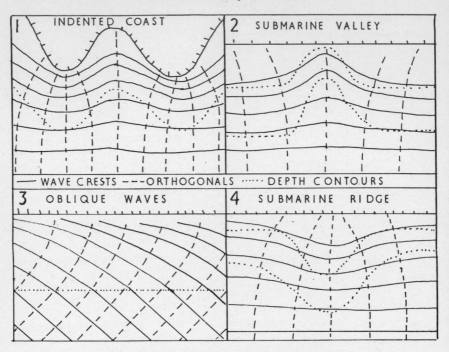

FIG. 1–6. Diagrammatic wave refraction patterns.

on the shore is the effect of wave generated currents. Some of these are directly due to wave refraction which, as has been shown, causes zones of convergence and divergence. These wave currents flow from the zones of energy concentration and high waves to areas of divergence and low wave energy values. They have been studied in some detail on the coast of California in the neighbourhood of the Scripps Institute of Oceanography where submarine canyons approach very close to the shore and the waves are long, thus giving favourable conditions for the generation of such currents. Longshore currents due to wave action can also be generated close inshore when waves approach the coast obliquely. These currents, unlike the former type, are more pronounced in shorter waves which suffer less refraction before they reach the coast and therefore lie at a greater angle to it and can generate relatively rapid longshore currents.

Another type of wave-induced current which may or may not be related to the first type is the rip current. It may be the result of the landward transport of water by mass movement. The water moving shorewards must escape to the sea in some way and this may be achieved by the formation of localized seaward directed currents (see fig. 1–7). Their speed may attain 2 knots where they are concentrated in the surf zone, but once through the surf zone they tend to spread out and lose their velocity. More detailed references are given to these topics in chapter three in which they are treated more fully.

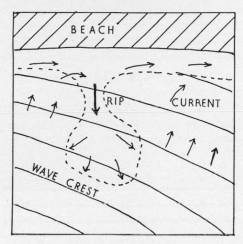

FIG. 1–7. Diagram to show rip currents.

Summary

Ideal waves are defined by their height, length, period and velocity; the last three properties are connected by $L = C\,T$ and L (feet) is $5 \cdot 12\ T^2$ (seconds) when waves are in water deeper than half the wave length. Height and length are related to give the steepness ratio H/L. Waves in the generating area are known as 'sea', outside it they are called 'swell'. Where two or more sets of waves, coming from different directions, are present they interact to become short crested, some swells may be long crested. Ideal waves are approximately sinusoidal in form. The energy of waves is given by $E = 41\ H^2\ T^2$ in ft. lb./ft. of wave crest/wave length. The water particles move in open circles whose diameter decreases at the rate of $\frac{1}{2}$ for every $1/9L$ downwards about. A slight mass transport of water occurs in the direction of wave motion. Waves grow by the transference of energy from the air and depend on the fetch, velocity and duration of the wind. They are propagated from the generating area and as they proceed lose energy by decrease of height but can be traced for thousands of miles.

In shallow water all their dimensions change except the period. The length and velocity decrease; the height, after an initial small decrease, increases rapidly near the break-point. Steepness increases rapidly near the break-point. Energy remains more or less uniform except on very flat coasts but may be concentrated or dissipated by refraction at different places along the shore. The particle orbits now become open ellipses and accelerations develop in the to and fro movement on the bottom. A wave breaks when d_b/H_b is about $4/3$ and breakers are of two types; a spilling breaker is more characteristic of a flat beach while plunging breakers occur often on steeper beaches. Where waves approach a vertical structure or cliff reflection occurs if the water is deep, but when it is such that the wave can trap air as it breaks on the structure shock pressures may be set up. Refraction occurs as the waves feel bottom and turns the wave crest more nearly parallel to the bottom contours. The orthogonals illustrate the distribution of energy along the coast. Concentration of wave energy may set up longshore currents and rip currents may represent the escape seaward of water carried landward by mass transport. Longshore currents may also be set up by short oblique waves.

3. *TIDES*

In contrast to the variable and unpredictable nature of the waves, the rise and fall of the tide is normally both regular and predictable; it exerts a considerable influence on the function of beach processes nevertheless. In this section the significance of the tide to beach problems is considered and a short account of the main factors on which its type and range depend is given.

The tide affects beach processes in two ways. Firstly, because of the rise and fall of the water level and, secondly, because it gives rise to currents. On a tideless coast the area of beach coming under any particular part of the wave action is small in dimensions and is limited by the size of the waves themselves, and as long as these remain constant the position of the break-point and extent of the swash will remain constant. This has an important bearing on the beach profile as will be fully explained in chapter 10. Where, on the other hand, the tidal range is considerable the break-point of the waves is never fixed in position for long periods and the effect of the swash can be exerted over a wide stretch of beach. This has an important bearing on the formation of certain types of beach profile and on the cutting of such features as wave-cut platforms.

The exceptionally high water levels which occasionally occur might be mentioned as they are often responsible for spectacular changes or damage to the coast and coastal structures. They are not tidal in origin but may appear to be related to the normal tidal rise and fall. The cause of such surges is usually due to abnormal meteorological circumstances. In extreme cases the height of the high water may be raised by up to 10 ft. above the predicted level, as occurred on the coast of Holland during the storm-floods of January–February 1953, with disastrous consequences to the sea defences. The height above the predicted level on the Lincolnshire coast was 7·8 ft., which was sufficient to cause considerable damage; but had the crest of the surge coincided with the normal high water the height of the tide would have been at least 2 ft. higher at high water, which would have greatly intensified the damage. Fig. 1–8 shows the actual and predicted tide curves.

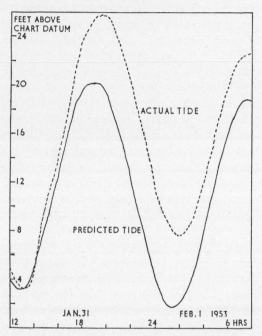

FIG. 1–8. The actual and predicted tide curve for Immingham on Jan. 31 and Feb. 1, 1953.

The variation of water level during the tidal cycle is probably of greater significance on many parts of the coast than the tidal currents. At one time many coastal features were explained by reference to tidal currents but they are now thought to be of less significance than wave action in the formation of many coastal land-forms. The fact that tidal currents are reversed at each change of tide reduces their capacity to move beach material. The flood current usually flows in one direction while the ebb current often flows with almost equal strength in the opposite direction. It must, however, be remembered that these two opposing currents will probably be acting at different levels on the beach, thus material on the upper beach may be carried in one direction by the flood tide at high water, while at low water this part of the beach will be exposed to the air and the lower part will be under the influence of reversed currents.

On the open coast tidal currents are rarely of sufficient velocity to enable them to pick material off the sea-bed and transport it alongshore, but even if they are weak they can move material that has first been thrown into suspension by the waves. In river mouths and estuaries, however, the currents may attain sufficient velocity to enable them to carry considerable quantities of material; for example, the strength of the tidal currents at the southern extremity of Orford Ness in Suffolk reaches 8 or 9 knots when the flood and ebb streams reach their maximum.

(a) Tide producing forces

The general principles of modern tidal theory which explain the type and range of the tide will be briefly discussed to enable the cause of this factor to be more fully appreciated. Before attempting to consider the tides as they occur in the oceans and seas the tide producing forces will be briefly mentioned. These forces are caused by the gravitational attraction of the Sun and Moon on the Earth and are, therefore, closely related to the movement of these three bodies. Their movements are somewhat complex as neither the Earth in its orbit round the Sun nor the Moon in its orbit follow circular paths; also the Earth's orbit or ecliptic lies at an angle of $23\frac{1}{2}$ deg. to the equator, while the Moon's orbit lies at an angle of 5·9 deg. to the ecliptic. The result is that the value of the tidal forces at any one place vary with the change in declination of the Sun and Moon, giving a complex pattern of tidal forces. These are, however, susceptible to harmonic analysis by which method the complex curves may be simplified. Before considering this analysis it should be remembered that owing to its greater distance away the forces due to the Sun are only 0·46 those of the Moon. The cube of the distances more than balances the one power of the masses of the Sun and Moon as both quantities enter into the formula which gives the tractive force of the bodies. $T=\dfrac{3g}{2}\dfrac{M}{E}\dfrac{e^3}{r^3}\sin 2C$. T is the tractive force, g is gravity, M and E the mass of the Moon and Earth respectively, e the Earth's radius and r the Moon's distance and C the angular distance of the point measured at the centre of the Earth from the line of centres. It is important to make it clear that it is the tractive force exerted by the Moon or Sun which is important rather than the direct attractive force; this latter force acts only in a direction perpendicular to the Earth's surface while the tractive force acts horizontally along the surface. The tractive force has a maximum value of 0·000,000,084 g when the Moon is at its mean distance.

When the Moon is overhead at the equator (zero declination) the tractive forces are symmetrical, producing two maxima and two minima during one lunar day (24·8 solar hours) and the actual value of the force varies with the latitude. This is called the semi-diurnal tide-producing force. If, however, the declination of the Moon is not zero the forces no longer remain symmetrical. Their value can most easily be appreciated, for a lunar declination of 15°N, by considering fig. 1–9. From the stereographic projection the direction and value of the tractive force at latitude 30°N can be found for every hour, giving the complex curve shown in fig. 1–9 (b). This curve can be simplified by splitting it up into its northerly and easterly components as shown in fig. 1–9 (c). It is apparent that even these curves are not symmetrical. The process must be carried one stage farther and these curves again split up into their component symmetrical curves. Fig. 1–9 (d) shows the northerly component. The resulting curves clearly differ in that one has two maxima and the other only one. The tide producing force has now been split up into its semi-diurnal and diurnal components. The diurnal component is, therefore, a function of the declination of the moon; it is nil when the declination of the Moon is zero and a maximum when the Moon's declination is greatest. The semi-diurnal force on the other hand will be reduced at times of high declination. The forces due to the Sun will be similar to those of the Moon but smaller and their period will be that of solar time not lunar.

(b) Types of wave motion in tides

So far only the actual forces have been mentioned but the oceans will react to these forces in a way that can be related to them and analysed in a similar way, although the relationship is not always very apparent. This is because the actual oceans are very different from an ideal ocean covering the whole world with very deep water. In order to appreciate the reaction of the oceans to these forces the types of wave motion and the effect of the rotation of the earth of these types of movement must be mentioned.

One type of wave motion is the progressive wave, whose main characteristics are that the maximum flow occurs at the crest of the wave in the direction of propagation and at the trough in the opposite direction; its velocity, c, is given by $c = \sqrt{gd}$, where d is the depth of the water. The wave velocity depends, therefore, only on the depth of water. If a progressive wave advances against a vertical barrier it will be reflected from it to form the second type of wave, the standing or stationary wave. When a perfect reflection takes place in this way an equal wave moves in the opposite direction to the primary one and reacts with it in such a way that at the maximum and minimum elevations there are now no

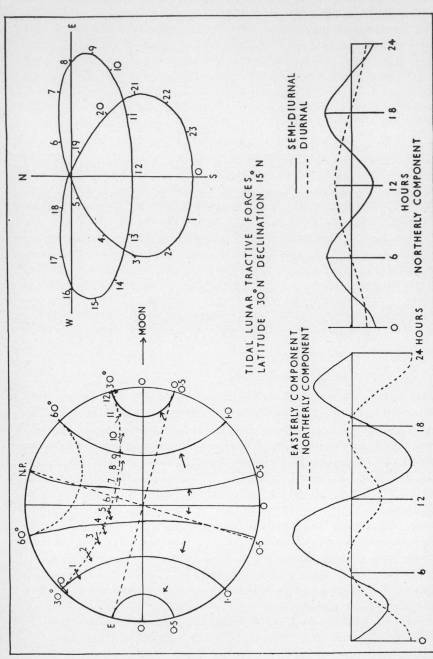

TIDAL LUNAR TRACTIVE FORCES.
LATITUDE 30°N DECLINATION 15 N

SEMI-DIURNAL
DIURNAL

NORTHERLY COMPONENT

HOURS

EASTERLY COMPONENT
NORTHERLY COMPONENT

Fig. 1–9. Lunar tractive forces for a lunar declination of 15°N. at latitude 30°N. (After Doodson and Warburg.) A.M.T. Figs. 1–9, 10, 11, 12, 14, 15 and 16 are reproduced by permission of the Controller of H.M. Stationery Office and the Hydrographer of the Navy.

currents, while when the surface is flat the streams reach their maximum velocity as shown in fig. 1–10.

This type of wave may also be formed in an enclosed basin by oscillating the water within it. In a standing wave of this type the water will oscillate about a nodal line so that when the water reaches its maximum slope the streams will be nil but when the surface is flat they will reach their maximum velocity. The period of oscillation of such a basin, having one central nodal line, is given by $T = \dfrac{2L}{\sqrt{gd}}$, where L is the length of the basin and d is its depth. Thus the period of the stationary wave or standing oscillation is equal to that of a progressive wave whose length is twice that of the basin. The natural period of oscillation of any body of water will, therefore, depend largely on its dimensions, its length and depth. This is very important as it is now thought that the tides in the ocean are mainly of the standing oscillation type.

The tides cannot, however, be closely related to the simple standing oscillation as another important modifying factor must be taken into account. This is the rotation of the earth or the gyratory force. This movement has the effect of deflecting moving particles to the right of their path in the northern hemisphere and to the left in the southern hemisphere. The force may also cause a transverse gradient to build up making the water on the right of the current at a higher elevation than that on the left in the northern hemisphere. The adjustment may take place either by transverse streams or by developing a transverse gradient or by a combination of both.

(c) Effect of the earth's gyration (amphidromic systems)

The application of the gyratory force to a standing oscillation may now be considered. In a rectangular basin as shown in fig. 1–11 it will, in the absence of gyration, be high water at one end and low water at the other with no currents at hour 0. At hour 3 the surface will be flat but a current will be flowing west across the nodal line, hour 6 is a reverse of hour 0 and hour 9 of hour 3, completing the sequence. Adding the effects of gyration the subsidiary elevations and currents shown in the figure will occur. When the current is flowing strongly west at hour 3 it will build up a gradient giving high water at the north of the basin at this time; at hour 9, when the current is flowing east, this secondary elevation will be at the south end of the basin; in between subsidiary currents will be directed southwards at hour 6 and north at hour 0. These two sets of movement combined are called an amphidromic system because the tide, instead of oscillating about a nodal line, now moves round a nodal point. It will be seen that high water now progresses round the basin in an anticlockwise direction in the northern hemisphere.

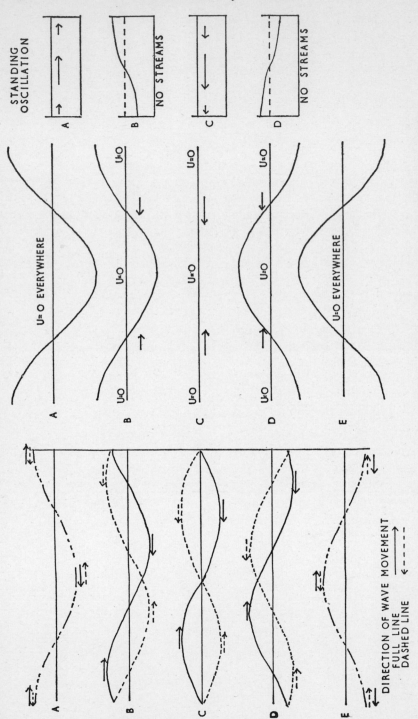

FIG. 1-10. Reflected progressive wave and standing oscillation. (After Doodson and Warburg.) A.M.T.

If the currents are now considered it will be apparent that they are also moving anticlockwise round the basin, at high water the current, therefore, is moving in the same direction as the wave crest, while at low water it is moving in the opposite direction. Now this is a characteristic of the progressive wave, the type of motion is now like that of a progressive wave moving round a point, anticlockwise in the northern hemisphere and clockwise in the southern hemisphere. The range of the tide will be greatest round the coast and least in the centre near the amphidromic point where it is nil.

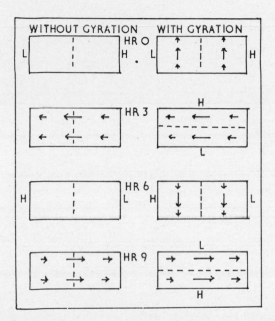

FIG. 1–11. Standing oscillation modified by gyration. (After Doodson and Warburg.) A.M.T.

(d) Oceanic tides

To a greater or lesser degree it appears that the tides in the oceans as well as the adjacent seas are based on the operation of a series of amphidromic systems. The response of the different water bodies to the tide-producing forces depends to a large extent on the principle of resonance. It has been shown that any body of water has a natural period of oscillation dependent on its dimensions; if this natural period of oscillation approximates to the period of one of the tide-producing forces it will naturally react to that period and a state of resonance will be set up. Harris, at the end of the last century, was one of the first to emphasize the importance of resonance; he drew a co-tidal chart of the oceans divided into oscillating areas, but because he ignored the rotation of the earth his map lacks reality. The co-tidal chart constructed by Sterneck in 1920 shows a pattern of amphidromic systems in the Atlantic Ocean.

Most of the coasts of the Atlantic Ocean have tides which are predominantly semi-diurnal in type, the diurnal inequality of the tide is therefore small. This is because the Atlantic Ocean is of dimensions which respond most readily to the period of the semi-diurnal tide producing forces. On the Pacific coasts, in British Columbia and California, for example, there is a marked diurnal inequality of the tide, one high water being much higher than the other. This is probably due to the fact that the Pacific Ocean is large enough to react to the diurnal as well as the semi-diurnal tide-producing forces. In tides of this type there is a variation of the tide as the moon progresses through its cycle of declination, the inequality being greatest at times of high declination and, therefore, the diurnal factor is greatest also. In some parts of the Pacific Ocean the tides appear to follow the sun instead of the moon, as for example in Indo-China and Tahiti, this can be explained if the area is near the amphidromic point of the lunar tidal system but far away from that of the solar tidal system.

The same principle of resonance can be applied to gulfs and seas as has been applied to the main ocean basins. The Bay of Fundy, with its very high tidal range, has a natural period of oscillation of between 11·6 and 13 hours, which corresponds closely to the tidal semi-diurnal period. This area is also interesting in that it does not appear to respond so much to the normal spring and neap tidal periods, related to the co-operation or otherwise of the Sun and Moon, as to the variation in distance of the Moon from the Earth; this is called an anamolistic tide or perigee/apogee tide.

(e) Tides around the British Isles

The North Sea also demonstrates the point of resonance. Its dimensions are such that it responds to the tidal movements in the open Atlantic to produce three amphidromic points as shown in fig. 1–12. The position of the points as shown on the Admiralty Chart No. 301 (5058) (see fig. 1–13) demonstrate the effect of friction, which has not yet been mentioned. Friction, in a shallow sea like the North Sea, has the effect of moving the amphidromic points eastwards away from the source of tidal energy which approaches from the north and moves anti-clockwise round the basin.

The tidal chart of the English Channel shows a further stage in this process. Here the amphidromic point has moved inland and is said to have become degenerate. This has the result of greatly decreasing the tidal range on the English coast in the neighbourhood of the Isle of

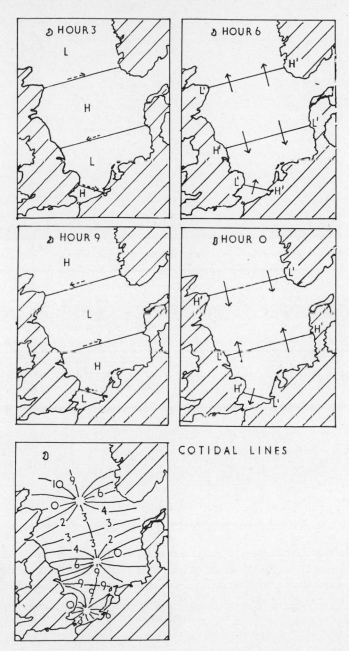

FIG. 1–12. Tides in the North Sea. The figures in the lower map refer to times of high water. (After Doodson and Warburg.) A.M.T.

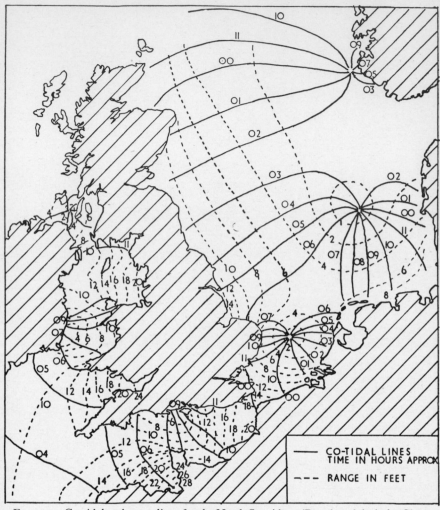

FIG. 1–13. Co-tidal and range lines for the North Sea tides. (Based on Admiralty Chart No. 5058 with the permission of H.M. Stationery Office and the Hydrographer of the Navy.)

Wight in relation to the range on the French coast, which is very great in the region around St. Malo. Again this is probably due to friction influencing the position of an amphidromic point which should have been in the centre of the channel in the absence of friction, with the tide moving anticlockwise round it, that is eastwards along the French coast and westwards along the English coast. This same feature is also apparent in the southern Irish Sea where there is a degenerate amphidromic point off south-east Ireland south of Dublin.

(f) Shallow water effects

The presence of an area of low tidal range off the south coast of England is one of the factors which helps to explain the interesting double tidal phenomena which occur around the Solent. This feature is probably due to a shallow water effect. It can best be appreciated by considering the deformation which a progressive wave undergoes as it enters shallow water as shown in fig. 1–14 (a). The smooth sine form

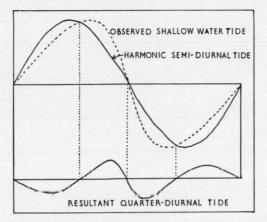

OBSERVED SHALLOW WATER TIDE

HARMONIC SEMI-DIURNAL TIDE

RESULTANT QUARTER-DIURNAL TIDE

FIG. 1–14. Shallow water tidal modification of a progressive wave. (After Doodson and Warburg.) A.M.T.

of the wave is modified because at the crest of the wave the water is deeper. As the speed depends on the depth of water this results in an acceleration of the wave crest and a retardation of the trough causing the form of the wave to become asymmetrical, with a steep front and gentle back slope. This asymmetrical curve can be split into its component parts in the same way as before, the two curves consist of a large sine curve and a smaller asymmetrical curve having two maxima to the one of the main curve. Because the curve of small amplitude has two crests it is called a quarter-diurnal tide as the original was a semi-diurnal tide curve. It can itself be split into its component sixth, eighth and higher species of tide, by the same technique of harmonic analysis. These curves have a phase lag of about 90 deg. so that they can never combine to give double high or low water.

When a standing oscillation enters shallow water it appears that the deformation is such that when the tidal curve is analysed harmonically the phase lag is often about 0 deg. or 180 deg. as shown in fig. 1–15 (a and b). This means that the semi-diurnal tide is high when the quarter-diurnal tide is high or low respectively. Thus with a phase relationship of o deg. the two curves combine to give a double low water if their amplitudes are suitable, while if the phase relationship is 180 deg. a double high water should result.

In order to form a double high or low tide most simply the amplitude of the quarter-diurnal tide must be more than $\frac{1}{4}$ of the semi-diurnal tide, or the sixth-diurnal tide must be more than 1/9 of the semi-diurnal tide. This is most likely to occur with respect to the quarter-diurnal tide near the node of the semi-diurnal tide. Fig. 1–15 (c) shows that this is also likely to be near the maximum of the quarter-diurnal tide if they occur in a closed channel as shown. These conditions

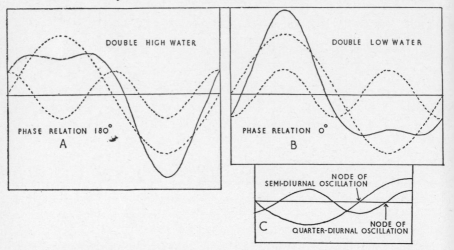

FIG. 1–15. Shallow water tides. A. Double high water. B. Double low water. C. Relation of $\frac{1}{2}$ and $\frac{1}{4}$ diurnal nodes. (After Doodson and Warburg.) A.M.T.

are well fulfilled in the Solent area, which is near the node of the degenerate amphidromic system in the English Channel. Freshwater, Isle of Wight, illustrates the formation of a double low water by the simplest means. The phase relation is +176 deg., the semi-diurnal tide has an amplitude of 2·02, the quarter-diurnal tide has an amplitude of 0·53, giving 4×0·53=2·12. The conditions at Portland are favourable for the formation of a double high water, with a phase relation of −002 deg. but the amplitude relationship is not quite suitable, four times the quarter-diurnal tide is not quite equal to the semi-diurnal tide. However, the sixth and higher species of tides fulfil the necessary conditions to produce a double high water.

(g) Tidal streams

So far little has been said about the pattern of the tidal currents on the open coast. Their reversing nature in the immediate vicinity of the beach has been mentioned, but in this environment their movement is necessarily restricted to one dimension. A little farther offshore, however, it can be observed that tidal currents are usually rotatory in character. A combination of the streams shown for different hours on fig. 1–11 is shown in fig. 1–16 for an ideal amphidromic system. Everywhere the pattern is one of anti-clockwise rotatory currents in the northern hemisphere. These become more asymmetrical towards the edge of the basin.

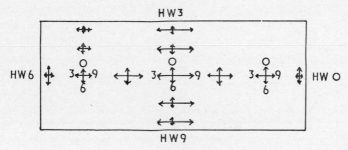

FIG. 1–16. Tidal streams in an ideal amphidromic system. (After Doodson and Warburg.) A.M.T.

Another type of rotatory tidal currents may be set up by the effect of the gyration of the earth on a progressive wave in a fairly narrow channel where the compensation is achieved by the development of transverse currents rather than by the setting up of subsidiary gradients. The streams in this instance will rotate clockwise in the northern hemisphere.

Much of the material for this section has been based on the Admiralty Manual of Tides (1941) by Doodson and Warburg,[13] which provides one of the best accounts of modern tidal theory and observation.

Summary

The tidal rise and fall has an important effect on beach processes and the occasional exceptionally high tides may be catastrophic; tidal currents may be significant locally.

Tides are produced by the gravitational attraction of the Moon and Sun and the tractive force, which is the significant one, can be split up into its harmonic semi-diurnal and diurnal components for both lunar and solar periods. The diurnal forces are due to the declination of the Moon. Progressive and stationary waves are important in tidal theory, the former move with a velocity dependent only on the depth, $c = \sqrt{gd}$; a reflected progressive wave has all the properties of a standing oscillation or stationary wave. In this type no currents exist at high water but they reach their maximum when the water surface is flat. The period of a standing oscillation depends on the length and depth of the water body, $T = \dfrac{2L}{\sqrt{dg}}$. A state of resonance will be set up when the period corresponds to the period of the tidal forces. The effect of the rotation of the earth on a standing oscillation is to produce an amphidromic system. High water appears to move anticlockwise round an amphidromic point of no tidal change with the maximum streams at high water in the direction of movement.

Oceanic tides are based on a series of amphidromic systems, whose dimensions are such that a state of resonance can be set up. Observations of tides round the British Isles show that three amphidromic systems exist in the North Sea; the amphidromic points have moved east due to friction, giving a greater range on the English coast than the Continental coast. One degenerate amphidromic point is found inland of the Isle of Wight in the English Channel. Near the Isle of Wight, where the semi-diurnal tide is reduced in amplitude, shallow water effects produce a relatively large quarter-diurnal tide, this causes the occurrence of double high and low waters at some places. Tidal streams are usually rotatory a little distance offshore, in amphidromic systems this rotation is anticlockwise in the northern hemisphere.

4. *WINDS*

The last factor to be considered is that of the wind. This is an important factor in its own right as well as being the cause of the waves in the ocean, and exerting a considerable influence on the height of the tide. In considering the effect of wind on a coast it is important to differentiate between the prevalent, or most common wind direction, and the dominant, or most effective wind direction. Where the two directions coincide as, for example, on the west coast of Britain, the coast is known as a windward coast; where the two directions differ, as on the east coast of England the area is a lee shore. Here, although westerly winds still predominate, it is the northerly or easterly winds which exert the most marked effect on the coast processes. The winds may perhaps most usefully be differentiated as onshore, alongshore and offshore winds, as it is their relation to the direction of the coast-line which is most important. An onshore wind, while helping to produce local seas, will also generate currents within the water. These currents are not normally very strong but they can be very effective in moving material first thrown into suspension by the waves. Strong onshore winds also help to raise the water level abnormally high, thus enabling the waves to reach parts of the coast usually beyond their reach. Alongshore winds, which are often accompanied by oblique waves, are very important in a consideration of the movement of material laterally along the coast. This is a very significant factor in the study of many areas of coastal erosion.

Offshore winds, on the other hand, will tend to reduce the energy of waves advancing on to the coast, especially those of local origin, while giving fuller play to the swells derived from a distant storm area. At the same time the water level will be somewhat lower than normal and a wind-generated current directed onshore on the bottom will probably be developed. Observations made at Les Karantes, on the south coast of France, showed that there was a correlation between the strength of the wind and the height of the water level. This relationship is shown in

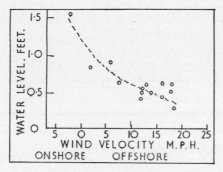

Fig. 1–17. The effect of an offshore wind on the water level at Les Karantes, in the Mediterranean Sea

fig. 1–17, in which the water level has been corrected for the very small tidal range of the area (0·6 ft. at spring tide and 0·2 ft. at neap tide). The total variation was more than 1.2 ft.

The wind is also significant on a sandy beach, particularly one with a large tidal range as a very considerable quantity of sand can be blown from the beach; with an onshore wind it will be blown inland, to form coastal dunes where the conditions are favourable, but with an offshore wind it will be blown into the shallow water immediately offshore. Sand-trap observations of the amount of sand being blown across the beach by a Beaufort Force 6 wind were made on the Lincolnshire coast. These showed that the wind carried 22 grams/min./cm. width of sand.

Summary

Prevalent and dominant winds must be distinguished; the two directions coincide on the west coast of the British Isles, but differ on the east coast, where the dominant winds come from the north. Onshore winds help to generate local seas and produce currents which have an important effect on the movement of material. They also tend to raise the water level above normal. Alongshore winds can be important in the movement of material along the coast, while offshore winds tend to reduce the part played by local waves and allow far travelled swells to affect the beach. They also cause a lowering of the water level normally. The wind is also important in the formation of coastal dunes.

REFERENCES

[1]Silvester, R., 1956, A model study of littoral drift at Bunbury Harbour, W.A. *Inst. of Eng.*, Australia **28**–29.

[2]British Standards Institute, 1947, British standard code of practise.

[3]Inman, D. L., 1952, Measures for describing the size distribution of sediments. *Journ. of Sed. Pet.* **22**–3, pp. 125–45.

[4]Chapman, G., 1949, The thixotropy and dilatancy of a marine soil. *Journ. of Marine Biol. Assoc. of U.K.* **28**, pp. 123–40.

[5]Valentin, H., 1954, Der Landverlust in Holderness, Ostengland von 1852 bis 1952. *Die Erde* 3–4, pp. 296–315.

[6]The report of the Royal Commission on coast erosion 1911.

[7]Trask, P. D., 1952, Sources of beach sands at Santa Barbara, California, as indicated by mineral grain studies. *B.E.B. Tech. Memo*, **28**.

[8]Baak, J. A., 1936, Regional petrology of the south North Sea.

[9]Pugh, D. C., 1953, Etude mineralogique des plages Picardes et Flamandes. *Bull. d'inform. Com. Cent. d'Oceanog. et d'Études des Côtes.* **5**–6, pp. 245–76.

[10]Trask, P. D., 1955, Movement of sand around the southern Californian promontories. *B.E.B. Tech. Memo.* **76**.

[11]Williams, W. W., 1947, The determination of the gradient of enemy-held beaches. *Geog. Journ.* **109**, pp. 76–93.

[12]Bigelow, H. B., and Edmonson, W. T., 1947, Wind waves at sea, breakers and surf. *Hydrog. Off. H.O.* Pub. **602** (*U.S. Navy*).

[13]Doodson, A. T., and Warburg, H. D., 1941, Admiralty manual of tides. H.M.S.O. Hydrog. Dept. Admiralty.

CHAPTER 2

METHODS OF RESEARCH

1. *THEORETICAL*

IN the first chapter some of the main factors on which the character of the beach depends were discussed briefly. From the discussion it will be apparent that waves play the major part in shaping the beach and coast, it is natural, therefore, that a considerable part of the research into beach processes and coastal development should be based on a study of waves and their effect on the beach. It is also in this field that theoretical work is perhaps most satisfactory; waves are amenable to mathematical analysis in an ideal form, which, even if it does not bear much relation to the waves of the sea, provides fundamental concepts of wave motion and character. The generation of waves in deep water has been considered from the theoretical point of view by Jeffreys (1925),[1] Sverdrup and Munk (1947),[2] Phillips (1957)[3] and others, and will be considered in more detail in chapter 3, pp. 55–60. The need for precise data concerning the character of sea and swell during the planning and carrying out of amphibious operations during the Second World War has led to a great increase in the knowledge and theory concerning all aspects of wave data. This has been actively promoted since the war by the National Institute of Oceanography in Great Britain.

The character and properties of ideal waves in deep water are now fairly well known from the theoretical point of view, but problems still remain in forecasting the complex wave characteristics in the ocean which are partly related to the limitations of the meteorological data on which they must be based. When waves enter shallow water, where they break and eventually loose themselves on the shore, they become subject to an increasing number of variables; mathematical treatment must necessarily become more complex. Other techniques can be used to supplement mathematical analysis.

It is partly the large number of variables involved in beach problems which make their solution difficult. One mathematical technique which has been used to deal with the numerous variables is dimensional analysis. A complex series of variables can be reduced to dimensionless ratios, which are functions on which the particular feature under consideration depends. Take, for example, the beach slope and the factors on which it depends, which may be given in the following symbols: $i\,h\,l\,p\,v\,d\,u\,s\,E\,g$.

i .. beach slope, dimensionless
h .. wave height, L feet
l .. wave length, L feet
p .. wave period, T seconds
v .. sand settling velocity, LT^{-1} ft./sec.
d .. density ML^{-3} lb./cubic ft.
u .. viscosity $ML^{-1}T^{-1}$ lb./ft./sec.
s .. sand medium diameter L ft.
E .. wave energy ML^2T^{-2} ft.-lb.
g .. acceleration of gravity LT^{-2} ft./sec./sec.

Taking E, l and v as three variables which include all three quantities, mass, time and length, and solving dimensionless equations for all the other variables in turn the following six dimensionless ratios are arrived at: $i=f\left(\dfrac{h}{l}\ \dfrac{vp}{l}\ \dfrac{v^2l^3d}{E}\ \dfrac{l^2vu}{E}\ \dfrac{s}{l}\ \dfrac{lg}{v^2}\right)$ The beach slope is a function of these dimensionless ratios. Thus it becomes apparent that the beach gradient depends on the wave steepness h/l; the sand size, which is itself a function of the settling velocity, is also a significant factor as shown by the second ratio, $\dfrac{vp}{l}$, as p and l are dependent on each other. The wave length as shown by the ratio $\dfrac{s}{l}$ is also an important factor. It will be shown in chapter 10, pp. 321–329, that these variables are in fact those which determine the gradient of the beach.

2. *EXPERIMENTAL*

(a) Scale problems

Because of the large number of variables involved both theoretical analysis and full-scale observations of beach processes are frought with difficulty. For this reason the experimental approach to the problems is all the more attractive because the variables can be brought under control and isolated in the controlled conditions of the model wave tank. Observations of beach changes and measurement of wave characteristics are also greatly facilitated. The range of problems which can be investigated by means of models is large; they can be used to study how closely waves follow the theoretical pattern and motion, calculated mathematically, both in deep water and as they move into shallow water and break. The movement of beach material and the form of the beach profiles may be studied in profile and in plan, while the effect of different waves and the wind on a variety of beach types can be measured. But unless these experimental results can be applied to their full-scale counterparts they are of relatively little value, specially from a practical point of view. Therefore, it is relevant to consider the problem of scale in the application of the results of model experiments to beaches in nature.

Various aspects of ideal waves in deep water, including wave form, velocity, orbital radii and mass transport can be reproduced in a model wave tank with a very good correlation with the theoretical values. As the waves move into shallow water the degree of correlation with theoretical values often decreases considerably, although this does not necessarily mean that the model behaves differently to the natural counterpart. Some studies, however, such as that by Johnson (1949)[4] shows a close correlation with empirical relationships derived from observations on a particular beach. A 1 : 40 model of the Scripps beach in California shows that model values of the relationship between wave steepness and depth of breaking agree closely with the empirical curve. (H_0/L_0 v. d_b/L_0) Model results indicate that there may be some discrepancy between the theoretical figures and the actual ones. So far model experiments have not contributed substantially to the solving of the problem of wave generation.

Models can be used to study the movement of beach material and the character of beach profiles in general, or to study particular problems on a model of a specific area. In both these instances the material forming the beach is a vital factor in the analysis. The conversion of the size of beach material from model to nature and vice versa is difficult and has led to considerable difference of opinion. One argument is put forward by Bagnold (1940)[5] and is based on the requirements of geometrical similarity which will be discussed on pp. 42–43. He considers that the beach profile should be similar if the ratio, $R,=H/d$, where H is the wave height and d is the diameter of the material, is constant for the model and prototype. The ratio R increases as the material becomes finer and as the waves increase in height, for a fine sand beach, where the median diameter of the sand is 0·20 mm., R would be 6000 for a wave only 1·2 m. in height. In order to imitate these conditions in a model wave tank if the wave height was 12 cm. the diameter of the material would have to be 0.02 mm.; this value is below the limit of fine sand. To imitate high storm waves the material would have to be even finer in grade. When sand is used in the model tank it would simulate shingle on a natural beach if the scale were considered in this way. There are, however, many respects in which sand and shingle beaches differ in nature; their profiles are different and they affect and are affected differently by the waves. It would appear unlikely, therefore, that sand in a model tank would give reliable data concerning a shingle beach in nature. On the other hand sand in nature is no more likely to be simulated by silt or clay in the tank as geometrical similarity would suggest it should.

One relevant factor in this discussion is the velocity required to initiate movement of material on the bottom. It has been shown by Hjulstrøm (1935)[6] and others that this velocity for a bed of uniform material depends on the size of the particles. The most easily eroded particles are those with a diameter between 0·1 and 0·5 mm.; particles both smaller and larger than this size require a considerably higher velocity to initiate movement. Thus if silt or clay grade material were used in a model tank to simulate sand in nature it would require a higher velocity to move it from the bed than the natural counterpart, the force available, however, would only be the model waves instead of the full size waves with their higher velocities. Once the material is in suspension, however, different laws come into force; the finer material in the tank would not be deposited until the velocities were very much lower than those which would allow the coarser material to settle on the bed. The ratio between the material size and the erosion velocity will differ from the ratio between the material size and the settling velocity in the tank and in nature. Other properties of the sediments are also important, the cohesion of the finer particles will effect their movement while the different rates of percolation through sediments of different size is very significant as will be discussed in detail when the gradients of the beach are considered (see pp. 321–329).

The factors mentioned above have led some workers, notably Meyers (1933),[7] to go to the opposite extreme. He considers that, if the gradient of the beach is an important factor in the experimental work, the same material should be used in the tank as on the natural beach, if comparable gradients are to be obtained. At the steeper limits of the experimental and natural gradients the results agreed well but for the flatter natural slopes the differences became considerable. The flatter natural gradients were about 1 : 100 for fine sand while the comparable experimental slopes were only 1 : 11·6. These results indicate that this solution to the problem is also not entirely satisfactory.

The value of model results would be greatly increased if it were possible to formulate exact laws connecting the model beach results to their natural counterparts. An attempt to assess the reliability of model results has been made by the Beach Erosion Board (1933).[8] They compared the results obtained in a large wave tank with those obtained in a smaller one. All the dimensions including the sand size were reduced to scale for the models in the ratio 1 : 2; for the larger model the sand size was 0·56 mm. and for the smaller 0·28 mm. It was found that there was a close agreement in the resultant beach profiles for the three wave lengths used for this experiment. The gradients on the swash slope did not agree exactly and the reason for this discrepancy will be discussed in chapter 10. For the linear scales smaller than 1 : 2 the sand diameter was kept at 0.28 mm. But even so a good agreement with the larger model was maintained up to a scale of 1 : 3·5. When the scale between the models was 1: 4·5 there was still a general similarity of profile although the smaller model reacted less quickly to the waves than the larger model. Johnson (1949)[4] mentions a similar set of experiments made by the U.S. Waterways Experimental Station (1940) when wave tanks on the scale 1 : 2 : 3 were used for the tests. Using a beach slope of 1 : 5 similar waves produced very similar results and there was a close agreement of the stable slopes.

These results suggest that there is a reasonable correlation between the results of model experiments and the behaviour of natural beaches under similar conditions. One type of wave will produce a storm profile in both model and natural beach while the opposite type will build up a normal profile. On the other hand the critical wave characteristic which will determine which type of beach will be formed appears to differ slightly from model to counterpart and indeed from one natural beach to another, as will be discussed in chapters 4 and 8 (see pp. 126, 250). The similarity noted by Lewis (1943)[9] between features formed in a small lake in Iceland, whose greatest fetch was less than 500 yds., shows that the same processes can produce similar results on widely differing scales. One of the features formed in this small lake in some respects closely resembled the great shingle structure of Chesil beach in Dorset; both on their very different scales turn to face the dominant waves.

Another scale problem associated with wave action in a model tank has been discussed by Bagnold (1946).[10] He notes that the ripples which form in the sandy bed of the model are very much greater in proportion to other features than their full-scale counterparts. These relatively large ripples exert too great a drag between the water and the bed thereby exhausting the waves too soon. In order to overcome some of the scale difficulties concerning the character and behaviour of the bed material Bagnold (1947)[11] has carried out experiments with material of much smaller density than normal quartz sand in the hope that it might react to the smaller tank waves in a way more similar to natural sand and full-size waves. The material he used was ground perspex with a density of 1·18. His conclusions, however, suggest that the low density material does not give useful results in the study of beach profiles, although it is useful in studying the action of waves in deeper water where the velocities are lower. It can also be used with advantage in experiments with wind in a model tank as will be mentioned in chapter 6 (see pp. 208, 209), when the currents generated are too slow to move quartz sand.

(b) Model laws

Model laws have been developed by Froude to enable different parameters to be converted to scale. His derivation of the model laws has shown that the model must be undistorted, that geometrical, kinematic and dynamic similarity must be maintained between model and nature. Fig. 2–1 shows the relations between model and prototype in an undistorted model. The co-ordinates of point C in the prototype are a and b while those of the model point C' are a' and b'. Therefore $b/b'=a/a' =A$, where A is a constant defined as the length ratio, assuming geometrical similarity between model and prototype.

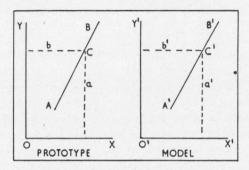

FIG. 2–1. Diagram to illustrate the derivation of model laws.

In discussing the kinematic similarity between model and prototype the time ratio must be fixed. From the figure the time taken for a point to travel from B to C is equal to t, and from B' to C' is equal to t'. This gives the ratio of velocities C as $V/V'=\dfrac{CB/B'C'}{t \ / \ t'}= At'/t$, now if $t/t'=B$ (where V is the velocity in the prototype and V' is the velocity in the model and B is a constant and is defined as the time ratio.) V/V' is now equal to A/B. The acceleration ratio is similarly A/B^2.

In discussing dynamic similarity a ratio of forces must be considered. The forces of inertia and gravity only will be considered. The inertia in nature on a particle of volume Q is Qra (where r is the density and a the acceleration). The inertia on a model particle is $Q'r'a'$. Therefore the ratio of forces Fi is $Qra/Q'r'a'$, $Q/Q'=A^3$ and $a/a'=A/B^2$. If the ratio of densities is R then $Fi=\dfrac{RA^3\times A}{B^2}=\dfrac{RA^4}{B^2}$ R is 1 if the same fluids are used in the model as those in nature. The ratio of the gravity forces Fg are $Qra/Q'r'a'$ and $Fg=RA^3\times 1$ as gravity is the same in nature and the model. The same ratio of forces must hold for gravity and inertia therefore $Fi=Fg$, therefore if R is 1, $A^4/B^2=A^3$, $A/B^2=1$, $A=B^2$. Considering the ratio of velocity $C=A/B$, therefore $C=B$. From this Froude's law follows, $A=B^2=C^2$ which states that the time and velocity scale are equal to the square-root of the linear scale. Froude has also shown that it is impossible to use a geometrically distorted model in the study of gravity waves.

For any model in which wave action is an important aspect the model must not be distorted. However, it has been found that when constructing models of particular areas to study some specific problems that good results are obtained by using a vertical exaggeration of scale. This applies particularly to models of harbours and river mouths in which tides and currents are of prime importance. For most areas the range of tide in the model would be negligible without vertical exaggeration.

(c) Description of model apparatus

There are two different types of model apparatus which serve different functions. One type is designed for a specific area and which usually aims to solve a particular engineering problem. This type of model is usually associated with such features as harbours and breakwaters and problems of coastal defence or the tidal stretch of rivers. As this type of model is associated largely with specific engineering problems and has been described in detail by Allen (1947)[12] it is not necessary to consider it further here. It might be pointed out that in this type of model, such as that of the Severn estuary, there is nearly always a vertical exaggeration of scale which is chosen so that the behaviour of the model can be made to simulate known changes in the prototype and from this future changes can be extrapolated and the effect of structures on the régime examined.

The second type of model is one designed to establish fundamental relationships between the different factors which affect the character of beaches under wave action. Such models can provide empirical data which can then be checked against full-scale phenomena or they can be used to check theoretical data. Many examples of the use of models for both these purposes will be considered in the following chapters. The apparatus used by workers for different problems vary but they can be divided into two main groups. One type is three dimensional; in it studies of movement both normal to the shore and parallel to it can be made. Others are narrow and are used to study the processes which operate normal to the shore in two dimensions. The latter type is rather simpler as the variables introduced by three dimensional movement are eliminated, this type will be considered first.

As an example of a long narrow wave tank the one in the Geography Department at Cambridge may be described. The lay-out of the wave tank is shown in fig. 2–2, it was 30 ft. long but only $9\frac{1}{2}$ in. wide and about 2 ft. deep. The waves were generated by a curved paddle which was fitted to a 0·25 h.p. engine. The wave heights could be adjusted by varying the eccentricity of the arm attaching the paddle to the motor, giving a range in deep water from 2 to 10 cm. The wave length was varied by use of a system of gears which gave periods of 0·75 sec., 1·5 sec. and 2·2 sec. Variations between these values could be obtained by use of electric resistance. Wave heights were measured with a point and hook gauge at the required depth and the period of the waves was timed by stop-watch, using the average of 10, from this figure the wave length in deep water could easily be calculated. Owing to the limited depth available true deep water waves could not be generated so that direct measurements of length would have been of limited value. As shown in fig. 1–3 the wave height does not begin to increase rapidly till d/L is about 0·05; for most purposes, therefore, the wave height measured in the deeper part of the tank gives an adequate value for the deep water wave height.

In addition to the paddle for generating waves a fan, to simulate the effect of an onshore wind, was set up over the wave generator as shown in the figure. This fan produced winds of up to 35 m.p.h. but the wind could be varied to give the required velocity. The wind velocity was measured with a small anemometer over the beach area or where required. The results of experiments with the fan in operation are discussed in chapter 6 (see pp. 207–213).

A baffle was placed behind the wave paddle to absorb any effect of disturbance in the water behind the paddle. At the other end of the tank a sand beach on a smooth wood floor was built. The profile could be recorded easily by reference to a grid of strings stretched across the glass window in the tank at 2 cm. intervals. The beach extended over a distance of about 3 m. from the top of the tank and was built of quartz sand of fairly uniform size, which had been passed through a sieve of twenty meshes to the inch to give a median diameter of 0·41 mm.

Many of the experiments made in this tank were concerned with the measurement of the volume of material moved along the beach under varying conditions. Some of these are described in chapter 4 (see pp. 121–127). The experiments were made by trapping sand in a trap designed to measure the sand moving both onshore and offshore. The trap, which extended across the full width of the tank, was divided into two portions by a central division running the length of the trap as shown in the inset in fig. 2–2. Sand travelling onshore fell into the portion nearest the sea while sand moving offshore would fall into the other half. The difference between the two amounts gives the net quantity of sand moved and the direction in which it is moving. It appeared from tests that the width of the half trap which was 2·5 cm. was enough to prevent sand from by-passing the trap nearest to it, except, perhaps, under the largest waves near their break-point where the turbulence was greatest. Up to 400 grams of sand was caught in the traps during the normal run of five minutes. This type of tank can be used for studies of the transport of sand and for experiments on the formation of beach profiles such as those discussed in chapter 5.

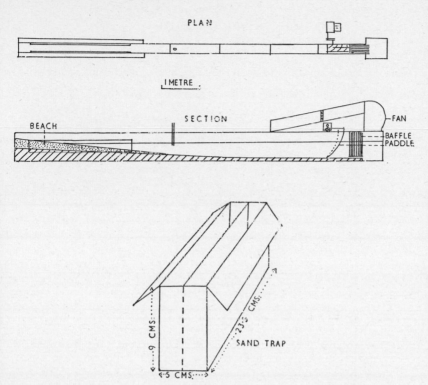

FIG. 2–2. The wave tank in the Geography Department of Cambridge University. The trap used to determine the direction and amount of sand transport is shown.

An example of the larger type of three dimensional tank is that used by Saville (1950)[13] to study the character of longshore currents and the transport of material alongshore. The results of his studies are considered in chapter 3 (pp. 111–112) and 4 (pp. 144–147). The lay-out of the tank is shown in fig. 2–3, which gives the dimensions of the tank and the alignment of the beach at an angle to the wave generating flap. Various precautions were taken to ensure that the movement of sand along the beach simulated the conditions on an infinitely long beach in nature.

A considerably larger three-dimensional model reproducing the shore in the neighbourhood of Dunwich, Suffolk, on a horizontal scale of 1 : 30 has been built up by the Hydraulics Research Board, it is described in the report for 1956.[14] The model reproduces 3,000 ft. width of beach

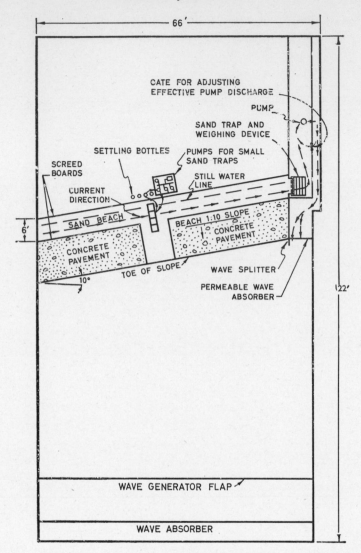

FIG. 2–3. Plan of wave tank used to study longshore transport. (After Saville.)

extending 1,800 ft. offshore, there is a slight vertical exaggeration giving the vertical scale the ratio of 1 : 20. This enables the natural tides and waves to be reproduced on the model. The waves were made with a new type of pneumatic wave generator. The aim of the experiments was partly to test the effectiveness of various types of groynes in stabilizing the beach under the action of oblique wave, these approached the shore at 30 deg. to normal, the wave height being 2 ft. on the prototype in deep water. The sand used in the model was 0·15 mm. compared to 0·45 mm. in the prototype, the results of the experiments are mentioned in chapter 4 (see p. 147).

For studying some problems, such as the formation of ripples, experiments have been done by oscillating a carrier containing sand through still water. In this way the longer accelerations associated with wave action in nature can be more easily simulated than in a normal wave tank where the waves must of necessity be much smaller than natural ones. Experiments of this type, carried out by Bagnold (1946)[10], are described in chapter 4 (pp. 128–130). The application of this technique is restricted to a rather small range of problems and cannot be used to study the actual beach. The use of models does in general, however, provide a very useful method of tackling some of the very complex problems associated with beach development and wave characteristics.

Summary

Models can be used for the study of waves in deep water and shallow water, the character of beach profiles built by the waves, and the movement of sediment on the bottom. The problem of scale is important in the latter problems particularly; two possibilities are suggested, either the ratio, R, of wave height to sand size may be kept constant, or similar material may be used in tank and nature. Neither produces exactly comparable results but probably the latter is in general more satisfactory. On the whole model beaches simulate with reasonable accuracy the character of known changes on natural beaches in response to differing waves.

Model laws state that a model used to study waves and their effect must be undistorted both geometrically, kinematically and dynamically. The time and velocity scales must equal the square-root of the linear scale. Models of harbours, river estuaries and other areas in which tidal forces are significant, however, must usually use a vertical exaggeration.

Models can be designed to study engineering and other problems in specific areas or they can be used to establish fundamental relationships between the beach and waves, wind and other forces. The latter type can be divided into two groups; the model which studies processes acting normal to the shore and which is long and narrow, and the three dimensional model where processes acting both normal to and along the shore can be studied.

3. *FIELD OBSERVATIONS*

Although much useful information both on the general nature of wave action on the beach and on specific problems of coastal engineering can be gained from models, the final aim of coastal studies is to understand the forces at work on the beaches in nature. For this purpose it is essential to make full-scale observations of many different processes and features. These vary from the generation of waves in the open ocean to the movement and character of the beach material at and near the water line and must also include a study of the backshore zone.

(a) Nomenclature

The nomenclature used throughout this book when referring to the beach zone will be given. The term 'beach' will be used to include the backshore, foreshore and offshore zones as defined in fig. 2–4. The term 'backshore' is used for the zone above the limit of the swash of normal high spring tide and is, therefore, only exceptionally under the direct influence of the waves. On a rocky coast it will include the cliffs and on a low coast it may consist of sand dunes or mature salt marsh. The 'foreshore' zone includes all that part of the beach which is regularly covered and uncovered by the tide. On a tideless beach this zone will be very narrow, only extending the distance between the limit of the swash and the backwash of the larger waves. The 'offshore' zone extends from the uppermost point always covered by water to a depth at which substantial movement of beach material ceases, under normal circumstances, or becomes very small. Ripple formation and minor changes of level will take place to much greater depths. The limit of this zone is discussed in more detail in chapter 4 (pp. 132–138).

Fig. 2–4 shows a diagrammatic composite sand and shingle beach profile. The 'berm' is a terrace formed in the backshore zone above the limit of the swash at high tide to form a flat terrace or sometimes a ridge with a reverse slope. The berm is sometimes double. Ridges are sometimes found exposed on a tidal sand beach at low water. The term 'ridge' is used only for features which are, for part of the time at least, above the water level. Below low water the positive features on the sandy floor in the offshore zone are called 'submarine bars'. The term 'bar' implying that the feature is never exposed above the water level, a property which is emphasized by the term 'submarine'. Such features have in the past been referred to by other names such as 'offshore bars' and 'low and ball'. The latter term is ambiguous, it has been used both for sand ridges and submarine bars by different authors. The features described by Cornish (1898)[15] seem to be sand ridges, while those discussed by Evans (1940)[16] under the title 'low and ball' are found in Lake Michigan which is tideless and these features must, therefore, be submarine bars.

The hollows found on the landward side of the ridges and submarine bars of sandy beaches are termed respectively 'runnels' and 'troughs'. The runnel in a tidal beach carries the water draining off the beach as

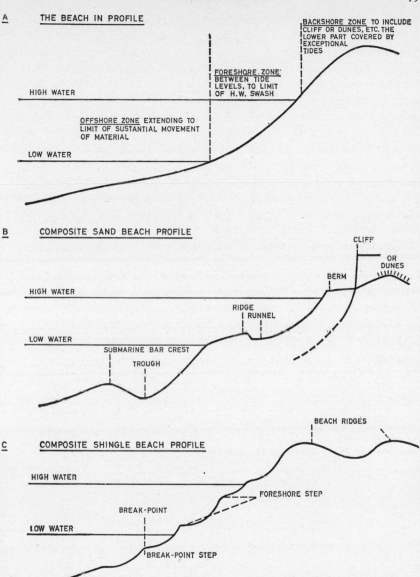

A <u>THE BEACH IN PROFILE</u>

BACKSHORE ZONE TO INCLUDE CLIFF OR DUNES, ETC. THE LOWER PART COVERED BY EXCEPTIONAL TIDES

FORESHORE ZONE BETWEEN TIDE LEVELS, TO LIMIT OF H.W. SWASH

HIGH WATER

OFFSHORE ZONE EXTENDING TO LIMIT OF SUSTANTIAL MOVEMENT OF MATERIAL

LOW WATER

B <u>COMPOSITE SAND BEACH PROFILE</u>

CLIFF

OR DUNES

BERM

HIGH WATER

RIDGE RUNNEL

LOW WATER

SUBMARINE BAR CREST

TROUGH

BEACH RIDGES

C <u>COMPOSITE SHINGLE BEACH PROFILE</u>

HIGH WATER

FORESHORE STEP

BREAK-POINT

LOW WATER

BREAK-POINT STEP

FIG. 2–4. Beach Nomenclature: A. The Beach in profile. B. Composite sand beach profile. C. Composite shingle beach profile.

the tide falls and is flooded first by the rising tide. The trough of a submarine bar is always under water.

A larger feature which is built permanently above the limit of high tide, but which is separated from the shore by a lagoon or channel will

B.C.–E

be referred to as a 'barrier beach' or 'island', following Shepard (1952).[17] Such features have often in the past been referred to as offshore bars, but the term barrier appears appropriate as the feature separates the land from the open sea and is thus a barrier to movement on and offshore.

The features typical of a shingle beach differ from those found on a sand beach, confusion is therefore avoided if they are referred to by different terms. The features which are built considerably above the limit of the storm waves may be called 'backshore' or 'shingle' 'beach ridges', while the term 'swale' is suitable for the generally shallow depressions which separate such ridges. The smaller features built up between the tide marks may be called 'foreshore steps' which indicates the part of the beach where they are found. Another step is often found at the break-point of the waves and to differentiate this from the former it may be referred to as a 'break-point step'.

The terms used for the constructional features of the beach zone in plan are illustrated and discussed in chapter 12, figure 12–6 shows them diagrammatically, they need not, therefore, be mentioned here. The terms 'down-wave' and 'up-wave' will be used when discussing the longshore movement of material to indicate the dominant direction towards which and from which beach material is moved respectively.

Table 2–1 gives, as far as possible, the equivalent terms in other languages.

TABLE 2–1

Terms used	French	Nomenclature German	Dutch	Swedish
Beach	Plage	Strand		Strand
Berm	Terrase de plage	Strandterrasen		
Beach ridge (shingle)	Levees de plage, bancs de galet	Strandwalle	Strandrug	Strandvellar
Barrier beach or island	Cordon littoral	Kustendammwall, Nerhung Lido	Shoorwall vrije or losse strandwall	
Lagoon	Lagune, étangs (littoraux)	Lagune Haff		Laguner
Ridge (sand exposed at low water)	Crêtes pre-littoraux	Schwellen	Aangroeiinsrug	
Runnel (exposed at low water)	Sillons pre-littoraux		Zwin	
Submarine bar (never exposed)	Barre	Sandriff, Barre	Strandbank	Revel
Submarine bar trough	Creux		Rifftalen	Trâg

(b) Problems considered

SITUATION. The beaches themselves may be considered first. Observations on the beach should include information concerning their position with relation to fetch and the wind régime of the area, the lateral extent of the beach along the coast which is intimately linked with the general form of the coast. The nature of the hinterland is of importance as the beach sediment is often partly derived from inshore. The offshore zone is also very important as the character of this zone has a marked effect on the waves which reach the coast and on the supply of material from offshore sources.

BEACH MATERIAL AND ENVIRONMENT. On the beach the character of the backshore area must be examined; the type of artificial defences must be included, where these are present. The material of which the beach is composed must be studied in detail; both its lateral and perpendicular arrangement is important. The form of the beach profile must be considered and its changes from time to time require investigation. The profile should, if possible, be continued downwards from the low water line to a depth equal to the limit of wave action under normal circumstances. A study of the material in deeper water is also of interest in assessing the movement of material alongshore in deeper water. This latter problem is not one which it is easy to solve; it is nevertheless one of great importance in a study of the beach and coast development.

WAVES. The factors responsible for the movement of the material on the beach and the resultant form of the beach profile must be taken into account. The waves are the most important of these factors, it is necessary, therefore, to observe or compute from available data, such as synoptic meteorological charts, the nature of the wave attack on the coast. This requires a knowledge of the significant wave height, wave length and direction of approach throughout the period under consideration. Precise measurements of these quantities along the entire coast is clearly impossible with present equipment, various techniques have been devised to enable these wave characteristics to be deduced from meteorological data which are more readily available. These techniques can then be checked at those localities where the necessary wave recording apparatus is available. As well as the wave dimensions and direction the detailed movement of the water within the wave must be considered, as it is this which moves the material and determines the beach character. Different techniques are required for this type of observation.

TIDES, WIND. The tidal régime and tidal currents must also be taken into consideration at any particular place, such data are often available from tide tables but sometimes they must be measured. Wind observations for the immediate locality are also necessary for a full study of any particular beach.

TIME FACTOR. The observation of all the relevant data must be continued over a considerable period of time to enable the effect of as many as possible combinations of waves, wind and tide to be observed. It is not possible to isolate the many variables in nature, the observations must, therefore, continue long enough to provide samples of many types. It may then be possible to explain the character of that particular beach and to arrive at relationships which can be applied to other areas of similar type; the results of model experiments can also be checked. Such work requires frequent surveys of the beach so that the observed changes can be correlated with the measured changes in the waves; the more frequent are the surveys the more likely that the changes in the beach profile can be related to the measured variation in the waves. The frequency of the surveys required will naturally depend on the variability of the waves and to a certain extent on the character of the beach as some beaches react more rapidly than others. Shingle, for example, reacts to a change in wave type very much more rapidly than fine sand and hourly surveys may show considerable changes. On the other hand occasional surveys are also of value as they may show whether that beach undergoes seasonal or tidal cycles, as has been shown to occur on some beaches, or whether the beach is undergoing more or less continuous erosion or accretion. Beach cycles of this type can take place over a considerable number of years, of the order of twenty, in some areas. The fluctuations of the beach at Sumner, near Christchurch, New Zealand, discussed by Scott (1955),[18] illustrates this point.

SURVEYS. The actual methods of survey will be discussed in the appropriate chapters, where they are referred to in more detail. Some interesting new techniques, such as the use of radio-active isotopes, have been developed fairly recently to study the movement of pebbles and sand on the shore. These experiments are discussed in chapter 4 (see pp. 154–158).

Summary

The nomenclature used is discussed. Observations on a natural beach should include a consideration of their situation and exposure. The beach material must be studied in detail over all the beach zones. Measurement or estimate of wave size is essential and the tidal régime must be ascertained. Observations of the changes on the beach must be carried out over a considerable period of time as well as over short periods when the changes can more easily be correlated with changes in the wave characteristics.

4. HISTORICAL DATA

The use of historical material can often add much of interest to the study of a particular coastal area. This material is more relevant to the development of the coast than the beach, although there can be interesting implications as far as the beach is concerned. Naturally such studies can only be carried out where the historical material goes back a reasonable time and the nature of the evidence will vary considerably from place to place. In chapter 11 two areas are considered in detail from this point of view; the Lincolnshire coast has been a coast of erosion since the thirteenth century, while the Dungeness and Romney Marsh area of Kent is an area of deposition, where the historical data goes back to the invasion of Julius Caesar.

The use of maps to establish changes in coastal outline can also be valuable, although it is rare to get sufficiently accurate maps to make precise measurements of the rate of change before the first edition of the Ordnance Survey, published during the nineteenth century, in Britain. Hydrographic surveys probably provide an exception to this generalization, but they are normally restricted to areas of importance to navigation such as harbours. The data they give of the offshore zone is, however, often of considerable value.

REFERENCES

[1] Jeffreys, H., 1925, On the formation of waves by wind. *Proc. Roy. Soc. A.* **107**, pp. 189–206.

[2] Sverdrup, H. U. and Munk, W. H., 1947, Wind, sea and swell—theory of relationships in forecasting. *H.O. Pub.* 601, U.S. Navy Dept.

[3] Phillips, O. M., 1957, On the generation of waves by turbulent wind. *Journ. Fluid Mechs.* **2**–5, pp. 417–45.

[4] Johnson, J. W., 1949, Scale effects in hydraulic models involving wave motion. *Trans. Am. Geoph. Un.* **30**–4, pp. 517–25.

[5] Bagnold, R. A., 1940, Beach formation by waves—some model experiments in a wave tank. *Journ. Inst. Civ. Eng.* **15**, pp. 27–52.

[6] Hjulstrøm, F., 1935, Studies of the morphological activity of rivers as illustrated by the river Fyris. *Bull. Geol. Inst. Uppsala* **25**.

[7] Meyers, R. D., 1933, A model of wave action on beaches. Thesis for M.Sc. Univ. of Calif. Doc. **91**.

[8] Beach Erosion Board, 1933. Interim report.

[9] Lewis, W. V., 1943, Miniature spits and embankments on a lake shore in Iceland. *Geog. Journ.* **102**, pp. 175–9.

[10] Bagnold, R. A., 1946, Motion of waves in shallow water, interaction between waves and sand bottom. *Proc. Roy. Soc. A.* **187**–1008, pp. 1–15.

[11] Bagnold, R. A., 1947, Model experiments with light materials. *Journ. Inst. Civ. Eng.* **4**, p. 447.

[12] Allen, J., 1947, *Scale models in hydraulic engineering.*

[13] Saville, T., 1950, Model study of sand transport along an infinitely long straight beach. *Trans. Am. Geoph. Un.* **31**–4, pp. 555–65.

[14] Hydraulics research, 1956, *D.S.I.R.*, H.M.S.O. Pub. 1957, pp. 33–36.

[15] Cornish, V., On Sea beaches and sand banks. *Geog. Journ.* **11**, 1898, pp. 628–51.

[16] Evans, O. F., 1940, The low and ball of the eastern shore of Lake Michigan. *Journ. Geol.* **48**, pp. 476–511.

[17] Shepard, F. P., 1952, Revised nomenclature for depositional coastal features. *Bull. Am. Assoc. of Petrol. Geol.* **36**–10, pp. 1902–12.

[18] Scott, W. H., 1955, Sea erosion and coast protection at Sumner, N.Z. *N.Z. Engineering* **10**, pp. 438–447.

CHAPTER 3

WAVES

1. WAVES IN DEEP WATER

Ideal waves

THE fundamental dimensions and character of waves in deep water have already been mentioned in chapter 1, including the formulae which relate the wave velocity, length and period. These formulae were developed by Airy[1] in 1842. A few years later Stokes[2] in 1847 extended the theory to waves of finite height; his solution required that the velocity should depend to some extent on the wave height and that the orbital movement was in the form of open circles, indicating the existence of mass transport. Stokes did not obtain a rigorous solution although he worked out the formulae to a fifth approximation. Levi-Civita,[3] however, in 1925 proved that the series was convergent for deep-water waves, while Struik[4] in the following year obtained an exact solution for finite depths. The form of the waves in Airy's analysis is sinusoidal, but for waves of finite height the form approximates to a trochoid.

Another theory of wave motion has been developed on the assumption that the waves are exactly trochoidal. This theory was developed independently by Gerstner[5] and Rankine,[6] in 1802 and 1863 respectively. It shows that the orbits of the particles are exactly circular and hence does not allow for mass transport; this has been shown to exist, for example by Mitchim (1940).[7] The results of this theory are very similar to those of Airy for low waves in deep water, it also has the advantage that the formulae are much simpler than those of Stokes' theory and provides exact solutions for the motion of particles, the wave form, energy and velocity. The theory was extended for shallow water conditions by Gaillard (1904).[8]

The two wave theories which have just been mentioned require different forms of motion in the water. The Airy-Stokes theory demands that the flow be irrotational. It appears that the theory of Stokes which requires both irrotational flow and mass transport is closer to reality than the simpler theory of Gerstner and Rankine, where the flow is rotational and no mass transport is allowed.

One of the most important properties of the irrotational theory of Stokes is the mass transport; its velocity at the surface, which is proportional to the square of the wave steepness, is very small compared to the wave velocity, this value becomes very small for low waves and is negligible for very low waves. The volume of mass transport is given by $H^2\sqrt{\dfrac{g\pi}{32L}}$ per unit width of wave crest, this value has been checked experimentally by Mitchim, H is the wave height and L the wave length.

The trochoidal wave of Gerstner's theory of wave motion requires rotational water movement and can be defined fairly simply. The wave form in deep water is given by $x = R\theta - r\sin\theta$ and $y = R - r\cos\theta$ where L is $2R$ and H is $2r$, the height of the crest above still water is given by $\dfrac{H}{2} + 0.7854\,\dfrac{H^2}{L}$ and the depth of the trough below still water level is given by $\dfrac{H}{2} - 0.7854\,\dfrac{H^2}{L}$. Thus it can be seen that the crest height is greater than the trough depth. The energy of the wave is given by the formula $E = \dfrac{wLH^2}{8}\left(1 - 4.93\,\dfrac{H^2}{L^2}\right)$ which is the total kinetic and potential energy per wave length. For flat waves it is apparent that this formula is the same as that already given for the low sinusoidal waves. Although the actual form of ideal waves in deep water is fairly well established when it comes to a discussion of the generation of waves in the sea, knowledge is much less advanced. This aspect is, however, of greater significance from the point of view of the beach as it determines the type and character of the waves reaching the shore.

2. WAVE GENERATION

(a) Theory—Jeffreys, Sverdrup and Munk, Eckart, Phillips

The generation of waves depends on the transference of energy from the wind to the sea but the exact method whereby this is achieved is not yet fully known. Some of the theories put forward to explain this will be discussed briefly.

JEFFREYS. One of the theories put forward to explain the generation of waves is the sheltering theory of Jeffreys (1925).[9] He assumes that the air flow is laminar over the windward slope of the wave and turbulent on the lee slope. It is assumed that the lee side of the wave form is sheltered by the crest and low velocities are found here. The normal pressure thus differs between the windward and lee faces. If the wind velocity exceeds the wave velocity energy is transferred from the air to the water. The tangential friction is ignored in this theory. One important factor in his analysis is the 'sheltering co-efficient', s, which is related to that proportion of the windward slope of the wave which offers resistance to the wind; from his calculations he found s to be about 0·27. His theory accounts reasonably satisfactorily for the initial generation of waves when their steepness is very low, but as the waves increase in steepness his value of s appears to be too great. Experiments by Stanton and others (1932)[10] showed that the sheltering coefficient was only 1/10 of Jeffreys' value. The conclusion is reached that drag must be taken into account to explain the growth of waves as the observed sheltering coefficient is much smaller than the theoretical one.

SVERDRUP AND MUNK. The rough turbulent theory developed by Sverdrup and Munk (1947)[11] is based on rough turbulent flow which applies when the wind speed is over 7 m./sec. (Force 4 Beaufort scale). Above this velocity ripples of small dimensions are formed on the wave surface and these alter the type of surface from hydrodynamically smooth to hydrodynamically rough. This concept of a critical speed has since been criticized by Munk (1957)[12] who originally put it forward. It now appears that there is no critical wind speed (see p. 58). The air flow is considered to be similar to that suggested by Jeffreys, an eddy forming on the lee side of the wave. The sheltering coefficient used for this theory is about 1/20 of Jeffreys, s being 0·013. It is suggested that the tangential stress of the wind, which is an important factor in this theory, varies with the square of the wind velocity above a certain figure. The waves acquire energy from the wind by tangential stress when the water particles move in the same direction as the wind, and energy is lost when the particles move against the wind, but because of mass transport there is a net gain of energy. Because the wave velocity is much greater than the velocity of the particles within the wave it is possible for the wave velocity to exceed the generating wind velocity; the limit would be reached when the particle velocity equalled the wind speed. When the waves are moving faster than the generating wind the energy transfer is in two directions; the waves are gaining energy by tangential stress but are losing it by the pressure of the wave form on the wind. Energy is also converted into heat by turbulence. The wave will continue to grow until the loss of energy equals the gain. The whole energy of the tangential and normal stress of the wind goes into the wave, and causes an increase of height and length; the increase in height is more important when the wave is moving slower than the wind, but when the wave speed exceeds the wind velocity most of the energy goes to increase the wave velocity. The proportion of energy increasing the height and length is determined by the relation between the wave steepness and wave age. Observation fits fairly well with the theoretical curve and provides a basis for the forecasting of wave height.

ECKART. Eckart's theory (1953)[13] of wave generation applies to the open ocean with fully turbulent flow. Normal pressure in the form of gusts are assumed to be distributed at random, independent of the waves already formed. One disadvantage of the theory is that sheltering is ignored. The gusts producing the waves are assumed to be similar, moving over the water with the speed of the wind which is constant. Owing to the lack of observations of the wind pressure it is not possible to check the results of calculations using the theory; it does, however, appear that the simplest model, without taking sheltering into account, and considering only the normal pressure, is not sufficiently accurate.

PHILLIPS. One of the most recent and promising theories of wave generation is that put forward by Phillips (1957).[14] He assumes that a turbulent wind at a given moment starts to blow over a surface previously at rest. The pressure on the surface fluctuates in a distribution which is a stationary random function of position and time. The study aims to discover the properties of the surface displacement at subsequent periods. Eckart has already attempted to solve a similar problem, but it appears that his assumption of the pressure distribution was not sufficiently random to give accurate results, his predicted wave heights being too small. The random distribution assumed by Phillips is an important part of his analysis, which involves a type of resonance. The turbulent nature of the wind is an essential factor in the growth of waves and causes random stresses on the water surface; these include both normal stress or pressure and tangential shear stress. Eddies, in the air stream, are carried by the wind, and change as they move, so that the stress distribution moves across the surface with a certain velocity dependent on the wind speed; this convection velocity of the stress fluctuations is defined as the velocity of the frame of reference, U_c, in which their frequency scale is least, or their time scale is greatest. This velocity is very nearly equal to the wind velocity as measured from a ship.

The fluctuating pressure upon the water surface is held responsible for the birth and early growth of waves. An analysis of the surface would show a wide variety of wave numbers and frequencies in both two dimensional space and time. The components of the pressure fluctuations acting on the surface generate small forced oscillations. These fluctuations affect the amplitude components on the surface. If the pressure distribution includes components whose wave numbers and frequencies coincide with possible dimensions of free surface waves a type of resonance is set up and the continued presence of these particular frequencies in the pressure distribution will generate surface waves whose amplitude will increase. Thus, if it is assumed that the frame of reference is not changing in character but is moving with the convection velocity, and one of the wave frequencies generated is moving with the same velocity, then the two move together and there is no differential movement and growth can continue. This, however, ignores the evolution of the stress pattern so is an over-simplification; if the pressure pattern is changing slowly the growth of the wavelets is reduced.

At first the surface may be assumed to have no effect on the pressure distribution but this will not last for long as small ripples will soon form which have a considerable effect on the velocity distribution in height or the mean velocity profile. In considering the long gravity waves it appears that these do not affect the pressure distribution. The viscosity of the water is ignored, which is probably justified for all but the shortest waves. The motion is then irrotational. These results apply when the mean square slope is small so that the surface boundary condition can be considered linear. At later stages of growth the non-linear effects may become important.

In the initial generation of waves the minimum velocity is given by $C_{min}=(4gTs/\rho)^{\frac{1}{4}}$, ρ is the water density, Ts the surface tension at the inter-face, C_{min} is the minimum velocity. The wave length of the critical waves is about $L_{cr} \doteq 2\pi(Ts/\rho g)^{\frac{1}{2}}$; for water $\rho=1$ gm. cm.$^{-3}$ Ts is 73 gm.sec.^{2}, g is 980 cm.sec.$^{-2}$, then C_{min} is 23 cm.sec.$^{-1}$ and the critical wave length $L_{cr}=2\pi/n_{cr}$ is 1·7 cm. n is the wave number. The initial waves generated may travel at directions almost perpendicular to that of the generating wind as this increases in force. Some observational evidence supports this view. The minimum wind velocity which may generate resonance waves is 23 cm.sec.$^{-1}$ but a smaller wind velocity will disturb the surface although waves will not continue to grow. The most probable value for U_{min} appears to be o, although values up to 790 cm./sec. have been proposed by different workers. The wave generated with very low winds may not be visible to the naked eye. That U_{min} is probably o is made more likely owing to the demonstrated impossibility of laminar flow except under artificial conditions.

Considering the development of waves after the initial stage of growth it can be shown that the mean square wave height is directly proportional to time. The wave spectrum is independent of time until the mean square slope increases beyond a certain point when non-linear factors become significant. This is reached first for the shorter waves; it appears, therefore, that the direct proportionality of wave height to time does not change till the largest waves reach the limiting value of mean square slope. It is shown that for light winds the spectrum is narrower, and therefore the waves appear more regular. The wave spectrum can be defined by the following formula $\bar{\xi}^2 \sim \dfrac{\bar{\rho}^2 t}{2\sqrt{2}\bar{\rho}^2 U_c g}$ where $\bar{\xi}^2$ is the mean square surface displacement, $\bar{\rho}^2$ is the mean square turbulent pressure on the water surface, t the time elapsed, U_c the convection speed of the surface pressure fluctuations and ρ the water density. These terms cannot be directly applied to observations made in the oceans but the formula can be expressed in different terms with reasonable accuracy; the relationship between the mean square turbulent pressure and the recorded wind velocity is one of the more difficult to define; Longuet-Higgins (1952)[15] has shown that the significant height H is related to $\bar{\xi}^2$ by the formula $H^2 = 8\bar{\xi}^2$ approximately. The formula can now be given as $\dfrac{gH}{U^2} \sim 6 \times 10^{-4} \left\{ \dfrac{g\,T}{U} \right\}^{\frac{1}{2}}$, the accuracy of the constant is quite low as the value of $\bar{\rho}^2$ is not certain. This formula gives results which agree well

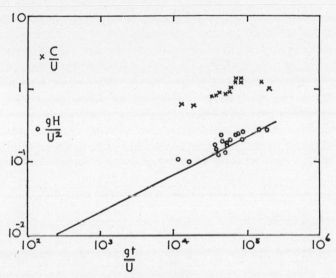

FIG. 3–1. The relationship between wave height and wind speed and duration. (After Phillips.)

with observations given by Sverdrup and Munk over a relatively restricted range of duration. The wave heights observed are close to the computed values (see fig. 3–1).

It has been shown that although waves can exist with a velocity equal to or greater than the wind velocity they will be relatively inconspicuous.[16] The predominant waves are those whose velocity is about three-quarters the wind velocity. This was early recognized in the empirical rule suggested by Cornish (1934)[17] that the 'average' storm sea travels with a velocity about 80 per cent of the wind velocity. This brings out a very important point in the study of the generation of waves; there is never one period and one height of waves generated. A storm at sea produces a spectrum of waves[18] which range in size from small ripples to waves travelling faster than the generating wind. This greatly complicates the analysis of the sea and the calculation of the wave pattern from the observed wind characteristics of force direction and duration.

Summary

Various theories have been put forward to explain the way in which energy is transferred from the wind to the waves. Jeffreys sheltering hypothesis is based on variation of normal pressure on the windward and lee side, but owing to too high a value of the sheltering coefficient it cannot account for the continued growth of waves. Sverdrup and Munk base their theory on turbulent flow and tangential stress, whereby energy is transferred from wind to water when these move in the same direction. Eckart's and the more successful theory of Phillips are based on the movement of pressure fluctuations due to the gustiness of the wind, the former theory does not allow sufficiently random pattern to account for the development of the waves and also does not allow for sheltering. A type of resonance is set up according to Phillips which assists the transference of energy from the air to the water. None of the earlier theories explained adequately the growth of the waves. Waves generated by the wind are of many lengths and heights so forming a spectrum of waves, in the generating area energy can be transferred from the short to the longer waves as the dominant length increases and the maximum length corresponds to the greatest wind velocity.

(b) Wave propagation and decay

The discussion so far has been largely concerned with the generation of waves within the area where they are growing under the influence of the wind. Many of the waves reaching the shore, however, have been generated by winds a great distance away and may have travelled for thousands of miles across the oceans. A useful technique whereby wave records could be analysed and used to study the propagation of swell has been recorded by Barber and Ursell (1948).[19] The basic assumption of

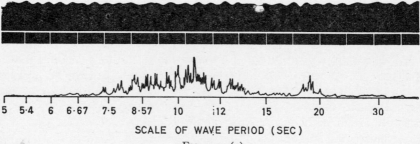

SCALE OF WAVE PERIOD (SEC)

FIG. 3-2. (*a*)

Typical wave record and spectrum. (After Darbyshire.)

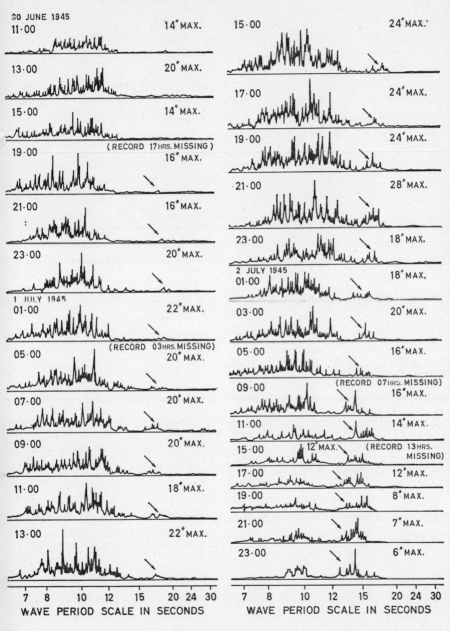

FIG. 3–2. (b)

Wave spectra at Pendeen, Cornwall, 30 June to 2 July, 1945. (After Barber and Ursell.)

their analysis is that the wave trains travel at a speed equal to half the wave velocity.

One problem was to obtain reliable wave data in a form suitable for analysis. Wave records were analysed in a special instrument to provide a Fourier amplitude spectrum of the wave period which gives a series of peaks depending on the period of the components of the mixed wave trains. A measure of the period and height of the different groups in the spectrum is thus obtained. A typical wave record and spectrum is shown in fig. 3–2: (a) shows the wave record as obtained from the measuring instrument on the ocean floor, as well as the spectrum, (b) shows a series

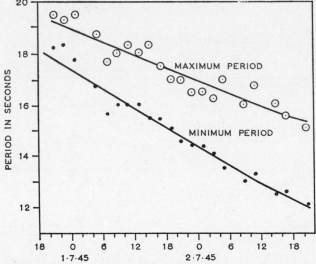

FIG. 3–3. Maximum and minimum periods limiting the frequency band from the tropical storm of 26 to 28 June, 1945, in the wave spectra of 1 and 2 July. (After Barber and Ursell.)

of spectra for a $2\frac{1}{2}$-day period; the height of the waves is indicated by the pressure in inches while the peaks in the curve indicate the most important frequency bands. As an example of the analysis of wave spectra the period from 30 June to 2 July, 1945, may be taken. During this period the swell from a small intense depression reached the coast of Cornwall, where the wave recorder was situated. The tropical hurricane could be followed on the synoptic charts as it moved northwards along the east coast of the United States of America, reaching its greatest intensity on 26–27 June off the coast between Cape Hatteras in North Carolina and Nantucket, Mass. which is about 2,700 to 3,000 nautical miles from the Cornish coast. The spectra shown in the figure indicate that the first effects of the storm were apparent at 1900 on 30 June; the waves concerned had a period of about 18 sec. Subsequently the wave period band increased in width as the periods became shorter; they decreased to 13–15 sec. by 2 July. There is some irregularity in this decrease, indicated on fig. 3–3, due to the interference effect of tidal streams near the wave recorder. From the time of arrival and period of

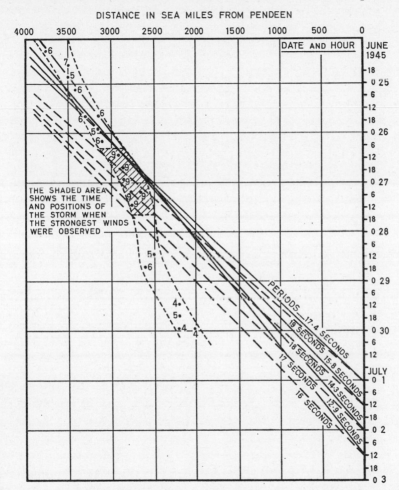

FIG. 3–4. Propagation diagram for waves reaching Pendeen between 24 June and 2 July, 1945. (After Barber and Ursell.)

the waves a propagation diagram can be drawn as shown in fig. 3–4, the time is plotted against the distance from Cornwall. On the diagram the position of the storm centre is shown at different times, the full straight lines refer to the minimum period and the dashed to the maximum at any one time of arrival. The lines indicate that the shortest waves are generated first and the longest when the wind reaches its maximum.

The crossing of the lines shows that the shorter waves are nearly all overtaken by the longer waves before they reach the coast. The conclusions drawn from this study strongly suggest that wave trains of different periods can be propagated independently with a speed equal to half the wave velocity. It also appears that there is an upper limit to the wave period which can be generated by a given wind but that this limit increases with increasing wind strength.

Summary

Barber and Ursell have shown that waves can travel for long distances from the generating area at the group velocity of the wave train; this is half the wave speed. All the waves forming the complex wave spectrum travel at their own appropriate group velocity, depending on their length.

(c) Empirical formulae and wave forecasting

SVERDRUP AND MUNK (1947)[11] collected many wave observations in order to establish empirical relationships between the variables affecting the growth and character of waves. A later analysis of the same data with all available subsequent material was made by BRETSCHNEIDER[20] in 1952. The curves he has drawn use the same dimensionless parameters as Sverdrup and Munk, these are C_o/U v. gF/U^2 and gH/U^2 v. gF/U^2, where C_o is the deep water wave velocity in ft./sec., U is the average surface wind speed in ft./sec. and knots, F is the fetch length in feet or nautical miles and H is the significant deep water wave height in feet. These curves are shown in fig. 3–5. The figures refer to the significant wave; this is a wave whose height is defined as the average of the highest $\frac{1}{3}$ of the waves, the significant period is the average period of the high groups of waves. This period is divided into the period of observation to obtain a wave number, and this is used to calculate the $\frac{1}{3}$ highest waves. The curves shown in the figure give all the necessary wave characteristics, including their velocity and their height, the steepness ratio and a term related to the duration of the generating wind tU/F, where t is the duration of the wind in seconds. This curve gives the time required for the generation of waves of maximum energy for that particular fetch and wind velocity, indicating that after this time has elapsed there will be no further increase of height and length.

WAVE ATTENUATION. When the generating wind dies down or the waves move out of the generating area they cease to grow and gradually attentuate with time and distance. It has already been shown that their velocity does not vary but their height is modified. It is the modification of wave height as the waves decay in moving across the ocean that is most important from the point of view of the beach. The attenuation of swell with time and distance from the generating area is the main cause

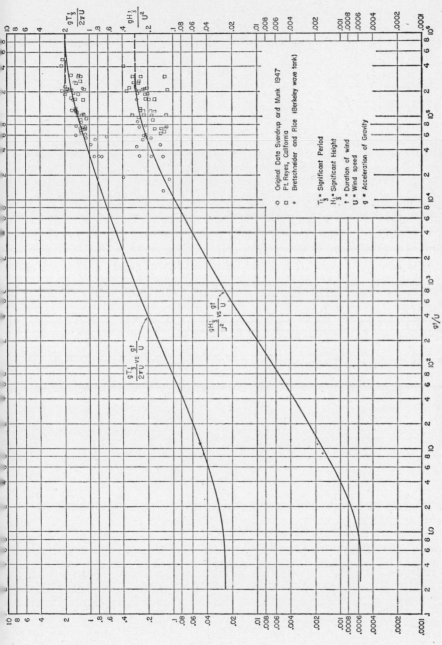

FIG. 3–5. (*a*) Fetch graph for deep water. (After Bretschneider, B.E.B.)

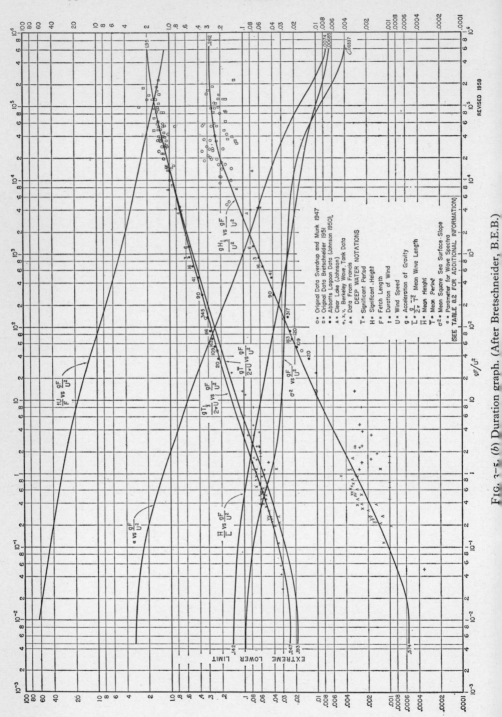

FIG. 3-5. (b) Duration graph. (After Bretschneider, B.E.B.)

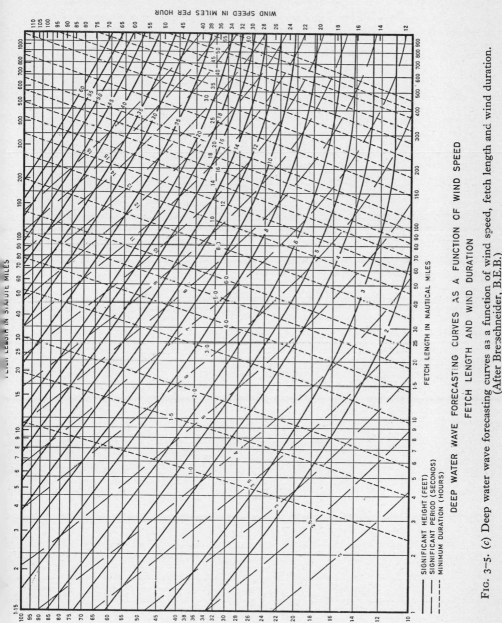

DEEP WATER WAVE FORECASTING CURVES AS A FUNCTION OF WIND SPEED
FETCH LENGTH AND WIND DURATION

FIG. 3–5. (c) Deep water wave forecasting curves as a function of wind speed, fetch length and wind duration.
(After Bretschneider, B.E.B.)

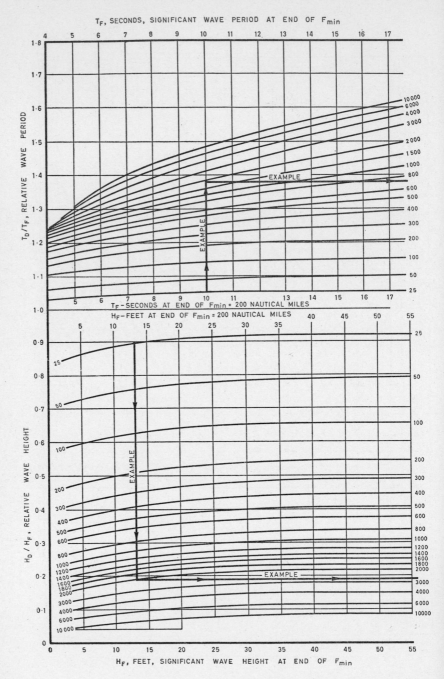

Fig. 3-6. Forecasting curves for wave decay.

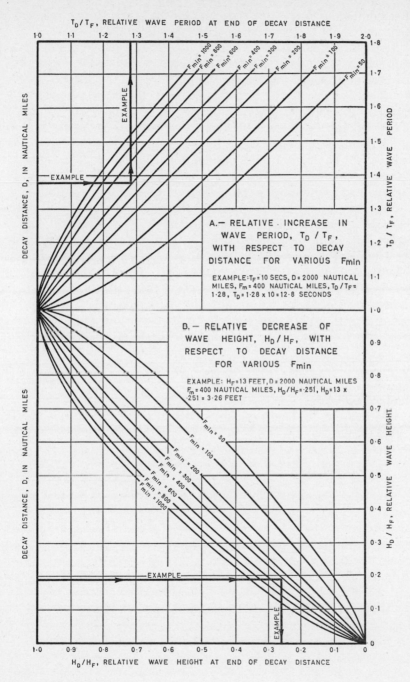

T_D/T_F, RELATIVE WAVE PERIOD AT END OF DECAY DISTANCE

DECAY DISTANCE, D, IN NAUTICAL MILES

T_D/T_F, RELATIVE WAVE PERIOD

EXAMPLE

F_{min} = 1000
F_{min} = 800
F_{min} = 600
F_{min} = 400
F_{min} = 300
F_{min} = 200
F_{min} = 100
F_{min} = 50

A.— RELATIVE INCREASE IN WAVE PERIOD, T_D/T_F, WITH RESPECT TO DECAY DISTANCE FOR VARIOUS F_{min}

EXAMPLE: T_F = 10 SECS, D = 2000 NAUTICAL MILES, F_m = 400 NAUTICAL MILES, T_D/T_F = 1·28, T_D = 1·28 x 10 = 12·8 SECONDS

B.— RELATIVE DECREASE OF WAVE HEIGHT, H_D/H_F, WITH RESPECT TO DECAY DISTANCE FOR VARIOUS F_{min}

EXAMPLE: H_F = 13 FEET, D = 2000 NAUTICAL MILES F_m = 400 NAUTICAL MILES, H_D/H_F = ·251, H_D = 13 x ·251 = 3·26 FEET

F_{min} = 50
F_{min} = 100
F_{min} = 200
F_{min} = 300
F_{min} = 400
F_{min} = 800
F_{min} = 1000

DECAY DISTANCE, D, IN NAUTICAL MILES

H_D/H_F, RELATIVE WAVE HEIGHT

EXAMPLE

H_D/H_F, RELATIVE WAVE HEIGHT AT END OF DECAY DISTANCE

(After Bretschneider, B.E.B.)

of the different effect of sea and swell on the beach; hence it is one of the main reasons for the importance of exposure of the beach.

Bretschneider has drawn a series of empirical graphs shown in fig. 3-6 from which the change in wave height and period as the waves decay can be found, using as one parameter of the graph the relation between the decay length and the fetch length D/F, the other parameters are dimensionless ratios of height and period to decay distance. The higher and steeper the waves are as they leave the fetch area the more rapid will be the reduction of wave height; for a wave period of 10 sec. and a fetch distance of 100 nautical miles and an initial height of 20 ft., after 200 nautical miles decay the wave height will be less than 10 ft., while after 1,600 nautical miles it will be only 4 ft.

According to the curves given by Bretschneider the period during the same distance would have increased to nearly 12 sec. It is this apparent increase in wave period which can be misleading. It has already been shown that wave trains move with a velocity equal to half the wave velocity. With time the height of the waves in the different wave period groups will vary relative to one another, therefore the period of the highest wave need not remain constant, although each wave train still moves with the appropriate velocity. The dispersion of the wave spectrum, which naturally follows from the concept of travel at the appropriate group velocity, also affects the apparent wave heights which are made up of the superimposition of many different wave trains to form the wave spectrum. Bretschneider does not consider the waves as a complete spectrum.

Observations by Donn (1949)[21] made near Cape Cod confirm the findings of Barber and Ursell with regard to the group velocity of travel of swell; the increase in period shown on the decay graphs of Bretschneider was not apparent in their observations.

NEUMANN. More recently data has been presented in another way by Neumann (1953),[22] giving results which differ somewhat from those of Bretschneider. His work is largely theoretical in character and is based on the complete wave spectrum. Examination of the wave spectrum shows that the wave energy is concentrated in a relatively narrow band; the range of periods within this band determines the actual wave pattern. Until recently, owing to the limited instrumental data concerning the character of waves in the generating area in deep water, use was made of visual observations. The most easily observed dimension is the length of time between successive crests. This figure can be called the apparent 'period' $\bar{T}$ of the waves. These 'periods' can be related empirically to the speed of the generating wind, each wind producing a certain range of periods with a well defined maximum, which increases with the wind velocity. These empirical relationships can be supported theoretically.

Considering the spectrum, the wave components with a significant amount of energy cover a well defined band of the f scale, where f is $1/T$. A 20-knot wind, for example, covers a range of $f=0.083$ to $f=0.30$, or 12–3 secs. at with a maximum period $f_{max}=0.124$ or $T_{max}=8.1$ sec. There is a very rapid increase of energy, which is proportional to the square of the spectral wave height, as the wind increases. The frequency of the optimum band is given by $f_{max}=\dfrac{2.475}{U\ kts.}$ and $T_{max}=0.405\ U$. The total energy is shown to be proportional to the fifth power of the wind speed in a fully developed sea with composite wave motion. The wave heights can be considered in terms of the average height, the height of the highest $\frac{1}{3}$ of the waves, or the highest $1/10$ of the waves. The relationship between these values has been found from wave records and theory by Longuet-Higgins (1952)[15] giving the following results:

$$H_{av}/H_{\frac{1}{3}} = 0.65 \text{ (from wave records) } 0.625 \text{ (theory)}$$
$$H_{\frac{1}{10}}/H_{\frac{1}{3}} = 1.29 \text{ (from wave records) } 1.27 \text{ (theory)}$$

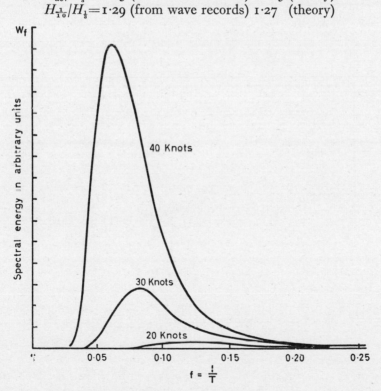

FIG. 3–7. (*a*) Wave spectra for fully arisen sea at a wind speed of 20, 30 and 40 knots, respectively. (After Neumann, B.E.B.)

These values can be related to the computed wave energy. The wave height can also be related to the wind velocity by the formula H (cm.) $=0.9 \times 10^{-5}$ (U cm./sec.)$^{2.5}$ this fits closely to the observed upper limit of the wave height, but further data are desirable. This figure, however, agrees with the relationship already given for the total energy which depends on U^5 as the height depends upon $U^{2.5}$.

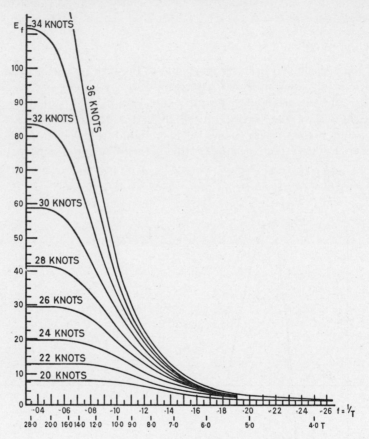

Fig. 3–7. (*b*) Co-cumulative power spectra for ocean waves at wind velocities between 20 and 36 knots. (After Neumann, B.E.B.)

Neumann has developed a graphical representation of the wave spectrum in a diagram he calls the co-cumulative power spectrum. Fig. 3–7 shows the curves for winds of speeds between 20 and 36 knots. The ordinate scale is in units of E, which can be converted into wave heights, as it is a function of the wave energy, the abscissae is in f or T units, the wave period, so that the wave height and period for the whole range of the spectrum can be found. From this graph the significant range of period can be found by ignoring the upper 5 per cent and lower 3 per cent of the curve. Table 1 gives the resulting upper and lower limits of the wave periods and table 2 the period of the most energetic wave and $\tilde{T}$, together with the various wave heights.

TABLE 1

Significant range of periods in fully arisen sea at different velocities. (U)

U knots	T_l sec.	T_u sec.	U knots	T_l sec.	T_u sec.
10	1·0	6·0	34	5·5	18·5
12	1·0	7·0	36	5·8	19·7
14	1·5	7·8	38	6·2	20·8
16	2·0	8·8	40	6·5	21·7
18	2·5	10·0	42	6·8	23·0
20	3·0	11·1	44	7·0	24·0
22	3·4	12·2	46	7·2	25·0
24	3·7	13·5	48	7·5	26·0
26	4·1	14·5	50	7·7	27·0
28	4·5	15·5	52	8·0	28·5
30	4·7	16·7	54	8·2	29·5
32	5·0	17·5	56	8·5	31·0

TABLE 2

Characteristics of fully arisen sea

U knots	$\tilde{T}$ sec.	T_{max} sec.	H_{av} ft.	$H_{\frac{1}{4}}$ ft.	$H_{\frac{1}{10}}$ ft.
10	2·8	4·0	0·88	1·41	1·79
12	3·4	4·8	1·39	2·22	2·82
14	4·0	5·6	2·04	3·26	4·15
16	4·6	6·5	2·85	4·56	5·80
18	5·1	7·2	3·80	6·1	7·8
20	5·7	8·1	5·0	8·0	10·2
22	6·3	8·9	6·4	10·2	12·8
24	6·8	9·7	7·9	12·5	16·0
26	7·4	10·5	9·6	15·4	19·6
28	8·0	11·3	11·3	18·2	23·1
30	8·5	12·1	13·5	21·6	27·6
32	9·1	12·9	16·1	25·8	32·8
34	9·7	13·6	18·6	29·8	38·0
36	10·2	14·5	21·6	34·5	43·8
38	10·8	15·4	24·7	39·5	50·2
40	11·4	16·1	28·2	45·2	57·5
42	12·0	17·0	31·4	50·1	63·9
44	12·5	17·7	36·0	57·7	73·4
46	13·1	18·6	39·7	63·5	80·6
48	13·7	19·4	44·4	71·0	90·4
50	14·2	20·2	48·9	78·0	99·4
52	14·8	21·0	54	87	110
54	15·4	21·8	59	95	121
56	15·9	22·6	64	103	130

T_{max} is period of the most energetic wave in spectrum.

$\tilde{T}$ is average 'period'.

Neumann has also presented curves and tables showing the effect of fetch and wind duration on the generation of waves. He has superimposed lines of constant duration and fetch on the curves of wave generation already mentioned. The limiting effect of these factors can be easily

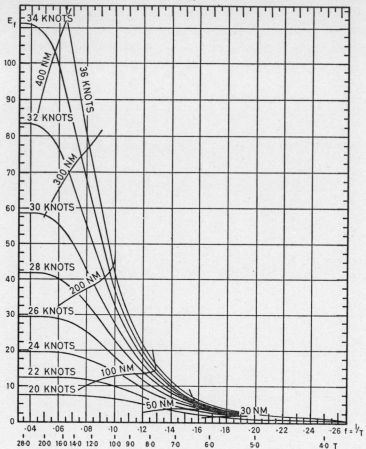

FIG. 3–7. (*c*) Co-cumulative spectra for wind speeds from 20 to 36 knots as a function of fetch. (After Neumann, B.E.B.)

assessed in terms of wave period and height. It is clear from the fig. 3–7 (c, d) that as the wind speed increases so the fetch and duration required for the generation of a full sea increase.

Further refinements in the actual process of preparing a forecast are described in H.O. Publication 603 (1955).[23] The character and position of the storm in relation to the point for which a forecast is required is taken into account by the use of filters. These allow for the angular spreading of the waves, which results from the variation in direction of wave travel within the storm area. Filter I considers a line source of waves and determines which wave directions and periods affect any point not in the direct path of the generating storm. Filter II takes into account the effect of the fetch over which the storm winds are blowing

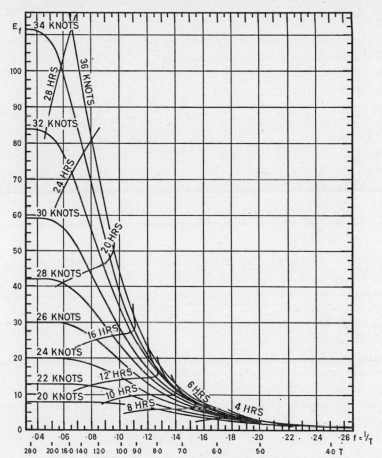

Fig. 3–7. (*d*) Co-cumulative spectra for wind speeds from 20 to 36 knots as a function of duration. (After Neumann, B.E.B.)

and calculates the arrival of waves generated near the rear of the storm. Filter III considers the situation in which the storm area is moving at about the speed of the generated waves and hence storm and waves arrive almost simultaneously. Filter IV estimates the result of a rapid cessation of storm winds and the resulting reduction in height of the waves generated by them. All synoptic situations must be simplified for analytical purposes, but the importance of the width of the fetch is made clear, in its effect on the wave height and the width of the wave front.

ROLL AND FISCHER. A modification of the wave spectrum method of forecasting the state of the sea devised by Neumann and Pierson has been put forward by Roll and Fischer (1956).[24] They point out that two empirical formulae for the mean wave energy in a particular small period or frequency band given by Neumann give different values for the period of the wave of maximum energy, T_{max}. One formula uses the wave period and the other the frequency; T_{max} is given by differentiation, the first formula gives T_{max} as 0·641 U (U in m./sec. and T in sec.) the second gives T_{max} as 0·785 U. Neumann only gives the latter formula. The difference is due to the different powers of T which enter the formulae and can be resolved if the period and frequency relationship is taken logarithmically and not linearly, as Neumann does. With this modification the second formula now yields the result $T_{max}=0·641\ U$ so that the two formulae now agree.

The expression derived for the increment of energy can be integrated to give the total wave energy from the previous formula if it is extended to all frequencies between 0 and ∞. The total energy is given in terms of the wind speed as follows:

$$E = \frac{c\ \rho\ \pi^2}{16g}\ U^4 \ (ergs\ cm.^{-2})\ \rho\ \text{is density and}\ c\ \text{is a constant}$$

This formula relates the wave energy to the fourth power of the wind speed and not the fifth as given in Neumann's formula. The wave energy is proportional to the square of the wave height, which Sverdrup and Munk have shown to be proportional to the square of the wind speed, the fourth power is therefore more likely to be correct than the fifth.

Roll and Fischer derive the constant c in the above formula by two methods which give the value as c is $1·96 \times 10^{-2}$, Neumann gives the value of c as $8·27 \times 10^{-4}$ (sec.$^{-1}$) for the constant from observations. A direct comparison of the two values is not possible because they relate to different forms of the energy equation and have different dimensions.

The constant given by Roll and Fischer can be tested by relating the wave energy to the mean height of the apparent sea, $\widetilde{\overline{H}}$. Taking the value given by Longuet-Higgins for $\widetilde{\overline{H}}=1·772\sqrt{E}$ and using the previous formula in which c is taken as $1·96 \times 10^{-2}$, $\widetilde{\overline{H}}= \dfrac{0·275}{g} U^2$. This value agrees satisfactorily with that given by Sverdrup and Munk (1947) (0·26) and Rossby and Montgomery (1935) (0·30). There is, however doubt about the derivation of the values as they are based on visual observations of the significant wave height, $\widetilde{H_{\frac{1}{3}}}$. The correlation of this value with $\widetilde{\overline{H}}$ the mean height, of the apparent sea is doubtful. According to the present analysis for a fully developed sea $\widetilde{H_{\frac{1}{3}}}=2·832\sqrt{E}$, which according to the relation given by Longuet-Higgins and the formula already used gives $\tilde{H}_{\frac{1}{3}} = \frac{0 \cdot 44}{g} U^2$. This value is very high and casts some doubt on the value of c which does not yet appear to be very satisfactory. The constant c depends on whether the relationships of Neumann, which have been used so far, do in fact correctly relate the apparent and true wave size. It seems possible that the value of c is too great.

Walden (1956)[25] has suggested a new value for the constant c as $0 \cdot 48 \times 10^{-2}$ which gives the formula $\tilde{H}_{\frac{1}{3}}$ as $\frac{0 \cdot 22}{g} U^2$ instead of $\frac{0 \cdot 44}{g} U^2$. The factor $0 \cdot 22$ is lower than those of Sverdrup and Munk and Rossby and Montgomery but it appears to give satisfactory results.

DARBYSHIRE. Darbyshire (1952)[26] has analysed the generation of waves by storms in fetches of varying length on an experimental basis; some measurements were made in the open ocean with fetches of 100–1,000 miles, others in the Irish Sea with fetches of 40–100 miles and for the shorter fetches Lough Neagh was used, with fetches of 1–10 miles. The aim of the analysis is to establish the spectral distribution of wave energy in the storm area. The wave spectrum is analysed to give a series of sine waves whose periods are submultiples of the duration of the record and whose heights are proportional to the heights of the peaks of the spectrum.

The wave energy is given by $\frac{1}{8} g \rho H^2$ for a wave of height H, the total energy will, therefore, be $\frac{1}{8} g \rho \Sigma H^2_n$, where H_n is the height of the nth peak in the spectrum. From this the equivalent height of a hypothetical wave having the same energy as the complicated wave train can be calculated and related to the maximum observed height. The equivalent height H_T can be found in the same way for any given wave period band of 1 sec., T, i.e. $T - \frac{1}{2}$ to $T + \frac{1}{2}$. These heights can then be related to the strength of the generating winds and the length of fetch.

It was found from the analysis that the maximum wave period in seconds is about $\frac{1}{3}$ of the maximum gradient wind in knots. The period of the highest waves was found to be about $\frac{1}{4}$ of the mean gradient wind speed in knots, U_g, this value held for fetches of considerable length. The value of the equivalent height, H, is given by $H = 0 \cdot 027 U_g^{\frac{3}{2}}$ (H in feet, U_g gradient wind in knots).

All the relationships given were derived from observations in fetches greater than 100 miles; they indicate that for waves of 13 sec. period, which was the maximum considered, an increase of fetch would not significantly change the relations H_T/T and T/U_g. The rather surprising conclusion was reached that the wave characteristics become more or less independent of the fetch after 200–300 miles.

Silvester (1955)[27] has drawn graphs for Darbyshire's formulae which are given in fig. 3–8, the first relates the wave height for different wind speeds to the fetch. The wave height is given in terms of the mean wave height, H_{mean}, which is the average of all waves, and which is taken as 1·0; then H, the equivalent height, is 1·2 H_{mean}. The significant height is 1·6 H_{mean}, and the maximum height is 2·4 H_{mean}. The significant period can also be related to the wind velocity and the fetch, F, by the formula, shown in the second graph, $T_s = 0·24\ U_g\ (1 - exp\ (-0·23\ F)^{\frac{1}{2}})$ (T_s in sec. U_g in knots and F in nautical miles.) Computation of these data from the observed heights and periods of Sverdrup and Munk[11] give a satisfactory agreement.

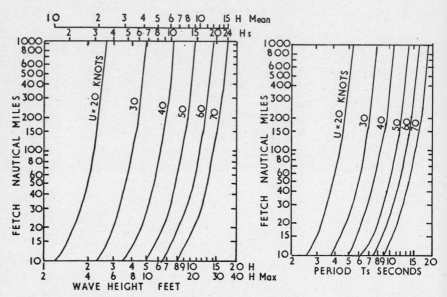

Fig. 3–8. Graph relating wave height and fetch for varying wind speeds and wave periods and fetch for varying wind speeds for the formulae of Darbyshire. (After Silvester.)

The steepness of the waves is important and is given by $0·149/U_{\frac{1}{2}}$ where U is surface wind for a fully developed sea. This factor depends on the square root of the wind velocity and on the stage of development of the waves if they are not yet fully developed. The latter factor can be given in terms of the ratio of wave speed to wind speed according to Sverdrup and Munk (C/U). The steepness of the highest waves is then equal to $0·163/U^{\frac{1}{2}}\ (C/U)$. The work of Darbyshire (1952) which has just been discussed is based upon observations made largely at Perranporth in Cornwall in the Irish Sea and Lough Neagh in Northern Ireland.

More recently Darbyshire (1955)[28] has analysed wave data recorded in deep water by the Ocean Weather Ship '*Weather Explorer*', situated in the North Atlantic Ocean at 61°N, 15° 20′W and 52° 20′N, 20°W. These observations were carried out by a shipborne wave recorder, between February 1953 and January 1954 (see p. 92). It was found that the formulae already given, which apply to waves generated in relatively shallow water over the continental shelf, cannot be applied accurately to waves generated in deep water. Empirical results of the analysis indicate that the effect of fetch is small after 100 miles, in deep as well as shallow water. The period of the longest wave was found to depend on $2 \cdot 3 \ U_g^{\frac{1}{2}}$ instead of $U_g/3$, while the period of the highest wave was $1 \cdot 64 \ U_g^{\frac{1}{2}}$ instead of $U_g/4$. The value of the equivalent height is now $H = 0 \cdot 0038 \ U_g^2$. This indicates that in deep water lower wave heights are generated with winds under 50 knots but at higher speeds greater heights are found. The ratio of wave steepness to wind speed for a fully developed sea for deep water equals $0 \cdot 00028$, this means that it increases linearly with wind speed, whereas in shallow water it decreases; the points plotted on the graph, however, show a large scatter. In both shallow and deep water the steepness of the waves increases as the fetch increases till the equilibrium value is attained.

Darbyshire (1956)[29] has since filled in a gap in the studies of the wave generation which had previously concentrated on the fetches of less than 1 mile or greater than 100 miles by studying the wave generation in fetches of lengths up to 100 miles. He has re-analysed observations made on Lough Neagh in the light of the results obtained from the analysis of the deep ocean records already mentioned.

On Lough Neagh two wave recorders were used; one was fixed at the north-east corner of the lake, and the other was portable and was used in several different positions. Wind speeds and direction were obtained from the anemograph situated at Aldergrove on the north-east shore of the Lough. The wind speeds were multiplied by 3/2 to give the equivalent gradient wind. A relationship between the maximum wave height and the wind speed is given by H_{max} (ft.)$= 0 \cdot 0032 \ U_g^2$ (knots^2) and T_s (sec.)$= 0 \cdot 67 \ U_g^{\frac{1}{2}}$ (knots$^{\frac{1}{2}}$) where T_s is the significant period. For the open sea the formulae were $H_{max} = 0 \cdot 0076 \ U_g^2$ and $T_s = 1 \cdot 64 \ U_g^{\frac{1}{2}}$. The same ratio of $0 \cdot 41$ holds between the short fetch wave height and the large fetch wave heights and between the short and long fetch periods. If the ratio of the wave height at any fetch to that in infinite fetch is termed y its value can be given in terms of x, the length of the fetch in nautical miles. Darbyshire gives the following formula for y which best fits his plotted data $y = (x^3 + 3x^2 + 65x)/(x^3 + 12x^2 + 260x + 80)$ this formula provides a good fit for fetches between $\frac{1}{4}$ and 100 miles, the curves are shown in fig. 3–9.

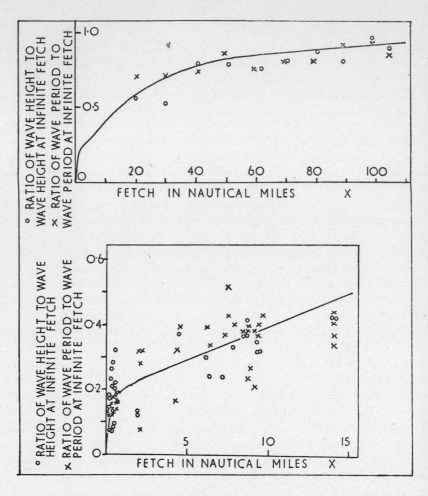

FIG. 3–9. Relationship between wave characteristics and fetch related to infinite fetch. (After Darbyshire.)

ATTENUATION. Since so many waves reach the coast after a long period of decay, the changes which take place after the waves cease to be generated are very important. The problem of the attenuation of swell has been considered recently by Darbyshire (1957).[30] He analysed the wave records of the *Weather Explorer*, considering decay distances of 400–1,600 miles. In the analysis H_T is used, which is the square root of the peaks for each 1 sec. period interval; it is the height of the simple sine wave having the same energy as the total energy of the spectrum for that period interval. The values of H_T for each wave period tend to reach a maximum value at a particular time; the wave propagation lines from these points meet at the centre of the storm. The value of T_{max}, the maximum wave period with a measurable H_T value and T_s the period with the highest H_T value could be determined. T_{max} was found to depend on the gradient wind according to $T_{max}=2\cdot30\ U_g^{\frac{1}{2}}$ and $T_s=1\cdot64\ U_g^{\frac{1}{2}}$, with U_g in knots and T in seconds. From the plots of the results it appears that the ratio, $H_T/H^0{}_T$, where $H^0{}_T$ is the value of H_T for the generating area, does not vary with the period and velocity of the following winds. These values are shown on fig. 3–10 and it can be seen

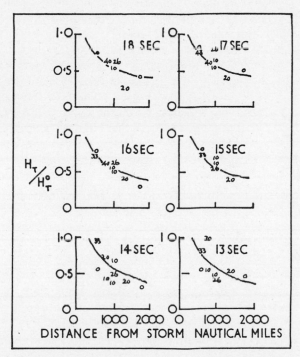

FIG. 3–10. Reduction of wave height in relation to distance from storm centre and strength of following winds. (After Darbyshire.)

that they do not affect the curves. The reduction in wave height appears to depend largely on the decay distance, D, according to the formula $H_T/H^0{}_T=(300/D)^{\frac{1}{2}}$, where D is in nautical miles. This is a simpler relation than that proposed by Bretschneider, but it also shows the very considerable reduction in wave height with decay distance.

The reduction in height is the result of three possible causes; firstly, dispersion, although the effect of this factor is reduced by using only a narrow frequency band for the analysis. Secondly, loss of energy due to air resistance and turbulence; these factors depend on the wave period, which has been shown to be insignificant in this respect, and therefore they are not important. The third factor is divergence which probably causes the observed effect. Computed and observed values of wave height and period for swell at Casablanca agreed to within 25 per cent, using the relations given, most of the results being considerably better.

In estimating the wave pattern in any coastal area it must be borne in mind that swell travels a very long distance without losing its identity. If it has been generated by strong winds of long duration, to give it a relatively low steepness value, it will have a slow rate of attenuation. For example, Wiegel and Kimberley (1950)[31] drew attention to the presence of swell on the coast of California, during the summer months, which had originated in the south Pacific Ocean between 40° and 65° south and 120°–160° west. This swell normally had a significant breaker height of 2–6 ft., but reached a maximum of 10–12 ft., it had a very long period of 12–18 sec., sometimes reached 22 sec. and had probably travelled up to 7,000 miles. This swell would not have been considered if only the relatively local weather situation had been taken into account, it is nevertheless very important in a consideration of the beach processes.

COMPARISON OF DIFFERENT METHODS OF WAVE FORECASTING. The state of wave forecasting from meteorological data is such that it is not yet possible to choose definitely between the different methods put forward. One may give better results in one area, while another may suit somewhere else. It is likely that in many areas local conditions may have to be taken into account.

Sverdrup, Munk and Bretschneider's curves are entirely empirical and only attempt to give a value for the significant wave heights and lengths. Neumann's method, with the later modification of Roll and Fischer, is largely theoretical but they do attempt to consider the whole spectrum of the waves. Darbyshire's results are based on more precise measurements than the other methods, and adopt a more experimental approach.

A comparison of the three techniques of forecasting wave heights has been recorded by Dearduff (1955),[32] for a storm off California. As Darbyshire pointed out, the decay of the waves appears to be largely due to divergence; the width of the fetch is thus an important factor. For example if one fetch is twice as wide as another it will, for the same decay conditions, produce waves $\sqrt{2}$ higher than the other. The particular storm considered occurred in October 1950 and the various wave heights recorded and forecast, using the same fetch pattern, are shown in fig. 3–11. It can be seen that the Neumann, or wave spectrum technique, gives waves much higher than the other methods, and twice as high as the observed waves. One reason may have been due to the comparative difficulty of using the original curves of Neumann. Another point which applies to all methods of forecasting waves is the difficulty of analysing the synoptic chart correctly to give an accurate value for the fetch, length and width, the wind direction and force. The same fetch and wind force were used for the different forecasting methods. In this example it appears that the Bretschneider method gives the most reliable estimate of the wave height. Until the newer methods have been tested more thoroughly it is premature to be dogmatic about the relative merits of the different techniques. Neumann's curves have been redrawn to make their application easier in the form of distorted co-cumulative spectra graphs. These are discussed in detail in the manual for forecasting waves published by the U.S. Hydrographic Office.[23] In any case one of the major problems of deciding on the appropriate fetch pattern and wind

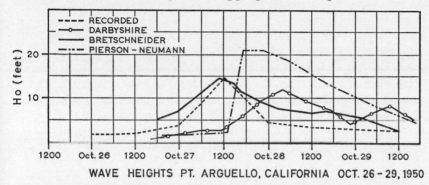

WAVE HEIGHTS PT. ARGUELLO, CALIFORNIA OCT. 26 - 29, 1950

FIG. 3-11. Correlation of three different techniques of forecasting waves with observed wave heights. (After Dearduff, B.E.B.)

character must remain relatively subjective, and the synoptic chart over the sea may not be a true representation of reality. James (1954)[33] has discussed an example of the application of the wave spectra method to wave forecasting, and shows that there is an excellent agreement between the forecast and observed data, using the Neumann-Pierson technique. Use of this technique for preparing wave charts for shipping has been discussed by James (1957)[34] who states that the prognostic charts have been found rather accurate, 85 per cent of the forecast heights were within ±4 ft. of observed heights, many of which were over 25 ft.

One difficulty in attempting to assess the relative accuracy of the different methods is the lack of detailed measurements of complete wave spectra in the oceans. Neumann and Pierson (1957)[35] have recently made a detailed comparison of four different families of curves with one measured wave spectrum. The first is that given by Darbyshire in 1952 from the wave recordings off Cornwall, the second is Neumann's of 1953 and 1954, the third is a modification of Darbyshire's earlier work based on wave recordings made in the open ocean, lastly Roll and Fischer's modification of Neumann's original curves are used. One difficulty found in comparing the different methods, is that Darbyshire has used the gradient wind, derived from synoptic charts, while the other methods use the surface wind speeds. It is difficult to relate gradient winds accurately to surface winds for different conditions. The gradient wind formulae have been correlated with the surface wind ones by taking the surface wind as two-thirds the gradient wind.

Neumann and Pierson do not consider that the modification of their curve made by Roll and Fischer is necessary. The difference arises owing to the use of different scales by the two methods; Roll and Fischer's is logarithmic and their own is a linear frequency curve; other workers suggest that it is not possible to decide between the relative merits of the two techniques at present.

In all the spectra the fully developed sea depends only on the wind strength, the Neumann and Darbyshire spectra grow from high to low frequency with increasing fetch and fixed wind speed. The differences between the spectra are quite considerable particularly with high winds and long fetches. The areas under the Darbyshire spectrum and the Roll-Fischer spectrum vary as U^4 but the Neumann spectrum varies as U^5. The variation of wave energy at the high frequency end of the spectrum varies such that $E_f \, 1/f^5$ for Roll-Fischer, $E_f \, 1/f^6$ for Neumann and $E_f \, 1/f^7$ for Darbyshire.

The stereo wave observation project (S.W.O.P.) attempted to measure a wave spectrum at sea, using a wave pole developed by the Woods Hole Oceanographic Institute. One problem was the elimination of swell and waves from other directions, the spectrum determined was developed by an $18·7$ knot wind measured at 18 ft. elevation, which lasted at least 10 hours. The spectrum calculated from the observations has been compared with the three different theoretical spectra; compared to Darbyshire's spectrum the peak of the theoretical spectrum is too far to the left, giving a maximum height at too long a period. The Roll-Fischer curves come nearer but now the peak of the theoretical curve for $18·7$ knot wind is too far to the right, implying too low a period for the maximum height, which is a little too low. Of the three spectra the Neumann one fits best giving the correct period for the maximum height wave.

The significant height of the waves can be given in the three formulae approximately as follows: Darbyshire $\bar{H}_{\frac{1}{3}} = 6·18 \times 10^{-5} \, U_g^2$ or $1·39 \times 10^{-4} \, U^2$ (U is surface wind. $U = 2U_g/3$.) Roll-Fischer $\bar{H}_{\frac{1}{3}} = 2·667 \times 10^{-4} \, U^2$ which is also Sverdrup-Munk-Bretschneider's value, Neumann $\bar{H}_{\frac{1}{3}} = 7·065 \times 10^{-6} \, U^{2.5}$, $\bar{H}_{\frac{1}{3}}$ in cm., wind in cm./sec. These formulae only apply to fully developed seas, which are rarely obtained for the higher wind values, hence it is difficult to check the curves. It would appear that the Darbyshire results are too low and that the $U^{2.5}$ law gives more reliable results in this one instance; however, the observed wave spectrum is open to various interpretations from the measurements on which it is based.

Bretschneider (1957)[36] has considered the various powers of the wind speed which have been proposed to govern the height of waves, and concludes that the square of the wind speed is the correct value rather than the 5/2 power and that at high wind speeds, above 35 knots, the Neumann method is liable to error.

The average period also appears to fit the observed data most closely from the formula of Neumann. Darbyshire gets too long periods for low wind speeds implying that the orbital velocity is greater than the wind velocity at low speeds. The wave steepness value for the formula of Roll-Fischer, which gives a constant steepness for all wind speeds, appears to be much too high, 0·175 for the highest 1/10 waves and 0·14 for the highest $\frac{1}{3}$; Darbyshire's results, on the other hand, appear to give rather too low steepness values for slow wind speeds according to Neumann and Pierson. They consider that the Roll-Fischer results lead to waves with impossible statistical properties they will not, therefore, be discussed further.

Darbyshire (1957)[37] gives an example of the use of his own and the Neumann-Pierson-James formula to determine wave dimensions generated by winds averaging 40 knots on 8–10 October 1954 at 59°N, 19°20′W. Darbyshire's prediction in this instance, although rather lower than the recorded values at some times, is much closer than the Neumann method value, where the results are very much too high. Other examples given also show that Darbyshire's results are closer to the measured heights and periods.

Roll (1957)[38] has shown that 1,232 measurements of waves in the North Sea are much closer to the computed values of Darbyshire than Neumann, whose results are too high by 50 per cent or more, especially for higher fetch and durations. These waves were, however, generated over a shallow bottom and Pierson has critized the method of presentation.

Cartwright (1957)[39] has drawn attention to the importance of the air-sea temperature difference in the generation of waves; for example Fleagle (1956)[40] has shown that an 11° decrease of air temperature relative to sea temperature causes a doubling of wave height for the same wind speed. This factor may account for some of the scatter between the recorded and computed values.

Darbyshire considers that a fetch of 100 nautical miles is all that is needed to generate a full sea for a wide range of wind speeds, while Neumann requires increasing fetches and durations for increasing wind speed, thus a 50-knot wind requires 1,420 nautical miles and 69-hours duration. The extreme rarity of such conditions make it difficult to test the upper part of the scale. Records of a severe storm in the North Pacific gave observed wave heights of 48 ft., these were generated by winds of 45–55 knots blowing for 33 hrs. in a fetch of 500 nautical miles. Forecasts by Neumann and Bretschneider both agreed with this value but Darbyshire's results gave a height of only 36 ft. According to Neumann it appears therefore that Darbyshire's results are liable to be too low for high winds and long duration. However, Darbyshire (1957)[37] has pointed out that the value of 48 ft. could be 20–30 per cent in error; a reduction of this order would bring the value into agreement with instrumental observations under similar conditions in the Atlantic Ocean. At low velocities Bretschneider's curves give too high waves probably owing to dead sea in some of the data used.

Observations show that on Lake Superior where the fetch is of the order of 100–250 nautical miles waves much greater than 20 ft. are not produced while in the open Atlantic over long fetches 60 ft. waves are developed. Ursell (1956)[41] has pointed out that Cox and Munk's (1954) work on sun glitter of the sea surface is consistent with Neumann's spectrum but not with Darbyshire's.

Summary

Four different methods of empirical forecasting of waves are considered. The Sverdrup-Munk-Bretschneider curves relate empirically the significant dimensions of the waves to the generating wind's velocity and duration and to the fetch. They are derived from observations of waves in the ocean and at the coast. Bretschneider has also produced curves to illustrate the attenuation of waves, as a function of decay distance, for height decrease and period increase.

Neumann has produced curves and tables to illustrate semi-empirical approach to the forecasting of the complete theoretical wave spectrum for different wind speeds. He also considers the effect of duration and fetch. The range of period and apparent period of waves are related to wind velocity; the wave heights are derived from the energy of the spectrum from relationships set up by Longuet-Higgins. Roll and Fischer have subsequently put forward a modification of Neumann's theoretical formulae in which they relate the wave energy to the fourth power of the wind speed and not to the fifth as in Neumann's formula.

Darbyshire has also produced a wave spectrum method of forecasting waves from an analysis of many observations made in the open ocean, coastal stations, seas and lakes. The generation of waves was found to differ in the shallow water coastal stations and the deep ocean, in the former the equivalent wave height depended on $U_g^{3/2}$ while in the open ocean it depended on $U_g{}^2$. Darbyshire found that waves reached their maximum size in a fetch of little more than 100 nautical miles. He also worked on the attenuation of swell; from his analysis he derived the formula $H_T/H_T{}^0 = (300/D)^{\frac{1}{2}}$ (D in nautical miles). The cause of the attenuation is probably divergence of the wave front.

Various attempts to test the value of the different methods are not very conclusive in their results. This is partly due to the difficulty of measuring the wave spectrum in the ocean. In one test Bretschneider's results fitted the observations best but in others Neumann's seemed to approximate most closely to the observed values. Darbyshire's results appear to fit very closely observed data at Casablanca and adequately in the North Sea. It seems likely that Neumann's results may give wave heights which are much too high; this is partly due to the use of observed heights in the derivation of the curves, rather than measured heights, as it is very easy to over-estimate wave heights. The earlier methods of Sverdrup, Munk and Bretschneider should be superseded by the newer spectrum technique but until more accurate observations are available wave forecasting will not become an exact process.

(d) Wave observations

Owing to the difficulty and doubt of forecasting waves which the foregoing account should have made clear, it is of value to obtain a statistical summary of the probable pattern of wave attack, from observed values, in any area. Some attempts to do this in different areas will be mentioned.

Saville (1954)[42] attempts to analyse the probable pattern of wave attack for four stations on the east coast of the U.S.A. in percentage of time that waves from different directions and of varying height may be expected to come. The results were based on Bretschneider's curves for deep water and have been modified by the use of refraction formulae to obtain the shallow water wave pattern. The refraction diagrams were complicated by the Hudson Canyon which caused the orthogonals to cross in a complex pattern. To check the accuracy of the data wave recorder observations were made in a depth of 20 ft. for the period from April 1948 till October 1949. The computed and observed waves agreed well for heights up to about 5 ft. but for higher waves the disagreement increases considerably. This was thought to be due to the method used for refraction analysis, which tended to over-emphasize the convergence effect of waves coming from due east, one of the assumed directions; waves coming from only 5 deg. to either side would be considerably less refracted. This indicates the danger of generalizing the direction of attack to 16 points of the compass. A great improvement between the observed and computed data was obtained by splitting all the waves in each segment arbitrarily into three groups, and asigning each part its appropriate refraction value, derived from a diagram such as that shown in fig. 3–18 (p. 99).

From an analysis such as Saville's (1954) it is possible to calculate the total number of occasions on which waves of a certain height and period group will come from each direction, in the form of a diagram as shown in fig. 3–12. This is based on a statistical analysis of the data, which also gives the frequency with which waves of specified height may be expected to occur, thus at one station near Cape Cod 20-ft. waves may be expected on 2 per cent of days, while a 10-ft. wave will probably occur

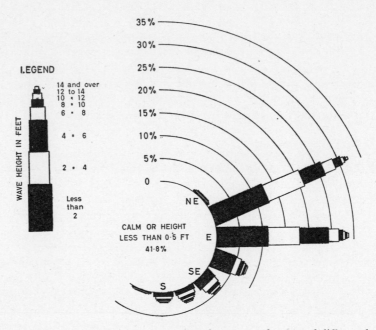

FIG. 3–12. (*a*) Wave rose to show percentage frequency of waves of different height coming from various directions off New York Harbour Entrance. (After Saville, B.E.B.)

on 16 per cent of days, but a 36-ft. wave will only be expected once every three years. This sort of data is of great value in a study of the processes at work on any particular stretch of coast, and in a consideration of coastal defence problems.

Neumann and James (1955)[43] in their analysis of the same stations have divided the wave roses into seasonal divisions which gives a more detailed picture of the wave pattern. Their results have not been modified for shallow water and as a result will not be as accurate as those of Saville for coastal areas. They could be adjusted by use of refraction diagrams. Because of this limitation they cannot be compared directly

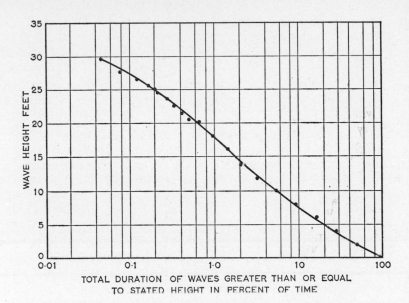

FIG. 3–12. (*b*) Frequency of occurrence of waves above a given height. (After Saville, B.E.B.)

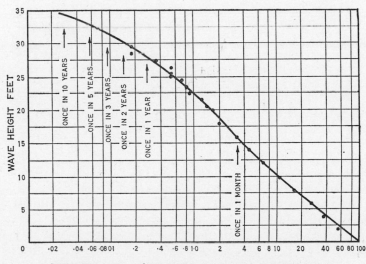

FIG. 3–12. (*c*) Total duration of waves greater than or equal to a stated wave height. (After Saville, B.E.B.)

with the near-shore observations. The computed and observed wave parameters agree quite closely for sea and swell.

Somewhat similar data have been published by Darbyshire (1955).[44] The observations he uses were made in the North Atlantic at the positions 61°N, 15°20′W, and 52°30′N, 20°W and these are compared with records taken at Perranporth on the coast of Cornwall. The observations in mid-Atlantic were made during the period February 1953 to January 1954 while those for the coastal station are for the period between February 1946 and January 1947. The results are shown by plotting the percentage time that the wave height falls between two limits, i.e. 40–50 ft., 30–40 ft., 25–30 ft., 20–25 ft., 15–20 ft., 10–15 ft., 5–10 ft., and below 5 ft., for each month; the mean wave period of each group is also shown.

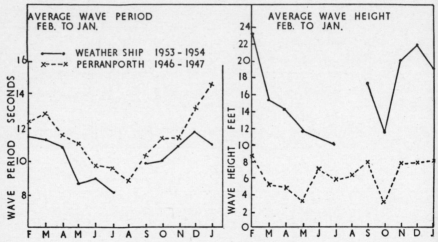

FIG. 3–13. Average monthly wave period and height for Perranporth and mid-Atlantic Weather Ship. (After Darbyshire.)

The significant wave periods (mean period of highest $\frac{1}{3}$ waves) are analysed in a similar way and the corresponding mean heights given. The results show that the wave heights in the open ocean are very much greater than in coastal waters; 40–50 ft. waves are not uncommon in the winter months in the open ocean but waves over 20 ft. only occur for a small percentage of the time in the coastal waters. On the other hand the significant period of the waves is much longer on the coast; periods over 15 sec. are much more common on the coast than in mid-ocean, on the coast they may occur for as much as 45 per cent of the time in some months, but they never exceed 5 per cent in mid-ocean in the winter. It must be remembered that the two years compared are not the same at both stations. It does appear that the process of wave generation is not so efficient in shallow water, possibly due to tidal streams, higher waves being generated in mid-ocean. The shorter period waves are also probably attenuated by the same cause resulting in the predominance of the longer waves at the coast. Fig. 3–13 shows the average monthly significant period and wave height at the two stations. In general the longer and higher waves occur during the winter months, although this relationship is not very marked for the wave heights at Perranporth, owing to high values in June and August.

The statistical distribution of wave height has been calculated by Jasper (1955).[45] The figures given above are actual means for one particular year but the data of this type can also be expressed statistically. The data used by Jasper consists of 12,000 observations from U.S. Weather ship data; he expresses the data in the form $y = A \, exp - (\log x - \log a)^2/b^2$, y is the probability density, x is the significant wave height and a most probable value of x. Darbyshire (1956)[46] has fitted this formula to three years' observations of the O.W.S. *Weather Explorer* in three positions in mid-Atlantic including the two already given and 59°N, 19°W. By plotting the data so that the y axis is the time percentage that any given height is exceeded and the x axis is the maximum wave height the scales can be arranged so that the points fall on a straight line if the logarithmic normal law holds. This was found to be true for values between $4\frac{1}{2}$ and 45 ft. but not outside these limits (see fig. 3–14A). The logarithmic normal distribution can be plotted by dividing the waves into 1-ft. groups and plotting the percentage in each group (see fig. 3–14 B). The points plotted fall almost on the curve given by $y = 6 \cdot 6 \, exp - (\log x/9)^2 /0 \cdot 126$. This curve fits the observations for the three separate years plotted independently showing that there is no significant variation in the pattern from year to year. Plots for different seasons do show some variation in pattern with the time of year, the following curves fit each seasonal group:

Dec.–March	$y = 6 \cdot 6 \, exp - (\log x/14)^2/0 \cdot 065$
April–July	$y = 9 \cdot 2 \, exp - (\log x/ \ 8)^2/0 \cdot 104$
August–Nov.	$y = 6 \cdot 1 \, exp - (\log x/ \ 8)^2/0 \cdot 137$

Wave data for Casablanca and Perranporth have been analysed in a similar way and the following relationships hold for these areas; Casablanca $y = 18 \, exp - (\log x/3 \cdot 5)^2/0 \cdot 137$ for four years 1952–5 (see fig. 3–14 C and D). Perranporth for 1946 gives $y = 13 \, exp - (\log x/4)^2/0 \cdot 199$ (see fig. 3–14 E). The figures show graphically the percentage frequency at which different wave heights might be expected to occur.

WAVE RECORDING METHODS. Shallow water wave recording instruments have been in use for many years, but methods of measuring waves in deep water, and finding the direction of waves in shallow water, have only been developed fairly recently. One method of measuring waves in the open ocean consists of a graduated pole attached by 200 ft. of wire to a drogue to hold it in position.

An instrument, devised at the National Institute of Oceanography, and described by Tucker (1952),[47] has been developed for use in ships. The instrument is contained in the hull of the ship. It measures the height of the water surface above a point on the ship's hull and the height of this point above a reference plane. The addition of the two amounts gives the height of the water surface above the reference plane and is, therefore, independent of the ship's movement. A small hole is

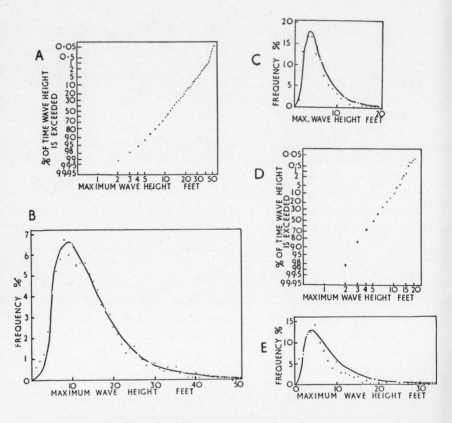

FIG. 3–14. (*a*) Graph of per cent time a value of maximum wave height is exceeded against the value of maximum wave height for all Weather Ship data. (*b*) Frequency of occurrence of value of maximum wave height against the value of maximum wave height for all Weather Ship data. (*c*) The same data for Casablanca. (*d*) Graph of per cent time a value of maximum wave height is exceeded against the value of maximum wave height for Casablanca. (*e*) Frequency of occurrence of value of maximum wave height against the value of maximum wave height for Perranporth in 1946. (After Darbyshire.)

bored in the ship's hull at a point 10 ft. below the water line, where the instrument is installed. Because the units are mounted at this depth short waves of less than 4 sec. are not recorded. Waves 30 ft. high have been measured in a gale Force 9 wind. The accuracy of the instrument is of the order of $\pm$10 per cent.

Another instrument devised recently is described by Barber (1954).[48] The technique, which was developed in Waitemata Harbour, New Zealand, provides a measurement of the energy distribution in different directions for waves of a narrow frequency band. Tests showed that the direction of maximum energy coincided with the wind direction at the time of observation. The instrument can be used at shore stations to measure the direction of travel of swell, and if the instruments are set out parallel to the bottom contours, and these are straight, wave refraction can be ignored.

Summary

It is possible to calculate statistically the frequency with which waves of various heights are likely to occur. Wave roses may also be constructed to show the proportion of time that waves of various heights come from different directions. Examples of these methods are given for the east coast of U.S.A.; weather ship data from mid-Atlantic and coastal data for Perranporth, Cornwall and Casablanca, North Africa are discussed. A method of observing waves with a ship-borne wave recorder gives results which are $\pm$10 per cent accuracy. A technique for measuring direction of approach of waves has also been devised recently.

3. *WAVE REFRACTION DIAGRAMS*

Before the waves reach the coast they must travel over the shallowing water of the offshore zone where they are influenced by the submarine relief as soon as they feel the bottom. The long swells and storm waves are particularly affected owing to their great length. In order to achieve a reliable estimate of the pattern of wave attack on any coast the effect of wave refraction must be taken into account. Because wave refraction depends on the nature of the offshore relief each area must be treated individually, although, as has already been mentioned, certain general principles apply. Before considering the implications of wave refraction the method of constructing wave refraction diagrams will be considered.[49]

(a) Method of construction of wave refraction diagrams

An accurate chart showing the bottom configuration to a depth equal to half the longest wave to be considered is necessary; the direction of approach of the waves in deep water and their period or length must be known. The latter information can either be observed or calculated by the techniques already considered. The refraction diagrams show wave crests and orthogonals; the latter lines, which are everywhere at right-angles to the wave crests, indicate the distribution of wave energy along the coast. The energy between equally spaced orthogonals in deep water should be equal and this remains nearly true as they are traced into shallow water, where they converge or diverge according to the relief.

If detailed refraction diagrams are required for any stretch of coast it is often useful to use a small scale chart, on a scale of about 1 : 100,000, to trace the waves into water about 1,000 ft. from the shore. More detailed diagrams can then be constructed for a small area by transferring the wave crests from the smaller to the larger scale, which might be about 1 : 12,000. On the large-scale chart the waves can then be followed into very shallow water. On the smaller scale charts wave crests may be drawn at intervals of about $10 L$, but on the large scale ones every other wave crest can be shown.

A table should first be prepared giving for each depth the following information: L/L_o, which is the length at the depth specified relative to the deep water length which can be obtained from fig. 1–2, this should be converted into an actual distance to the scale of the chart for the chosen number of crest intervals, nL. A diagram is then constructed on tracing paper, showing for each successive depth, the appropriate length proportional to the wave length, nL, in that depth to scale. A line is drawn joining the centre points of this diagram, which is then cut out. On the chart a line is drawn to represent the direction of wave advance in deep water; where the wave continues to advance in deep water each wave crest can be drawn parallel to the last and at a distance proportional to nL on the chart. When the wave enters shallow water its length decreases and it is no longer straight crested. Each crest is followed landwards from offshore by placing the cut-out scale on the chart in such a position that the centre line cuts the required depth contour at the same depth line on the scale, while the straight edge of the scale is made tangent to the preceding wave crest. The point where the depth line cuts the curved edge of the scale indicates the next position of the wave crest. This is explained in fig. 3–15. A series of points are marked in this way, using each depth contour in turn, they are then joined up to make a smooth line showing the succeeding position of the wave crest, in this way the crests can be traced into very shallow water. The ease with which this can be done depends to a considerable extent on the complexity of the bottom contours.

Once the wave crests have been drawn the orthogonals can be inserted on the chart. These are equally spaced in deep water and are drawn everywhere parallel to the wave crests, an example of a wave refraction diagram is shown in fig. 3–16. Where the bottom topography is complex it is sometimes found that the wave crests and orthogonals cross, an example of this is discussed by Munk and Traylor (1947).[50] They drew diagrams for part of the Californian coast where submarine canyons, which approach closely to the shore, cause sudden marked refraction. The diagrams showing the crossing of orthogonals were checked by photographs; these confirmed that the wave crests did in

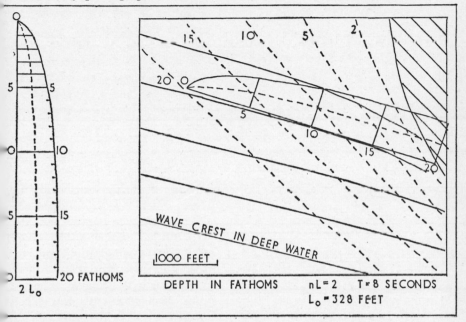

FIG. 3–15. Diagram to illustrate method of construction of wave refraction diagrams.

fact cross, as shown on the diagrams. Further information on the crossing of orthogonals is discussed by Pierson (1951).[51]

The orthogonals which indicate the distribution of energy along the coast are perhaps more important than the wave crests. A method has been developed by Arthur, Munk and Isaacs (1950)[52] whereby the orthogonals can be drawn without the first step of constructing the wave crests; this tends to eliminate some of the error involved, which is cumulative, as the waves are traced progressively inshore. The error becomes greater as the number of wave crests on the scale increase because the scale covers an increasing range of depth. The orthogonals can be constructed either towards deep or shallow water. The ratio of the wave velocity at two successive contours is calculated relative to the deep water value. Considering fig. 3–17 the mean contour between the

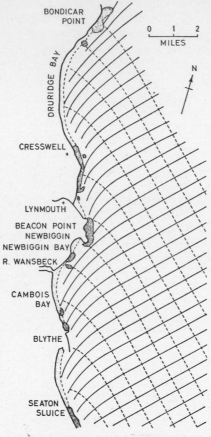

BONDICAR POINT

DRURIDGE BAY

CRESSWELL

LYNMOUTH
BEACON POINT
NEWBIGGIN
NEWBIGGIN BAY
R. WANSBECK

CAMBOIS BAY

BLYTHE

SEATON SLUICE

0 1 2
MILES

N

FIG. 3–16. Wave refraction diagram for part of the coast of Northumberland.

two shown is drawn by eye. The orthogonal cutting contour 1 is produced to cut the mean contour at P'. Then $P'R$ is drawn perpendicular to AP' and equal to unity on any convenient scale. Next c_1/c_2 is drawn on the same scale from R to cut QP' produced at S. PB, the new direction of the orthogonal, is drawn perpendicular to SR so that $PB=AP'$. For reasonable accuracy the angle a, should be less than 15 deg. and $\triangle c/c_1$ should be less than 0·2. The orthogonals can be traced continuously in this way. A diagram such as that shown in fig. 3–17b facilitates the calculation of the wave velocity for any depth in relation to the deep water velocity and hence c_1/c_2 can easily be found. Dunham (1951)[53] has compared the value of the two methods and comes to the conclusion that the crestless method is more likely to be accurate, as it avoids the two steps, necessary in the first method, to obtain the orthogonals. In fact the earlier method is considered obsolete by Pierson, Neumann and James (1955)[23] who advocate the crestless method described above.

(b) Results of wave refraction and other methods of showing refraction

From refraction diagrams the zones of convergence and divergence of wave energy become apparent; this variation of energy is apparent at the coast by a reduction of wave height in areas of divergence, as opposite submarine canyons or in bays, while in areas of convergence the wave heights are greater, opposite submarine ridges and on headlands. The variation of wave height sets up significant longshore currents which will be discussed in more detail on pp. 112–117. The effect of wave refraction on the wave energy and characteristics

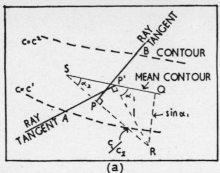

(a)

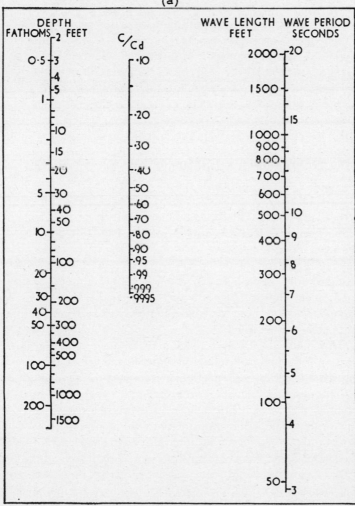

(b)

FIG. 3-17. (*a*) Diagram to illustrate the construction of wave rays. (*b*) Diagram to relate wave period, length, and velocity to varying depths. (After Arthur, Munk and Isaacs.)

along the coast is very important in considering beach processes and movement of beach material.

The refraction diagrams so far discussed only show the detailed conditions which would be expected to occur for one wave length, coming from one direction, along a considerable stretch of coast. It is possible, however, to construct a diagram in which data for a number of different wave directions and periods are considered together for one particular locality. An example of such a diagram constructed by Munk and Traylor (1947)[50] is shown for the Scripps Pier in California. The refraction diagram, fig. 3–18, is given in terms of K_b and a_b for wave periods between 6 and 16 sec. and directions from south-south-west to north-north-west. The factor K_b approaches unity as the waves become shorter and as their direction of approach becomes more normal to the coast. K_b is known as the refraction factor and refers to conditions at the break-point, it is related to the wave energy and is apparent in changes of wave height; these are given by the formula $H/H_o = \gamma K$, $H_b/H_o = \gamma_b K_b$. $K_b = \sqrt[3]{S_o/S_b}$ where S is the distance apart of the orthogonals on the refraction diagram, the suffix $_o$ referring to deep water and $_b$ to break-point. K_b, in terms of wave velocity and angle of approach for straight beach and parallel contours, is given by $K_b = \left[\dfrac{\cos 2\,a_o}{1 - (C_b/C_o)\sin a_o^2} \right]^{\frac{1}{6}}$

The constants are only applicable to one depth and are intended to allow for the effect of friction and diffraction, the latter allows energy to flow across the orthogonals. The former factor will be considered in more detail later (see pp. 100, 101), but it appears from the good agreement between forecast and observed wave heights, that both these factors are relatively unimportant in areas where refraction is great. The angle a_b determines the angle between the wave crest and the shoreline as explained on the figure. Diagrams of this type, therefore, provide very useful evidence concerning the relative effectiveness of waves approaching from different directions.

In a mathematical treatment, Longuet-Higgins (1956)[54] discusses the modification of certain wave characteristics as the waves are refracted on entering shallow water, with particular reference to the changes in crest length. The observed increase of crest length can be explained by the refraction of the waves. The length of crest relative to wave length depends on the angular deviation of the wave components, the smaller the deviation the greater the crest length to wave length ratio. The length of the wave crest is affected by refraction in two ways; firstly, if the waves are of the same length but vary in direction the waves are collimated to become more parallel to the coast, their angular deviation is reduced and their crest length is increased. Secondly, if the waves come from the same direction but vary in length, they are refracted by

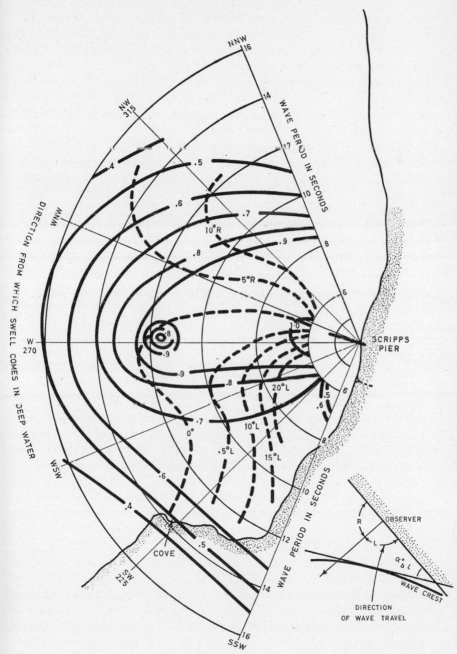

FIG. 3–18. Wave refraction diagram for Scripps Pier. (After Munk and Traylor.)

differing amounts, and their angular difference increases and they become shorter crested as a result. In deep water the second type would be long crested but the crests would split up in shallower water as refraction takes effect. These two possibilities are proved mathematically. In general it appears that an increase of crest length is more common than a decrease. This sometimes takes place as the result of a combination of longer swell with shorter waves; the longer waves, which are usually longer crested, are amplified more than the shorter leading to an increase of crest length. This analysis does not apply to high waves or to waves which steepen at their crests and break.

In considering the changes in amplitude it is shown mathematically that waves approaching a coast obliquely increase less than those approaching normally. A graph is drawn to facilitate numerical calculation of this effect.

Summary

Wave refraction diagrams can be drawn, for any given wave length and direction of approach in deep water, along any stretch of coast where the alignment of the bottom contours is known. The orthogonals on these diagrams show where wave energy is concentrated along the coast. The data for waves of different lengths coming from various directions can be assembled in another type of diagram which refers only to one point on the coast.

4. *WAVES IN SHALLOW WATER*

Some of the aspects of waves in shallow water have already been mentioned, but they will be considered in more detail in this section The water movement in the waves near the shore will also be considered as a problem, associated with mass-transport. Before discussing this problem the cause of changing wave height as the waves approach shallow water, other than the effect of refraction, will be mentioned. The water movement in breakers and the character of longshore currents will also be considered.

(a) Changes in wave height

Waves change in height and length as they enter shallow water; the effect of the change in wave length has already been discussed in considering the process of wave refraction. It has also been shown that this process has a marked effect on the wave height. The other causes of variation in wave height may be mentioned. The increase of wave height with decreasing depth was shown in fig. 1–3, p. 14, this change depends on Stoke's theory of wave motion in shallow water and can be verified by observation. There are, however, factors which modify this theoretical increase in wave height as the waves enter shallow water near their break-point.

One cause of a decrease of wave height is bottom friction. The problem has been considered theoretically by Putnam and Johnson (1949)[55] and Putnam (1949).[56] It is pointed out that the development of ripples is largely responsible for the loss of energy which is reflected in a reduction of wave height; this is more important than the roughness of the sand. This effect is only really significant when the bottom is shallow, and its slope is very flat, such as the coast of the Gulf of Mexico. The reduction of wave height is much greater for a gradient of 1 : 300 than it is for one of 1 : 10. The changes in wave height, from this cause, do not become apparent for the first 60 per cent of the distance from the point where d/L_o is 0·5 to the break-point. In the analysis the friction factor was taken as 0·01 and considered to be constant; this may not be justified. The vertical velocity of water flow was ignored, which is probably allowable in view of its low value compared with the horizontal velocities. Owing to the reduction of wave height bottom friction causes the waves to break in shallower water. The maximum reduction for a 5-ft. wave in deep water with a period of 12 sec. was 21 per cent of its frictionless value, and for a 6-sec. wave of the same height it was 22 per cent, this applies to a bottom slope of 1 : 300. If the bottom slope is 1 : 10, for a 12-sec. wave of the same height, the maximum reduction in height would be less than 1 per cent.

The effect of percolation is even less marked and would only be significant on a flat slope in shingle which is unlikely to occur in nature. The term is used to describe currents set up by the waves within the bed material, which are rapidly attenuated by friction. The maximum effect is to reduce the wave height by 7·3 per cent for a 1 : 300 slope, for a 5-ft. wave of 12-sec. period, or 8·7 per cent, for a 6-sec. wave with a permeability of 100 Darcys. Bretschneider and Reid (1954)[57] have developed graphs for computing the values from the formulae of Putnam and Johnson.

(b) Water movement and mass transport in shallow water

When considering the movement of material by waves the character of the mass transport in shallow water becomes significant, as it must have some effect on the bottom material and the material in suspension. The theoretical side of this problem has been discussed recently by Longuet-Higgins (1953)[58] while experimental data on this topic were discussed by Bagnold (1947)[59] and more recently by Russell and Osorio (1957). In water where d/L is $1/2\pi$, according to the classical theory of Stokes, there is a steadily increasing landward velocity, which is nil at the bottom and increases to a maximum in the direction of wave advance at the surface.

This theoretical pattern has not been found in observations such as those of Bagnold (1947), who found that the reverse flow in fact occurred; there was a strong forward movement on the bottom with a slower seaward drift in the upper part of the model tank. The dividing line between the landward and seaward flow varied between 0·2 and 0·35 d (depth), while the backward movement was about $\frac{1}{5}$ of the forward thrust along the bottom. Caligny and Bouasse also found this

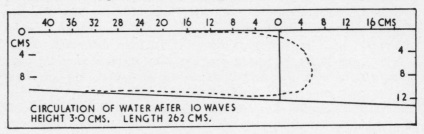

CIRCULATION OF WATER AFTER 10 WAVES
HEIGHT 3·0 CMS. LENGTH 262 CMS.

FIG. –19. Water movement in a model tank to show forward thrust on the bottom and surface with seaward flow in the centre.

forward movement on the bottom, the former (1878)[60] found that the surface water also moved in the direction of wave propagation. Experiments carried out in the model tank at Cambridge showed the same pattern of water movement as that found by Caligny. The experiments were made with dye which was dropped into the water in a depth of 12 cm. as a thin thread, its subsequent movement after the passage of ten waves was recorded. In nearly all runs the same pattern was observed; the bottom water moved rapidly forward while the central water moved back a smaller distance and the surface water moved forwards, this pattern is shown in fig. 3–19. The amount of seaward movement in the central layers appeared to depend on the deep water wave height, increasing with increasing wave height in a constant depth, although there was a considerable scatter of the data. At a depth of 40 cm. with a short wave of 77 cm. length, which would therefore be in deep water, it was found that there was no landward movement on the bottom. It increased rapidly, however, as the depth decreased as shown in fig. 3–20. In the deep water there was still a landward movement on the surface so that the observations now agreed with the theoretical concept of the classical wave theory.

The forward thrust on the bottom was found to be dependent on the character of the bottom; it only occurred when the bottom was of smooth sand, as soon as the bed became rough with ripples the forward thrust was no longer observed. The presence of ripples greatly increased the turbulence of the water and prevented the forward movement of the thread of dye. The same result was also recorded by Bagnold (1947). He also noted that when the dyed tongue of water approached closely to the break-point of the waves, the tongue moved vertically upwards and became dispersed by turbulence, near the surface the dyed water started to drift away from the beach. Dye dropped into the water in front of the break-point became dispersed in front of it, but did not move seaward of the break-point. This double circulation system agrees with observations made in nature.

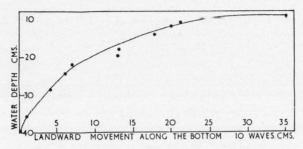

FIG. 3–20. Graph relating landward movement of water on the bottom to water depth.

The theory developed by Longuet-Higgins (1953)[58] accounts for the forward velocity on the bottom by considering the boundary effects and the viscosity of the water, which leads to markedly different results from those derived from the classical theory of Stokes. The velocities observed by Bagnold agree well with the values predicted by the theory, and more recent experimental work by Russell and Osorio (1957) confirm the theoretical work of Longuet-Higgins for the bed velocities.

(c) Water velocity in shallow water and breakers

The mass transport discussed in the last section indicates the general drift direction of the water at different depths, but the actual velocities of the particles of water is also important in the movement of material. From observations described by Inman and Nasu (1956)[61] it was found that the particle velocities agreed fairly closely with the theoretical values for the solitary wave theory. A mathematical treatment of waves in shallow water is given by Stoker (1957)[62] including a discussion of the solitary wave theory. In this theory, which applies to waves in very shallow water only, each wave is independent of its neighbours; the wave consists only of a crest, whose velocity is largely dependent on the depth of water and the wave height, $C=\sqrt{g\,(H+d)}$, where d is the depth below the trough. Each crest is separated from its neighbours by flat water in which the particles are at rest. The water particles under the wave crest move in the direction of propagation of the wave; the theoretical maximum velocity at the bottom is shown in fig. 3–21, relating the bottom velocity to the depth for various heights. For any one wave height the velocity increases for decreasing depth and it increases rapidly with increasing wave height for any given depth. According to the theory the particles are virtually at rest at a distance of 10 d from the wave crest horizontally. As the wave crests approaches the particles

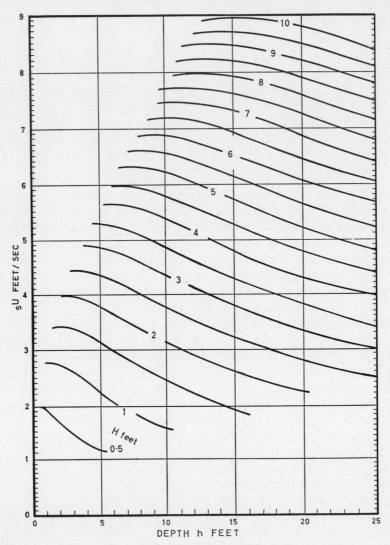

FIG. 3–21. Relation between bottom velocity and depth of water for various wave heights. (After Inman and Nasu, B.E.B.)

move up and forward, as the crest passes the particles slow down and move downwards to a new position of rest. It is probable that a slow uniform return velocity is superimposed on the landward velocity, so far considered. This would slightly reduce the landward velocity under the wave crest and produce a seaward velocity under the trough.

Observations made to test the theoretical velocities given in fig. 3–21 consisted of measurements of orbital velocities from the Scripps Insti-

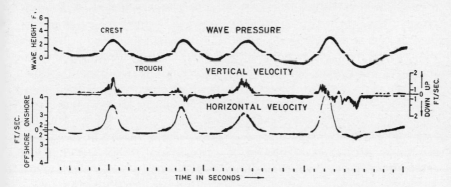

FIG. 3–22. Profile of a wave off Scripps Pier with related orbital velocities in horizontal and vertical directions. (After Inman and Nasu, B.E.B.)

tute pier together with instrumental and visual observations of the wave characteristics. The orbital velocities were measured with a current meter set at 0·82 ft. above the bottom, which consisted of well-sorted fine sand of median diameter of 0·18 mm., with a gradient of 1 : 35. The current meter was designed to record both vertical and horizontal velocities at the point selected. It was just seaward of the breaker zone, in water varying in depth from 5 to 15 ft. In the interpretation of the results many sources of error have to be considered; the horizontality of the meter and its direction relative to the wave approach are important and affect particularly the relatively low vertical velocities. Another difficulty was the acceleration of the currents between the trough and crest, to overcome this difficulty only the maximum trough and crest velocities were considered; this reduces the value of the results but eliminates the necessity of making so many assumptions. The wave meter was mounted on the same tripod as the current meter and was calibrated by reference to visual observations on a graduated staff near the orbital velocity meter tripod.

In relating the observed to the theoretical group velocity the analysis of the data necessitated the treatment of each wave individually. For each series of waves the wave profile from the pressure gauge and the orbital velocities are plotted together as shown in fig. 3–22. The graphs relating the orbital velocity to the wave profile show that the velocity appears to follow the wave form closely; the velocity is greatest, not at the highest point, but where the wave form is changing most rapidly. Where the waves become asymmetrical near the break-point, the orbital velocities are also asymmetrical. These were always directed on-shore under the wave crest, where velocities are nearly always greater than the seaward velocity under the wave trough.

The results have been compared to the theoretical velocities obtained from the solitary wave theory, and the Airy-Stokes shallow water progressive wave theory, by plotting the observed orbital velocities against the wave height for different depths. The curves of the theoretical values were added for comparison. Because the period affects the orbital velocity in the Stokes' theory the theoretical curves are drawn for three different periods. The relation between the observed and theoretical velocities showed a considerable scatter on all the graphs, but particularly for the lower wave heights. This may be in part due to the decreasing sensitivity of the meter at low velocities, and the consequent greater possible error of observation. In general the observed points agreed more closely with the solitary wave theory. The agreement with theory for the solitary wave was better for wave periods over 6 sec. because the shorter period waves tend to be associated with lower orbital velocities. The agreement was best in those waves whose profiles were relatively simple. The increase in particle velocity was almost linear with increasing wave height; 6–7 ft./sec. was recorded for waves about 5 ft. high in depths of 7–8 ft.

The study of orbital velocity just described was carried out just seaward of the break-point. Owing to difficulty of observations it was not possible to obtain reliable full-scale data for the breaker area. Observations in a model tank have been made by Iverson (1952).[63] The study aims to establish relationships between the breaker characteristics, the wave dimensions, and the beach slope. The experiments were made in a model tank having smooth bottom slopes of varying angles from 1 : 10 to 1 : 50. The breakers were studied by means of moving photographs of the waves, into which recognizable particles, of the same specific gravity as the water, had been introduced. From these results the particle velocity and the change in form of the breaking wave could be found. The results are correlated with the beach gradient and the wave steepness. The waves as generated were not true deep water waves, but their deep water steepness could be found by computation; the length, being derived from the measured period, presented no difficulty, but the true deep water height could not be determined so readily. Fig. 3–23 shows the relationship between the wave steepness and the breaker index, which is the ratio of breaker height to deep water height, H_b/H_o for two different versions of the deep water wave height. One is derived from the laboratory data and the other from the theoretical relation between deep water and breaker wave height. Both graphs, however, show the effect of beach slope on the breaker index. On the whole the steeper the slope the greater the breaker index; it is about 40 per cent higher on a 1 : 10 slope than one of 1 : 50. The form of the breaker is

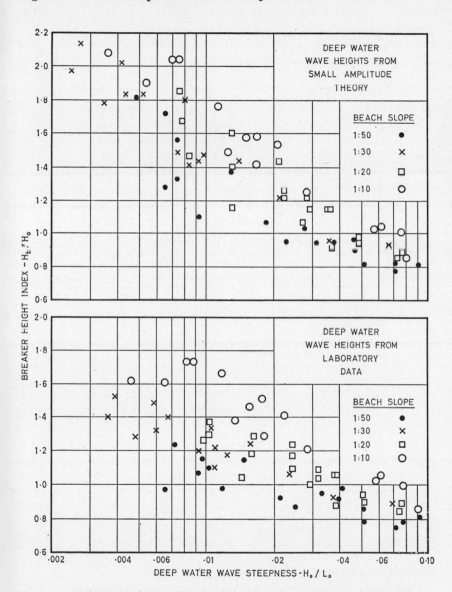

FIG. 3–23. Relationship between breaker height and deep water wave height and wave steepness and beach slope in model experiments. (After Iverson.)

also different; as the slope becomes steeper the breaker is steeper in front and flatter behind and has a greater tendency to plunge.

Velocities were also determined from the photographs, these included: backwash and crest velocities, the former were obtained by averaging all velocities in the region of the minimum depth. With high backwash velocities there is a tendency to produce plunging breakers. With high steepness values the breakers tended to spill, but with very low values they tended to surge, particularly on the steeper slopes. The pattern of velocity actually measured in breaking waves is shown in fig. 3–24. The

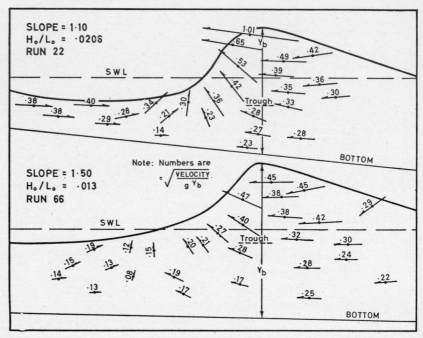

FIG. 3–24. Direction and speed of movement in a breaking wave on flat and steep slopes. (After Inverson.)

form of the breaker is shown and as the two extreme beach slopes are represented this factor can be evaluated and shows the steeper front slope on the steeper beach. Values for different wave steepnesses are shown, the velocity is given in the form $\sqrt{\dfrac{\text{velocity}}{g \text{ crest elevation}}}$; as would be expected the maximum velocity is found near the crest of the wave.

(d) Surf beat or long waves

The discovery of waves very much longer than normal waves is of interest because, although the waves are much lower than normal waves, they may influence the velocities of the water particles under wave action and, owing to their great length, they may be effective in much deeper water than normal waves. They have been termed 'long waves' or 'surf beat'. Munk (1949)[64] has recorded the presence of surf beat, with a period of about 2 min. and heights about 1/11 that of the normal waves, which are related to groups of high waves which raise the water level temporarily at the shore. The surf beat represents about 1 per cent of the wave energy returned seawards from the shore. Where the normal waves in deep water was 4·5 ft. and 8-sec. period the surf beat had a height of 0·6 ft. at the break-point of the normal wave whose height was 6 ft. here. The respective horizontal orbital velocities were 0·62 and 5·9 ft./sec. It has been calculated that in a depth of 20 ft. the surf beat was 0·47 ft. high with a horizontal orbital velocity of 0·30 ft./sec. compared to 2·5 ft./sec. of the normal wave. In depths in excess of 200 ft. the horizontal orbital velocity associated with the surf beat exceeds that of the normal wave although both are small.

Long waves of 1-5 min. period were recorded by Tucker (1950)[65] on the coast of Cornwall whose heights correlated closely with that of the normal waves. A high group of ordinary waves were followed by a group of long waves after about 4–5 min., the time it would take the waves to travel to the shore and back to the recorder 1,000 yds. off-shore, it is, therefore, suggested that the long waves are formed by groups of high waves breaking on the beach. The long waves reach heights of 5 in. for ordinary waves of 6 ft., i.e. 1/12, there being a linear correlation between the two. The cause of the long waves appears to be related to an increase of mass transport landwards in the breaker zone which causes an acceleration both on- and offshore, the depression between the two resulting elevations has been observed in the record and is followed by the reflection of the shoreward elevation from the beach.

Similar long waves have been recorded by Darbyshire (1957)[66] at Tema, Ghana; their period was between 1 and 10 min. with most activity in the range 2–4 min. Their amplitude approximated to 1/20 of the normal waves, their maximum height being about 5 in. These waves were formed partly by the acceleration of water towards the shore and partly by deformation of the wave form.

(e) Longshore currents

i. THEORY. Before considering the experimental work and observations made on longshore currents the theoretical approach to the problem made by Putnam, Munk and Traylor (1949)[67] will be discussed. The theoretical results can then be tested against the observations. The problem has been approached from two different aspects, firstly the energy approach and, secondly, the momentum approach. If a specific volume of water landwards of the break-point of the waves, as shown in fig. 3–25 is considered, the total energy entering this volume over a width of beach, dx, is $C\,E\cos\alpha\,dx$, where C is the wave velocity, E is the mean energy per unit surface area of the breaking waves, and α is the angle between the wave crests at the break-point and the shore. Only a small part of this energy is actually used to generate longshore currents, much of it is lost in the breaking of the wave and in other ways. Energy is also lost by frictional resistance of the bottom. The frictional force per

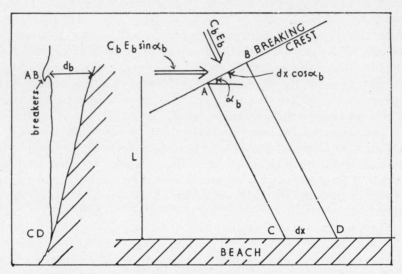

FIG. 3–25. Diagram to illustrate the theoretical analysis of longshore currents. (After Putnam, Munk and Traylor.)

unit width of beach is given by $k\rho V^2 l^1 dx$, and the rate at which energy is lost in the volume $ABCDE = k\rho V^3 l^1 dx$ where k is a friction parameter, V is the velocity of the longshore current and l^1 is the distance along the sea-bed to the break-point. l^1 can be taken as l, $d_b/l = m$ where m is the beach slope. If a steady state is assumed the energy entering the area must equal the loss of friction so that $s_t CE \cos\alpha \sin\alpha\; dx = k\rho V^3 dx\; d_b/m$. Using formulae derived by the solitary wave theory, V can be given in terms of the wave height, period, angle of approach and beach slope as follows $V = K[(m\,H_b^2/T)\sin 2\alpha]^{\frac{1}{3}}$ where K^3 is $0·871\; g(s_t/k)$, s_t is the sand surface texture and k is a function of the hydraulic roughness of the beach which thus also affects the velocity of the current. These formulae apply to a steady state current in an area where there is no interruption of the current due to obstructions on the beach. Observations have shown that the steady state is achieved remarkably quickly; 5 min. is sufficient for the current to reach a steady state after a train of waves starts to break on the beach, and such a current will reach its full value only 200 yds. from an obstruction such as a break-water.

The second method of approach is the momentum one; this considers the momentum given to a volume of water which is put into motion in the direction of wave propagation when the wave breaks. A component of this movement is directed alongshore and this provides the energy of the longshore current. In fig. 3–25 the cross-sectional area of the breaking wave crest is Q, C and L are its velocity and length respectively, a its angle to the shore and ρ the density of the water. The average momentum per unit surface area $\rho QC/L$. The component of momentum flux parallel to the shore equals $c \sin a\ (\rho QC/L) \cos a\ dx$. Considering the balance of frictional drag along the bottom, the velocity of the current V can be given by $V=(a/2)[\sqrt{1+4C\sin(a/a)}-1)]$ and $C=(2\cdot88\ g\ H_b)^{\frac{1}{2}}$ and $a=(2\cdot61\ m\ H\ \cos a)/(kT)$. k is given by $k=(2\cdot61\ m\ H\ \cos a)$ $(C\sin a - V)/TV^{2*}$ so that V may now be found in the same terms as before. The same limitations apply and the results apply only to a beach which is straight and of uniform bottom slope. k was found by the substitution of observed data in the formula above* for the different types of beach tested from which values of K and s_t were determined in the table. s_t is the sand surface texture which was found to be comparable for the natural and laboratory sand although k was very different in each case.

Beach	k	K	s_t	
Field	0·0078	8·2	0·15	
Lab 1	0·0397	5·12	0·19	Natural sand bonded with cement
Lab 2	0·0070	11·02	0·33	Sheet metal or smooth concrete
Lab 3	0·385	—	—	$\frac{1}{4}$ in. pea-gravel

ii. MODEL EXPERIMENTS. Saville (1950)[68] has conducted some experiments into the movement of sand along the shore in a model tank 66×122 ft. (see chapter 2, pp. 45, 46). Part of this work was devoted to a study of the longshore currents, and their observed velocity has been compared to the theoretical velocity as determined by Putnam, Munk and Traylor. In the experimental tank in which the observations were made the waves approached the shore at an angle of 10 deg. in deep water, breaking on a beach with an initial gradient of 1 : 10. The velocity of the longshore current was obtained by timing the movement of dye over a 10-ft. length parallel to the beach, it ranged between 0·066 and nearly 0·4 ft./sec. The observed current showed an increase of strength as the waves steepened. This can be explained partly by the refraction of the longer, less steep waves, which approach the beach at a smaller angle and as a result set up slower longshore currents. The current was reduced as the wave length increased but an increase in wave height caused an increase in velocity. The highest waves were also the steepest which accounts for the positive correlation of both these factors with the longshore current velocity.

In order to compare the observed and predicted current the friction factor, k, must be known. This was determined from the observed velocities and found to be $k=0.0135$. The graph showing the relationship between the theoretical momentum approach and observed velocities indicates a good agreement between the two values; they are mostly within 10 per cent of each other until the steepness value becomes very low.

The maximum current velocity was always along the break-point bar in the tank; there was a very rapid reduction in speed outside the bar, while inside it the current also slackened but rather less rapidly, in fact here the velocity remained fairly uniform over a considerable range.

iii. FIELD OBSERVATIONS. One of the most comprehensive surveys of coastal and longshore currents to be obtained on an open coast is that reported by Shepard and Inman (1950).[69] The area studied was around the Scripps Institute in south California. The coast here is fairly straight, but the southern beaches are partly protected from the south by La Jolla Point. The offshore relief is, on the other hand, very complex; two submarine canyons come close to the shore, while between these the continental shelf slopes gently seawards at 1.3 deg. This complex bottom topography has a marked effect on the refraction of the longer period waves reaching the coast, as has been indicated. The resultant longshore currents are also important.

The methods used to measure the circulation of water near the shore were fairly simple; measurements outside the breakers were made with triplanes, or current-crosses, attached by line to small surface floats. The triplane thus showed the direction of drift below the surface at any required depth. The surface currents were measured by drift bottles. The positions of the triplanes and bottles were determined during the observations by horizontal sextant angles to fixed positions onshore from a boat. Depths were obtained by soundings during the observations. The triplanes could not be followed into shallow water as they grounded, so that other techniques had to be used in the surf zone. Here the surface currents were observed by means of dye, while the bottom currents were obtained by use of a weighted ball. On some occasions numbered floats were released beyond the breaker zone and followed into the surf, and were later recovered from the beach; these observations were made on days of no wind. Wave characteristics were recorded visually and instrumentally at the same time as the current observations were made.

In interpreting the results of these observations various different types of currents can be distinguished; there are the deep water coastal currents, which dominate the longshore movement outside the breaker zone, they are fairly uniform in velocity and depend mainly on wind-driven ocean current or tidal currents. The nearshore currents are related largely to the action of the waves along the shore; these are the most important from the point of view of the beach processes. These currents are a combination of several distinct water circulations; firstly, there is the mass-transport velocity already considered, acting in a shoreward direction. Secondly, longshore currents are present due to the oblique approach of the waves to the beach, to wave refraction and to variations in water level along the coast, resulting from the uneven shoreward transport of water by mass-transport. Thirdly, the seaward flow may be divided between uniform seaward return flow and the irregular seaward flow in rip currents, the former flow may be related to the seaward movement in intermediate depths already considered in experimental data. The extent to which the coastal currents affect the shallow water is variable being greatest on a steep beach with weak wave action.

The general pattern of circulation was found to vary with different types of waves. The wave period, height, and the direction of deep water approach were the most important variables. For the longer waves the direction of approach is not so important because these waves suffer marked refraction. As a result zones of convergence and divergence are strongly developed and these in turn induce rapid longshore currents, flowing away from the zones of convergence; these currents may flow against the direction of wave approach. They turn seaward as rip currents some distance away from the convergences. Weaker currents flow out from the heads of the submarine canyons. Where the outflowing currents meet there is a tendency for deposition to take place.

The maps in fig. 3–26 indicate the nature of the circulation under different wave conditions. The shorter waves, which approach the coast normally, do not suffer such marked refraction, as a result the zones of convergence are not so marked, and rip currents are smaller and more numerous. When short waves approach at a considerable angle to the coast, the longshore currents are almost continuous in the direction of wave approach, and may reach velocities of 1 knot or more. The longer waves showed a few, much more marked zones of convergence with associated rapid rip currents.

In considering the variation of currents with depth, it was found that 73 per cent of the observations showed the same direction from surface to bottom, while most of the remainder showed a diagonal offshore movement at the bottom and an alongshore movement at the surface. Only 1 per cent showed a surface onshore and a bottom offshore move-

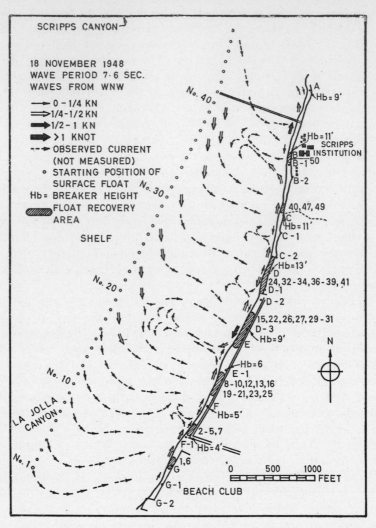

FIG. 3–26. (*a*) Typical nearshore circulation pattern resulting from waves less than 10 seconds period approaching normal to the Scripps beach and a southerly flowing coastal current. (After Shepard and Inman.)

ment. It should be remembered, however, that the observations were made under calm conditions.

An analysis of the rip currents and their associated longshore feeder currents has been made by McKenzie (1958)[70] from observations on the sandy beaches of New South Wales, Australia. He has generalized from many observations to conclude that in heavy seas a few strong rips are produced which may be fed by longshore feeder currents up to

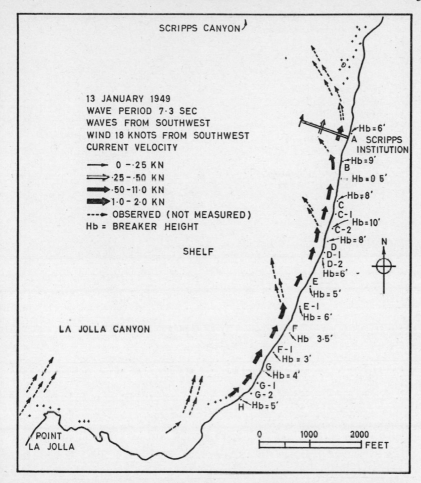

SCRIPPS CANYON

13 JANUARY 1949
WAVE PERIOD 7·3 SEC
WAVES FROM SOUTHWEST
WIND 18 KNOTS FROM SOUTHWEST
CURRENT VELOCITY

→ 0 – ·25 KN
⟹ ·25 – ·50 KN
➡ ·50 – 1·0 KN
➡ 1·0 – 2·0 KN
---→ OBSERVED (NOT MEASURED)
Hb = BREAKER HEIGHT

SHELF

LA JOLLA CANYON

Hb = 6'
A SCRIPPS
INSTITUTION
Hb = 9'
B
Hb = 0 5'
Hb = 8'
C
C - 1
Hb = 10'
C - 2
Hb = 8'
D
D - 1
D - 2
Hb = 6'
E
Hb = 5'
E - 1
Hb = 6'
F
Hb 3·5'
F - 1
Hb = 3'
G
Hb = 4'
G - 1
G - 2
H Hb = 5'

N

POINT
LA JOLLA

0   1000   2000
|_____|_____| FEET

FIG. 3–26. (*b*) Typical nearshore circulation pattern resulting from short period storm waves approaching the Scripps beach from the south-west. (After Shepard and Inman.)

a half-mile long and from a few inches to 6–8 ft. deep. These currents and the rips themselves cut channels along the beach and through any sand banks which may be lying parallel to the shore. He found that each pattern of wave approach tended to produce a characteristic pattern of longshore currents and rips, with smaller waves the rips were smaller but more numerous.

Summary

As waves approach shallow water they lose height slowly, due to friction, if the beach slope is very flat and to a much lesser extent by percolation. The mass transport of water under wave action, in shallow

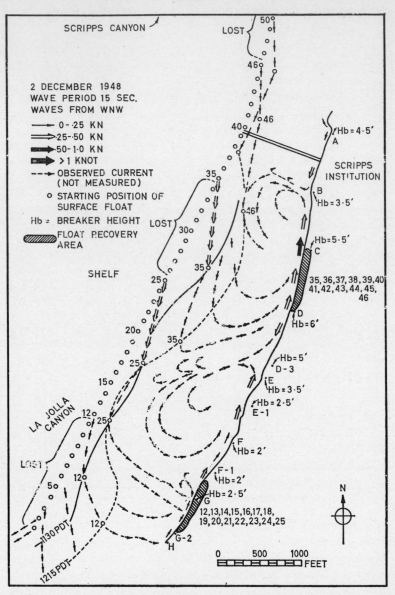

FIG. 3–26. (c) Typical nearshore circulation pattern resulting from long waves of 15 second period coming from west-north-west. (After Shepard and Inman.)

water, produces a landward movement on the bottom and a seaward return flow at higher levels when the flow is not turbulent. It has been found that theoretical velocities of flow on the bottom agree fairly closely with the solitary wave theory from observations made off Scripps pier, except for the lower waves. The increase in particle velocity was almost linear with increasing wave height. Measurements have also been made of the particle velocities recorded in breaking waves and backwash. The breaker index, H_b/H_o, increases for decreasing wave steepness and increasing beach slope.

The theory of longshore currents is discussed in relation to the energy and momentum approaches, both of which give formulae relating the velocity of the longshore current to wave height, period, beach slope, beach roughness and direction of wave approach. Model experiments made to test the momentum theory showed that the experimental values agreed well with the theoretical ones (mostly to within 10 per cent); the velocities increased with increasing wave height and steepness. Field observations of longshore currents showed that with long waves marked zones of convergence and divergence developed and strong rip currents formed; the currents were most continuous and strongest alongshore when short waves approached the shore obliquely.

LIST OF SYMBOLS

H	Wave height, $r=\frac{1}{2}H$, H_T equivalent height, $\bar{\bar{H}}$ Mean height of apparent sea
L	Wave length, $R=\frac{1}{2}L$
c	Constant
C	Wave velocity
M	Volume of mass transport
g	Force of gravity
E	Wave energy
w	Weight of 1 cubic ft. of water
s	Sheltering coefficient
U_c	Velocity of frame of reference—nearly equal to wind velocity measured from ships
Ts	Surface tension at interface
ρ	Water density
n	Wave number $=\dfrac{2\pi}{L}$
$\overline{\xi^2}$	Mean square surface displacement
$\overline{p^2}$	Means square turbulent pressure
t	Time elapsed
U	Surface wind speed
U_g	Gradient wind speed
F	Fetch
T	Wave period $\tilde{T}$ Apparent period T_s Significant period
D	Decay distance

f	Frequency $= 1/T$
K_b	Refraction factor at break-point
S	Distance apart of orthogonals
d	Depth of water
m	Beach slope
V	Longshore current velocity
k	Friction parameter
s_t	Sand surface texture
l'	Distance along sea bed to break-point
l	Horizontal distance to break-point
a	Angle of wave crest with shore

SUFFIX

	Lower
u	Upper
o	Deep water
b	Break-point
$\frac{1}{3}$	Significant height or period, average of highest $\frac{1}{3}$
$1/10$	Average of highest $1/10$
max	Highest of 100 or maximum
min	Minimum
cr	Critical
av	Average

REFERENCES

[1]Airy, G. B., 1845, On tide and waves. *Encycl. Metropolitana* **5**, pp. 241–396.
[2]Stokes, G. G., 1847, On the theory of oscillatory waves. *Trans. Camb. Phil. Soc.* **8**, p. 441.
[3]Levi-Civita, T., 1925, Détermination rigoureuse des ondes d'ampleur finie. *Math. Ann.* **93**, pp. 264–314.
[4]Struik, D. J., 1926, Détermination rigoureuse des ondes irrotationelles périodiques dans un canal a pronfondeur finie. *Math. Ann.* **95**, pp. 595–634.
[5]Gerstner, F., 1802, Theorie der Wellen. *Abh. Konigl. Bohm. Ges. Wiss.* pp. 412–45.
[6]Rankine, W. J. H., 1863, On the exact form of waves near the surface of deep water. *Phil. Trans. Roy. Soc.* pp. 127–38.
[7]Mitchim, C. F., 1940, Oscillatory waves in deep water. *Mil. Eng.* **32**, pp. 107–9.
[8]Gaillard, D. D., 1904, *Wave action in relation to engineering structures.*
[9]Jeffreys, H., 1925, On the formation of water waves by wind. *Proc. Roy. Soc. A.* **107**, pp. 189–206.
[10]Stanton, T. E., Marshall, D. and Houghton, R., 1932, The growth of waves on water due to the action of the wind. *Proc. Roy. Soc. A.* **137**, pp. 283–93.
[11]Sverdrup, H. U. and Munk, W. H., 1947, Wind, sea and swell—theory of relationships in forecasting. *H.O. Pub.* **601**, *U.S. Navy Dept.*
[12]Munk, W. H., 1957, Comments on ref. 36.
[13]Eckart, C., 1953, The generation of wind waves over a water surface. *Journ. Applied Physics* **24**, pp. 1485–94.
[14]Phillips, O. M., 1957, On the generation of waves by turbulent wind. *Journ. Fluid Mechs.* **2**, 5, pp. 417–45.

[15]Longuet-Higgins, M. S., 1952, On the statistical distribution of the heights of sea waves. *Journ. Marine Research* **11**, pp. 245–6.

[16]Russell, R. C. H. and Macmillan, D. H., 1952, *Waves and tides.*

[17]Cornish, V., 1934, *Ocean waves and kindred geophysical phenomena.*

[18]Deacon, G. E. R., 1949, Waves and swell. *Q. J. R. Met. Soc.* **75**, 325, pp. 227–38.

[19]Barber, N. F. and Ursell, F., 1948, The generation and propagation of ocean waves and swell I. Wave periods and velocities. *Phil. Trans. Roy. Soc. A.* **240**, pp. 527–560.

[20]Bretschneider, C. L., 1952, The generation and decay of wind waves in deep water. *Trans. Am. Geoph. Un.* **33**, 3, pp. 381–9.

[21]Donn, W. L., 1949, Studies of waves and swell in the western North Atlantic. *Trans. Am. Geoph. Un.* **31**, 4, pp. 507–16.

[22]Neumann, G., 1953, An ocean wave spectra and a new method of forecasting wind generated sea. *B.E.B. Tech. Memo.* **43.**

[23]Pierson, W. J., Neumann, G. and James, R. W., 1955, Practical methods for observing and forecasting ocean waves by means of wave spectra and statistics. *Hydrog. Off. Pub.* **603**, *H.O. U.S. Navy.*

[24]Roll, H. U. and Fischer, G., 1956, Eine kritische Bemerkung zum Neumann-Spektrum des Seeganges. *Deutsche Hydrog. Zeitschrift* **9**, 1, pp. 9–14.

[25]Walden, H., 1956, Vorschlag zur Änderung der Neumannschen Konstanten c bei der Berechnung der Wellenhohe aus der Windstarke. *Deutsche Hydrog. Zeitschrift* **9**, 1, pp. 14–17.

[26]Darbyshire, J., 1952, The generation of waves by wind. *Proc. Roy. Soc. A.* **215**, pp. 299–328.

[27]Silvester, R., 1955, Practical application of Darbyshire's method of hind-casting ocean waves. *Australian Journ. Appl. Sci.* **6**, 3, pp. 261–6.

[28]Darbyshire, J., 1955, An investigation of storm waves in the north Atlantic Ocean. *Proc. Roy. Soc. A.* **230**, pp. 560–9.

[29]Darbyshire, J., 1956, An investigation into the generation of waves when the fetch of the wind is less than 100 miles. *Q. J. R. Met. Soc.* **82**, pp. 461–8.

[30]Darbyshire, J., 1957, Attenuation of swell in the north Atlantic Ocean. *Q. J. R. Met. Soc.* **83**, pp. 351–9.

[31]Wiegel, R. L. and Kimberley, H. L., 1950, Southern swell observed at Ocean-side, California. *Trans. Am. Geoph. Un.* **31**, 5, pp. 717–22.

[32]Dearduff, R. F., 1955, A comparison of the deep water forecasts by the Pierson-Neumann, the Darbyshire and the Sverdrup-Munk-Bretschneider methods with recorded waves for Point Arguello, California for 26–29 Oct. 1950. *Bull. B.E.B.* **9**, 1, pp. 5–13.

[33]James, R. W., 1954, Wave forecast based on the energy spectra method. *Trans. Am. Geoph. Un.* **35**, 1, pp. 153–60.

[34]James, R. W., 1957, Application of wave forecasts to marine navigation. *U.S. Hydrog. Off. Sp. Pub.* (p. 32).

[35]Neumann, G. and Pierson, W. J., 1957, A detailed comparison of theoretical wave spectra and wave forecasting methods. *Deutsche Hydrog. Zeitsch.* **10**, 3, pp. 73–92 and **10**, 4, pp. 134–46.

[36]Bretschneider, C. L., 1957, Review of ref. 23. *Trans. Am. Geoph. Un.* **38**, 2, pp. 264–6.

[37]Darbyshire, J., 1957, A note on the comparison of proposed wave spectrum formulae. *Deutsche Hydrog. Zeitsch.* **10**, 5, pp. 184–90.

[38]Roll, H. U., 1957, Some results of comparison between observed and computed heights of wind waves. Chap. 24 Proc. Sym. on the behaviour of ships in a seaway. *Wageningen* pp. 418–26.

[39]Cartwright, D. E. and Darbyshire, J., 1957, Discussion of Chap. 7, Neumann, G. and Pierson, W. J. A comparison of various theoretical spectra. Proc. Sym. on the behaviour of ships in a seaway. *Wageningen* pp. 16–24.

[40]Fleagle, R. G. 1956, Note on the effect of air-sea temperature difference on wave generation. *Trans. Am. Geoph. Un.* **37**, 3, pp. 275–7.

[41]Ursell, F., 1956, Wave generation by wind. Chap. 6 in *Surveys in mechanics*, ed. by Batchelor, G. K. and Davies, R. M., C.U.P., pp. 216–49.

[42]Saville, T., 1954, North Atlantic wave statistics hindcast by Bretschneider, revised Sverdrup-Munk method. *B.E.B. Tech. Memo.* **55.**

[43]Neumann, G. and James, J. W., 1955, North Atlantic coast wave statistics hindcast by the spectrum method. *B.E.B. Tech. Memo.* **57.**

[44]Darbyshire, J., 1955, Wave statistics in the north Atlantic Ocean and on the coast of Cornwall. *The Marine Observer* **25,** 168, pp. 114–18.

[45]Jasper, N. H., 1955, Chap. 34 Proc. 1st Conf. on 'ships and waves' Coun. of Wave Res. and Soc. of Naval Arch. and Mar. Eng.

[46]Darbyshire, J., 1956, The distribution of wave heights. A statistical method based on observations. *Dock and Harbour Auth.* **37,** pp. 31–34.

[47]Tucker, M. J., 1952, A wave-recorder for use in ships. *Nature* **170,** pp. 657–9.

[48]Barber, N. F., 1954, Finding the direction of travel of sea waves. *Nature* **174,** pp. 1048–50.

[49]Johnson, J. W., O'Brien, M. P. and Isaacs, J. D., 1948, Graphical construction of wave refraction diagrams. *U.S. Hydrog. Off. Pub.* **605.**

[50]Munk, W. H. and Traylor, M. A., 1947, Refraction of ocean waves; a process linking underwater topography to beach erosion. *Journ. Geol.* **55,** pp. 1–26.

[51]Pierson, W. J., 1951, The interpretation of crossed orthogonals in wave refraction phenomena. *B.E.B. Tech. Memo.* **21.**

[52]Arthur, R. S., Munk, W. M. and Isaacs, J. D., 1952, The direct construction of wave rays. *Trans. Am. Geoph. Un.* **33,** 6, pp. 855–65.

[53]Dunham, J. W., 1951, Refraction and diffraction diagrams. Chap. 4, Proc. 1st Conf. on Costal Eng. 1950 Council of wave research, pp. 33–49.

[54]Longuet-Higgins, M. S., 1956, The refraction of sea waves in shallow water. *Journ. Fluid Mech.* **1,** 2, pp. 163–76.

[55]Putnam, J. A. and Johnson, J. W., 1949, The dissipation of wave energy by bottom friction. *Trans. Am. Geoph. Un.* **30,** 1, pp. 67–74.

[56]Putnam, J. A., 1949, Loss of wave energy due to percolation in a permeable sea bottom. *Trans. Am. Geoph. Un.* **30,** 3, pp. 349–56.

[57]Bretschneider, C. L. and Reid, R. O., 1954, Modification of wave height due to bottom friction, percolation and wave refraction. *B.E.B. Tech. Memo.* **45.**

[58]Longuet-Higgins, M. S., 1953, Mass transport in water waves. *Phil. Trans. Roy. Soc. A.* **245,** pp. 535–81.

[59]Bagnold, R. A., 1947, Model experiments with light materials. *Journ. Inst. Civ. Eng.* **27,** p. 447.

[60]Caligny, A. F. H., 1878, *C.R. Acad. Sci.*, Paris., **87,** p. 10.

[61]Inman, D. L. and Nasu, N., 1956, Orbital velocity associated with wave action near the breaker zone. *B.E.B. Tech. Memo.* **79.**

[62]Stoker, J. J., 1957, Water waves. *Inter. Sci. Pub.*, New York.

[63]Iverson, H. W., 1952, Laboratory study of breakers. *Nat. Bur. of Stand. circ.* **521,** pp. 9–32.

[64]Munk, W. H., 1949, Surf beats. *Trans. Am. Geoph. Un.* **30,** pp. 849–54.

[65]Tucker, M. J., 1950, Surf beats: sea waves of 1 to 5 min. period. *Proc. Roy. Soc.A.* **202,** pp. 565–73.

[66]Darbyshire, J., 1957, Sea conditions at Tema Harbour. *Dock and Harbour Auth.* **38,** pp. 277–8.

[67]Putnam, J. A., Munk, W. H. and Traylor, M. A., 1949, The prediction of longshore currents. *Trans. Am. Geoph. Un.* **30,** 3, pp. 337–45.

[68]Saville, T., 1950, Model study of sand transport along an infinitely long straight beach. *Trans. Am. Geoph. Un.* **31,** 4, pp. 555–65.

[69]Shepard, F. P. and Inman, D. L., 1950, Nearshore circulation related to bottom topography and wave refraction. *Trans. Am. Geoph. Un.* **31,** 2, pp. 196–212.

[70]McKenzie, P., 1958, Rip current systems. *Journ. Geol.* **66,** 2, pp. 103–13.

Chapter 4

MOVEMENT OF MATERIAL ON THE BEACH

In this chapter the movement of beach material in the foreshore and off-shore zones will be considered with particular reference to the part played by the waves. Evidence of both model experiments and full-scale observations will be considered in the movement of material both normal to the shore and alongshore. The grading and sorting of beach material will also be discussed.

1. *MOVEMENT OF MATERIAL NORMAL TO THE SHORE*

(a) Model experiments

The experiments which will be described were carried out in the wave tank in Cambridge University, to study the direction and amount of sand moved at varying depths under different conditions. The material used was medium grade sand with a median diameter of 0·41 mm., many of the experiments were carried out with the aid of a trap which has already been described (see pp. 43 45). Its chief value was that it enabled the amount and direction of the net volume of sand moving normal to the beach to be determined. The experiments were carried out with a variety of beach gradients, in varying depths of water, and with different bottom conditions and wave characteristics, so that the effect of each of these variables could be determined. The experiments can be considered in two parts; those made outside the break-point of the waves and those made inside it, because different processes operate in these two zones.

i. SAND MOVEMENT OUTSIDE THE BREAK-POINT. One of the most interesting features of this movement is that in 98 per cent of the observations the net movement was in a landward direction. The few exceptions involved very small amounts and were obtained with very steep waves. This result can be explained by reference to the character of the orbital movement on the bottom discussed in the last chapter, where it was shown that the maximum velocity occurred under the wave crest in a landward direction. It is also suggested by the tank experiments describing the movement of dye in wave action, where a strong landward thrust on the bottom was observed; this movement may be of less significance because the landward movement continued when the bottom was rippled, under which conditions the landward thrust no longer occurred. The variable amount of landward movement outside the break-point could be explained by reference to the effect of the following factors:

    (*a*) Wave height
    (*b*) Wave period or length
    (*c*) Water depth or distance from the break-point
    (*d*) Beach gradient
    (*e*) Bottom character—rippled or smooth

As only one sand size was used the effect of this factor was not determined.

Wave height. The wave height is clearly an important factor in determining the amount of material moved landwards, as shown in fig. 4–1.

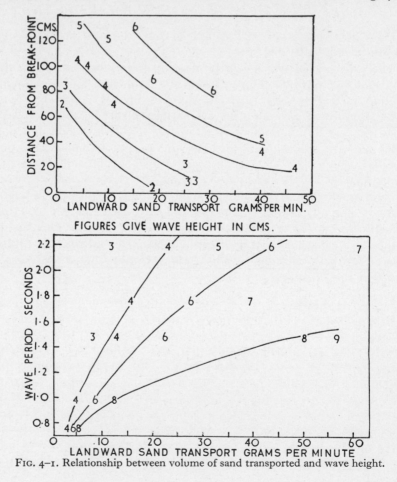

FIG. 4–1. Relationship between volume of sand transported and wave height.

For any given wave period at a specific distance from the break-point the amount transported increases very rapidly with increasing wave height.

Wave period. The same graphs show that changes in wave period also affect the amount of sand moved. As the period lengthens, for any given wave height, so the volume of sand moved is greater. The greater volume of transport with lengthening wave period is more rapid as the waves become higher, which is the result of the increase in the energy of the wave. A long wave may be expected to move more sand in the same depth of water owing to the smaller value of d/L, which is one of the parameters determining the horizontal amplitude of movement on the bottom. Thus for a short wave with L 100 cm. in a depth of 20 cm. d/L will be 0·2, but for a wave 300 cm. in length d/L will be 0·067, this will produce a theoretical amplitude of oscillation of 0·6H for the short wave and 2·3H for the long wave.

Wave steepness. It appears that the wave steepness is not so fundamental in this movement because by holding the length constant and increasing the height the steepness will be greater, but by using a constant height and lengthening the period the steepness will be decreased. Both changes have been shown to increase the volume of landward transport.

Depth. As would be expected the volume transported is considerably greater as the water becomes shallower and the break-point is approached; the maximum transport occurs near the break-point of the waves. The same argument as that used to explain the increase of transport with lengthening waves can be applied in this instance as well; again the d/L ratio is decreased as the break-point is approached. The depth at which no movement takes place is a function of the wave height and length; for the larger waves used the limit at which movement ceases was not reached in the tank. For the lower waves the limit of movement appeared to be reached when the depth exceeded 0·015–0·02 of the wave length, i.e. d/L greater than 0·015; the transport of sand became very small in these depths.

Beach gradient. The beach gradient affected the transport of sand as would be expected; the flatter slopes allowed greater transport of sand. The gradients used were 1 : 12, 1 : 15 and 1 : 20. The graph in fig. 4–2 shows the effect of changing gradient at different distance from the break-point for one wave height and length. This result can be explained by the influence of the force of gravity.

Character of bottom. The experiments already discussed were made with an initially smooth sand bed but before the end of the usual run of 5 min. the bed had nearly always become rippled. Another series of experiments was made to determine the effect of the character of the bed on the volume of transport. The bed was made smooth at the beginning of the run as usual but as soon as ripples started to form the waves were stopped. One wave length and height were used and the gradient was kept at 1 : 15; the experiments were made in varying depths.

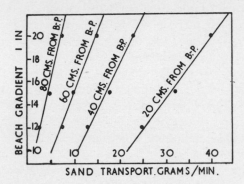

FIG. 4–2. Relationship between volume of sand transported and beach gradient.

From the graph in fig. 4–3 it can be seen that for any given distance from the break-point the sand transport on a smooth bed was considerably less than that on a rippled bed. The scatter of the points for the rippled surface is partly accounted for by the number of ripple crests passing over the trap during the run. A plot of the ratio of sand transport on a smooth bed to that on a rippled bed, T_s/T_r, against the water depth shows the effect of rippling is much more marked in the deeper water; here the ratio T_s/T_r is about 0·2 while in shallow water it increases to over 0·5. When the bottom is rippled sand movement begins in deeper water than on a smooth bed. One reason for this result is probably the

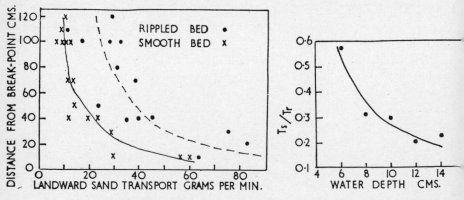

FIG. 4–3. Relationship between volume of sand transported and character of the bed.

greater turbulence in the lower layers when rippling develops, much more sand is raised into suspension; the turbulence is demonstrated by the dispersal of the thread of dye on a rippled bottom, which remains as a unit on a smooth bottom. There is little sand in suspension when the bottom is smooth and therefore transport must be achieved by rolling of grains of sand on the bottom. A more detailed consideration of the effect of rippling on the movement of bed material and the reason for the development of ripples will be discussed in a later section (see pp. 128–132).

Summary

Model experiments showed that the transport of sand on the bottom outside or seaward of the break-point was practically always in a landward direction. The volume transported increased as the waves became higher, as the period increased, as the energy increased, as the depth decreased, as the beach became flatter and as the bottom became rippled.

ii. SAND MOVEMENT INSIDE THE BREAK-POINT. As has already been stated the movement of sand outside the break-point was almost always landwards in the experiments described. Inside the break-point, however, the movement was not so regular. Different factors are of importance in determining the direction of movement in this zone. Only one row of breakers could be formed in the tank used so that it was not possible to simulate conditions that obtain on flat beaches in nature, when surf or broken water covers a wide stretch of beach. Landward of the break-point in the tank the action of the swash and backwash become important elements in the movement of material as they also do on a natural beach. It must be remembered that the waves in the tank were not at first working on the equilibrium profile, but on a uniform slope which for most of the experiments discussed was 1 : 12. It will be shown that this gradient is flatter than the equilibrium gradient (see chapter 10, pp. 341–345); this fact probably had some influence on the direction of movement of material in the very shallow water. Had the slope been steeper than the equilibrium gradient a different result would probably have been obtained.

The importance of wave height and period on the movement outside the break-point has been discussed but inside the break-point their effect is less easy to demonstrate. This is because the sand is not moving in a constant direction. It was found that the direction of movement inside the break-point depended on the wave steepness. This can be demonstrated by plotting the amount and direction of transport against the water depth as shown in fig. 4-4. The landward transport is shown to the left of the axis while the seaward transport increases to the right of the axis. The break-point must also be shown as it is here that there is an abrupt change in the pattern of movement. Each graph is drawn for one specific wave length, the wave height varies giving three wave steepness values on each graph. Clearly the waves of different steepness will break in varying depths of water dependent on their height, as is shown. The position where the maximum transport occurred, with a few exceptions, was found to be in a landward direction just seaward of the break-point.

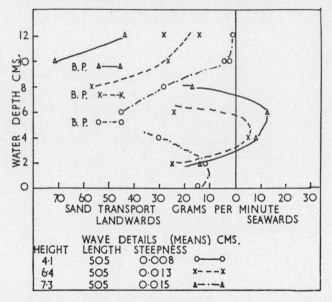

Fig. 4-4. Direction of transport of sand in relation to wave steepness inside the break-point.

The steepest waves, with a steepness of more than 0·04, moved relatively little sand outside the break-point, probably because they were very short. Inside the break-point they moved a very large volume of sand seaward, which decreased with decreasing depth. Seaward movement inside the break-point was apparent for all waves above a critical steepness; below this steepness value sand was moved landwards in all depths, although the amounts were less than those just outside the break-point. The critical steepness under the conditions of the experiment was about 0·012.

This result agrees with the well-known fact that steep waves are destructive on a beach while flat waves tend to build up the beach. It, therefore, gives confidence in the applicability of model experimental results to beaches in nature. It must not be supposed, however, that the same critical steepness will apply under all conditions. The size of the beach material is one of the factors of importance in determining the value of the critical steepness; as only one size of sand was used in the experiments discussed the effect of this variable was not determined experimentally. In other experiments the critical steepness varied between 0·03 and 0·025, Scott (1954)[1] found that a destructive effect was obtained with a steepness value of 0·019, which lies nearer to the value found in the experiments under discussion.

The result of the experiments may be explained by the velocities of the swash and backwash respectively. The swash acts with a high velocity for a short period and the backwash with a lower velocity for a longer period. Assuming a constant wave length, the volume of water descending the beach increases as the wave height increases. The period remains constant so that the amount lost by percolation remains constant. The increased volume will cause increased velocities in both swash and backwash; these will be raised above the critical velocity for sediment transport in both directions of flow as the wave steepness increases. When the velocity of the backwash is above the critical velocity the sand will be moved seawards owing to the longer duration of the backwash current. The greater turbulence associated with higher waves will also help to put sand in suspension so that it can be more easily moved. The return flow relating to the mass transport velocity will be relatively great for the higher waves and will be most strongly felt in the shallow water inside the break-point.

Further experiments were made on a much flatter gradient of 1 : 40 to examine the effect of this variable. On this flatter gradient the waves broke in a series of rather feeble breakers, the nearest likeness to surf waves that could be achieved. The results showed that these waves reacted in a similar way to waves with similar characteristics on a steeper beach; the steep waves were destructive inside the break-point and the flat ones were constructive throughout the tank. The gradient, therefore, does not alter the results of the experiment although the volume of sand moved was affected. In the deeper water outside the break-point more sand was moved on a flatter gradient but inside the break-point the reverse was true. This may be explained by the much greater horizontal distance over which the wave energy was dissipated inside the break-point on the very flat gradient compared to the steeper slope.

Summary

Inside the break-point of the waves in the model tank the direction of transport of sand depended on the steepness of the waves. Waves with a steepness in excess of 0·012 moved sand seawards while flatter waves moved it landwards in all depths. Similar results were obtained on gradients of 1 : 12 and 1 : 40.

iii. RIPPLE FORMATION. Some mention of the effect of ripple formation on the amount of sand moving outside the break-point has already
been made; in this section the mode of formation and dimensions of the
ripples will be considered in more detail. Observations have been made
both in ordinary wave tanks and by oscillation of a curved cradle, containing sand, through still water. One very detailed study has been made
by Manohar (1955)[2] using both theoretical and experimental data. His
data apply largely to the effect of shallow water waves in relatively deep
water; he states that the formulae for bed movement and ripple formation refer to depths of about 25 ft. He discusses in detail the nature of the
boundary layer and concludes that ripples only form when the flow in
this layer is turbulent. Because his analysis applies mainly to deeper
water, where the water velocity landward and seaward has less differential value, his results are not directly applicable to the formation of
ripples and movement of sediment near the break-point of the waves.

The experiments made by Bagnold (1946)[3] were also carried out by
oscillating a curved cradle through still water in a simple harmonic
motion. A series of angular velocities was used for a number of different
semi-amplitudes, R, from 25 to 0·5 cm.; the range of velocities used
covered the speed at which sand first started to be disturbed to a velocity
at which the whole sand bed started to move off the cradle. A second
series of experiments was made to measure the ripple drag. The motion
of the water was studied by using a camera which was fixed to the cradle
and therefore moved with the ripples. The photographs revealed the
presence of small eddies and large vortices. Bagnold has described two
very different types of ripples which are formed by different forces, but
are superficially similar in appearance. The similarity arises because both
depend on the maximum angle at which sand in water is stable, which is
about 30 deg.

When sand movement first starts at the lowest water velocity capable
of initiating movement the sand grains first move by rolling, the distance
at first being short as only the maximum acceleration raises the speed
sufficiently to move the sand. The grains in time form into a pattern of
transverse crests only a few grains high, which oscillate to and fro with
the passing waves. These small crests eventually grow into a stable
pattern, whose spacing depends on the sheltering effect exerted by one
ridge extending to the next. The height of the ridge which determines
the width of the flow-shadow also determines the repetition distance.
The form of these rolling grain ripples depends on the size of the sand;
for the larger grains it may become part of a nearly circular arc in profile,
while in finer material flat troughs exist. There is no movement in the
troughs of ripples of this type and no vortices are set up. This type of
ripple will not form if the initial bed has inequalities of greater amplitude

than about 20 grain diameters. The speeds at which it will form vary from the critical speed which first initiates movement to about twice that speed.

If the speed is increased to more than twice the critical speed the stable system of rolling grain ripples suddenly breaks down and vortex ripples will be developed. The steep lee face increases beyond a stable height at one point first and a vortex forms creating a new type of ripple which rapidly extends from this initial position in both directions. Any irregularity on the bed is sufficient to initiate the formation of a vortex and the breakdown of the stable system; on an irregular bed the velocity need not be so high to initiate vortex type ripples. The effect of the vortex is to move sand grains from the foot of the ripple to its crest, thus controlling its size. With a long stroke the height of the ripple tended to decrease and with very long strokes and high velocity the length to height ratio became such that no vortex could develop due to the high mid-stroke speed, hence this type of ripple could not form; with very short strokes, on the other hand, the crests of the ripples remained sharply pointed.

The length of the ripples was found to be independent of the speed of oscillation for a variety of sizes and densities of grains; coal, steel and quartz grains were used with diameters varying from 0·25 cm. to 0·09 mm. The variation in size of the grains did, however, affect the length of the ripples. The effect of variation in the stroke of the cradle, R, was not shown in a variation in pitch, p, of the ripple except for the two largest grain sizes; in these materials the ripples suddenly became shorter as the R/p ratio reached unity, but remained at the same ratio as R decreased. The natural length of the ripple appears to be independent of the density of the grain and to vary nearly as the square-root of its diameter. The degree of sorting of the sand also had little effect on the length of the ripple, although experiments were made with sand of much more mixed character than most natural beach sands.

The length to height ratio of the ripples was nearly constant for the shorter amplitudes of oscillation at 4·5–5 but increased to nearly 8 as the value of R increased to the maximum value of 32 cm. A modification of the vortex ripple pattern occurred when R was reduced to about 1/6 of the length of the ripple or $p/6$. This pattern resembled a brick wall in that regular transverse bridges were formed between two crests and offset as with brick walling. This pattern has also been observed in nature in deep water with a short oscillation on a sandy bed, which is interesting confirmation that the model ripples behaved as their full-scale counterparts.

Experiments were made in a wave tank by Scott (1954)[1] in which he studied the formation of ripples created by the uneven accelerations of water in wave motion on a sloping beach. His experiments apply more nearly to the natural conditions of a sand beach near the break-point than do those already discussed, which were made in uniform depth with harmonic oscillation. The movement of the ripples in relation to the direction of the shoreline could also be studied and the effect of differential acceleration under the wave crest and trough could be evaluated, while the dimensions of the ripple could be related to the wave characteristics. Scott found that the ripples moved towards the land on the upper part of the profile but they moved seawards in deeper water. The position of the change in direction varied slightly from time to time but was mostly between 8 and 11 ft. from the waterline in about 1 ft. of water. The velocity of movement increased away from the point of change of direction. The landward movement of ripples in the shallow water is caused by more sand being pushed over the crest of the ripples than is carried seaward in suspension by the vortex which develops as the wave trough passes. This type of movement causes an asymmetrical form to develop; the landward slope is steeper while the form and type of movement appears to be exactly reversed in the deeper water where the ripples are moving seawards. In intermediate depths the ripples are more symmetrical, implying a more balanced movement. The landward movement of ripples in shallow water was more rapid when the waves were higher. In order to relate the movement of the ripples to the acceleration of the water particles in the waves, moving photographs were used to measure the orbital velocity of the particles. The accelerations were very much higher in a landwards direction in relatively shallow water, while in deeper water the accelerations became more equal and in one case, near the position of change of direction of the ripples, the seaward acceleration was greater. The length of the ripples agreed closely with the amplitude of oscillation of the water horizontally which agrees with Bagnold's results, when R/p is less than unity.

(b) Observations in nature

i. RIPPLES. Observations reported by Inman (1957)[4] on the formation of ripples under oscillatory waves in nature, have been made recently by swimmers with breathing apparatus off the coast of California; these throw interesting light on the full-scale formation of ripples on the sea-floor. The observations were carried out to depths of 170 ft. It was found that ripples were always present on sandy sea floors where the significant orbital velocity was somewhere between $\frac{1}{3}$ and 3 ft./sec. The length of the ripples measured varied from 0·14 to over 4 ft. The observations made included the length, height, symmetry and form of the ripple. From the results it was found that the ripples were of two types; some had flat troughs between the crests, which were called solitary ripples, while others had rounded troughs and were named trochoidal ripples. Whenever possible the wave dimensions were measured at the same time as ripple observations were made, from these the orbital velocity at the bottom could be calculated; this was done by using Airy's formulae for the deeper water and the solitary wave theory for shallower water near the break-point.

The size of the ripples was found to be related to the size of the sand of which they were formed; the larger ripples are associated with the coarser sand and the smaller with finer sand. The depth of water and exposure also affect the ripple size; ripples in deeper water and off exposed coasts tend to be larger than those in shallower water and more sheltered areas. Ripples in bays and lakes are the smallest. This relationship is due to variations in the amplitude of the orbital oscillation of the waves forming them. The steeper or trochoidal ripples are found in the deeper water and more sheltered sites and are formed by the development of vortices. The flat bottomed solitary ripples are found where the bottom velocities and orbital amplitudes are greater, in shallow water and on finer sand, where the material is carried in sub-suspension in a layer of a few centimetres thickness. Where there was a large supply of sand the coarser grains were found on the ripple crest while the finest and densest grains were in the troughs; the finer sand was found at the crest where the supply was limited in areas of rocky bottom. It was found that the character of sand at the crest largely determined the dimensions of the ripples.

Observations of ripples on the bottom of the Black Sea off the coast of the Crimea have been made by Zenkovitch (1946)[5]. At a depth of 14 m. (45·8 ft.) he observed ripples from 90 to 110 cm. (2·95–3·6 ft.) in length and 7–10 cm. (2·75–4 in.) high which must originally have been 15 cm. (6 in.) in height owing to deposition of fine material in their troughs. The crests of the ripples in a depth of 13 m. (42·6 ft.) contained pebbles up to 6 cm. (2·36 in.) in length and an analysis of the material from the crest showed that it had a median diameter of 17 mm., the material in the trough had a median diameter of 3·5 mm. In a depth of 18 m. (59 ft.) the median diameter of the material at the crest was 3·0 mm. while that of the trough was 0·17 mm.

In comparing the results of the full-scale observations with those from model experiments it appears that in many ways the results are in agreement; there are, however, some points of difference. The model ripples did not reach as great a maximum length as natural ripples for the same sand size, while the longest ripples on natural beaches were in the deeper water where the velocities were slower. Manohar found that the longest ripples in the model were formed where the velocity was approaching the upper limiting value, while in nature the ripple length was reduced at higher velocities.

Summary

Studies of ripples by model experiment shows that two types exist with even accelerations, such as would occur in deeper water. On a smooth bed with low velocities rolling grain ripples are formed, if the speed is increased vortex ripples develop. The length of the ripple was found to be independent of the speed of oscillation but varied with the square-root of the grain diameter and with the amplitude of oscillation. With uneven acceleration, such as occurs in shallow water, the ripples appeared to move landwards, inland of a specific point, and seawards outside it.

In nature larger ripples are also associated with coarser material and formed where the orbital velocity lay between $\frac{1}{3}$ and 3 ft./sec., larger ripples were found in the deeper water and more exposed areas.

ii. DEPTH OF MOVEMENT. The amount of transport of material on the bottom under natural conditions is difficult to measure but it appears likely, both by analogy to experimental conditions and to theoretical considerations, that movement of material is, under normal wave conditions, in an onshore direction on the bottom outside the break-point. It has been shown by Ippen and Eagleson (1955)[6] from a consideration of theoretical and experimental data that the transport of sediment on the bottom under wave action is mainly a function of the hydrodynamic drag and the weight of the particle. One interesting result from their observations suggests that there is a null point at which the onshore transport of sediment becomes zero and seaward of which the transport is offshore. This seaward movement at depth is never rapid because in this zone the velocities of the water particles under wave action are only sufficient to move the grains by rolling and a little distance seaward of this point friction forces predominate and all movement ceases. The existence of this null point is also suggested by the change in direction of ripple movement which was noted previously, although it must be remembered that the direction of movement of the ripples does not necessarily determine the direction of net sand movement on the bottom; the ripples can be moving landward while the net transport is in a seaward direction at times.

As long ago as 1887 Cornaglia[7] put forward a theory in which he suggested that a neutral line existed; landward of it the bottom material moved landward while outside it the material travelled seaward. He supposed that the depth of the neutral line depended upon the character of the waves, the slope of the bottom and the size and density of the bottom particles. This depth reached a maximum of 10 m. (33 ft.) for the exposed beaches of the Mediterranean, while Timmermans (1935),[8] who also discussed the neutral line, suggested that its depth is $2\frac{1}{2}$ times the wave height, although this does not take into consideration the particle size which is clearly relevant.

Ippen and Eagleson, for a model beach slope of 1 : 15 and a range of steepness between 0·01 and 0·08, give the relationships governing the position of the null point as $(H/d)^2 \times L/H \times C/w = 11\cdot6$, where H is the wave height, L is the wave length, C is the wave velocity, d the local depth of water and w the terminal velocity of fall of the particles in fresh water. The wave characteristics refer to those at the point in question. The constant applies only to a slope of 1 : 15 and probably varies with slope (see fig. 4–5).

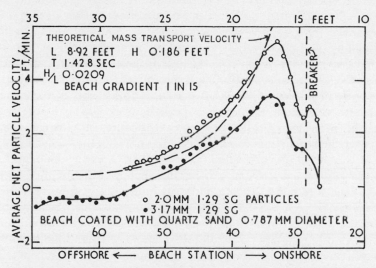

Fɪɢ. 4–5. Particle velocity related to distance offshore towards null point in the model tank. (After Ippen and Eagleson, B.E.B.)

The line of no movement would be closer inshore for coarse sediments on a natural beach and this would have a sorting effect on the distribution of particle size. The sorting of the particles as a result of the differential velocities will be considered in the next section; in this section the depth of the so-called neutral line is of importance as it will determine the maximum depth to which waves cause movement of material on the bottom. In general it appears that the offshore motion on a natural beach will be very much less in volume and importance than the onshore movement and can be ignored for most purposes.

The waves first feel the bottom effectively when the depth is equal to half the wave length, but it is not till the depth is much shallower that any appreciable amount of sand is transported and changes of the bottom contours resulting from it can take place. It is difficult to obtain precise data on this point and evidence is often conflicting due to the many variables which can affect the depth of movement. The existence of strong tidal or other currents in deeper water may be effective in some areas, where sediment would not otherwise be disturbed at the depth in question. Another difficulty is to obtain precise measurements of the amount of movement taking place in deep water. The accuracy of most types of hydrographic survey is not sufficiently great to record small changes of elevation resulting from bottom movement in deep water.

Some of the most precise data concerning the movement of material in fairly deep water on the bottom is reported by Inman and Rusnak (1956).[9] They carried out observations to a depth of 70 ft. on the shelf off La Jolla, California. The accuracy of the observations was such that the standard error in the determination of the sand level was ± 0.05 ft.; the method of survey will be considered in more detail in the next chapter (see pp. 196, 197). The changes in level recorded at depths of 70 ft. were of the same order of magnitude as the irregularities of the bottom so that it was difficult to determine their exact value. On the whole the magnitude of recorded changes decreased with increasing depth and were small for depths greater than 30 ft. The changes of sand level over the period of observation was about 0.15 ft. at a depth of 70 ft., 0.16 ft. at a depth of 52 ft. and 0.29 ft. at 30-ft. depth while in 18 ft. of water it was 0.62 ft.; for all except the shallowest depth the surveys ranged over a period of forty months or more. There was a steady decrease of sand size which was very fine on the whole, from shallow water outwards; at 18 ft. the median diameter was 0.15 mm., at 30 ft. it was 0.12 mm. and at 52 and 70 ft. depths it was 0.11 mm. The maximum change in level can be seen from the graph shown in fig. 4–6. The amount of change at 18 ft. was probably rather greater in total amount than indicated and exceeded 2 ft. at times, while the rod at 6 ft. was buried during the winter.

The depths at which the bottom movement becomes small was found to be similar to those just discussed by Trask (1955).[10] He was concerned with the transport of material round the rocky peninsulas of part of the Californian coast, which he studied by detailed analysis of the sediment characteristics in different depths and positions. He was able to show that material does move around the headlands of Point Arguello and Conception although this movement cannot take place on the beach itself as the headlands descend into relatively deep water and only small and isolated beaches occur at intervals along the coast.

Some interesting information concerning the state of the sea bed was observed off the Californian coast by divers, which has a bearing on the question of the depth at which waves can move the bottom material. The

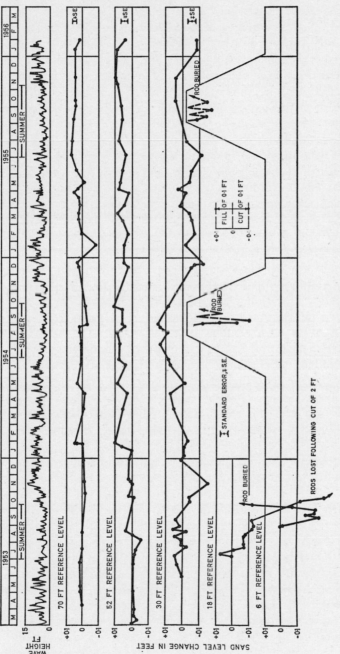

FIG. 4–6. Changes in sand level at various depths off the Californian coast. (After Inman and Rusnak, B.E.B.)

depth at which ripples were first developed on the sea bed was about 50 ft. and there was evidence of slight wave movement to a depth of 60 ft. Below 60 ft. to a maximum depth of 130 ft. the sea bottom was covered by a fine powdery deposit like brown 'rust' and the water was quite quiet, but at a depth of about 45 ft. the passing waves were observed to disturb the sand grains. The median diameter of the sand at 45 ft. was 0·149 mm. On another profile ripples were first encountered at a depth of 58 ft.; it may, therefore, be concluded that in this area movement of the bottom was limited under those wave conditions to quiet deposition in depths greater than 60 ft. Trask divides the sea bed into three zones above a depth of 60 ft.; beyond this depth is a passive zone of little or no movement, while between 60 and 30 ft. is a zone intermediate in character, in which sand is moved at intervals, an active zone extends between 30 ft. to the surf zone, and finally there are the surf and beach zones.

Later observations by Inman (1957)[4] have shown that in depths of 70 ft. the 'rust' reported by Trask is not a permanent feature of the sea bed. According to Inman's observations a quiescent state, in which 'rust' can form and burrowing animals can destroy the ripple pattern, is found for about 39 per cent of the observations. This state of the sea bed can develop in a few hours after the orbital velocity falls below that necessary for the formation of ripples. The period of quiescence at 52 ft. is 12 per cent, while at 30 ft. it is 0 per cent. Ripples were also measured at depths of 110 ft. and observed at a depth of 170 ft., it may be concluded, therefore, that during periods of strong wave activity the waves can cause some movement of material at very considerable depths although such movement is not likely to cause much change in the profile. Shepard and Inman (1951)[11] do show that changes in level at a depth of 100 ft. off the Scripps pier may rarely amount to as much as 1–2 ft.

On the other hand the dumping of beach fill in a depth of about 40 ft. showed that movement in this depth was very slow, Harris (1955),[12] the dumped material did not move landwards with any speed to replenish the beach. The beach concerned is at Long Branch, New Jersey and was steep and narrow, being in need of replenishment. To nourish the beach 601,991 cubic yds. of sand was dumped in water $\frac{1}{2}$ mile offshore where the depth was 38 ft. at mean low water. Surveys of the offshore area and dumping ground were made before, during and after the dumping operations. According to the analysis of Manohar, it was found that, by correlations with wave observations, only 3·4 per cent of the waves were able to move the stock-pile of sand; the minimum size of waves capable of moving the stock-pile were 4 ft. high with a period of 6 sec. These dimensions were only exceeded for 3·4 per cent of the waves measured.

After four years the stock-pile, which had been originally in the form of a ridge 7 ft. high, 750 ft. wide and 3,700 ft. long, had been flattened out but was still substantially intact. It was concluded that this method of beach nourishment had little influence on the processes operating along the shore itself where the annual loss was 156,000 cubic yds. after the dumping, only slightly less than the pre-dumping figure of 177,000 cubic yds. These results indicate that substantial movement of sand is a very slow process in a depth of 40 ft., but that the larger waves are able to effect slow changes at this depth. During the four-year period from July 1948 to October 1952 there was a slight decrease in the median diameter of the sand on the stock-pile area, this was 0·34 mm. when dumped in the offshore zone, where the original sand size was 0·39 mm., it was found to be 0·32 mm. in 1952.

Experiments reported by Inose and Shiraishi (1956)[13] made with radio-active sand at Tomakomai, Hokkaido, Japan have shown that sand of median diameter of 0·13 mm. starts to move at a depth of 6 m. (19·7 ft.) when the wave height exceeds 5·8 ft.

The observations which have already been discussed apply mainly to sand; it is probable that shingle can only be moved in depths considerably less than those in which sand is moved. Observations of the movement of radio-active pebbles have been carried out on the east coast of England at Orfordness, Suffolk, by Kidson, Carr and Smith (1958).[14] These showed that, for the duration of the observations over a period of about six weeks, pebbles in a depth of 30 ft. of water were not moved by the waves, but similar experiments off Scolt Head Island in Norfolk, showed that pebbles were moved to a depth of 18–24 ft. by moderate waves of about 3 ft. height at the break-point.[15] Where the tidal currents are very strong, the movement of shingle may occur at considerably greater depths, in fact where a tidal current of 4½ knots occurs between Hurst Castle Spit and the Isle of Wight shingle has been scoured in a depth of 32 fathoms.[16] Where there are no tidal currents the depth of movement of shingle has been suggested to be only 6 ft. below the lowest tide level. Bagnold (1940)[17] from the results of model experiments with the equivalent of shingle finds that the depth at which movement ceases is equal to the height of the waves, which determines the edge of the shelf (shown in fig. 4–7) regardless of the size of the shingle in the off-shore zone. The capacity of tidal currents to move material is discussed in chapter 5, pp. 202–205; it is shown that movement can take place in depths of 540 ft.

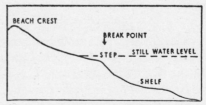

FIG. 4–7. Diagram of model shingle beach.

Summary

Sand does not appear to move substantially even off exposed coasts in depths greater than 40 ft. although waves can produce ripples and occasionally greater changes in level at greater depths of over 100 ft. The evidence with respect to shingle is more conflicting, it seems that strong tidal currents are necessary for substantial movement of shingle at depth, but moderate waves can move shingle in depths of about 20 ft.

iii. SEASONAL AND TIDAL CHANGES. The movement of beach material normal to the coast is mainly responsible for the very considerable changes which occur from time to time on the foreshore and in the off-shore zone. Such changes are seasonal in some areas but more erratic in others. The areas which undergo a seasonal variation of beach characteristics are mainly those which have a regular seasonal change in climatic conditions, with corresponding variation in wave action on the beach. The extent of the periodic fluctuation of the beach is partly dependent on the variability of the waves, but perhaps the most important factor is the nature of the beach material; the coarser the beach material the greater will be the changes of elevation of the beach. Changes in level of 2 or 3 ft. in one week have been recorded at Marsden Bay, County Durham, where the median diameter of the sand was about 0·36 mm., while on the much finer sand beach of Rhossili Bay, South Wales, where the median diameter of the sand was 0·23 mm. the change in sand level over a period of a week was limited to 1 or 2 in. On shingle beaches the changes are much more rapid and greater; on one occasion at Chesil beach near Abbotsbury a change in level of 5 ft. was recorded over a period of only one or two hours, the shingle here has a median diameter of 0·45 in. (11·4 mm.).

A similar relationship between the rapidity of beach changes and the size of the beach material has also been noted by Shepard on beaches in California (1950);[18] where the sand size is large, median diameter 0·5 mm., the changes were much greater and more rapid than on finer sand beaches. The reason for this variation is related to the gradient of the beaches, which is dependent partly on the size of the beach material as will be considered in detail in chapter 10 (see pp. 321–323). On the steeper beaches the waves break close inshore and their energy is dissipated over a relatively narrow beach zone; the greater power of the backwash is also important.

The foreshore and offshore zone along the Scripps Institute pier in California shows the seasonal changes in level very clearly. Fig. 4–8 shows that the beach changes, as recorded in the profiles for spring and autumn, reverse with the seasons; there is a marked fill on the upper part of the profile over the summer season with a cut in deeper water,

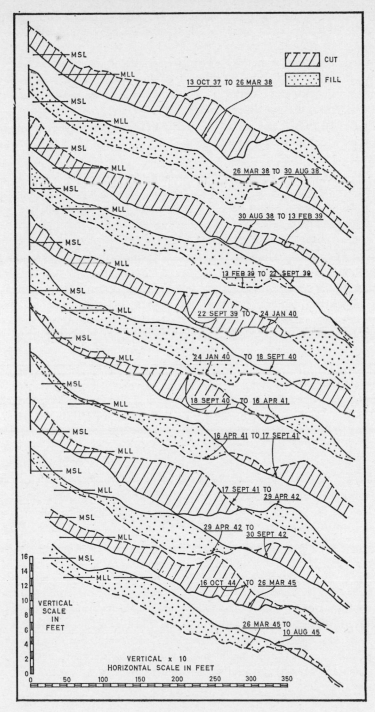

FIG. 4–8. Seasonal changes on Scripps Pier profile. (After Shepard, B.E.B.)

which indicates that the source of material being deposited on the upper beach is at least partly derived from the offshore zone by transport normal to the shore. During the winter season the reverse change is recorded, with loss of material from the top of the profile and deposition below. These changes can be related to the wave characteristics as will be considered in more detail in the sections dealing with constructive and destructive waves (see pp. 250, 280).

The tide may also produce cyclic changes on beaches in some localities which have very interesting biological consequences. On some of the beaches of California, at Long Beach and to a certain extent at La Jolla, there is a regular change in sand elevation with the tidal cycle of spring and neap tide. The problem is discussed by Thompson (1919)[19] and Lafond (1939)[20] who show that a few days after neap tide the beach, a few feet below mean tide level, reached its minimum elevation, while the beach a short distance above the mean tide level reached its maximum height. The reverse changes occurred after the spring tide; the cut now occurred at the higher level and the fill below mean tide level. This change in the elevation of the sand on the beach is used by a species of fish, *Leuresthes tenuis* or grunion, to protect their eggs after spawning. They lay their eggs two or three days after spring tide above mean tide level, the eggs are then buried by sand during the neap tide period when deposition occurs at this level. When the next spring tides occur and this sand is again removed the eggs are ready to hatch, after having been protected by sand. The spawning of the grunion takes place during the period from March to August when the sand movements resulting from tidal action are most constant; during other times of the year the changes in sand level due to variation in wave size are much greater than those due to tidal action and they, therefore, mask the latter changes. The changes in level are related to the different levels at which the waves act during different parts of the tidal cycle but the exact mechanism is still somewhat obscure. In most areas the waves are too variable for such changes to be observed, for this reason it was not possible to detect changes of this type due to the tidal cycle on a beach in County Durham where weekly surveys were carried out for quite a long period to determine whether such tidal changes were apparent.[21]

iv. SAND IN SUSPENSION. In considering the movement of beach material, particularly on a sand beach, the amount of material in suspension is an important factor; this material can be carried in the direction of the littoral currents even if these are of low velocity. The movement of sand in suspension is partly in a direction normal to the shore but it may also be carried parallel to the shore by the longshore currents. Quantitative data from observations made at Long Branch, New Jersey, were published in the *Interim Report* of the Beach Erosion Board (1933)[22] and are shown graphically in fig. 4-9. It can be seen that only near the break-point of the waves is the proportion of sand moved in suspension as great as 5 per cent of the total sand moved, this amounts to about 17,000 parts per million by weight. At a point only 25 ft. seaward of the break-point the quantity of sand in suspension had fallen to only 4,000 parts per million, while it was less than 1,000 parts per million 275 ft. farther seawards. It is only at the break-point itself that the sand in suspension extends evenly from the bottom to the surface; in the swash the sand grains are fairly evenly spaced throughout the depth of the water layer but in the backwash the movement is confined to a layer close to the bottom. Seaward of the break-point the level to which sand in suspension rises depends partly on the height of the waves; at a point 600 ft. from the shore there is very little sand above 10 ft. from the bottom except for waves over 10 ft. high, while for all waves, sand in excess of 2,000 parts per million is not found above about 2 ft. from the bottom.

More recently a field sampler, devised to measure the amount of sediment in suspension, has been described by Watts (1953).[23] It is an instrument of the pump type working by suction; a nozzle was held vertically downwards, at right-angles to the horizontal velocities, during the experimental stage of the development of the instrument in a tank. The sampler was calibrated in the laboratory where known volumes of sand concentrations could be used at specified velocities of flow in the tank; various widths and velocities of flow in the nozzle could be tested. It was found that the instrument was much more accurate when the nozzle velocity was greater than the velocity in the tank. If the nozzle velocity was twice the maximum orbital velocity of the wave motion and the nozzle width was ½-in. the results were correct to within 15 per cent even without a correction factor.

The field tests were carried out off the pier at Mission Bay, California, as the equipment is bulky. Runs were made for 5 min. and 290 observations were made, of these 238 were inside the breakers and 52 outside; these observations provided 170 acceptable figures inside and 22 outside the breakers. Clogging of the nozzle by seaweed reduced the nozzle velocity below the allowable minimum in some of the runs, which could not be used. The results show some scatter but the mean of several values is probably fairly accurate. The results are plotted for different wave heights at several levels from the bottom and in varying depths of water. One example gives a mean value of 241 parts per million with a maximum of 482 parts per million and a minimum of 155 parts per million where the depth of water was 6·1-8 ft. and the waves 2·1-3 ft. high at 2·1-3 ft. above the bottom. The greatest volume of material in

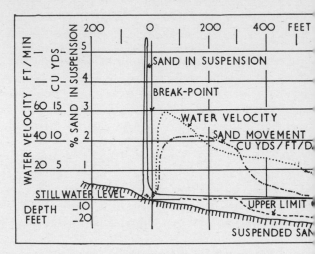

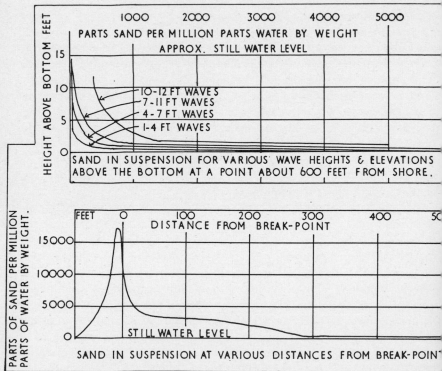

FIG. 4–9. Sand in suspension in relation to wave height, water depth and position of break-point. (After B.E.B.)

suspension was found in depths of 4–8 ft. just inside the break-point. The results of these measurements are shown in fig. 4–10. The median diameter of the sand in suspension was 0·14 mm., while on the foreshore it was 0·22 mm. grading down to 0·10 mm. at a depth of 50 ft., the median diameter was 0·15 mm. at depths between 0 and 20 ft. With

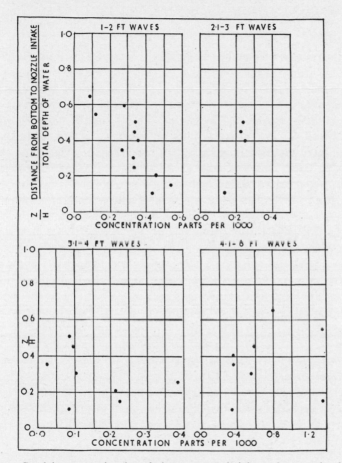

FIG. 4–10. Sand in suspension in relation to wave height and water depth. (After Watts, B.E.B.)

different velocities of littoral currents flowing alongshore it is possible to calculate the total littoral drift of material in cubic yards in suspension, this will be referred to again in the next section.

Summary

The maximum amount of material in suspension occurs near the break-point where 17,000 parts per million have been found, but this amounts to only 5 per cent of the total amount of sand moved. A new device for measuring sand in suspension has been developed which showed that the greatest volume of material in suspension occurred in depths of 4–8 ft., just inside the break-point.

2. *LONGSHORE MOVEMENT OF MATERIAL*

(a) Theory

The movement of material alongshore is one of the most important processes at work on the coast. It is responsible for the development of a large number of shore features such as various types of spits which will be discussed later (see chapters 8 and 12), as well as being an important factor in coastal erosion (see chapter 9); it is also one of the most difficult factors to measure accurately on natural beaches. In this section, therefore, the model experiments which have been made to study this problem will be discussed, and the techniques which have been developed to study this movement in nature will be mentioned.

Longshore movement takes place primarily in two zones along the beach; beach-drifting occurs along the upper limit of wave action and is related to the swash and backwash of the waves. It is clearly most effective when the waves approach at a considerable angle to the shore; it will be a powerful force on a steep coast which does not allow much wave refraction and where the waves are short, which also limits refraction. The other major zone of longshore movement is in the surf and breaker zone where the largest quantity of material is in suspension and which can be carried by the relatively weak longshore currents. These currents will tend to be irregular in direction with long waves, which suffer considerable refraction, thus setting up strong zones of convergence and divergence and hence variable longshore currents.

A theoretical analysis of the longshore component of littoral currents has already been discussed (see chapter 3, pp. 109–111), these currents will clearly affect the transport of sediment alongshore where it is thrown into suspension by the waves.

(b) Model studies

Model studies of sand transport along a straight beach with differing angles of wave attack have been made by Saville (1950)[24]. He used a model tank 66 × 122 ft. in plan and 2 ft. deep, which has already been described in chapter 2 (see pp. 45 and 46, and fig. 2–3). A beach was constructed at one end which was 6 ft. wide, the gradient extending offshore as a sloping ramp of concrete. The initial slope used was 1 : 10, and the size of the sand was 0·30 mm. A trap was fixed at the down beach end with a pump to ensure that the sand transport was not upset by currents at the end of the tank, giving the effect of an infinitely long beach. Traps were fixed at various levels in the centre of the tank to measure the bed-load transport. Sand was introduced at the up-beach end of the tank at the same rate as it moved out at the down-wave end.

It was found that once stability had been reached after a period of about 2–3 hours the amount of sand transported remains relatively constant. The traps were divided into four parts so that the transport in different zones on the profile could be measured. The transport of beach material took place in two main zones; one was the zig-zag transport on the beach in the form of beach-drifting, the other was the transport in suspension in the breaker zone over the submarine bar. The type of transport was found to vary with the wave characteristics; for steep storm waves about 60 per cent of the transported material was carried in suspension, for low, flat waves, only a small percentage was carried in suspension. The different zones in which the transport took place are clearly shown in fig. 4–11, (a) shows that transport under steep waves takes place mainly on the submarine bar in the breaker zone while (b) shows that with flat waves the transport takes place largely by beach drifting in the swash zone on the foreshore. The critical steepness causing a change in transport from beach-drifting to transport in suspension occurred with a steepness H/L ratio of 0·03.

An interesting result of the observations in the wave tank, which was confirmed by later experiments is the fact that there is an optimum wave steepness between 0·02 and 0·025 at which there is a maximum amount of total transport. There is a very rapid decrease for lesser steepness ratios, the peak value was also three times that taking place with very steep waves. In order to arrive at this result the points plotted were for different values of wave energy, as it was found that the wave energy had a marked effect on the amount of sand transported. It must be remembered also that these results were obtained on a beach in equilibrium, which is not likely to occur in nature. The relationship between the model and prototype also gives rise to uncertainties; in the model the strength of the alongshore current alone was not great enough to move the sand grains although it might well be fast enough to do so in nature.

These tests of Saville have been extended by Shay and Johnson (1953)[25] to examine a greater range of direction of approach of the waves. All Saville's results were obtained with waves that approached the beach at 10 deg., while the later observations extended the range to angles up to 50 deg. The maximum longshore movement of material was found to occur when the waves approached at an angle of about 30 deg. to the shore. The rate at which the transport takes place also slows down with time if the waves causing it are in process of adjusting the beach profile to a new equilibrium slope.

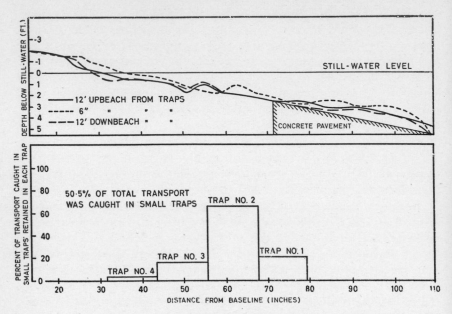

FIG. 4–11. (*a*) Model study of sand transport, beach profiles and total transport with steep waves. H/L 0.0597. (After Saville.)

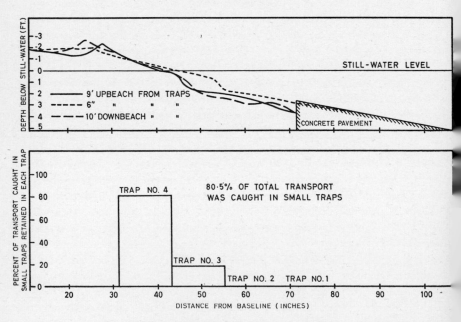

FIG. 4–11. (*b*) Model study of sand transport, beach profiles and total transport with flat waves. H/L 0.0151. (After Saville.)

The results of these studies, which give very interesting data concerning the processes of longshore drifting in a model tank, cannot be applied directly to a natural beach because of the other factors which complicate the problem in nature. The experimental conditions did not take into account irregularities of the coastal zone, the tide, the changing wave characteristics, nor the effect of the wind. On the other hand it is very difficult to make precise observations directly of the amount of sand being transported alongshore in nature; for this reason alone the model experiments are of value.

Experiments are being carried out by the Hydraulics Research Board (1956)[26] to examine the longshore movement on the model of a particular stretch of coast at Dunwich in Suffolk and to assess the effect of different types of groynes on the movement. The model profile, which is on a horizontal scale of 1 : 30 and a vertical scale of 1 : 20, has been moulded to represent that of the beach at Dunwich and the waves and tidal range have been adjusted by trial and error till the profile remains in equilibrium. The direction of wave approach was fixed at 30 deg. north of normal and their size according to the scale would be 2 ft. in deep water increasing to 3 ft. at the break-point. The amount of longshore movement was measured by collecting the sand in trays, each covering the equivalent of 60 ft. width of beach in the prototype or 2 ft. in the model. The total transport was the equivalent of 455,000 cubic yds. per year in the prototype on an open beach with no groynes over a width equal to the three upper trays, or 180 ft. The movement was found to be greatest around the high tide position and about half this value in the zone immediately above low tide level, the tidal range being the equivalent of 6 ft. in nature. The amount moved below low water level was very small. It was shown that groynes, 180 ft. long normal to the shore and 3 ft. above the beach level, greatly reduce the volume of longshore transport of sand. The groynes which were spaced 360 ft. apart reduced the transport to the equivalent of 120,000 cubic yds. per year. This experiment gives some information concerning the maximum amount of longshore movement which may be expected in a particular place, but owing to the use of the optimum direction of wave approach and only one wave size it cannot give the actual value of longshore movement that does in fact take place at Dunwich.

(c) Observations and calculations of longshore transport in nature

i. SAND BEACHES. It is not possible to measure directly the transport of sand along a shore; however, where suitable conditions have been available estimates have been made of the longshore transport in different areas and under different wave conditions. Such studies can be made most readily where the natural movement of sand alongshore has been interrupted by some barrier, such as a groyne or break-water of a harbour. By repeated surveys it is then possible to arrive at an estimate of the volume of material accumulating on the up-wave side of the barrier and the amount of material lost by erosion on the down-wave side. In some cases more accurate volumetric figures are available where sand has either been dredged from the up-wave side or deposited by dumping on the down-wave side. Such studies are clearly easier to make where there is a dominant direction of drift along the coast; without this there will be no longshore transport over a period of considerable duration in any case. Estimates of the amount of longshore transport have been made for various parts of the coasts of the United States including California, Florida and New Jersey; these will be mentioned as they give comparative figures of longshore movement under different conditions of wave action which can probably find a wider application to other areas where similar wave characteristics are found.

Data on the longshore drift of sand have been collected over a considerable period of time from Santa Barbara, California (see fig. 4–12 and inset) which has been reported by Johnson (1953)[27]. In 1929 a break-water was constructed to form a harbour at Santa Barbara which completely intercepted the west to east longshore movement of sand. The result of the construction of this break-water has been to cause silting in the harbour and on the up-wave beaches, and erosion down-wave for a distance of at least 10 miles along the coast after only a few years. To overcome this problem a system of harbour dredging and feeding of the down-wave beaches was initiated in 1935. From surveys of the harbour it has been possible to calculate the annual accretion in the harbour since 1932; the average amount of annual transport for the period 1932–51 is 279,650 cubic yds. per year. Since 1950 more precise figures from more frequent harbour surveys are available and can be correlated with wave recordings which were not available for the earlier period. The wave recorders were fixed in 30 ft. of water off the break-water at Santa Barbara and 10 miles to the west in 40 ft. of water, wind observations were also available but no recordings of the direction of approach of the waves were made; it is known, however, that except for a very few days in the year, the waves were such as to cause an easterly drift of sand. The period of detailed observations extended from April 1950 to the end of February 1951, which was an average period as far as sand transport is concerned. The median diameter of the sand moving into the harbour was about 0·2 mm. The results of the more detailed surveys revealed several occasions when the daily rate of transport was much higher than the average daily value; these periods were in general those with greater wave power, where the wave power is expressed as $E/2T$, where E is the wave energy and T the period. On one occasion the transport was much greater than usual which was probably due to a more oblique approach as the wave power was not above average. In all observations the wave steepness was low, never exceeding 0·017; by analogy with model experiments transport should have been taking place in the shallower water and therefore nearly all of the drift alongshore should have been trapped in the harbour. Even more frequent surveys were found to be necessary if precise relationships between waves and transport are to be established and a device to measure the direction of approach of the waves was also found to be essential. Some reasonably accurate information can be obtained on the direction of approach of waves by the system of hindcasting from synoptic charts and construction of wave refraction diagrams which have already been discussed.

A more recent study of longshore movement is reported by Savage (1957)[28] in a discussion of the sand bypassing project at Port Hueneme, California. This plan was put into operation to attempt to alleviate severe beach erosion. The area under consideration is 65 miles north-west of Los Angeles (see fig. 4–12), the harbour consists of an entrance protected by jetties extending down to a depth of 30 ft. in a natural salient of the coast. A submarine canyon extends right into the mouth of the harbour, which was built during the period 1938–40. The beaches north of the harbour have been accreting since observations were first made in 1855, while the coast south of the harbour had been remarkably stable during the same period. Since the building of the harbour the downwave or southern beaches have eroded rapidly and sea-walls have had to be built. The predominant wave direction in the area is from the northwest, particularly in the summer, during which period the waves tend to be rather lower than in winter, when a greater proportion come from directions other than north-west. These deep water waves are modified in direction and height by refraction. The presence of offshore islands protects the area from north-westerly waves and refraction reduces their height so that they rarely exceed 4 ft. The mean tidal range is 3·7 ft. with a diurnal range of 5·4 ft. mean higher high water to mean lower low water, the extreme range is 10·5 ft.

It appears that most of the material moving along the coast in the neighbourhood of Port Hueneme comes from inland via the Santa Clara river (see fig. 4–12). Estimates of the amount of material added to the up-wave beaches north of the jetties suggest that about 400,000 cubic yds. per year of sand are deposited in this area, while about 1,200,000 cubic yds. per year of material are moved along the coast from the downwave area. This amount has been lost from the down-wave beaches since the construction of the harbour works. It would appear, therefore, that the total transport along this coast is about 1,200,000 cubic yds. per year of which $\frac{1}{3}$ remains on the up-wave beaches and $\frac{2}{3}$ is lost into the Hueneme canyon. Some material, probably only a small amount, may be lost by wind erosion. Later surveys and computation between 1948 and 1952 confirm that the total rate of annual transport is about 1,100,000 cubic yds. per year.

To attempt to stabilize the down-wave beaches extensive dredging operations from the up-wave area to the eroded area were started in September 1953 and by June 1954, 2,032,703 cubic yds. had been moved to the down-wave beaches, surveys were carried out during this period and subsequently. It was estimated that from June 1954 to June 1955 only 812,000 cubic yds. reached the dredging area which is considerably less than the previous estimate of 1,200,000 cubic yds. per year although some material was probably lost into the canyon. On the down-wave beaches immediately adjacent to the harbour 1,400,000 cubic yds. was lost from the beach during the year June 1954 to June 1955, while 3–4 miles farther down-wave from the harbour 415,000 cubic yds. was lost. This figure is probably too small for the average movement in this area. Later surveys showed an acceleration in this longshore transport.

Another estimate of longshore movement of sand in California was made by Caldwell (1956)[29] for the area near Anaheim Bay (see fig. 4–12). In this area jetties had been constructed during 1944, which served as a trap for longshore transport of sand and hence provided suitable conditions for the correlation of the amount of longshore movement with wave data. The building of the jetties interrupted the normal movement of sand to such an extent that the down-wave area to the south of the structures had to be artificially replenished. The transport of this beach fill was carefully measured in a series of seven surveys between March 1948 and August 1949. The wave data correlated with the amount of transport included estimations of wave energy from synoptic charts, analysis of wave records from gauges of two types and photographic data. The results of the different techniques indicated that the hindcast data provided reasonably accurate values from which the alongshore component of wave energy could be calculated. By considering the angle of approach of the waves to the shore the total energy in ft./lb. transmitted alongshore is given by the formula $E = (41 \, T \, H_s^2 \, n \, (\tanh 2\pi \, d_s/L_s)$

$t \sin \alpha \cos \alpha$, where n is equal to $\frac{1}{2} \left[1 + \dfrac{4\pi \, d_s/L_s}{\sinh 4\pi \, d_s/L_s} \right]$, T is the period, H_s is the wave height in depth d_s, and L_s the wave length in feet in depth d_s, α is the angle of the wave crest with the beach at the point of analysis, t is the time in seconds over which the energy E is transmitted. The alongshore wave energy was averaged for the six periods between the surveys. In four of these periods the net direction of alongshore energy was directed to the south and only on one occasion was the direction of drift of material contrary to the computed alongshore wave energy, which in any case was a very small amount. In fig. 4–13 the amount of transport alongshore in cubic yards per day has been correlated with the wave energy, the figure also includes data of a similar type

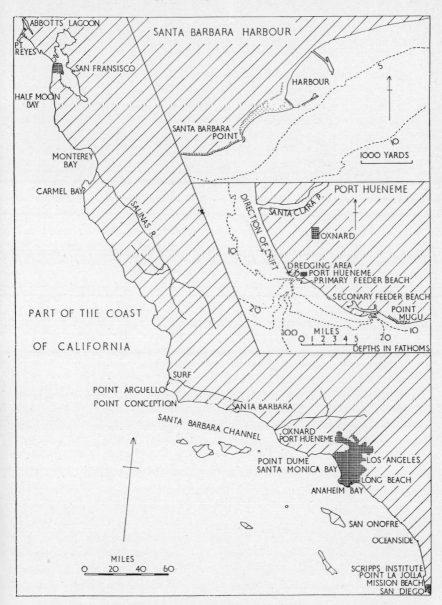

Fig. 4–12. Map of California to show places mentioned. Inset of Santa Barbara and Port Hueneme.

derived from observations made in Florida. These measurements are reported by Watts (1953)[30] and the two sets of data show a similar correlation which suggests that this technique of analysis has a wider application. The relationship between the variables plotted can be expressed as $Q_i = 210 \, E_i^{0.8}$, where Q_i is the intensity of alongshore sand movement in cubic yards per day and E_i is the intensity of alongshore energy in millions of ft./lb. per foot of beach per day.

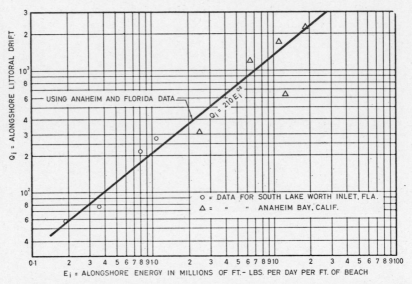

FIG. 4–13. Volume of sand transported alongshore in California and Florida. (After Caldwell, B.E.B.)

The size of sand on the beach in California near Anaheim Bay varied between 0·30 and 0·48 mm. The finer material was found to the south and represented the original beach material while the coarser sand was found to the north and represented the beach fill, as these figures apply to the first survey. At the end of the period the northerly area had a median diameter of 0·36 mm. and the southerly part one of 0·39 mm., this change is due to the transfer of the fill south by longshore movement.

The movement of sand along the coast at South Lake Worth inlet in Florida has already been mentioned. Here the drift is to the south and it has been estimated that about 200,000 cubic yds. move alongshore in a year. There is a fairly strong selective action in the size of the sand moving south; only the coarser particles are moved southwards as is shown by an analysis of sand size at various parts of the beach. All the sand is fairly coarse as the median diameters range from 0·33 mm. to 0·84 mm.

Farther north along the Atlantic coast of the United States measurements of longshore movement, reported by Watts (1956)[31] have been made on the beaches in front of Ocean City, New Jersey, shown in fig. 4–14. This area is now suffering erosion due to changes in configuration of the channels through the Great Egg Inlet immediately to the north-east of the beach under consideration. The deepening of the

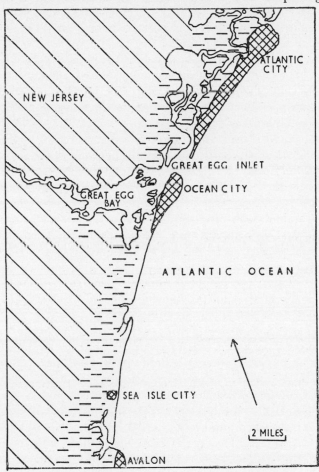

FIG. 4–14. Map of part of the coast of New Jersey.

channel through the inlet has reduced the amount of sand travelling alongshore to the Ocean City beaches from the north-east, which is the dominant direction of movement on this coast. During the period 1842–1949 the Ocean City beach had advanced seaward and towards the north-east into Great Egg Inlet as a result of accretion of material. A little farther north along the coast at Atlantic City the amount of sand moved southwest has been estimated to be about 400,000 cubic yds. per year; this amount must reach the Great Egg Inlet each year. The shifting of the channels in the inlet has meant that about 50,000 cubic yds. per year has been lost from the Ocean City beaches between 1930 and 1950. In order to make good this loss it was decided to put beach fill on the foreshore in this area; 2,550,000 cubic yds. of sand were placed on the beach between May and July 1952. This sand was of very fine grade of about 0·16 mm. median diameter; this is finer than the natural sand of the beach which was about 0·23 mm. at the mid-tide line. It was found that quite a large proportion of the finer part of the fill was taken offshore to a depth of about 12 ft.; later it moved alongshore to replenish the neighbouring beaches. The loss in the Ocean City beach area may be partly due to its position which lies farther seaward than the adjoining beaches, and as a result it is more liable to erosion.

The depth at which the longshore movement of sand took place was in general in the shallower water along the beach or in the surf zone to a depth of about 20–30 ft. It is often suggested that the presence of rocky headlands on the coast prevents the movement of material along the shore. This is certainly true as far as the beach and foreshore zone is concerned and probably often applies also to the surf zone. Baak (1936) has put forward very convincing evidence in support of this view. From a heavy mineral analysis of the sands of the west coast of Brittany and Normandy he has shown that each bay in this area of varied geology has its own particular type of heavy mineral assemblage in the sand. The material is absolutely local in character and sand from this part of the French coast does not pass through the Straits of Dover.

Further evidence on this point is given by Zenkovich (1946)[5] who states that the shingle in a small bay on the south coast of the Crimean Peninsula in the Black Sea was of local origin; no shingle can move into or out of the bay along the shore round the rocky headlands enclosing it; each bay contains only material of local origin.

Trask (1955),[10] as has already been mentioned, has worked on this problem of transport around rocky headlands along the Californian coast north of Los Angeles. He suggests that the uniform slope and uniform sorting of the sediments, particularly between 30 and 60 ft. depth, together with their uniform size, is strong evidence that sand migrates along the coast between Surf and Point Conception in depths between 30 and 60 ft., and that in this zone the sand can move past the headlands which prevent the movement of material along the foreshore and surf zones.

The use of radio-active isotopes for studying the movement of sand on beaches is being developed by several workers.[32,33,13] A recent experiment in this field has been reported by Davidsson (1958),[34] from work done in Sweden. Some of the earlier experiments in this field were made by use of activated glass sand. This technique tends to produce sharp splinter-like grains which do not closely simulate the natural sand; Davidsson overcame this disadvantage by allowing the crushed glass particles to fall through a hot flame thus rendering them more spherical, and therefore more like the actual sand of the beach where the experiments were carried out. The beach, situated on the west side of the island of Måkläppen, is of quartz sand with a diameter between 0·2 and 0·6 mm., but mainly in the finer part of this range. Active longshore movement takes place along the coast; it is in a northerly direction owing to the predominance of west to south-west winds. The radio-active sand was placed on the sea-floor in an area less than $\frac{1}{2}$ m. square and its movement was traced mainly in the swash zone by using a scintillation counter which was moved along a system of squares across the beach. During the experiments the direction and dimensions of the waves were measured or calculated from the type of curves discussed in chapter 3.

The longshore movement was studied on a small recurved spit where the activated sand was laid in a line 2 m. long from the upper limit of the swash to the break-point of the waves. After $\frac{1}{2}$ hour the radio-active sand was found in two lines, one at the limit of the swash and the other immediately inland of the break-point, which had extended alongshore for 11 and 8 m. (36 and 26·2 ft.) respectively. The sand did not move into depths greater than 25 cm. (9·8 in.) at which depth a terrace was formed by the breaking waves. The sand moved in a down-wave direction. After $1\frac{1}{2}$ hours the sand had moved farther down-wave but there was also a slight movement in the reverse direction where the sand had first been deposited. After 3 hours, the final stage recorded, most of the activated sand had reached the tip of the spit about 21 m. (69 ft.) away from the starting point.

An extensive plan of coastal observations including measurements of longshore movement of sand have been planned for the Dutch coast[35] (1957) in connexion with the plan to dam the estuaries of the Scheldt delta. Radio-active tracers will be used to establish the longshore movement using techniques devised and tested in a model flume. The authors of this report describe devices to measure bed-load but state that such techniques are not suitable under the oscillating flow associated with waves. The area under consideration suffered very serious flooding in the storm surge of 1953 (see pp. 283–288) and since this date beach observations have been intensified.

Experiments on the use of radio-active sand in rather greater depths have been carried out off Sandbanks, Dorset, on the south coast of England by the Hydraulics Research Board (1956).[26] The sand was activated with the isotope scandium-46 which has a half-life of 85 days. The size of the material, which was a type of glass was median diameter of 0·18 mm. compared to the median diameter of 0·22 of the beach sand. Current observations showed that tidal currents in the area selected did not exceed 1 ft. per sec., which was too low to move the sand. The activated sand was deposited at a point 2,800 ft. offshore in a depth of 19 ft. The activated sand was dropped from a height of 8 ft. above the sea-bed which caused a considerable scatter of the finer particles which may have spread 550 ft. during the first hour after injection. The subsequent movement of the activated sand was traced over a period of four months by using Geiger-counters. The activated sand moved very little during the first six weeks after its injection when the weather was relatively calm; however, during early November, 1955, a period of south-easterly gales produced waves which moved the sand to the north and north-east and caused a general scattering of the original patch. The conclusions reached as a result of these tests showed that the tidal currents were not capable of moving the sand nor were the waves of relatively calm weather, the storm generated waves did, however, cause a movement of material in this depth of water. The experiments showed that radio-active sand could be traced for at least four months.

ii. SHINGLE. Under the auspices of the Coastal Physiography section of the Nature Conservancy in conjunction with the Atomic Research station at Harwell some interesting experiments have been carried out on the east coast of England which are reported by Kidson, Carr and Smith (1958).[14] The experiments were carried out off the Suffolk coast. At a point 700 yds. offshore about 1½ miles north of the distal end of the shingle spit of Orford Ness 600 radio-active pebbles were dumped in water whose depth varied from 19 to 28 ft. according to the tide level. A further series of 2,000 radio-active pebbles were placed 12 yds. seaward of low-water level 400 yds. north of the tip of the spit in mid-January 1957. These pebbles had been taken from the beach and a radio-active coating was applied to each at Harwell before they were deposited on the sea floor. The isotope barium 140-lanthanum 140 with a fairly short half-life of 12 days was used, this enabled the pebbles to be traced for a period of about 6 weeks.

After their dumping the movement of the pebbles was measured as often as weather conditions permitted. The position of the pebbles is traced by means of two instruments, one for use below water level and one to locate pebbles driven up on to the foreshore and exposed at low water. The under-water instrument is less sensitive and consists of three Geiger-counters mounted on a sledge which is towed behind a launch and attached by tube to headphones; a dial then records the proximity of the radio-active pebble on the sea bottom. It will locate pebbles over a band 3–4 ft. wide, so very accurate positioning is needed to locate the pebbles and a large number of sweeps was required to be sure of locating them all. Once located the point is fixed by horizontal sextant angles to known positions on shore. The instrument used on the foreshore was a Scintillation-counter, which can locate a single pebble 15 ft. away horizontally and at a depth of 6–9 in. beneath the surface of the beach. It is possible to locate one radio-active pebble amongst the many millions on the beach.

During the period of observation which lasted about six weeks the pebbles in deep water did not move at all but those in the shallower water spread out up to more than a mile north of their original position. The mean distance which the 93 pebbles located in the first four weeks of observation, had moved was 600 yds. to the north. During this period southerly winds prevailed and the wave heights never exceeded 2 ft. However, during the fifth week of the experiment northerly winds occurred and these caused a very rapid southerly movement of the shingle, which is the dominant direction of movement. When northerly winds were blowing during two or three days some of the pebbles moved south to the distal end of the spit and up its inland side for a distance of about 500 yds., others moved across the mouth of the river Orr to Shingle Street on the southern shore as well as on to the shingle bank which dries out at low tide at the mouth of the river. This shows that river mouths provide little obstacle to the longshore transport of shingle even though tidal currents of 7–8 knots occur at ebb and flood of spring tides at the mouth of the river. The experiments also showed that the direction of movement of the shingle is closely related to the direction of approach of the waves, which, in the relatively enclosed North Sea, is closely connected with the wind direction. When this is opposite to the dominant direction, the beach material will then be moved in the reverse of its prevailing direction, but waves coming from the dominant direction are much more effective in causing longshore movement.

Summary

Model experiments on longshore transport of sand showed that with steep waves most of the sand moved along in the breaker zone, half in suspension and half along the bed. With flat waves 80 per cent of the sand moved along the bed and nearly all of this was moving in the swash zone. The optimum wave steepness for longshore movement was between 0·02 and 0·025, while most sand was moved alongshore when the waves approached at 30 deg. to the shore.

Estimates of the volume of sand moving alongshore on natural beaches has been calculated from beach surveys of areas where this movement is interrupted by break-waters or similar features. A figure of nearly 280,000 cubic yds. per year is given for Santa Barbara, California, while

1,100,000 cubic yds. per year has been suggested for Port Hueneme, California. A relation between the volume transported across a given line and the wave energy shows that the two factors increase together as $Q_i = 210 \, E_i^{0.8}$. An estimate of 400,000 cubic yds. per year is given for the sand transport off Atlantic City, New Jersey. The movement of sand alongshore can take place at depths down to 30–60 ft., but where rocky promontories extend into deep water shingle and sand cannot move along the foreshore as shown by mineralogical studies which prove that each bay has only local sand.

The use of radio-active sand and pebbles has made quantitative study of longshore movement of material easier. The method is still in an early stage of development and has not been used on a very large scale.

3. MATERIAL GRADING

(a) Methods of description

Some of the classifications of sediment by grain size have already been mentioned (see chapter 1, pp. 3, 4); methods of description used to compare material from different localities or at different times will now be considered. The most common measure of sediment size is the median diameter, which is given by the 50 per cent line on a cumulative curve on which size distribution in sediment is usually plotted. The size distribution is often found by sieving samples in a nest of sieves but some authorities believe that the settling tube technique is more reliable, particularly for fine sediment (Inman, 1953).[36] Inman (1952)[37] has suggested the mean diameter as another measure to describe the central tendency; he obtains this by calculating the mean value between the 16th and 84th percentile on the cumulative curve in ϕ units ($\phi = -\log_2$ diameter in mm.), thus $M_\phi = \frac{1}{2} \, (\phi_{16} + \phi_{84})$. Where the distribution of particle sizes is symmetrical the mean and median are the same, but they differ for asymmetrical distributions. A measure of the dispersion or sorting of the sediment can be given, according to Inman, by the formula $\sigma_\phi = \frac{1}{2} \, (\phi_{84} - \phi_{16})$, this is half the distance between the 16th and 84th percentiles. The ϕ deviation measure, σ_ϕ, gives the standard deviation in terms of Wentworth units because one ϕ unit is equal to one Wentworth division. This is made clear by reference to fig. 4–15. Another method of expressing the degree of sorting is that used by Trask (1932) where the sorting coefficient is defined as $S_o = \sqrt{Q_1/Q_3}$, Q_1 and Q_3 represent the lower and upper quartiles respectively, that is the diameters of the 25th and 75th percentiles on the cumulative frequency curves. This method of expressing sorting is probably rather more common than the ϕ deviation measure. In Trask's notation the nearer the sorting coefficient is to unity the better sorted is the sediment.

Where the mean and median differ the skewness of the sediment is no longer zero in the ϕ notation; the measure of skewness can be defined by the formula $a_\phi = \frac{1}{2} \frac{(\phi_{16} + \phi_{84}) - Md_\phi}{\sigma_\phi} = \frac{M_\phi - Md_\phi}{\sigma_\phi}$. The skewness is negative if the distribution is skewed towards the larger particles and positive if it is skewed towards the finer sizes. The Trask skewness coefficient is rather different again and is given by $S_k = Q_1 \, Q_3 / M_d^2$, where M_d is the median diameter, this is also rather a simpler formula to

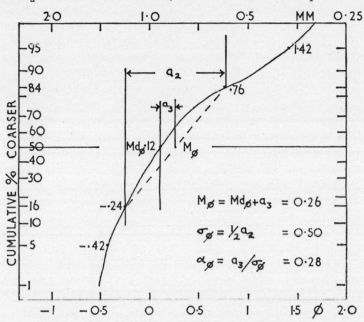

FIG. 4–15. Graph to illustrate measures for describing sediment size and character. (modified after Inman.)

apply than the ϕ skewness measure and has been much used. The advantage of the ϕ units is that they give approximate graphical values of definite statistical moment measures describing the frequency distributions, such as the mean, standard deviation and skewness.

(b) Sampling methods

It is often desired to relate the sediment size or samples from different localities or to relate it to the beach slope or some other parameter; for this purpose it is useful to have some measure of the reliability of different sampling techniques. Because the size of the sediment often varies from place to place on a beach it is unlikely that one sample will give an adequate description of the character of the beach material.

Krumbein and Slack (1956)[38] have investigated this problem for two different environments; one is the sandy and gravelly shore zone of part of Lake Michigan near Waukegan, Illinois and the other is the sandy shore at Ocean Beach, Maryland. The sediments on Lake Michigan were very mixed and the environment included sand dunes as well as a beach with berms of mixed sand and a few pebbles so the problem of describing the sediments acurately was complex.

The observations made on the ocean beach are probably of greater interest here, as they included the analysis of underwater sediments. One series of samples was taken above low water along six profiles of which the outside ones were spaced 1,600 ft. apart, while four profiles were spaced 100 ft. apart in the centre; three of these centre profiles were extended 2,000 ft. seaward to a depth of 30 ft. The above-water samples were taken in pairs every 50 ft. along the profiles and 16 on each end profile. These can be used to consider the variation in size in different zones across the beach and variations along the beach. The analysis of the results shows that there is no significant difference between the means obtained from the four centre profiles, but the upper and lower samples taken on the backshore and foreshore respectively do show significant differences. If the value of the mean sand size for this particular part of the beach is required all the 64 samples may be used and this result compared with different combinations of samples. Taking all the samples, the ϕ median diameter is 1·67 or 0·314 mm., the computed standard error for this value is 0·08 or a relative error of 4·8 per cent; taking all four profiles but only one sample at each the relative error is 5·4 per cent; taking all four profiles but only one sample from the backshore and one from the foreshore the relative error is 6·6 per cent; taking all samples from only one profile the relative error is 9·6 per cent; taking one sample from one profile the relative error is 19·2 per cent, but if a pair is taken from only one profile the error is 16·8 per cent. When the analysis was extended to the outer profiles along the beach the relative errors calculated were on the same order but rather larger reaching a maximum of 24·7 per cent for only one sample.

The under-water samples were taken every 250 ft. from low tide level along three profiles, they were taken with a double tube sampler with the samplers fixed 18 in. apart. All except one pair of samples were satisfactory; using each of the pairs separately to compute the mean diameter the figures were 0·145 mm. and 0·168 mm., but discarding the poor sample the figures were 0·150 and 0·157 mm., which shows how one bad sample can affect the result. The standard error of the results of this sampling pattern was less than 10 per cent, and the conclusion was reached that the additional effort of collecting double samples was not necessary to keep the error under 10 per cent. To arrive at a sound value of the mean particle diameter samples must be taken from the different beach zones in proportion to their width, extending from the backshore to about 30 ft. depth, if one zone is very variable more samples should be taken from this zone. It is also advisable to take samples from more than one profile along the beach; if, for example, five beach zones are covered by the profiles, six profiles providing 30 samples, one from each zone per profile, should provide an adequate number for analysis; this should provide a relative error of not more than 10 per cent at the 95 per cent confidence level.

Summary

Beach sediment grading can be defined either in mm. on the Wentworth scale or in ϕ units, where $\phi = -\log_2$ mm., the latter method allows the size distribution in the sample to be described graphically in a way related to the statistical analysis of the frequency distribution. The following moment measures are of value:

Central tendency, $M_{d\phi}$ — Median — 50 percentile on cumulative curve
$$M_\phi - \text{Mean} - \tfrac{1}{2}(\phi_{16} + \phi_{84})$$
Dispersion (sorting) $\sigma\phi$ — Deviation measure $-\tfrac{1}{2}(\phi_{84} - \phi_{16})$
$$a\phi - \text{Skewness} - \frac{M_\phi - M_{d\phi}}{\sigma\phi}$$
Sampling of a beach should include a number of samples from beach zone, including under-water samples. These should be taken along a number of profiles in proportion to the width of the zones on the beach.

4. SORTING OF BEACH MATERIAL

(a) Theory

When the movement of material was considered earlier in this chapter the importance of the differential velocity on the bottom was stressed. This difference between the shoreward and seaward acceleration under wave action also has the effect of sorting the sand in particle size parallel to the shore. If the beach were to be composed of uniformly graded sand so that the mean and median diameters are the same, Ippen and Eagleson (1955)[6] suggest that this uniformity will be disturbed by the waves. They suggest that in deep water some of the finer particles will move offshore and some will move onshore, the latter will travel all the way to the break-point. As the water becomes shallower so larger and larger particles will be capable of movement and will move onshore, so that a greater proportion of coarser particles should be found as the water becomes shallower. The median diameter should therefore increase as the water becomes shallower. The general direction of transport outside the break-point is towards the shore as far as the break-point so it might be expected that at this point the sand shows a poor degree of sorting as sand of all grades will tend to accumulate at this point and this has in fact been found to be true.

(b) Model experiments

Some of the points mentioned in the previous section have been examined experimentally by Scott (1954).[1] The sand he used in the wave tank was originally well sorted but the action of the waves caused differential movement of the grains, thus changing the median diameter in different parts of the tank. The changes in median diameter indicated

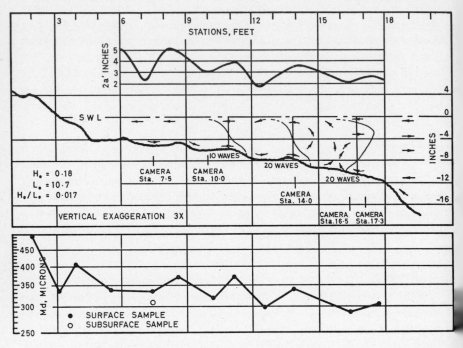

FIG. 4–16. Horizontal amplitude of orbital water motion (2a′), water drift and variation of median diameter along the final profile. (After Scott.)

that the coarser grains moved towards the beach while the finer grains moved offshore. Superimposed on this sorting it was found that the coarse grains collected on the tops of the break-point bars (see pp. 181–186) while the finer grains collected in the troughs. The variation in grain size is shown in fig. 4–16.

These changes could be correlated with the variation in orbital velocity which was relatively great in the shallower water and over the bar crests where the waves tended to break. The sorting of the grains of sand was influenced by the formation of ripples on the bottom. There is a correlation between the size of the sand and the horizontal amplitude of the orbital water movement, while the latter parameter also shows an increase when plotted against the decreasing water depth, although this is rather smaller than the theoretical value.

The sorting of the larger particles between 0·5 and 0·9 cm. in a wave tank has been described by Bagnold (1940).[17] He found that on the shelf from the point where movement first started to the foot of the step, the particles became smaller in size; they reached a minimum at the base of the steep slope leading up to the step (see fig. 4–7, p. 137). The largest particles were found on the steep slip face below the step, while the step itself as far as half way up to the beach crest was composed of particles of the mean size. Towards the top of the upper beach the size again increased till the maximum sized particles were found at the beach crest. Any finer particles amongst the shingle were removed to the deeper water beyond the shingle. This selective grading appeared to be confined mainly to the surface layer of pebbles except at the top of the beach crest and shows strong similarity to the grading of shingle beaches in nature.

(c) Observations

i. SORTING NORMAL TO THE SHORE. It is well known that on a beach of mixed sand and shingle the shingle is usually found at the top of the beach, which agrees with the experimental data just described. This can be explained by the fact that shingle is only in suspension actually at the break-point and therefore progresses by rolling on the bottom, where it is influenced by the differential velocity moving landward under the greater acceleration in this direction under the wave crests. The sorting of sand both on the foreshore and in the offshore zone is much more difficult to study as it is only apparent after careful sand sampling and analysis.

Many sandy beaches, particularly if the sand is fine, do not show any marked variation of sand size with the seasons or with changing wave conditions. Some coarser sand beaches are, however, very variable both from place to place and from time to time. It is generally true that the particle size is larger where the wave energy is greater; this can be applied both in time and space. Detailed work on the variation of sand size with the seasons has been carried out by Trask and Johnson (1955)[39] and Trask (1956)[40] on the beach at Point Reyes, California (see fig. 4–12). This is a variable beach facing the open ocean about 35 miles north-west of San Francisco; because of its variability it provides suitable conditions for a study of this type. The range of grain size lies between a median diameter of 0·35 mm. and 4·0 mm., although most of the samples lie between 0·56 and 0·77 mm. (0·84 and 0·38 ϕ units). The median diameter varies throughout the seasons; it is 0·77 mm. (0·38 ϕ) in February which is the maximum size, 0·710 mm. (0·50ϕ) in March, 0·62 mm. (0·68ϕ) June, 0·67 mm. (0·58ϕ) in May, 0·65 mm. (0·62ϕ) in August, 0·56 mm. (0·84ϕ) in October which is the smallest size and 0·62 mm. (0·68ϕ) in December, these figures are for the period October 1955 to August 1956 (see fig. 4–17). This shows that the finest sediments are found during the early autumn after the summer season, when the

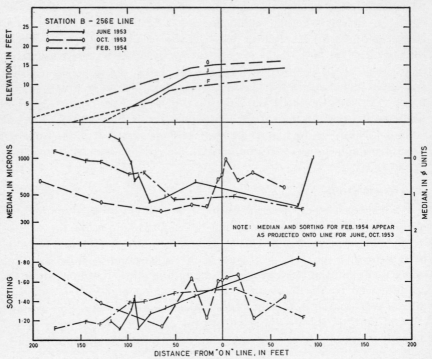

FIG. 4–17. Beach slope and elevation, median diameter of the sand and its sorting, for Abbotts Lagoon. (After Trask and Johnson, B.E.B.)

wave energy has probably been lower than during the winter season. The coarsest sand is found on the beach during February when the waves would have the most energy.

In considering the variation of sand size on the profile at any one time it is found that the finer sand is on the upper foreshore, with coarser sand on the lower foreshore and on the berm crest. The lower foreshore clearly receives more energy than the upper foreshore, which is at the limit of wave action, but it is less easy to explain the coarse sand on the berm crest. This may partly be due to the winnowing effect of the wind as the berm crest is only reached by very high water on rare occasions.

This particular beach shows poorer sorting than most beaches; as a result of its laminated nature many samples include more than one layer. In general there appears to be a rather crude correlation between sorting and sand size; the finer the sand the better the sorting. The best sorted sands tend to have median diameters of 0·15–0·20 mm., with finer material the sorting again becomes less good. It is perhaps significant that this size range is moved from the bed at the lowest velocity.

The variation of sediment size in deeper water has been studied by Inman (1953)[36] and Trask (1955)[10] in various localities along the coast

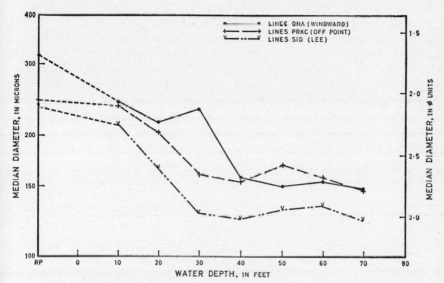

FIG. 4–18. Median diameter of sand in relation to water depth and exposure. (After Trask, B.E.B.)

of California. The latter has taken 175 bottom samples from depths of 80 ft. and less in the area around Point Arguello, Conception and Dume (see fig. 4–12). The median diameter of samples taken in the offshore zone decreased consistently with depth. For all profiles the sand between 0 and 40 ft. had a median diameter average of 0·165 mm. (2·6ϕ). Between 40 and 80 ft. the diameter varied between 0·145 and 0·150 mm. (2·8 and 2·74ϕ). The seaward decrease of grain size is at the rate of 0·02–0·05 mm. between 10 and 30 ft. per 10-ft. depth increase, between 30 and 60 ft. the sand was nearly constant while in greater depths it decreases in size at the rate of 0·005–0·015 mm. for each 10 ft. increase in depth. This is presumably the result of decreasing wave energy on the sea-floor as the depth increases.

The effect of the wave energy on the sand size on the foreshore is also shown by the decrease in median diameter from 0·311 mm. (1·7ϕ) on the windward beaches to 0·273 mm. (1·89ϕ) off the Points and 0·239 mm. (2·07ϕ) in their lee. Here the wave energy is reduced by refraction. The values for the three different exposures in the 20–40-ft. depths are 0·179 mm. (2·48ϕ) windward, 0·173 mm. (2·53ϕ) off the Points and 0·139 mm. (2·85ϕ) in their lee; for the 40–80-ft. depths the figures are 0·149 mm. (2·75ϕ), 0·154 mm. (2·70ϕ) and 0·130 mm. (2·95ϕ) respectively, these values are shown in fig. 4–18.

A detailed study of the variation of the beach and offshore sediments at La Jolla has been reported by Inman (1953).[36] He finds that the sediments are aligned in zones parallel to the shore, each zone having distinctive properties. A beach zone, surf and shelf zone and slope zone were differentiated. He found an area of coarser sediment and heavy mineral concentration at the edge of the shelf in depths of 60–90 ft., which may be related to tidal scour at the major break in slope or perhaps to the convergence of long period waves or surf beat. The following types are given: 1. Beach and foreshore with diameter of 0·165 mm. (2·6ϕ), best sorted; 2a. Surf zone, coarse and poorly sorted 0·203 mm. (2·3ϕ) which grades into 2b surf zone and shelf to 100 ft., 0·105 mm. (3·25ϕ) well sorted, very fine sand with less than 3 per cent silt; 3. The slope, 0·072 mm. (3·8ϕ) this zone shows increasing amounts of silt.

Experiments carried out by diving in the Black Sea, reported by Zenkovich (1946),[5] illustrate the effect of waves in sorting material unlike that of the rest of the bottom sediment. A mixture of dyed sand of equal quantities of the following grain sizes, 7–5, 5–2·5, 2·5–1, 1–0·5, 0·5–0·25, 0·25–0·1 and less than 0·1 mm., was placed between marked stones at a depth of 6 m. (19·7 ft.). The waves during the experiment were 80–120 cm. high (2·62–3·94 ft.) and their period was 5 sec. Samples were taken 11 min. after the placing of the material on the bottom at distance of 1 and 3 m. (3·28 and 9·84 ft.) on either side of the original strip. The results show that some of the larger grains moved shoreward while the finer grains (0·5–0·25) tended to move offshore. The grains of size 1–0·5 mm. appeared to be more or less in equilibrium, as they approximated to the size of the natural sand, whose median diameter was 0·6 mm.

ii. SORTING PARALLEL TO THE SHORE. The sorting of sediment normal to the shore appears to be related largely to the type of water movement and to the distribution of energy and it has already been suggested that variation in energy is partly responsible for variations in size parallel to the shore so that now specific examples of this effect may be considered.

One very good example of lateral sorting of sand is described by Bascom (1951)[41] in Half Moon Bay in California. This bay is protected at its northerly end from the prevailing swell from the north-west while the southerly end of the bay is fully exposed to the waves. This difference of exposure is reflected in a continuous decrease in particle size from the exposed southern end to the sheltered northern end of the bay. Four samples, from the points shown in fig. 4–19, have been taken at mid-tide level on the beach which have diameters of 0·65 mm. (0·63ϕ), 0·39 mm. (1·37ϕ), 0·20 mm. (2·31ϕ) and 0·17 mm. (2·56ϕ) respectively from south to north along the bay. It appears that in this locality the finer sand accumulates in the areas of least wave energy; that is either in the offshore zone or in the sheltered end of the bay where wave refraction reduces the height and energy of the waves very greatly.

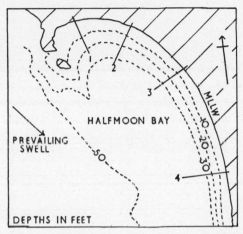

FIG. 4–19. Half-Moon Bay, California, showing position of samples. (After Bascom.)

A very striking example of the lateral sorting of shingle is found on Chesil beach in Dorset, mentioned in chapter 1. This beach which extends from Bridport in the west to Portland in the east is 18 miles long and for the last 12 miles of its length in the east it is separated from the coast by the Fleet as shown in fig. 4–20. The beach becomes wider and higher towards the east; at Abbotsbury, where it leaves the land about 6 miles from Bridport, it is 170 yds. wide and about 23 ft. above high water while at Portland it is 200 yds. wide and nearly 43 ft. high. Throughout its length the beach is made of shingle which varies evenly in size; the pebbles are small, being about the size of a pea at Bridport, at Abbotsbury they are about ½-in. in diameter grading to large shingle 2–3 in. in diameter at Portland where the beach joins Portland Island to the mainland.

Various views concerning the development of the beach have been put forward (Coode, 1853,[42] Prestwich, 1875,[43] Cornish 1898[44]), these

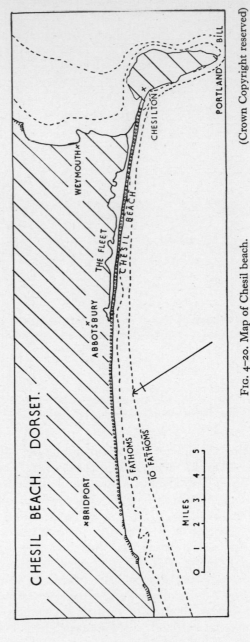

FIG. 4–20. Map of Chesil beach.

need not be considered in detail, but as yet there is no really satisfactory theory to account for the very even grading of the shingle. It is generally agreed that the main force causing the sorting of the pebbles is that of the waves. Chesil beach is aligned to face approximately the direction of approach of the dominant waves according to Lewis (1938)[45] which is from the south-west, these waves striking the beach more or less at right-angles would not cause any significant lateral movement of material or be seriously affected in energy distribution by wave refraction. Guilcher (1954)[46] shows a slight variation between the direction normal to the shore and that of the dominant wind vector and fetch directions. He gives the directions of the different factors as follows; the direction of maximum fetch is 224°30′, direction of the resultant of all onshore winds over Beaufort Force 4 is 215°30′ and the direction of simplification of the beach, which is the resultant of these two factors giving greater weight to the wind force, is 217°30′. The beach is not, however, quite straight and faces more to the south of south-west at its north-west end. In general it is true to say that the beach is perpendicular to the approach of the dominant waves. The next longest waves would probably come from west of south-west, these waves would produce an easterly drift of material and would probably reach the eastern end of the beach with more energy than the western end; they would therefore tend to drift the larger pebbles towards the east. The smaller waves generated in the English Channel would be capable only of moving the finer shingle westwards and in this way Lewis has suggested that the sorting would tend to take place.

The relative heights of the beach at Abbotsbury and Portland indicate that waves are able to throw larger shingle to higher elevations at the east end than the waves which can attack the central and western part of the beach. This suggests that the energy of the waves at the eastern end is much greater than that of the waves at the western end. It has already been shown that the largest particles tend to accumulate in the zones of greatest energy and there is no reason why this argument should not also apply to Chesil beach. The deeper water occurs off the south-east end of the beach which would help to concentrate the wave energy on the foreshore (see fig. 4–20). A study of the relative energy of the waves under different conditions along the beach taking into account the effect of wave refraction on the longer waves might help to solve this interesting problem. Observations made by Richardson (1902)[47] have suggested that pebbles larger than the average at any particular part of the beach move rapidly south-eastwards under normal conditions until they reach an area where the pebbles are of a similar size. The direction of movement of wreckage on the beach appears to be in general towards the east, this may be partly due to the fact that the tidal currents flow for 18 hours out of the 24 in a south-easterly direction along the beach, although the currents are not in themselves sufficiently rapid to move the shingle.

Summary

In general sediments show a gradual decrease in median diameter as the water deepens in the offshore zone. In the foreshore and surf zones distribution of particle size normal to the shore is more diverse. On a model beach of shingle the coarsest particles occur on the beach crest and the slip slope of the beach step, on a model sand beach there is a general decrease of size offshore with larger particles on the break-point bar crests and smaller ones in their troughs. In nature the coarser beaches show more variation, with fine material predominating after the summer and coarser after the winter in some areas. Coarser sand tends to collect on the berm crest and on the lower foreshore; the coarsest material is often found in the surf zone.

Sediment sorting laterally along the beach can be shown to be related to variation in wave energy; larger particles are associated with greater energy. A similar argument may account for the grading of shingle on Chesil beach, where the large shingle at the east must be affected by waves of greater energy as shown by the height of the beach above high water level, which is much greater than farther west.

BEACH CUSPS. These features are one of the more interesting minor shore forms which modify the normal regular sorting of material parallel to the shore. They are formed by the swash and backwash of the waves and, therefore, are found near the high water level on a tidal beach and tideless seas and lakes. According to Evans (1938)[48] they occur in all types of beach material from fine sand to gravel, but they are normally best developed in areas where the beach material contains a mixture of sand and shingle or on pure shingle beaches. They occur, for example, on Chesil beach near Portland, where the shingle is coarse, having a diameter on the average of 1–2 in. A very delicate balance between the beach profile and the characteristics of the waves is required for the cusps to form; if the conditions are suitable they will form very rapidly, and considerable changes in the conditions are usually required to remove the cusps.

Beach cusps have been described for a long time, but the method of formation and necessary conditions for their development are still open to doubt. Johnson (1919)[49] has collected most of the earlier theories on beach cusps and reached the conclusion that they are formed by selective erosion of the swash working on irregular initial depressions. The ultimate size of the cusps is related to the size of the waves; Johnson considered that the spacing of the cusps was roughly doubled as the wave height was doubled. Both he and Timmermans (1935)[8] thought that the cusps formed most readily when the waves were approaching the shore at right-angles. Evans (1938), on the other hand found that cusps could form under the action of both normal and oblique waves.

Evans (1938) has classified beach cusps into a number of different categories, some of which are dependent on features on the beach. The true beach cusps are, however, independent of fixed objects. From observation on Lake Michigan and other lakes Evans came to the conclusion that the cusps were formed by erosion of a previously built beach ridge by the waves. Small breaches in the ridge lead to the rapid development of cusps along the shore by deepening the breaks, the cuspate form being due to the parabolic paths of the water particles in the swash. The resulting cusps are spaced roughly equidistant, although, from several measurements of the cusp spacing, variation of 40 per cent were the minimum observed and they often varied in spacing by over 100 per cent.

Kuenen (1948)[50] has re-examined the problem of the formation of beach cusps and stresses the relative regularity of the features and the sorting of beach material that is typical of cusps on many beaches. The coarser material is carried to the back and horns of the cusp, while the finer sediment occupies the floor of the depression between the horns. Kuenen stressed the importance of deposition as well as erosion of material in the formation of the cusps, the horns being built up of material washed from the bays. The building up of the horns is assisted by the refraction of the swash in the bays, which carries the coarser particles to the edge of the bay. The sideways component of the swash also helps to concentrate the backwash along the edges of the horns. This lateral movement of the swash has also been commented upon by Bagnold (1940)[17] to explain the variation of gradient on a model beach. Bagnold compares the model beach with similar bays, spaced 12 m. (39·4 ft.) apart on the beach near Mersa Matruh, on the coast of Egypt. He notes that the swash piles up against the horns and is divided into two streams which swing round the head of the bay and unite to flow back, as backwash, down the centre of the bay; this is lowered by the more vigorous backwash. This scheme is rather different from that of Kuenen but both show the importance of the lateral movement of water in the formation of the cusp. The breaching of a beach ridge is no longer necessary to explain the initiation of cusps, they frequently occur where no such ridge is present, particularly on tidal beaches. Kuenen considers that there is an optimum depth of water in the bay, the hollow will grow as the depth increases at first, but as soon as the optimum is reached growth will be limited. This helps to account for the comparative regularity of the cusp spacing. As the waves grow in size, so the size of the cusp increases.

5. *DEPTH OF DISTURBANCE OF SAND BY WAVES*

Experiments have been made on several sandy beaches round the coasts of England and Wales to determine the depth to which waves disturb the sand in different positions on the beach and in various sand sizes.[51] The measured depth of disturbance has been correlated with the wave height and energy. The experiments were made by using dyed sand; a small quantity of sand was taken from the beach where the observations were to be made and dyed purple to contrast strongly with the natural colour of the sand. This dyed sand was placed in a vertical strip on the beach at low tide and the surface of the sand in the vicinity was then carefully smoothed. The site of the dyed sand was then marked by fixing two thin sticks about ¼-in. diameter and 2 ft. long in such a position that the dyed sand lay exactly on the line joining the pegs and at a known distance from them. These pegs also enabled the change in sand level to be measured; this was done by noting the length of peg above the sand surface both before and after the tide had risen over the area. The dyed sand was sufficiently far from the pegs to be uninfluenced by any minor scouring which might occur round them. After the tide had risen and fallen over the dyed sand the pegs were located and the position of the dyed sand marked, it was then undermined from below and the undisturbed column of purple sand was followed up until it came to an abrupt end at the point where the dyed sand had been dispersed by the action of the waves. The depth of disturbance was given by the distance from the top of the dyed sand to the surface and was measured to the nearest millimetre. Whenever possible observations were only made when the actual change in elevation of the surface of the sand was very small, because it was impossible to know whether the accretion or erosion of sand took place before or after the maximum disturbance of the sand.

The dyed samples of sand were placed in different positions on the beach so that at high water some of the samples were in a depth of up to 20 ft. of water, others were near the break-point while others were only in the zone of the swash and backwash of the waves. It is impossible by this method to measure the amount of disturbance in water deeper than that in which the maximum disturbance took place. The observations made to determine the depth of water in which the maximum disturbance took place were made at Rhossili, Gower Peninsula in South Wales, the beach here is wide and sandy and has a large tidal range of 26 ft. at spring tide (see fig. 7–1, p. 230). The sand is fine, having a median diameter of 0.23 mm. Owing to the large tidal range the dyed sand could be placed on the beach where it would be under 20 ft. of water at least at high tide.

The results of the experiments in which the sand was placed in a variety of positions on the beach indicated that the depth of disturbance was as great in the relatively shallow water under the swash and back-wash as it was under the break-point and in deep water as all the results were similar. It is perhaps relevant that the gradient of this beach is flat, being about 1 : 80, so that the waves formed spilling breakers rather than the plunging type and a wide surf zone was normally present. It was concluded that on a wide sandy beach the depth of disturbance is greatest at or slightly landward of the break-point in the surf zone, this is the area where the wave energy on the bottom reaches its maximum value and turbulence on the bottom is greatest.

In order to relate the depth of disturbance to the wave characteristics the depth of disturbance was plotted against the breaker height. It was found that the relationship was approximately linear as shown on fig. 4–21. The depth of disturbance in centimetres is about equal to the wave height at break-point in feet, thus a 3-ft. breaker will disturb the sand to a depth of 3 cm., which is a surprisingly small figure; this value applies to three of the four beaches on which observations were made, those of Rhossili in South Wales, Blackpool in Lancashire and Whitbeck in Cumberland. Although a similar relationship held for the fourth beach at Druridge in Northumberland the amount of disturbance on the latter beach was greater for a given wave height. The correlation between the two variables has been analysed statistically and regression lines have been drawn on the graph. The coefficient of correlation for the first three beaches is $r=0.9548$ and for the Druridge observations, which are fewer in number $r=0.859$, both these correlations are significant and show that the depth of disturbance of the sand is a function, partly at least, of the wave height.

As might be expected there is also a fairly close correlation between the wave energy and the depth of disturbance, the two parameters increasing together as shown in fig. 4–22. Again the observations for Druridge Bay produce a greater depth of disturbance than those of the other three beaches for the same wave energy. The correlation of disturbance depth with wave length was not close, indicating the greater significance of the wave height and the importance of wave height in the determination of the wave energy.

It has already been suggested that three of the beaches showed comparable depths of disturbance while the fourth showed a greater depth; this can be explained by considering the median diameters of the four sands. These are Blackpool 0.22 mm., Rhossili 0.23 mm., Whitbeck 0.29 mm. but Druridge has a median diameter of 0.40 mm. It is clear that the first three are fine sand while the last is considerably coarser. The depth of disturbance, therefore, increases as the material becomes

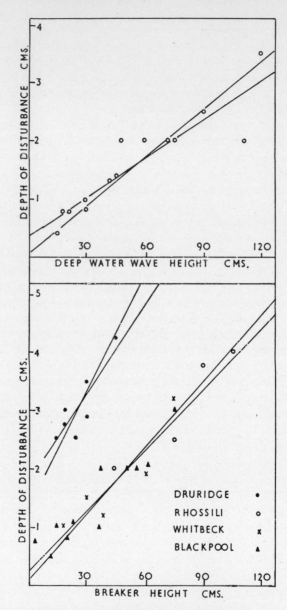

FIG. 4–21. Graph to show the relationship between wave height and the depth of disturbance of sand.

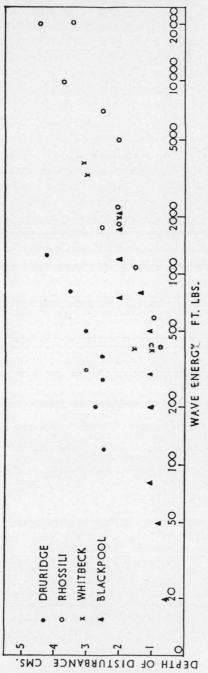

FIG. 4-22. Graph to show the relationship between the wave energy and the depth of disturbance of sand.

coarser. This agrees with the conclusions already reached that coarse beaches are much more mobile than fine beaches; this applies particularly to the zone landward of the break-point which has been shown to be the zone where the depth of disturbance is also at a maximum. On a coarser beach the zone in which the wave energy is dissipated is relatively narrow and hence the turbulence on the bottom is greater.

The observations show that the depth of disturbance in most sand beaches is relatively small and if the results obtained can be extrapolated for higher waves it seems unlikely that even very high waves of about 20 ft. would disturb the sand to depths greater than about 20 cm. or 8 in. It must be remembered that these depths imply that there is no change in elevation of the sand at the point of observation, a rather unlikely occurrence if really high storm waves are attacking the beach. The results of the experiment show that only a relatively thin cover of sand is enough to protect a wave cut bench beneath it from erosion by the sea, unless the cover of sand is removed entirely by destructive wave action, allowing the rocks beneath to be exposed to direct wave erosion. On a thick sand beach it is unlikely that all the sand will be removed except on very rare occasions, so that erosion of the wave cut benches can only occur with any reasonable speed where these are not protected by beaches.

Summary

Experiments have shown that the depth of disturbance of sand on beaches is a function of wave height and energy. There is an approximate increase of 1 cm. depth of disturbance for 1 ft. increase in wave height at break-point. The depth of disturbance is at a maximum in the shallow water of the swash zone and the surf zone. Increasing size of beach material causes an increase in the depth of disturbance.

REFERENCES

[1]Scott, T., 1954, Sand movement by waves. *Inst. Eng. Res.* Wave research Lab. Univ. of California.

[2]Manohar, M., 1955, Mechanics of bottom sediment movement due to wave action. *B.E.B. Tech. Memo.* **75.**

[3]Bagnold, R. A., 1946, Motion of waves in shallow water. *Proc. Roy. Soc. A.* **187,** pp. 1–15.

[4]Inman, D. L., 1957, Wave generated ripples in nearshore sands. *B.E.B. Tech. Memo.* **100.**

[5]Zenkovich, V. P., 1946, On the study of shore dynamics. *Trudy. Inst. Okeanologie* **1,** pp. 99–112.

[6]Ippen, A. T. and Eagleson, P. S., 1955, A study of sediment sorting by waves shoaling on a plane beach. *B.E.B. Tech. Memo.* **63.**

[7]Cornaglia, P., 1887, *Sul regime della spiagge e sulla regulazione dei porti* (On beaches).

[8]Timmermans, P. D., 1935, Proeven over den invloed van golven op een strand. *Leidische Geol. Med.* **6,** pp. 231–386.

[9]Inman, D. L. and Rusnak, G. A., 1956, Changes in sand level on the beach and shelf at La Jolla, California. *B.E.B. Tech. Memo.* **82.**

[10]Trask, P. D., 1955, Movement of sand around southern Californian promontories. *B.E.B. Tech. Memo.* **76.**

[11]Shepard, F. P. and Inman, D. L., 1951, Sand movement on the shallow inter-canyon shelf at La Jolla, California. *B.E.B. Tech. Memo.* **26.**

[12]Harris, R. L., 1955, Restudy of test shore nourishment by offshore deposition of sand, Long Branch, New Jersey. *B.E.B. Tech. Memo.* **62.**

[13]Inose, S. and Shiraishi, N., 1956, The measurement of littoral drift by radio isotopes. *Dock and Harbour Auth.* **36,** pp. 284–8.

[14]Kidson, C., Carr, A. P. and Smith, D. B., 1958, Further experiments using radio-active methods to detect movement of shingle over the sea-bed and alongshore. *Geog. Journ.* **124,** 2, pp. 210–18.

[15]Steers, J. A. and Smith, D. B., 1956, Direction of movement of pebbles on the sea-floor by radio-active methods. *Geog. Journ.* **122,** pp. 343–5.

[16]Russell, R. H. C. and Macmillan, D. H., 1952, *Waves and Tides.*

[17]Bagnold, R. A., 1940, Beach formation by waves; some model experiments in a wave tank. *Journ. Inst. Civ. Eng.* **15,** pp. 27–52.

[18]Shepard, F. P., 1950, Beach cycles in south California. *B.E.B. Tech. Memo.* **20.**

[19]Thompson, W. F. and Thompson, J. B., 1919, The spawning of the grunion. *Californian State Fish and Game Comm. Fish Bull.* **3.**

[20]Lafond, E. C., 1939, Sand movement near the beach in relation to tides and waves. *Proc. 6th Pacific Sci. Congr.* pp. 795–9.

[21]King, C. A. M., 1953, The relationship between wave incidence, wind direction and beach changes at Marsden Bay, Co. Durham. *Inst. Brit. Geog. Trans. and Papers* **19,** pp. 13–23.

[22]*B.E.B. Interim Report* 1933. Washington.

[23]Watts, G. M., 1953, Development and field tests of a sampler for suspended sediment in wave action. *B.E.B. Tech. Memo.* **34.**

[24]Saville, T., 1950, Model study of sand transport along an infinitely long, straight beach. *Trans. Am. Geoph. Un.* **31,** 3, pp. 555–65.

[25]Shay, E. A. and Johnson, J. W., 1953, Model studies on the movement of sand transported along a straight beach. *Inst. Eng. Res.* Univ. of Calif. Issue 7, Series 14 (unpub.).

[26]Report of the Hydraulics Research Board 1956 *D.S.I.R.* pp. 33–36. Pub. 1957.

[27]Johnson, J. W., 1953, Sand transport by littoral currents. *Proc. 5th Hydraulic Conf.* pp. 89–109.

[28]Savage, R. P., 1957, Sand bypassing at Port Hueneme, California. *B.E.B. Tech. Memo.* **92.**

[29]Caldwell, J. M., 1956, Wave action and sand movement near Anaheim Bay, California. *B.E.B. Tech. Memo.* **68.**

[30]Watts, G. M., 1953, A study of sand movement at south Lake Worth Inlet, Florida. *B.E.B. Tech. Memo.* **42.**

[31]Watts, G. M., 1956, Behaviour of beach fill at Ocean City, New Jersey. *B.E.B. Tech. Memo.* **77.**

[32]Forest, G., 1957, Observations du chariage littoral au moyen d'éléments radio actifs. *Journ. de la Marine No. sp. 'Nouvéautés Techniqués maritimes'.*

[33]Hours, R., Nesteroff, W. D. and Romanovsky, V., 1955, Methode d'étude de l'evolution des plages par traceurs radio-actifs. *Trav. Centr. Rech. d'Etudes Oceanogr.* **1,** 11.

[34]Davidsson, J., 1958, Investigations of sand movement using radio-active sand. *Lund Studies in Geog. Ser. A. Phys. Geog.* **12,** pp. 107–26.

[35]Arlman, J. J., Santema, P. and Svâsek, J. N., 1957, Movement of bottom sediment in coastal waters by currents and waves; measurements with the help of radio-active tracers in the Netherlands. Progress Report. *Deltadienst Rijkswaterstaat* pp. 56. See also *B.E.B. Tech. Memo.* **105** (1958).

[36]Inman, D. L., 1953, Areal and seasonal variations in beaches and near-shore sediments at La Jolla, California. *B.E.B. Tech. Memo.* **39.**

[37]Inman, D. L., 1952, Measures for describing the size distribution of sediments. *Journ. Sed. Pet.* **22,** pp. 125–45.

[38]Krumbein, W. C. and Slack, H. A. 1956, Relative efficiency of beach sampling methods. *B.E.B. Tech. Memo.* **90.**

[39]Trask, P. D. and Johnson, C. A., 1955, Sand variations at Point Reyes, California. *B.E.B. Tech. Memo.* **65.**

[40]Trask, P. D., 1956, Change in configuration of Point Reyes beach, California, 1955 to 1956. *B.E.B. Tech. Memo.* **91.**

[41]Bascom, W. N., 1951, The relationship between sand size and beach face slope. *Trans. Am. Geoph. Un.* **32,** 6, pp. 866–74.

[42]Coode, J., 1853, Chesil beach: description, with remarks upon its origin, the causes which have contributed to its formation, and upon the movement of shingle generally. *Mins. Proc. Inst. Civ. Eng.* **12,** p. 520.

[43]Prestwich, J., 1875, Chesil beach: origin, and the relation of the existing beaches to past geological changes, independent of the present coast action. *Mins. Proc. Inst. Civ. Eng.* **40,** p. 61.

[44]Cornish, V., 1898, On the grading of the Chesil beach shingle. *Proc. Dorset Nat. Hist. and Antiq. Field Club.* **19,** p. 113.

[45]Lewis, W. V., 1938, Evolution of shoreline curves. *Proc. Geol. Assoc.* **49,** pp. 107–27.

[46]Guilcher, A., 1954, *Morphologie Littorale et Sous-Marine*, Paris.

[47]Richardson, L., 1902, *Proc. Dorset Nat. Hist. and Antiq. Field Club.* **23,** p. 123.

[48]Evans, O. F., 1938, The classification and origin of beach cusps. *Journ. Geol.* **46,** pp. 615–27.

[49]Johnson, D. W., 1919, *Shore processes and shoreline development.*

[50]Kuenen, Ph. H., 1948, The formation of beach cusps. *Journ. Geol.* **56,** pp. 34–40.

[51]King, C. A. M., 1951, Depth of disturbance of sand on sea beaches by waves. *Journ. Sed. Pet.* **21,** pp. 131–40.

CHAPTER 5

BEACH PROFILES—EXPERIMENTAL RESULTS AND SURVEYING TECHNIQUES

IN this chapter the results of experiments in a model wave tank on the nature of beach profiles and the factors influencing their form will be considered. In the second part methods of survey and presentation of the results for natural beaches will be discussed. An analysis of the formation of different profiles in nature will be left to chapter 10 when all the relevant data on which such an analysis must be based will have been mentioned.

1. *EXPERIMENTAL RESULTS*

The advantage of model experiments, designed to investigate the formation of beach profiles, is that the variables can be easily isolated. The effect of these variables will first be considered, then the two main types of resultant profiles will be described and the factors on which they depend assessed. Some early experiments on beach profiles were carried out by Sweeting (1943)[1] in the long tank described in Chap. 2, which provided a basis for more detailed work.

(a) Effect of the material

The problem of scale in a model tank, where the nature of the material is of significance, has already been mentioned (see pp. 38–41) but the conclusion is reached, that with certain limitations characteristics of beaches in a wave tank do give useful information in relation to beach profiles in nature. Some of the beaches which Bagnold (1940)[2] discussed were the equivalent of shingle in nature according to his ratio $R=H/d$, where H is the wave height and d is the diameter of the particles; the profiles he obtained agreed closely with the known features of shingle beaches. His model beach profile showed a step at the break-point of the waves, this is also common in nature where a shelf often occurs below the step. The actual size of the material he used for his experiments was between 7 and 0·5 mm., the model shingle beaches being built with the coarser particles which are beyond the range of sand. A wave tank in which the effect of different sizes of sand could be studied has been described by Watts (1955),[3] Watts and Dearduff (1954)[4] and by Rector (1954).[5] The tank used was 85 ft. long and 14 ft. wide, being divided longitudinally into four equal parts each 3·5 ft. wide; sand of a different size was placed in each section with median diameters of 0·22 mm., 0·46 mm., and 3·44 mm., the fourth partition contained a mixture of the two coarser sands having a median diameter of 1·22 mm. It was found that the finest sand was the most mobile and differing wave conditions produced greater changes. This is the reverse of what would be expected for the shallower depths in nature, but may well apply to the deeper water outside the break-point where some of the changes recorded in the wave tank were taking place. It has already been explained why coarser beaches in nature are more mobile than fine beaches (see pp. 127, 138) landwards of the break-point. This is related to the steeper gradient associated with coarser beaches, while in the tank the initial gradient of 1 : 20 was the same for all sands. Rector has found that for any specific wave dimensions and wave steepness there is a greater tendency for the beach material to move shoreward as the grain size of the material increases. It was also found by Watts that the finer sand of 0·46 and 0·22 mm. produced more conspicuous bars than the coarser sand which again agrees with observations in nature, although Watts considered that at least some of the bars may have been due to reflection of the waves from the beach at the top of the tank. On the whole it appears that in the tank experiments the varying types of material react to the waves in a broadly similar way to the reaction of natural beaches of similar material, and that the exceptions can be explained.

(b) Effect of wave characteristics and the tide

Nearly all model experiments on the formation of beach profiles have shown that the most important wave characteristic on which the type of profile depends is the wave steepness. With steep waves a so-called 'storm' profile is formed while flat waves produce the 'summer' profile. The experiments discussed on pp. 121–127 on the transport of material inside and outside the break-point help to explain this fundamental difference; with steep waves the transport was seaward inside the break-point and landward outside it, this must clearly result in an accumulation of sand at the break-point. This forms the break-point bar which is one of the distinguishing features of the storm profile. With flatter waves it has been shown that material is moved landwards in all depths; there must, therefore, be an accumulation at the limit of wave action, hence the accretion associated with summer profiles can be explained. The value of the critical wave steepness varies somewhat in different experiments; Rector and Watts state that waves flatter than 0·016 will produce the summer profile. The experiments already described concerning the movement of sand showed that the critical steepness was about 0·012. It is likely that these variations depend partly on the size of material and the higher values are found with the coarser material.

The gradient also probably affects the critical steepness as mentioned on p.184.

Watts[3] has recorded a series of experiments to examine the effect of slight variations in the wave period in the formation of the beach profile; the variations were of 10 and 30 per cent covering periods of 10 min. and 1 hour of a total test time of 40 hours. The results showed that the 10 per cent change had little effect on the profiles which differed little from the standard test with uniform period. The 10 per cent variation in period did show some reduction in the formation of bars, while the 30 per cent change almost eliminated the bars. Changes in wave period of 25 per cent caused a 62 per cent change in the wave steepness, which was probably responsible for the changes in the formation of the bars.

Watts[4] also made a series of tests to show the effect of variation in water level to simulate the effect of a tide. The tidal range used was 0·5 ft. and 0·24 ft.; the former was the same as the wave height, 15 ft. from the generator. Both steep and flat waves were used. The greater tidal range was found to increase the amount of material moving but decreased the size of the bars. The importance of the tide will be mentioned again when the main types of profile are described in more detail.

Summary

The beach profiles produced in the model tank with different sized material seem to correspond fairly closely to the characteristics of their natural counterparts. Steep waves produce a 'storm' profile and flat waves a 'summer' profile in the model tank. The former is characterized by bars below the water level; these tend to be eliminated with variations of wave period and of water level.

(c) Break-point bars. Storm profile

There are two main types of profiles developed in sand in a wave tank dependent on the steepness of the waves. The steep waves produce a storm profile characterized by a bar at the break-point of the waves. Because this feature depends on the position of the break-point it is called a break-point bar. A series of experiments have been made to examine the characteristics of these bars in the wave tank. The experiments were carried out in the tank shown in fig. 2–2 and described on pp. 43–45. The bars form at the break-point of the waves where the sand moving landward outside the break-point accumulates with the sand moving seaward inside the break-point of steep waves. The crest of the bar never grows above the water level but reaches a definite equilibrium size (see fig. 5–1). The initial formation of the bar is easily explained but it is less easy to explain why it does not continue to grow above a certain height. The effect of the bar on the action of the waves

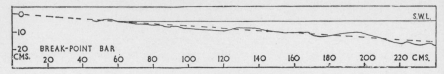

FIG. 5–1. Profile of a break-point bar formed in the model tank.

is probably responsible for this. When the bar reaches its maximum height it deforms the waves breaking on it so that they tend to reform landward of the bar. They can now apparently move the sand landwards inside the outer break-point, thus moving the surplus sand which has moved landwards from outside the breakpoint on to the beach across the bar trough. The bar reached maturity after about 30 min., but the water continued to deepen outside it after this time. Deposition was meanwhile taking place landward of the break-point on the foreshore despite the continued high value of wave steepness in deep water. The bar moved inland owing to the increase in the depth of water outside it which caused a landward shift of the break-point.

The effect of different wave characteristics and of other factors on the formation of the break-point bars may now be considered.

i. WAVE HEIGHT. The position and height of the break-point bar depends on the position of the break-point which is closely related to the height of the waves. The depth in which the wave will break is a function mainly of the wave height. The higher waves will produce a relatively large bar in deeper water. There is also a very close relation between the position of the bar on the profile, primarily determined by the wave height, and the height of the bar crest above the original profile. Fig. 5–2 and 3 illustrate the relationships and show that there is a constant ratio of 1 : 2 between the height of the bar crest above the original profile and the depth of water over the bar. The figure also shows that this ratio is independent of the beach gradient which varied from 1 : 10 to 1 : 20. If the form of the original profile and the position of the bar is known, it is possible to establish the depth of water over the bar crest from this relationship. The depth of water over the bar crest is also clearly related to the wave height which determines the position of the bar crest on the profile. If the wave height at break-point is known it is possible to deduce the depth of water over the bar crest. If this can be shown to apply to natural beaches the relationship can be of considerable value in some circumstances, such as the landing of boats on barred beaches.

ii. WAVE LENGTH OR PERIOD. The wave length does not itself appear to be an important factor in the formation of a break-point bar but it is

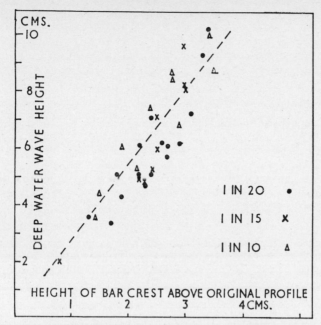

FIG. 5–2. The relationship between wave height and the height of the crest of the break-point bar above the original profile.

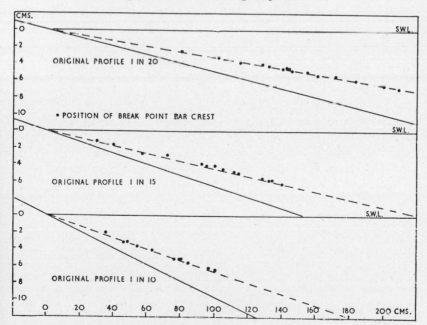

FIG. 5–3. To show the ratio of the depth of water over the bar crest in relation to the height of the crest above the original profile.

important in relation to the wave height as this determines the wave steepness.

iii. WAVE STEEPNESS. The fundamental importance of the wave steepness has already been discussed; it determines whether a break-point will form or not. The wave steepness affects the ratio of the trough depth to crest height of the bar. The steeper the wave the greater the depth of the trough landward of the bar in relation to the height of the crest from the original profile; the ratio of trough depth to crest height varies from 1·4 for a steepness of 0·0265 to 0·4 for a steepness of 0·013 on an original gradient of 1 : 15, the ratio is unity for a steepness of 0·022.

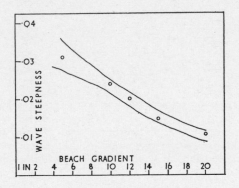

FIG. 5–4. Relationship between beach gradient, wave steepness and break-point bar formation. The upper line gives the approximate steepness at which the break-point bar is fully formed. The lower line indicates the steepness at which the break-point bar first forms.

iv. BEACH GRADIENT. The position and height of the fully formed break-point bar has been shown to be independent of the beach gradient. This factor is important, however, in relation to the wave steepness; it determines, for one sand size, the critical steepness at which the bar will form as shown in fig. 5–4. As the gradient becomes steeper so the critical steepness of waves which will form a break-point bar increases; for a gradient of 1 : 5 the steepness must exceed 0·034, but for a gradient of 1 : 20 the steepness need only exceed 0·0115. This is a fairly flat wave which will not form a fully developed bar trough. The variation in critical steepness which different workers have given as necessary for the formation of a barred profile may be partially explained by this factor.

v. CHANGE IN WAVE SIZE. Because the break-point bar is so dependent on the wave height it is clear that a change in its dimensions will affect the position and character of the bar. A large wave will form a bar in deep water. If the wave size is suddenly made smaller, without decreasing the steepness below the critical value for the conditions obtaining, a second smaller bar will be formed landward of the first at the break-point of the smaller waves. The smaller wave is unable to cause any very great change in the larger bar to seaward; this now comes under the action of unbroken waves, where the movement of material is landwards so there is a very slow landward shift of the large bar crest (see fig. 5–5).

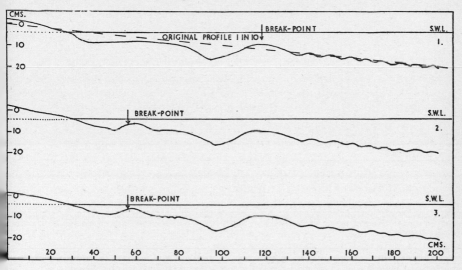

FIG. 5–5. Profiles to show the formation of two break-point bars: 1. Wave height 9 cms. Wave length 240 cms. Run 10 mins. 2. Wave height 3.7 cms. Wave length 88 cms. Run 10 mins. 3. Same waves as 2. Run 10 mins.

If the large waves now attack the beach again the smaller bar will be rapidly destroyed and the sand moved seaward on to the larger bar. A very slow change in the height of the waves will cause a bodily migration of the bar in the direction of the change of wave height; thus an increasing wave height will move the bar seawards as the break-point moves into deeper water, while a decreasing wave height will have the opposite effect.

vi. THE EFFECT OF CHANGING WATER LEVEL. The effect of a changing water level is similar to that of varying wave size because it also alters the position of the break-point, if the wave height remains constant. With a continually changing water level, as on a tidal beach, a break-point bar will never have time to form fully. A bar formed with a low-water level will clearly not be disturbed if there is a rapid rise of level, which will produce a similar change to a rapid reduction in wave height; if the change is slow enough the bar will move forward with the break-point.

If the water level starts to fall after a mature bar has been allowed to form in the wave tank the result is different. An experiment made to examine this process showed that the bar formed at the high water level was completely destroyed when the water level fell below the original position of the bar on the beach profile; the area where the waves previously broke now came under the action of the swash and backwash of the waves and this action destroyed the bar (see fig. 5–6). This indicates that a break-point bar cannot remain above the water level with a falling tide.

From these experiments it can be concluded that the break-point bar in the tank is dependent on the stability of the break-point for its formation and can only form where the wave steepness is above the critical value for the conditions of the experiment. The application of these results to full-scale beaches will be considered when natural beach profiles are discussed in chapter 10.

Summary

A break-point bar forms at the break-point of steep waves. The critical steepness increases with increasing beach gradient. The position of the bar depends on the height of the waves which determines the depth of breaking. The height of the bar crest above the original profile is half the depth of water over the bar crest. Two bars may exist together if small waves follow large steep waves, but the bar is destroyed by a falling water level and cannot exist above the still water level.

(d) Swash bars. Summer beach profiles

The flat waves which produce a summer profile in the wave tank will form a bar if conditions are suitable. This feature is in every respect different from the break-point bar already discussed; it is called a swash bar as it is formed in front of the break-point by the action of the swash and backwash of the waves. It has been shown that flat waves move sand towards the land in all depths both outside and inside the break-point; this sand must clearly accumulate at the top of the beach where it forms a swash bar in the wave tank. This type of bar, unlike the break-point bar, can be raised above the still water level and indeed above the limit of the swash of the waves. A profile of a typical swash bar is shown in fig. 5–7; it was built on a beach having an original gradient of 1 : 20 by waves 3·7 cm. high and 512 cm. long a wave steepness ratio of 0·007, the sand from which it is built had a median diameter of 0·41 mm. After a period of 10 min. sand had begun to accumulate landwards of the break-point. A slip slope facing landwards had formed after 11 min. at the angle of rest of the sand in water. It forms where the advancing sand was pushed over the growing accumulation of material by the construc-

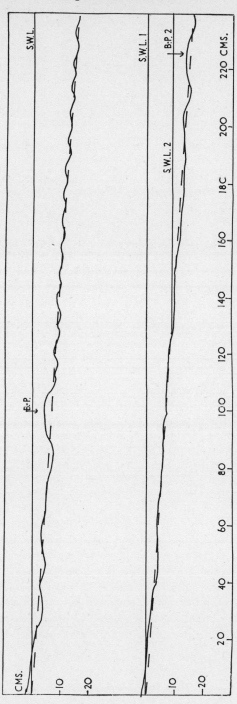

FIG. 5–6. The effect of a falling water level on a break-point bar.

tive action of the swash of these very flat waves. The position of the slip face was 20 cm. seaward from the original water line. Once the slip face had formed the growth of the bar was rapid till after 37 min. it had grown above the still water level nearly to the limit of the swash. The continued deposition of material by the swash on the bar crest gradually led to the elevation of the crest above the normal limit of the swash. The bar was now permanently above the level of wave action and extended practically across the tank. After a period of 45 min., when the profile was drawn, the bar was above the swash throughout its width, a deep lagoon was formed landwards of the bar in which the still water level was appreciably above that in the main part of the tank, as long as the waves were running. The bar crest in this particular example was 7 cm. above the still water level while the wave forming it was only 3·6 cm. high in deep water; the landward slope of the bar is steep, at the angle of rest of sand in water, while the seaward gradient varied with the size

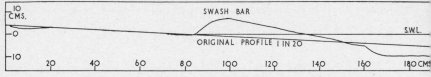

FIG. 5–7. A typical swash bar formed in a model tank.

of the wave forming the bar as will be discussed in detail in chapter 10 (see pp. 321–329). The deepening of the water outside the break-point shows clearly the source of the sand built into the swash bar; the position of the break-point is indicated by the abrupt change of slope at the foot of the swash slope, outside this 5 cm. of sand had been moved landwards with decreasing amounts farther offshore.

The effect of the different wave dimensions and other variables may be considered in relation to the characteristics of a swash bar.

i. WAVE STEEPNESS. Again wave steepness is fundamental to the formation of a swash bar; it must be lower than the critical value for the conditions obtaining. The value of the wave steepness below the critical minimum influences the amount of accretion. If the wave steepness is plotted against the ratio of crest height above the original profile to deep water wave height this ratio increases as the wave steepness decreases. This shows that a flatter wave is considerably more constructive in proportion to its height than a steeper wave. In this experiment the original gradient was 1 : 15 and the runs were continued till stability was reached.

ii. WAVE HEIGHT. The height of the wave exerts an important influence on the height of the mature swash bar as it determines the limit of swash up the beach. A graph shown in fig. 5–8 illustrates the relationship between the deep water wave height and the height of the crest of the swash bar above the still water level, it shows that the two amounts increase together at an almost linear rate for any one wave steepness value on a beach gradient of 1 : 10. The greater energy of the larger waves enables their swash to extend up the beach farther and thereby to build a higher swash bar.

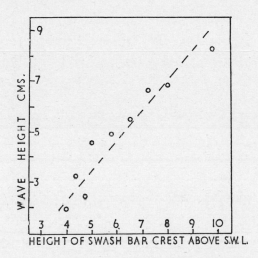

FIG. 5–8, The relationship between wave height and the height of the swash bar above still water level.

iii. WAVE LENGTH OR PERIOD. The effect of increased wave length is similar to that of the wave height if the wave steepness is maintained constant as the two parameters must increase together. The variation of wave length causes a change in the gradient of the swash slope which will be examined in chapter 10 (see pp. 323–325), which deals with the beach gradient.

iv. BEACH GRADIENT. A swash bar will only form if the original gradient of the beach is less than the gradient built up by the swash of the waves in their constructive action. Experiments were made using an original gradient of 1 : 2 which showed that however flat the waves they could not build up a swash bar on this gradient. If the original gradient is very flat, on the other hand, the swash bar is built to a considerably greater height above the original profile than it is on a steeper profile, for any given wave height and steepness. The bar is also formed farther seaward and a wider lagoon results, the lowest point of which is farther below the still water level than it is on a steeper original gradient. The bar forms a much more conspicuous feature as the original gradient becomes flatter.

v. CHANGE IN WAVE TYPE. A change in the size of the waves which does not alter their steepness ratio will not produce a very marked effect on the bar; if the waves are made smaller the bar will remain little altered, if they are increased in size the bar will be raised in height by the greater vertical reach of the swash of the more powerful waves.

If the waves are changed from the flat waves which formed the bar to steeper waves, which are destructive on the swash slope, the bar is likely to undergo erosion. This change of wave type was examined experimentally, the results are shown in fig. 5–9; a swash bar was formed

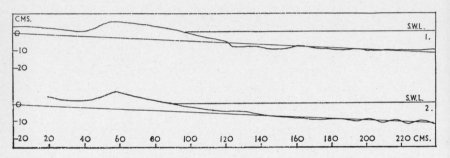

FIG. 5–9. The effect of steep waves on a swash bar. 1. Wave height 3.2 cms. Wave length 504 cms. Time of run 5 hr. 15 min. 2. Profile after 1 hr. of wave action by short waves.

by waves of steepness 0·006 on an original gradient of 1 : 20. These waves, which were 3·2 cm. high and had a period of 1·8 sec. built a swash bar to a height of 6 cm. above the still water level after 5 hrs. 15 min. The waves were then reduced in length to increase their steepness and were allowed to attack the mature bar for 1 hr. Their destructive action is shown by a considerable reduction in the volume of the swash bar but owing to their shorter length they were not able to wash over the bar, the position of which remained unchanged.

vi. CHANGE IN WATER LEVEL. The effect of changing the water level on the swash bar was also investigated in the wave tank. The effect of both rising and falling water levels were examined; a bar was first formed with a very low water level, the waves were then stopped and the level raised 13 cm. at which level waves of a similar deep water height formed a bar at the top of the beach after 40 min.; during this time the former bar, now deep under the water, was not disturbed by the waves as its crest was covered by 8 cm. of water. The water level was then slowly lowered 6 cm. to an intermediate position where a third bar was formed. During the fall in level the uppermost bar was not disturbed by the falling water level, but with the intermediate water level the outermost bar was affected by the waves as the depth of water over its crest was only 2 cm. This first bar was elongated and pushed forward but it did not loose its height or identity. The experiments showed that swash bars may exist at or above the water level and also below water level, although in this latter position their form is likely to be modified as they are affected by different processes.

It has been shown that two very different types of bars can be formed in the wave tank and that each type requires the opposite wave characteristics. One type of bar can never extend above the still water level, while the essential feature of the swash bar is the fact that it is built above the still water level at the limit of wave action. It is quite clear that one type of bar does not develop into the other; they are not merely two stages in one process but two different features.

Summary

A swash bar forms in front of the break-point of waves of low steepness where the original gradient is flatter than that built up by the waves. The height of the bar crest is raised above the still water level to the limit of the swash of the waves. This height is a function of the height of the waves forming the bar. A steeper wave, whose swash does not extend above the crest of the bar, will decrease the volume of the bar by destructive action on its seaward face. A swash bar is not disturbed by a falling water level and may exist on the beach, above, at or below the still water level, although in the latter position it is liable to be modified in form. The break-point bar and the swash bar are two distinct forms which cannot develop the one from the other.

(c) Time required to reach equilibrium in a model tank

The rate at which equilibrium profiles are formed in a wave tank is of interest in assessing the effect of different waves acting on beaches in nature for relatively short periods of time. From the experiments which have just been described it can be seen that the general character of the profile becomes apparent after the waves have been acting on it for only a short period of time; after only thirty minutes a well formed swash bar could develop, while a considerably shorter period of time was required for the growth of a break-point bar to its maximum height above the original profile. These profiles had not reached a state of static equilibrium, however, slow changes still being in progress throughout most of the profile.

Scott (1954)[6] has recorded the progressive changes in the beach profile during one of his experimental runs which was carried on over a period of 450 min. Fig. 5–10 shows a graph of the rate of change of the profile in terms of volume of sand moved per unit time. Although no precise volumes could be given the graph does show the relative rate at which the profiles change with time. The total net change is shown as curve 1, the other curves show various parts of the profile; the foreshore and inshore area are shown on curve 2, the area around the break-point bar is

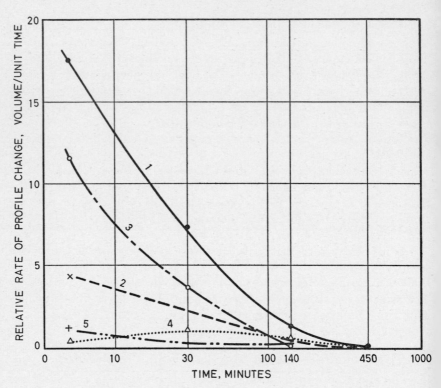

Fig. 5–10. The rate of change of beach profiles with time. (After Scott.)

shown on curve 3, while 4 and 5 cover the middle offshore and far offshore areas respectively. The rate of change is most rapid in the breaker zone while the break-point bar is forming, but when the profile of the bar is mature the greater changes take place in the nearshore zone inside the break-point. The curve for total movement, where the time is plotted on a logarithmic scale, showed that the rate of profile change decreases steadily with time at a logarithmic rate for the first 50 min. approximately, thereafter the change is at a slower rate and becomes very small after 140 min. practically ceasing after 450 min. or $7\frac{1}{2}$ hrs. These changes were brought about by changing the waves from a low to a higher steepness value, the waves during the run had a steepness ratio of 0·041 and they were attacking a profile previously built by waves of steepness 0·017. These waves had acted on the beach for 44 hrs. when slow changes in the profile were still in progress. These changes suggest that late in the formation of a profile the rate of change does not reach zero but instead begins to increase again. This is possibly due to the presence of standing waves in the channel. Thus it may be concluded that even in the controlled conditions and steady wave character in a model tank equilibrium is rarely completely reached when no changes at all are taking place along the profile. It is, therefore, much less likely that equilibrium is ever reached in nature where the waves are much more complex and additional factors such as tides and winds and irregular configuration of the coast make the variables much more complex. This makes it more difficult to apply the findings of experimental studies to natural conditions where it is very unlikely that perfectly formed bars of the types described will be found. Nevertheless, as will be shown later, it is possible to equate bars described with natural features which they appear to simulate.

2. BEACH SURVEYS

(a) Surveys above low tide level

One advantage of model beach profiles in a wave tank is that changes in the profile can be easily measured to any required depth of water but similar observations in nature are much more difficult to make. Where there is a considerable tidal range a large proportion of the beach may be surveyed at low water. This is usually done by levelling along a straight line at right angles to the coast from some fixed datum. An Ordnance Survey bench mark gives an accurate height which can be related to the tide levels by means of the tide tables. This is necessary as it is important to be able to plot the mean tide levels on the profile. The distances along the profile can usually be measured best by tacheometry as this avoids the actual measurement of distance along the beach which may be wet and muddy in parts.

In order to be able to relate changes in sand level and profile to the relevant wave and wind characteristics it is necessary to repeat the same beach profiles at intervals. The more frequent the intervals the better can the changes be correlated with the frequently changing pattern of wave action. It is not necessary to survey the profile by levelling each time observations are made if they are required at fairly short intervals, such as daily or weekly observations. On beaches which are not too frequented the variations in level on the beach from day to day can easily be measured by placing thin pegs in the sand along the surveyed profile at appropriate places and noting each day the length of peg standing above the sand. These pegs are not disturbed by the action of the waves and accurate changes in level can be recorded in this way. If the changes are required over longer periods of time more substantial markers must be fixed in the beach. Those that were put in the beach near Blackpool, during the period 1943–5 for daily measurements of this particular beach profile, were 2-in. scaffolding poles deeply buried in the beach so that they could withstand considerable changes of beach level and wave attack. Forty poles were fixed in the beach at significant points on the profile extending over a distance of 4,000 ft. horizontally and about 24 ft. vertically, as this is a very flat beach with a considerable tidal range. Clamps were fixed on each pole at a known height to facilitate the measurements which were made daily for a period and thereafter at weekly intervals. The poles were so firmly stuck in the beach that many of them were still standing in 1948 after a period of five years.

Some interesting techniques were devised during the war to establish the profiles of beaches which it was not possible to survey directly. Some of these techniques have been described by Williams (1947).[7] There are three main techniques which can be used under different circumstances; one is the water line method, which is applicable only to tidal beaches as far as the low water level. Another is the water transparency technique which is only applicable to beaches covered by very clear water with little or no wave action. The third, which Williams discusses in most detail, is based on the changes in wave length and velocity in shallow water; this is only applicable under suitable wave conditions when long clearly defined swell is reaching the beach. All methods require conditions under which good aerial photographs of the beach can be taken at suitable intervals.

The water line method consists of taking aerial photographs of the beach at known intervals during the tidal cycle and from tracings of the water line at different periods contours can be drawn on the beach and from these the beach gradient can be calculated. To interpret the data, information of the rate of tidal rise and fall must be known and a series of photographs taken at frequent intervals of time are required for accurate profiles.

The water transparency technique depends on the rate at which water of increasing depth absorbs the light and therefore affects the intensity of shading on the photograph. This technique can only be used in very clear water and requires different coloured filters for use in different depths, it is therefore limited to rather specialized conditions.

The third method depends on the fact that the wave length decreases with decreasing depth as mentioned in chapter 1 (see pp. 12, 13). If an aerial photograph contains part of the offshore region where the water depth is more than half the wave length, the deep water wave length can be measured on the photograph and converted into feet by reference to the scale of the photograph. The period of the waves can be ascertained from this data and their length in any depth can be found by reference to a set of curves as shown in fig. 1–2. The lengths of the waves as they move into shallow water as measured on the photographs can then be converted into the equivalent water depth and a plot of these depths gives a reasonably accurate profile of the beach. This method can only be used when suitable waves are reaching the beach; these must show well marked and even crest lines so that it is fairly certain that one major wave train is dominant in the wave spectrum. The changing velocity of the waves as they enter shallow water can also be used to establish the depth at any point in a similar way, but this requires accurately timed photographs.

(b) Surveys below low tide level

The last two methods of obtaining a beach profile mentioned above can be applied to beaches with little or no tidal range and can be extended below the normal low water on a tidal beach; they can also be used to determine the portion of the beach profile which is exposed at low water if the photographs are taken at high water. It has been found increasingly necessary to extend surveys of the beach profile below the low water level because changes in the offshore zone are closely related to changes on the foreshore, and offshore surveys are essential in estimating the amount of longshore transport of material. When tideless or small tidal range areas are being investigated it is necessary to make all the surveys under-water. This type of surveying poses very different problems from the surveying of the exposed part of the beach and cannot usually be done to as great a standard of accuracy as levelling on the exposed beach.

The most common method of offshore survey is by sounding with a lead line which gives sufficiently accurate results for most purposes. One of the problems associated with offshore surveying is to measure the distance between the surveyed points; the line of survey can be maintained straight by keeping two beacons on shore in line, while the measurement of distance can be done with horizontal sextant angles to two or more fixed beacons on shore whose positions are accurately known. This method has the advantage that it can be done by the crew of the boat but it is difficult to obtain accurate readings in a rough sea. An alternative method is to fix the position of the boat from which soundings are being made by plane-table angles from the shore, where the plane-table is set up at the end of a base line measured at right angles to the line of profile. More modern methods based on radio aids are also now available. If the profile is only required to extend to a depth of about 13 ft. it may be obtained by levelling from the shore if the gradient is not very flat. In this method the distances are obtained by tacheometry and requires the use of a specially designed staff 15 ft. long, it was divided into 10 cm. division by a system of coloured bands which dispense with the need for figures. The depths are estimated to the nearest centimetre with a level carefully adjusted to avoid collimation error because the sights cannot be made equal. This type of staff enabled readings to be made at a maximum distance of about 900 ft. with ease. In calm conditions the method probably gave results which were accurate to about 2 cm. in the tideless conditions in which it was used.

One of the disadvantages of the sounding technique is that only spot depths are recorded and unless these are made very frequently some of the irregularities of the bottom profile may be missed. This is overcome by using the more modern method of echo-sounding. This technique, with modern instruments specially designed for use in shallow water, can give depths which are accurate to about 3 in. It also has the advantage that a continuous profile is traced out by the recording pen on the revolving drum of the instrument.

Tests have also been made with other devices designed to give the under-water profile direct or in the form of changing gradients. One of the instruments was designed to be drawn along the sea bottom automatically recording the profile as it moved over the bed. Other instruments have been designed for observations of beach changes on steep shingle beaches. Tests were made on Chesil beach in which changes in the profile in and around the break-point of the waves over very short periods of time were recorded. The instrument consisted of a long pole to which a marker was fixed which could be manipulated from the shore, this recorded the level of the shingle at the position of a pole fixed in the beach. This method could only be used on shingle beaches where the gradient is very steep; on Chesil it varied between 1 : 5 and 1 : 2.

A new device has been reported by Inman and Rusnak[8] (1956) which yields much more accurate results but which requires special equipment. They also tested the accuracy of positioning for sounding and found that in a depth of 30 ft. 50 per cent of the observations fell within a radius of 5 ft. of the required point out of 45 tests; 80 per cent fell within a 10-ft. radius. The method of positioning used was to keep the boat on line by aligning two markers on shore and to fix the position along the line by horizontal sextant angle to a third fixed position on shore. These observations were made possible by the fixing of reference rods in the sea floor at the points tested. The rods used were of brass, $\frac{3}{8}$-in. in diameter and 4 ft. long, they were forced into the sand by observers wearing breathing apparatus. The rods were sited at depths of up to 75 ft. and buried in the sand to a depth of 3 ft. leaving 1 ft. exposed above the sand surface. These rods only caused very slight scour round their bases and were found more satisfactory than steel rods. At each reference point six rods were placed in the form of a T. In order to measure the changes of sand level all that was necessary was to visit the rods to measure the length protruding above the sand, the mean value for the six rods at each station then gave the change of level between the surveys. This method could not, however, provide the initial profile but was of great value for measuring accurately the change in level at any point.

(c) Accuracy and use of profiles

The most accurate method of under-water surveying is the direct measuring device just described, after which follows the echo-sounding technique. The accuracy of the direct measuring technique was evaluated by statistical analysis and it was shown that the average standard error of observation was about 0·05 ft. for the four stations measured, in depths varying from 18 to 70 ft.; the error became less farther from the shore. Sonic sounding was carried out at the same time as the under-water measurement of the reference rods to test the relative accuracy of the two methods. Five runs were made for each survey and the average taken to give a mean value. It was found that these five runs agreed much more closely with each other, having a range of 0·3 ft., than the average of five subsequent runs agreed with the appropriate direct measurements. The experimental accuracy of the echo sounding technique appears to be of the order of ±0·5 ft., at stations in depths of 30, 52 and 70 ft. of water. These figures show that the results which will be considered next are probably rather optimistic; this is partly due to the absence of an accurate value against which the changes could be compared. Only observations made at very short intervals could therefore be used, these have been shown to be more accurate than longer term changes.

The relative accuracy of lead-line sounding and echo-sounding has been discussed by Saville and Caldwell (1953)[9] for surveys carried out on Mission Beach, California. The probable error of the two methods of sounding was calculated statistically from the standard deviation, where $\sigma = \dfrac{\sqrt{\Sigma d^2}}{n}$, d is the profile deviation at fixed positions and the probable error is 0·6745σ. The echo sounder used under favourable conditions of uniformity gave a probable error of 0·07 ft., while the probable error of the lead line used in shallow water gave a probable error of 0·11 ft. as the deviation from the average profile or 0·20 ft. between successive profiles.

One use to which beach profiles may be put is for calculating the amount of material transported alongshore, derived from the volumetric change in beach material, based on a series of profiles. In this instance several profiles are surveyed across the area in question at various intervals along the beach and at different periods of time. It is assumed that the beach changes along the measured profiles are representative of the changes between the profiles; so that the closer the spacing of the profiles the more accurate will be the assessment of the volume of material added to or eroded from the beach. If the surveys are a considerable distance apart along the beach errors due to this wide spacing

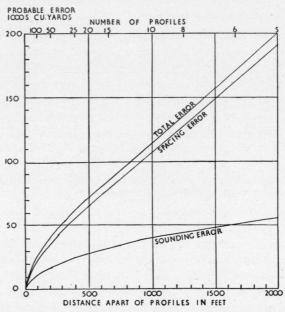

FIG. 5–11. Probable volume errors for 10,000 ft. of beach. Profiles 4,500 ft. long. The landward 500 ft. were sounded by lead-line, the remainder by echo-sounder. (After Saville and Caldwell, B.E.B.)

are liable to occur if the beach is at all variable. There are thus two sources of error inherent in the use of profiles for the calculation of long-shore movement or other volumetric changes of beach material; this double error is equal to the square-root of the sum of the squares of the two separate errors. The error in cubic yards equals $E = \dfrac{\sqrt{e_a^2 + e_s^2}\, L\, L'}{27}$, where L and L' are the length of beach between surveys and the length of profile, both in feet. The curves shown on the fig. 5–11 give the probable error for both lead-line sounding and echo-sounding. An example shows that on a stretch of beach 10,000 ft. wide, with a profile 4,500 ft. long, of which the outer 4,000 ft. are sounded by echo-sounding and the inner 500 ft. by lead-line, the error varies as follows for differing distances between surveys. If the spacing is 1,000 ft. apart, which would entail ten surveys, the probable error would be 113,800 cubic yds., if the spacing of profiles was 500 ft. the error would be 70,900 cubic yds. and if the profiles were surveyed every 200 ft. the error would be reduced to 39,800 cubic yds. These errors would be decreased by about 5 per cent if all the profile were surveyed by the more accurate echo-sounder. These figures show that for fairly small amounts of volumetric change the error due to inaccuracy of the surveyed beach profiles may lead to very misleading results, even if these are done with accurate instruments. The errors might be even larger than suggested as the sounding error may have been underestimated in this work.

(d) Amount of change in successive profiles

Beaches vary considerably in their relative mobility so that a technique whereby the variability of the beach profile from time to time may be assessed has been found useful. If a long series of beach profiles surveyed at various times along the same line on the beach, are superimposed they give some indication of the variability of the beach. In some instance the different surveys may lie close together indicating a stable beach (see fig. 7–1, p. 230). This type is most often associated with a fine smooth sand beach. Shingle beaches, also often smooth, are much more mobile and the superimposed profiles will spread over a greater height range. Where the beach profile consists of a series of ridges or bars which vary in position from time to time the profiles will cover a wide vertical range at any one point. If the highest points of all the profiles are joined by a curve this will indicate the height above which the material of the beach is unlikely to extend unless the conditions are very exceptional. Similarly if the lowest points of all the profiles are joined they indicate the level below which only exceptional erosion is likely to remove beach material. The longer the surveys have been made the less likely is the profile at any time to extend above or below these two curves. The zone between the two curves may be termed the 'sweep' zone, and may be defined as that portion of the vertical plane perpendicular to the coast line within which movement of beach material may take place by wave action.[10] In some instances the lower sweep zone profile, as the lower curve may be called, will be the foundation of the beach, for example the clay base of the beaches in parts of Lincolnshire, in some areas it is likely to be a rocky wave-cut platform. In other areas it may lie entirely in mobile beach material where the available supply of material is great. As shown in fig. 5–12 where a beach is ridged or barred the profile at any one time will never lie entirely along the upper sweep zone profile which is found by joining the crests of the ridges or bars on successive

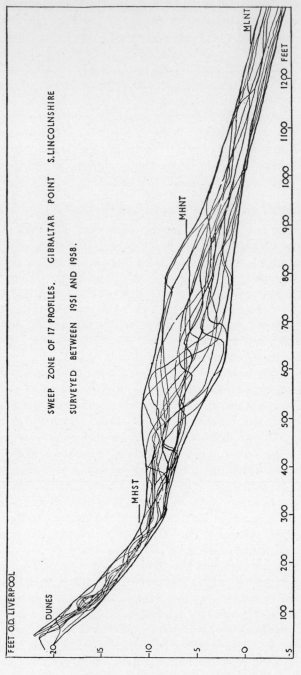

FIG. 5-12. (*a*) Sweep zone profile at Gibraltar Point, Lincolnshire.

profiles. On a smooth beach, however, it is quite possible for the profile to lie along the upper sweep zone profile; in this type the sweep zone itself will not be so wide vertically as it may be in the ridged and barred types.

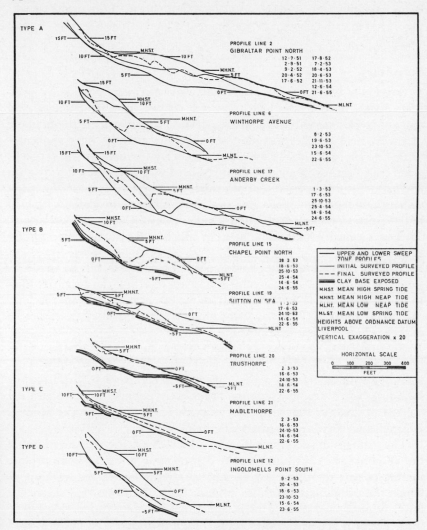

Fig. 5–12. (*b*) Sweep zone profiles along the Lincolnshire Coast.

Over a relatively short period of time the sweep zone indicates the maximum and minimum possible conditions of the profile of the beach. If sweep zones are constructed for any beach for different periods over a long time interval they can give useful evidence of secular changes along the coast. They can indicate the rate at which the coast is advancing or retreating apart from the short-term changes which are the result of variations in waves and wind. These long-term changes are shown by the movement of the whole sweep zone over the interval of years for which the observations are available. A change in the form of the profile resulting in a systematic change in the beach gradient can also be seen by this method.

Summary

Surveys of beach profiles above low water can best be made by levelling. Stakes fixed in the beach can be used to measure changes over daily or weekly periods. Techniques devised for measuring the gradient of enemy-held beaches include the water-line method, only applicable to the foreshore of tidal beaches and requiring frequent air survey. The water transparency method can only be used when the water is very clear and calm but can be used on both tideless and tidal beaches. The wave velocity and length methods also apply to both tidal and tideless beaches but require suitable long crested simple and well defined wave trains. The wave velocity method requires in addition accurately timed photographs.

Surveys below low water under normal conditions can be made by sounding with a lead-line or echo-sounding, levelling can be carried out to a depth of 13 ft. The more accurate measurement of changes in level can be obtained by divers making direct measurement of poles placed in the sea bed in deep water offshore.

The order of accuracy of under-water surveys is firstly, direct measurement, with an average standard error of 0·05 ft., secondly, echo-sounding with an error of 0·5 ft., although in comparison with lead-line sounding more accurate results have been obtained. In computing volume of material moved the accuracy depends largely on the number of profiles surveyed over a given length of coast.

The changes in successive profiles which constitute the variability of the beach can be illustrated by the construction of sweep zone profiles for the beach; the upper sweep zone profile indicates the level above which the profile is unlikely to extend, while the lower one shows the lower limit of the beach. This is sometimes the solid foundation but in some places it lies within the mobile beach material. The movement of the whole sweep zone indicates longer term beach changes.

3. *OFFSHORE BANKS*

One of the factors on which longer term beach changes depend in some areas is the slow migration of offshore banks. In considering the

significance of offshore changes in relation to coast and beach development the effect of tidal currents on the form and movement of offshore
sand banks is of importance. Van Veen (1950),[11] (1936)[12], has put forward a theory, which has been applied to the relevant offshore districts
of the coast of England by Cloet (1954)[13], (1954)[14] and Robinson (1956)[15],
and Robinson and Cloet (1953).[16] The theory concerns the form, and
to a certain extent the movement, of offshore banks and channels; the
form and pattern of the banks and channels are related to the position
and strength of the ebb and flood tidal currents and their sediment
carrying capacity. The channels formed by this process develop an
interdigitated pattern, some extending seawards and others towards the
shore. They develop best where the tidal flow is rectilinear and are
termed 'ebb and flood channels'. The currents associated with the rising
and falling tide tend to follow different paths, each of which scours
according to its capacity, with accumulation taking place as elongated or
parabolic banks between the tidal channels. Such channels and banks
can only form in areas where much loose sediment is available, they are
therefore found in the southern North Sea and Irish Sea; in both areas
a large amount of loose material was left as a result of glacial deposition,
much of this material has been resorted and formed into banks by the
tidal currents.

A particularly good example of these features is found in the Goodwin
sand area off Kent in the southern North Sea. Because of its danger to
navigation the area has been surveyed frequently and in detail, giving
evidence of the form and movement of this bank (Cloet 1954a)[13]. This
great sand bank has been more or less in its present position for a considerable time and is maintained in it by the interplay of ebb and flood
tidal currents. It has, however, gradually been moving since detailed
surveys were started in 1844. The feature as a whole is more or less
elliptical in shape with the major axis trending a little east of north, it
has a length of about 8–9 miles above 6 fathoms. To the north-west it is
separated by the Gull stream from Brake Bank which lies less than 2
miles off the Kentish coast between Deal and Ramsgate in Sandwich
Bay. The Goodwin area is cut at its south-western end by the flood
channel in Trinity Bay, another flood channel follows the coast between
Deal and Brake Bank; both are directed north. The intervening ebb
channels, directed south, flow down the Gull and round the east side
of the Goodwin Bank. The feature reaches its greatest width, across the
minor axis, where the two opposed streams are least able to counteract
each other. The whole of the Goodwin Bank is tending to rotate anti-
clockwise, its northern end moving west and its southern end east, and
it is widening slightly. Brake Bank, meanwhile, has been moving slowly
towards the shore.

Since the beginning of this century a deep cut has developed in the north-east part of the bank, forming Kellett Gut, first surveyed in 1926. It is 13 fathoms deep and cuts across the widest part of the bank. Its formation may represent an attempt of the ebb and flood tides to balance one another, or it may represent a stage in the formation of a new Brake Bank, as the north Goodwin Bank becomes farther separated from the south and the present Brake Bank moves towards the shore, on to which it may be welded. It appears that as the sediment content of a bank increases so it will tend to move towards the shore.

Evidence has been put forward by Robinson and Cloet (1953)[16] to suggest that the process of shoreward migration of offshore banks has already taken place to form the Stonar shingle bank, which lies inland of the present shingle and sand bank of Brake Bank. The Stonar Bank, extending south from Ebbsfleet now lies inland of a sand and shingle spit extending north from near Deal. The outer bank has grown northwards by longshore movement of material along the coast from the south. The Stonar shingle bank is an extensive feature nearly $2\frac{1}{2}$ miles long, 1,750 ft. across and extending down to a depth of 40 ft. below O.D. and reaching 16 ft. O.D. in height. It is formed of rounded flint shingle.

The offshore Brake Bank lies $1\frac{1}{2}$ miles from the coast and is 1,000–4,000 ft. wide and 4 miles long, much of it being in less than 2 fathoms. It has a steep slope of 1 : 40 facing landwards into the Ramsgate channel which separates it from the shore, its seaward slope is much flatter being 1 : 500. It is similar in form and composition to the Stonar Bank and it is suggested that this latter feature represents an earlier offshore bank which has slowly been driven landwards, either by tidal currents, causing an anti-clockwise rotation as is taking place in the Goodwin area, or by wave action. The Brake Bank is now moving onshore, probably by wave action moving shingle to its steep landward face. This may represent the process by which the Stonar Bank formed. A similar process may lead to the addition of material to the beach in other areas, for example some of the shingle of Orford Ness may be derived from offshore, as extensive beds of shingle have been located 5 miles offshore in this area. Recent experiments (Hydraulics research 1957)[17] with radioactive tracers have shown that sand on an offshore bank only $\frac{1}{2}$ mile away from the beach, about 6 miles north of Great Yarmouth, did not reach the shore over a period of about three months. It travelled south at a steady rate, under the influence of the tidal currents, reaching at least 2,000 ft. during the period of observations and it is likely that some of the sand travelled over a mile to the south. Despite a considerable variety of wave types none of the sand reached the coast and its movement was not affected by the changing wave pattern, which indicates that only the tidal currents influenced its travel, these had a resultant of 0·72 ft. per sec. on a southerly direction.

Minor features associated with offshore sand banks are the sand waves discussed by Cloet (1954b),[14] these waves are found in the North Sea on the northern part of Brake Bank; they vary from 1·5 to 7 ft. in height and 100 to 450 ft. in length and lie perpendicular to the run of the bank, their steeper slope faces north. The waves are associated with the tidal stream channels already mentioned and increase in size up the channel, currents of a maximum velocity of 3·2 knots have formed the waves on Brake Bank. From a study of the form of the waves Stride and Cartwright (1958)[18] have deduced the general nature of the circulation of sand in the southern North Sea, assuming that material is moving towards the steep side of the sand ridges. They find that sand is moving north along the coast of Holland in a belt about 40 miles wide, while it is moving south in a 10-mile belt off the coast of East Anglia. Off the East Anglian coast, however, some of the sand waves appear to be moving north, which may be due to their protection from the general southerly movement resulting in their response to ebb and flood tidal currents. The total volume moving north along the Dutch coast is estimated at 40 million cubic metres per year.

Sand waves have also been reported by Cartwright and Stride (1958)[19] in deeper water at a point 47°41′ N, 7°13′ W on the edge of the continental shelf south-west of Land's End. The waves here are found in 90 fathoms and have heights of 25 ft. with a maximum of 40 ft. and a mean length between crests of 2,800 ft. They are formed by tidal currents which must be strong enough to move sand in this depth, their form indicates a slow westerly movement out to the edge of the shelf. They are formed of sand of median diameter of about 0·5 mm.

Summary

Sand banks offshore form where a superfluity of material on the sea floor is shaped into banks by the ebb and flood tidal currents. They occur in areas where these currents are rectilinear; in avoiding their respective channels the ebb and flood currents form an interdigitating pattern of troughs between elongated or parabolic banks of sand or shingle. The Goodwin Sands, which are a good example of this feature, are slowly rotating anti-clockwise while the Brake Bank is moving shoreward. In some areas sand waves occur on the banks and these can give information concerning the direction of movement of material offshore. It appears to move south in general along the East Anglian coast and north along the Dutch coast. Sand waves occur in depths up to 90 fathoms on the edge of the continental shelf off south-west England.

REFERENCES

[1]Sweeting, M. M., 1943, Wave trough experiments on beach profiles. *Geog. Journ.* **101**, pp. 162–72.

[2]Bagnold, R. A., 1940, Beach formation by waves; some model experiments in a wave tank. *Journ. Inst. Civ. Eng.* **15**, pp. 27–52.

[3]Watts, G. M., 1955, Laboratory study on the effect of varying wave periods on beach profiles. *B.E.B. Tech. Memo.* **53**.

[4]Watts, G. M. and Dearduff, R. F., 1954, Laboratory study of the effect of tidal action on wave formed beach profiles. *B.E.B. Tech. Memo.* **52**.

[5]Rector, R. L., 1954, Laboratory study of the equilibrium profiles of beaches, *B.E.B. Tech. Memo.* **41**.

[6]Scott, T., 1954, Sand movement by waves. *Inst. Eng. Res.* Wave research Lab. Univ. of California.

[7]Williams, W. W., 1947, The determination of the gradient of enemy held beaches. *Geog. Journ.* **109**, pp. 76–93.

[8]Inman, D. L. and Rusnak, G. A., 1956, Changes in sand level on the beach and shelf at La Jolla, California. *B.E.B. Tech. Memo.* **82**.

[9]Saville, T. and Caldwell, J. M., 1953, Accuracy of hydrographic surveying in and near the surf zone. *B.E.B. Tech. Memo.* **32**.

[10]Barnes, F. A. and King, C. A. M., 1955, Beach changes in Lincolnshire since the 1953 storm surge. *East Midland Geog.* **4**, pp. 18–28.

[11]Van Veen, J., 1950, Eb en vloedschaar systemen in de Nederlandse getijwatern. *Tijd. van Let. Kon. Ned. Aardr. Gen.* **67**, p. 303.

[12]Van Veen, J., 1936, Onderzockingen in de Hoofden in Verband met de gesteldheid der Nederlandsche Kust.

[12]Cloet, R. L., 1954, Hydrographic analysis of the Goodwin Sands and the Brake Bank. *Geog. Journ.* **120**, pp. 203–15.

[14]Cloet, R. L., 1954, Sand waves in the southern North Sea and in the Persian Gulf. *Journ. Inst. Navig.* **7**, pp. 272–9.

[15]Robinson, A. H. W., 1956, The submarine morphology of certain port approach channel systems. *Journ. Inst. Navig.* **9**, pp. 20–46.

[16]Robinson, A. H. W. and Cloet, R. L., 1953, Coastal evolution of Sandwich Bay. *Proc. Geol. Assoc.* **64**, pp. 69–82.

[17]Report of the Hydraulics Research Board, 1958, Hydraulics research 1957. *D.S.I.R.* H.M.S.O. pp. 56–60.

[18]Stride, A. H. and Cartwright, D. E., 1958, Sand transport at the southern end of the North Sea. *Dock and Harbour Auth.* **38**, 447, pp. 323–4.

[19]Cartwright, D. E. and Stride, A. H., 1958, Large sand waves near the edge of the continental shelf. *Nature* **181**, p. 41.

CHAPTER 6

THE EFFECT OF WIND

THE wind, quite apart from its major function of generating waves, plays an important part in the movement of beach material. In this chapter model experiments made to establish the effect of onshore wind on sand movement will be described first. The full scale effects of wind action on the beach will then be considered and finally coastal dunes, which are wind formed features, will be considered briefly.

1. *MODEL EXPERIMENTS WITH AN ONSHORE WIND*

(a) **Water circulation**

It has been shown that under the action of waves in shallow water both the major acceleration of the water particles and the transport of sediment is predominantly in a landward direction outside the break-point. If this were true of all conditions it would appear that there should be a general tendency for accretion to take place; no mechanism whereby material can be moved seawards outside the break point has been demonstrated. It is true that in places rip currents can carry water and with it sediment through the breaker zone, but such movements are localized and are not found under all wave conditions and do not extend far beyond the breakers.

One factor which would appear to be capable of causing a seaward current along the bottom is an onshore wind. This causes a landward movement of the surface water, which it would be reasonable to assume must be compensated by a seaward current at a lower level. A series of experiments was made in the wave tank in order to examine the effect of an onshore wind on the water movement and sediment transport on the bottom both inside and outside the break-point. The experiments were made by fitting a fan above the wave generator, this enabled wind and waves to be generated together. The wave tank used has been described in chapter 2 (see pp. 43–45).

The first series of experiments were designed to study the pattern of water flow under the action of an onshore wind without wave action. The tank was not long enough for the wind of the strength used to generate any measureable waves itself; the water circulation examined, therefore, was the result of the wind only. The circulation was measured by using dye in depths from 8 to 18 cm. with winds varying from 10 to

13 m.p.h. In all depths the pattern was the same; a rapid landward flow on the surface, extending downwards to between $\frac{1}{3}$ and $\frac{1}{4}$ of the total depth at most positions, became a seaward drift on the bottom and in the lower part of the section. The maximum landwards current, where the wind velocity was 13 m.p.h. (580 cm./sec.), was 5·8 cm./sec. on the surface with a seaward current of nearly 2 cm./sec. near the bottom. With a greater wind velocity of 30–35 m.p.h. a series of measurements were made of the seaward velocity of water on the bottom by timing the travel of small wax balls of about 2 mm. diameter and a specific gravity of 1·1. The results are plotted on fig. 6–1, which shows that on a smooth sand bed of gradient 1 : 15 in depths of water ranging from about 3 to over 13 cm. there is a decrease of bottom velocity seawards from about 2 cm./sec. in a depth of about 3 cm. to a very low seaward velocity in depths greater than 12 cm. A landward velocity on the surface was maintained in all depths. This result can be explained easily; in a narrow tank of the type used there must be a return seaward of the water blown towards the shore, in shallow water this must be accomplished in a relatively narrow zone and hence a faster current is necessary, where the water is deeper the return flow can be spread through a greater depth of water and need not therefore be so rapid at the bottom where the velocity was measured. This distribution of velocity on the bottom under wind action is just the reverse of that under wave action alone; here the movement on the bottom is always landwards, although it increases in velocity towards the shallower water as it does in wind action as far as the break-point. Thus the expected seaward return current can be demonstrated in the tank but its velocity is not sufficient in itself to move grains of quartz sand. It will be shown, however, that this weak current can have a very significant effect on the movement of sand on the bottom when it is combined with wave action.

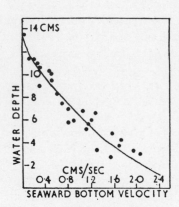

FIG. 6–1. Relationship between water depth and seaward bottom velocity with an onshore wind in the wave tank.

(b) Ground perspex experiments

The effect of the wind generated current on the bottom was tested by using perspex ground to a median diameter of 0·63 mm., this material was very light, having a specific gravity of only 1·18. It was, therefore, much more mobile than quartz sand and reacted to the low velocity of wind generated currents. The ground perspex was formed into a beach with a gradient of 1 : 15 and experiments were made in varying depths with a trap similar to the one used for the experiments described in chapter 4. The strength of the wind over the trap was 29 m.p.h. The results of the experiment are plotted in fig. 6–2 in which the water depth is plotted against the seaward transport of ground perspex in grams per minute over the width of the tank. The points plotted are the mean values for any depth. It can be seen that there is a very rapid increase in the amount of seaward transport as the water becomes shallower which agrees with the increase in velocity with decreasing depth. In depths over 6 cm. less than 5 grams per min. moved seawards but in a depth of

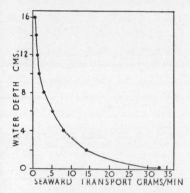

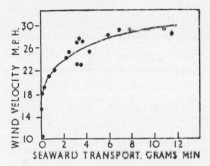

Fig. 6–2. Relationship between water depth and seaward transport of perspex sand under an onshore wind in the wave tank.

Fig. 6–3. Relationship between wind velocity and seaward transport of perspex sand under an onshore wind in the wave tank.

2 cm. the amount is nearly 15 grams per min. The agreement between the seaward velocity and the amount of ground perspex moved seawards can be demonstrated by plotting the two values against each other. They show a linear relationship with both values increasing together.

By placing the trap in a constant depth of water and varying the wind velocity at this point it can be shown that there is a very rapid increase of seaward transport, at this point, of perspex sand when the wind velocity exceeds 22 m.p.h., the experiment was made in a depth of 4 cm. on a beach gradient of 1 : 15. The relationship is shown in fig. 6–3.

(c) Movement of sand under wind and wave action

i. VOLUME AND DIRECTION OF MOVEMENT. The wind generated currents could not, under the conditions of the experiments, move the quartz sand grains. The effect of the wind, therefore, had to be studied together with that of the waves. This state is much more likely to occur in nature when the wind is usually accompanied by waves. It has already been pointed out that the direction of movement outside the break-point is in the opposite direction under wind and wave action. For constructive waves inside the break-point the direction of current flow will also be reversed, but for steep waves inside the break-point, under both wind and wave action, the flow is seaward and the two currents will reinforce each other. Experiments to verify these assumptions were made by trapping sand in a similar way to that already described (see pp. 43–45). The addition of wind generated currents modified both the gross and net transport of sand on the bottom. For a flat wave of steepness 0·01 on a beach gradient of 1 : 15 the gross transport without wind increased steadily till the break-point was reached and then fell off sharply. Similar waves combined with a wind of 28 m.p.h. moved a considerably lower gross volume of sand than was moved under calm conditions. The reduction would appear to be the result of the wave and wind currents partially cancelling each other and thus reducing the amount of sand moved. This reduction of volume transported was found to occur in all depths but was most marked in the vicinity of the break-point.

The net transport of sand is more important as changes in the beach profile are more dependent upon it. The effect of wind generated currents was examined on waves of two types, the steep destructive waves which move sand seawards inside the break-point and the flat waves which move sand landwards in all depths, and which build swash bars. Each run was made once without wind and then repeated with similar wave conditions but with a wind of 28 m.p.h. blowing over the tank. In all runs the beach gradient was 1 : 15.

For the runs made with steep waves, with H/L 0·046, but without wind, the curve plotted to show the amount of sand moved against the distance from the break-point is similar to those already discussed, showing a landwards movement outside the break-point and sea-ward inside it. The runs made with a strong onshore wind show that in all depths the seaward movement of sand is much greater in volume especially inside the break-point, where the seaward wind generated current has been shown to be strong (see fig. 6–4a). The effect on the movement outside the break-point is not very marked; both sets of observations show a certain amount of scatter in all depths. These results therefore confirm the supposition that the seaward currents in-side the break-point will reinforce each other to cause a greater seaward movement under a strong onshore wind.

The flat wave used had a steepness value of 0·01 and the plot of sand transport against proximity to the break-point showed landward trans-port in all depths reaching a maximum near the break-point. In this experiment the wind effect is more marked; in the deepest water the slight landward movement under calm conditions was reversed into a slight seaward movement under a strong onshore wind. In the shallower water outside the break-point the strong landward movement in calm conditions was considerably reduced under the action of the onshore wind; the position of maximum landward movement was no longer at the break-point but about 30 cm. seaward of it. Inside the break-point

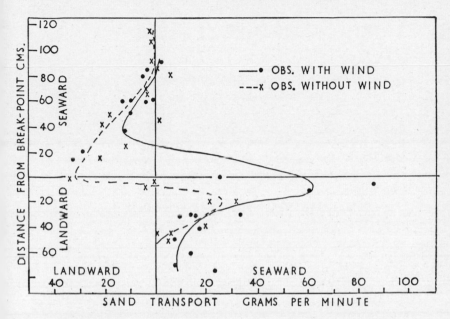

FIG. 6–4. (*a*) The effect of wind on the transport of sand with a steep wave, H/L 0.046.

the landward movement under calm conditions was again reversed to become a fairly marked seaward movement as shown in figure 6–4b. This result illustrates clearly the effect of the seaward wind current on the normal landward wave generated current. The wind currents are sufficiently strong to reverse the landward current in the shallowest and deepest water, in the former the wind current reaches its greatest strength where the wave current is rather weaker inside the break-point, while in the deeper water the wind velocity was strong and the wind generated current still appreciable in depths where the rather low wave used had little effect on the bottom. These experiments, therefore, show that the general landward movement outside the break-point may be reversed in some areas and that the effect of the wind is strongly felt inside the break-point, causing an increased or reversed seaward movement.

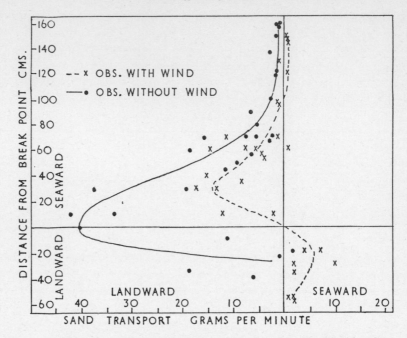

Fig. 6–4. (*b*) The effect of an onshore wind on the transport of sand with a flat wave, H/L 0.010.

ii. EFFECT ON THE BEACH PROFILES. It has been shown that a strong onshore wind can have a marked effect on the amount of sand moved on the bottom by waves. This must affect the development of beach profiles in the model tank. To examine this effect an experiment was made using a flat wave whose height was 4 cm. in deep water and whose length was 350 cm., giving a steepness of 0·0114. This would be expected to produce a swash bar in the wave tank as it was below the critical steepness. The experiment was carried out on a gradient of 1 : 15. The waves were allowed to shape the beach profile for a period of $1\frac{1}{2}$ hrs. after which time a profile as shown in fig. 6–5 had formed. This is typical of a flat wave, showing a well developed swash bar built at least

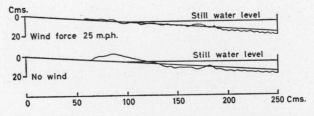

Fig. 6–5. To show the effect of an onshore wind on a beach profile built by flat waves.

5 cm. above the still water level while the deeper water shows a loss of sand owing to the landward transport to form the swash bar. The second profile shows the effect of the same waves which were accompanied by a strong onshore wind. The waves and wind were allowed to act for the same period of $1\frac{1}{2}$ hrs. The profile after the waves and wind had been acting together was very different from that formed by wave action only. The swash bar was completely lacking and the only deposition of sand was a very small area near the break-point of the waves. The waves, with the addition of the wind current, can be shown to be destructive under these conditions practically throughout the beach profile, which confirms the results of the experiments on sand transport under wind action combined with waves which would normally be constructive.

Summary

Model experiments have shown that an onshore wind generated seaward bottom currents, which increase in velocity with decreasing depth. When combined with wave action onshore winds increase the destructive effect of steep waves inside the break-point; with flat waves an onshore wind reduced or reversed the landward transport of material, having a particularly strong effect in shallow water in front of the break-point and in the deeper water outside it, where the direction of movement was reversed. This prevents the formation of a swash bar on the model profile under the action of flat waves.

2. *OBSERVATIONS IN NATURE*

If it can be shown that the results of the experiments on the effect of an onshore wind on sand movement are applicable to natural beaches, then it is clear that the frequency and intensity of onshore winds are a very important factor in the régime of the beach. These winds would reverse the effect of waves which would normally cause accretion on the upper part of the beach. A series of surveys were made on the east coast of England at Marsden Bay, County Durham, to study the effect of the wind on the movement of sand on the beach[1]. The wind is likely to have a double effect on the water movement on a natural beach; it will generate currents near the shore in a way similar to that discussed in the tank experiments, but it will also affect the character of the waves themselves. When a strong onshore wind is blowing it will often be accompanied by the steep waves of a locally generated sea which may be superimposed on and conceal a longer, lower swell. With a strong offshore wind, on the other hand, the height of the advancing swell will be reduced by the effect of a head wind and the waves reaching the coast will be very flat and therefore liable to move material up the beach towards high water level. Observations of the steepness value of the waves made at Marsden Bay confirms this argument. The mean deep water wave steepness measured with an offshore wind was 0·0014, with a maximum of 0·0060 for very short waves and a minimum of 0·0002. With an on-shore wind the mean steepness was 0·0059, the maximum being 0·010 and the minimum 0·002. It may therefore be assumed that, even without the effect of the wind generated currents near the beach, waves accompanied by a strong onshore wind will tend to be more destructive on the foreshore than waves working with an offshore wind.

The effect of the wind generated current will enhance the effect of the wind on the wave characteristics; it has been shown that an onshore wind generates a seaward bottom current, it is also very likely that an offshore wind will tend to produce an onshore drift on the bottom. In order to investigate the possible connexion between wind and beach changes wind roses were prepared for the weekly period between beach surveys which indicated the general pattern of wind during the week; in many cases the wind was predominantly onshore or offshore during the period. On this beach the prevailing westerly winds blow offshore, while the dominant winds are from an easterly and north-easterly quarter, but winds from north and north-east blow on to the beach from the direction of maximum fetch. The results of the observations showed that on thirteen occasions accretion occurred on the upper foreshore above mean tide level with an offshore wind, while erosion only took place on three occasions. With an onshore wind erosion took place thirteen times while accretion only occurred four times. On the lower foreshore below mean tide level the changes were reversed on most occasions. A good example of the effect of an offshore wind is shown in the profiles drawn for 11 and 17 November 1950, shown in fig. 6–6; during the whole period between surveys the wind blew offshore from a westerly point; the profiles shown in the figure show the accretion at the top of the beach and erosion below. During this period long, low swells reached the beach. The period between 17 and 25 November 1950, when the winds were blowing mainly between south and north-east in an onshore direction, was characterized by locally generated seas with short, high waves. The combined effect of wind and waves caused very marked erosion on the upper beach with accretion taking place near low tide level; at the south end of the bay sand was removed by the waves to a depth of about 3 ft., while the berm was largely removed. It seems that the results of the experiments made in the wave tank can be applied to natural beaches and that a strong onshore wind will generate seaward currents which will enhance the destructive conditions which would naturally be expected to occur with short, high seas generated by a strong onshore wind blowing in the vicinity of the beach under observation.

The effect of an offshore wind on the other hand is largely constructive in the shallowest water. The landward movement by the waves in this instance may be augmented by the direct action of the wind blowing loose sand from the backshore zone into the sea. This will be parti-

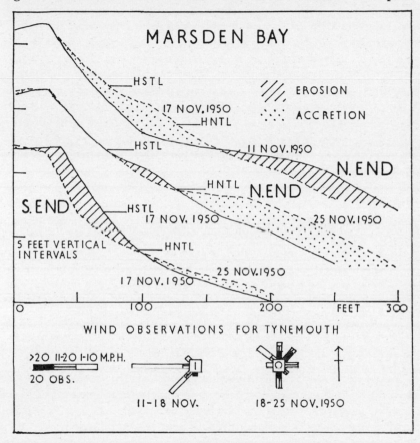

Fig. 6–6. Profiles of Marsden Bay, Co. Durham to show the effect of onshore and offshore winds.

cularly effective where the beach is backed by dunes and on tideless beaches where the sand is not damped by the tide at high water and is therefore more easily blown into the water by the offshore wind. This effect was observed on the tideless beaches of the Mediterranean where a fairly wide expanse of sand was exposed above the water line. This sand was protected to a certain extent by a hard salt crust which prevented the wind from blowing the sand beneath into the sea. Measurements showed that a 24 m.p.h. wind blew 95 grams of sand per ft. width of beach into the sea in 1 min. This caused accretion in the shallow water.

The wind sometimes blows along the shore rather than on or offshore and under these conditions it will tend to set up currents acting along the shore. Short waves may be generated which, because they are short in length, will not be strongly refracted and will therefore approach the shore at a very oblique angle. Both these oblique waves and the long-shore currents will cause considerable movement of material alongshore, particularly when the material is thrown into suspension by the waves, and can be moved by the wind generated currents as a result. Shepard (1950)[2] points out the importance of wind stress in the generation of longshore currents but states that it is difficult to separate currents due to this cause from currents generated by wave action directly. When he made observations calm days were chosen for preference, because the wind did not then affect the movement of the floats used for the observation of the surface currents or the triplanes used for current measurement at depth.

Summary

Full scale surveys have shown that natural beaches respond in a similar way to model beaches to onshore and offshore winds. The former, both by generating short, high seas and by giving rise to seaward currents, cause erosion on the upper foreshore. Offshore winds, which are usually accompanied by long swells, cause accretion on most occasions on the upper foreshore. Alongshore winds are significant in assisting the transport of material laterally along the coast.

3. *COASTAL DUNES*

When the wind is blowing onshore it has already been shown to be destructive in the shallow water by generating seaward currents. On the exposed part of the beach it is also likely to be destructive. At low water sand is exposed to the air and dries, it can then be blown off the beach by onshore winds, where under suitable conditions, it will accumulate to form coastal dunes. Such dunes will form most readily where a wide expanse of sand is exposed at low water, providing suitable material for the wind to carry inland. They will only form where the relief inland is suitable for the deposition of sand; thus dunes are unlikely to form where high cliffs occur immediately behind the beach as the wind cannot blow the sand on to the shore at these points. Where the ground behind the beach is low lying the sand can be blown inland to accumulate in dunes. The character of the dunes will vary according to their position in relation to the wind régime; on the west coast of Britain the sand can be blown inland by the prevailing and dominant winds which come from a south-westerly quarter, but on the east coast the sand can only be blown off the beach by the occasional easterly winds, the resulting dunes are therefore different. Those on the west coast show a greater tendency to form at right-angles to the wind direction and are often more extensive than those on the east coast.

One of the most significant differences between the dunes of the coast and those of the desert is the presence of vegetation on many of the former and the lack of it on the latter. The part played by vegetation is very important in the character of many coastal dunes. It plays an important part in the stabilization of the dune and also promotes its growth by providing a trap for the wind blown sand. There is a definite order of colonization by plants of developing dunes; this may differ slightly from place to place and it exerts an important influence on the character of the dune area. The most important dune plants are the grasses which flourish in loose sand. Of these marram grass (*Ammophila arenaria*) is the best known, this grass only grows well when it is being continually covered by fresh wind blown sand. Other grasses which are important dune builders are *Agropyron junceum* and *Elymus arenaria*. Some of the plants can withstand a certain amount of immersion in salt water, *Agropyron* can withstand rather more salt water than *Elymus* and therefore is frequently the first colonizer of shingle or sand ridges near the limit of high spring tides, and itself helps to trap sand to form the embryo dune. The marram follows it and grows well as long as sand is being added to the dune but when the dune becomes stabilized the marram dies off and its place is taken by such plants as Sea Buckthorn (*Hippophae rhamnoides*) and Dewberry (*Rubus caesius*) or Elder (*Sambucus nigra*) and many other plants grow as a soil begins to develop.

The southern part of the Lincolnshire coast illustrates the various phases of coastal dune development on a shore which is building out.[3] The beach here is wide and sandy, providing plenty of material at low tide to blow on to the dunes during easterly winds. There are two major dune ridges on this coast one of which is much older than the other; the inner one was frontal in 1779 and the outer ridge has developed since 1824,[4] and is probably only about ninety years old, while newer dunes can be watched in process of formation in front of the second main dune ridge at the present time (see fig. 8–4 (*b*), p. 259). The oldest ridge and the second main dune ridge shown in fig. 6–7 are both fully stabilized and colonized by mature vegetation, only on the outer foredunes, which are actively growing, are the typical dune plants to be found. The earliest colonizer on these dunes is *Cakile maritima* (Sea Rocket), and *Salsola kali* (Prickly Saltwort), which will colonize small wind-blown accumulations of sand

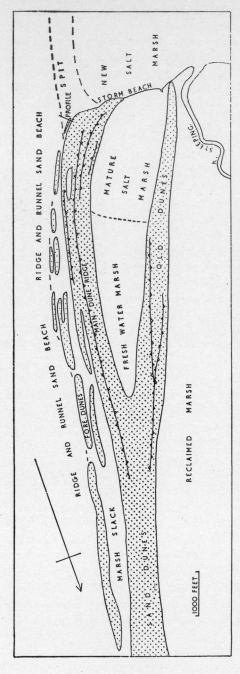

Fig. 6–7. Dune pattern at Gibraltar Point, Lincolnshire.

which have collected in the lee of some obstacle. On this beach a large amount of flustra collects near the high water level and this facilitates the accumulation of sand. The lowest level at which vegetation will colonize growing sand accumulation is about 12·25 ft. O.D. (Liverpool) where the mean high spring tide level is 10·9 ft. O.D. The height range of *Salsola kali* is between 12·25 and about 15 ft., at heights above about 14 ft. O.D. *Agropyron junceum* and *Ammophila arenaria* take over from *Salsola kali* and induce further upward dune growth. Under favourable conditions dune growth can be rapid. Fig. 6–8 shows that over 5 ft. of sand accumulated over a period of six years on the foredunes at Gibraltar Point, Lincolnshire, over a considerable horizontal distance. At higher levels *Elymus arenaria* grows in clumps. These plants have an important effect in helping to bind together the sand by their complex root system and thus they help to protect the dune from erosion. If the vegetation is weakened

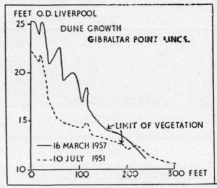

Fig. 6–8. Dune growth at Gibraltar Point, Lincolnshire.

for any reason, as by the trampling of people walking over the dunes, sand is exposed to the wind and the loose grains are blown away and in extreme cases blow-outs may occur. This will break up the even line of the dune crest and alter the form of the dunes. Dunes form an important protection to the coast if the hinterland is low lying as will be considered in detail in chapter 9.

(a) Types of coastal dunes

The variety of form and extent of coastal dunes is great; Smith (1954)[5] gives the height range from less than 10 ft. to over 200 ft. with a width of less than 100 ft. inland to many miles. The distribution of coastal dunes is very wide; they are found along much of the Atlantic coast of America, along the coast of Texas, on the Pacific coast they occupy $\frac{1}{3}$ of the coast of Oregon and considerable parts of the Washington and Californian coasts. In Europe dunes are widespread along the north coast of Germany, the coasts of Denmark, Belgium and north France and the Bay of Biscay. They are more scattered round the coast of Britain and the Mediterranean. Many other coasts also have dunes such as the desert coast of Peru, parts of Australia and the northern part of the North Island of New Zealand.

The main types of coastal dunes may be listed as follows according to Smith (1954):

1. Foredunes—mounds up to 10 ft. high adjacent and parallel to the beach.
2. U-shaped or parabolic dunes—arcuate sand ridges with open end toward the beach.
3. Barchans or crescentic dunes—steep slip-off slope on lee side facing away from the beach.
4. Transverse dune ridges—these trend parallel or oblique to the shore and are elongated perpendicular to the dominant winds. Their form is asymmetrical with steep lee slope and gentle windward slope.
5. Longitudinal dunes—these are elongated parallel to the wind direction and extend oblique or perpendicular to the shore and are symmetrical in form.
6. Blow-outs—these are hollows or troughs cutting into dunes of the previous types, large mounds with steep lee slopes occur landward of the larger blow-outs.
7. Attached dunes—these depend on some obstacle round which sand accumulates.

Of these groups the first and second are the most common types on many coasts. The colonization of the first type has already been mentioned, the second type will now be considered.

(b) U-dunes and their orientation

A study of the orientation of dunes in relation to the wind direction has recently been published by Landsberg (1956),[6] while Jennings has suggested slight modifications (1957).[7] The type of dune considered is probably the most common type in the British Isles and Europe and on part of the coast of America. Before considering their relationship to the wind forming and modifying them the chief characteristics and method of formation of parabolic or U-dunes may be mentioned. The part played by vegetation in the formation of the dunes is an important one. In its early stages the dune is an oval accumulation which may have a slip face on the lee side if it is moving fast, marram will be established on the front face but will be fairly sparce. The vegetation helps to anchor the flanks of the dune which tend as a result to drag behind the movement of the centre. This is the reverse of the movement of a desert dune where the flanks travel fastest, forming the horns typical of a barchan in areas where the wind is unidirectional. Dunes in this early stage are found at Forvie in Scotland and on the Danish coast at Raabjerg Mile near Skagen. The stages of evolution are shown in fig. 6–9. The mass of the dune diminishes by removal from the centre. During this phase, in which erosion is dominant, almost the whole surface of the dune becomes vegetated. The U-shape is now clearly seen opening towards the dominant wind direction. A small zone of bare sand may, however, occur near the forward edge of the dune facing up-wind with a very steep crest line. In time the dune becomes completely vegetated and gradually elongates its flanks by moving slowly down-wind in the centre, the erosion face is now eliminated. Sometimes the front face of the dune breaks through completely by the formation of a blow-out near the leading edge which

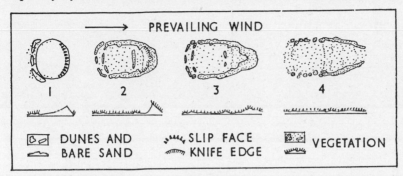

FIG. 6–9. U-dune formation. (After Landsberg.)

is least protected from the wind; the dune now consists of its two trailing flanks while a new dune forms in front, giving an *en echelon* pattern to the dune field. This final phase of the U-dune is not found in Britain or Denmark but does occur in Germany.

In order to relate the direction of the flanks of the U-dunes to the wind direction it is necessary to analyse the wind observations. Landsberg used a slightly modified form of the vector diagram method suggested by Bagnold (1951).[8] An earlier method of analysing wind is that used by Musset (1923)[9] in which he used the formula $c = \sum_{j=1}^{10} n\,j$, where n is the number of occasions a particular wind was recorded and j is the Beaufort force. Schou (1945)[10] modified this formula by using only winds of Force 4 or more on the Beaufort scale and calculating c for each vector of 45 deg. This formula does not take into account the fact, as shown by Bagnold (1941),[11] that the sand-moving power of the wind depends on the cube of the wind velocity above 10 m.p.h. A formula was used taking this into account which gives the vector terms as $b = s \sum_{j=3}^{12} n_j\,(v_j - V_t)^3$, where s is a scaling factor of 10^{-3}, j refers to the Beaufort force and V_t is 10 m.p.h., n is the number of occasions and v

is the wind speed in m.p.h. These figures calculated for all vectors can be drawn as a continuous figure to give the mean wind direction of all vectors. The second of the two formulae gives better results in all four examples, only two of the areas studied in Britain and Denmark give unsatisfactory results. In one of the two, the Culbin sands area of

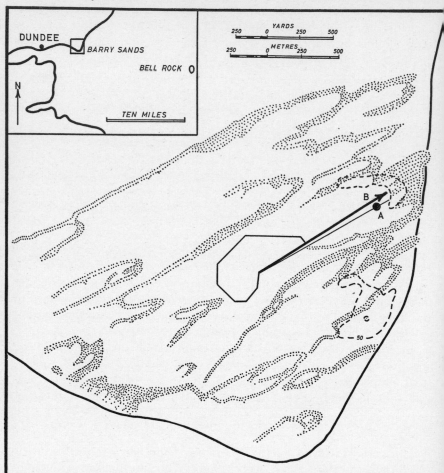

FIG. 6–10. (*a*) The relationship between dune orientation and wind direction. Sands of Barry. (After Landsberg.)

Morayshire both the techniques give a north-west wind, while Steers (1937)[12] has observed that the prevailing winds in the dune area is south-west, the figures used cannot, therefore, be typical of the dune area. One of the conclusions of this study is that the wind régime as defined by the second formula of Bagnold is a major factor in the orientation of U-dunes (see fig. 6–10a) the local siting of the observing stations and variations of local winds over the dune area affect the results in some instances.

More recently Jennings (1957)[7] has applied the formulae to dunes on King Island, Tasmania (see fig. 6–10b). He found that particularly for the dunes on the leeshore the relationship between wind direction and dune orientation was much closer if only the onshore winds were used for the construction of the vector diagram of wind direction. These winds have a clear advantage as far as dune formation is concerned in that the sand is derived from the beach so that only the onshore winds have access to it for dune building purposes. Where erosion is considered it may be argued that the vegetation cover is less complete on the windward side so that blow-outs are more likely to occur with onshore winds. There is still room for improvements in the technique; for example, the wind data are rarely available for the immediate vicinity of the dunes and the significant wind is that near the ground, which is rarely measured. Irregularities of the solid rock relief also affect the dune orientation as shown by the south-eastern part of King Island. On the whole the U-dune, which are amongst the most common type of coastal dune, can be related to the direction of the winds responsible for their formation.

(c) Transverse and Longitudinal dunes

Cooper (1958)[13] has recently described the coastal dunes of Oregon and Washington where, unlike most areas, parabolic dunes are rare, but 'transverse' and 'oblique' dune patterns are found. The latter type might be placed in the fifth group of Smith's classification as they have much in common with longitudinal dunes. He also mentions another type of dune referred to as 'precipitation ridge'. All these dunes differ from most of those already mentioned in that vegetation is not involved in their form and growth. This is partly because the main dune forming plant, marram grass, is not native to this part; it is only since the introduction of this grass that well stabilized foredunes have developed along the coast. Marram was introduced to San Francisco in 1869 and was brought to Coos Bay, Oregon in 1910.

The transverse dunes characteristic of much of the sand dune coast of Oregon and Washington are formed by the summer winds which blow mainly from the north and north-west. These dunes have long, gentle windward slopes of 3–12 deg. and steep slip face to leeward. There is a tendency for the distance between crests to increase inland over the range 25–50 m. (82–164 ft.). The ridges move under the influence of the summer winds while they tend to be destroyed by the south-westerly winds of the winter season, which is also the wet one. They form where the ground is reasonably level and where the sand supply is

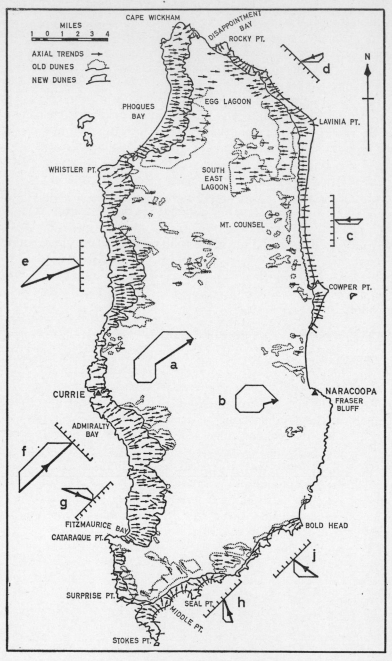

FIG. 6–10. (*b*) The relationship between dune orientation and wind direction. King Island, Tasmania. (After Jennings.)

adequate. This type of dune is found all over the world where suitable conditions prevail, one of these is the constancy of the wind direction for at least one season of the year. The direction of this wind is closely parallel to the lee projections which extend down-wind from the higher parts of the transverse crests. The trend of the main transverse dune ridge is almost perpendicular to the dune forming wind.

The second major type discussed is the oblique ridge, these only form where the sand is plentiful over a wide area and is fully exposed to both the seasonal winds, north-west to north in summer and south-west in winter. The alignment of the dune ridge is dependent on the relative importance of the two winds and lies along the mean direction of summer and winter winds, greater weight being given to the summer winds. The position of this type of ridge is more or less fixed and they are about 200–300 m. (655–985 ft.) apart with crests extending for over 1000 m. (3279 ft.). The summer winds tend to elongate the ridge while the winter winds which blow almost at right-angles to the direction of the ridge drive sand on to it, thereby adding to its bulk.

It is suggested that this type is ultimately stabilized to form a 'precipitation ridge' at the forest edge. This is the name used to describe the active slip face which forms in a mass of sand driven towards the forest edge. A large mass of sand is involved in the advancing precipitation ridge which gradually drives over and destroys the forest in its path.

Summary

Coastal dunes differ from desert dunes in the important part played by vegetation. The most significant plants are the sand loving grasses, particularly marram (*Ammophila arenaria*). The south Lincolnshire coast illustrates the stages of dune growth and colonization; early plants are *Cakile maritima* and *Salsola kali* followed by the grasses.

Dunes may assume a number of forms, but the parabolic or U-dune are amongst the most common. The orientation of these dunes is controlled by the velocity vector of the sand carrying winds.

In areas where vegetation does not play an important part transverse and oblique ridge forms are found, for example on the coast of Oregon and California, the former are formed by the summer winds, the latter depend on winds from two directions; they are larger and more stable in position.

REFERENCES

[1]King, C. A. M., 1953, The relationship between wave incidence, wind direction and beach changes at Marsden Bay, Co. Durham. *Trans. and Papers Inst. Brit. Geog.* **19**, pp. 13–23.
[2]Shepard, F. P. and Inman, D. L., 1950, Nearshore circulation related to bottom topography and wave refraction. *Trans. Am. Geoph. Un.* **31**, 2, pp. 196–212.

B.C.–Q

[3]Barnes, F. A. and King, C. A. M., 1951, A preliminary survey at Gibraltar Point, Lincolnshire. *Bird Obs. and Field Res. St. Gib. Pt. Lincs. Rep.* pp. 41–59.

[4]Barnes, F. A. and King, C. A. M., 1957, The spit at Gibraltar Point, Lincolnshire. *East Midland Geog.* **8,** pp. 22–31.

[5]Smith, H. T. U., 1954, Coast dunes. Coastal Geog. Conf., Feb. 1954 *Off. Naval Research.* pp. 51–56.

[6]Landsberg, S. Y., 1956, The orientation of dunes in Britain and Denmark in relation to the wind. *Geog. Journ.* **122,** pp. 176–89.

[7]Jennings, J. N., 1957, On the orientation of parabolic or U-dunes. *Geog. Journ.* **123,** pp. 474–80.

[8]Bagnold, R. A., 1951, Sand formations in south Arabia. *Geog. Journ.* **117,** pp. 77–86.

[9]Musset, M., 1923, Über Sandwanderung, Dunenbildung und Veränderung an der Hinterpommerischen Küste. *Zeitsch. fur Bauw.*

[10]Schou, A., 1945, Det Marine Forland. *Folia Geog. Dan.* **4.**

[11]Bagnold, R. A., 1941, The physics of blown sand and desert dunes.

[12]Steers, J. A., 1937, The Culbin sands and Burghead Bay. *Geog. Journ.* **90,** pp. 498–528.

[13]Cooper, W. S., 1958, Coastal sand dunes of Oregon and Washington. *Geol. Soc. Am. Memoir* **72.**

CHAPTER 7

CLASSIFICATION OF BEACHES AND COASTS

1. *CLASSIFICATION OF BEACHES*

THE classification of beaches can be made primarily on the character of the beach material, this gives the two major groups of shingle and sand beaches. This basis of classification is justified because the two materials react differently to the waves and the profiles typical of each material exert an influence on the waves which attack them. Further subdivision can be made most satisfactorily on the basis of the beach profile. A classification which will be justified in more detail in chapter 10 is given as follows:

1. Shingle beaches
2. Sand beaches (*a*) Tidal
                      i. Smooth profile
                     ii. Ridged profile
           (*b*) Tideless
                      i. Barred profile—straight bars
                                   —crescentic bars
                    ii. Smooth profile

The main characteristics of these different beach types will be described briefly and specific examples named. There is much less variety in shingle beach profiles than in those of sand beaches. Shingle beaches are nearly always steep and descend into fairly deep water with a step frequently forming where the waves break. Compared to sand grains the pebbles on a shingle beach are very well rounded and are usually well sorted. Their median diameter rarely lies near the lower limit of the shingle grade. There are, however, a few beaches which are built of material which actually comes within the coarse sand classification but which behave much more like shingle beaches than sand beaches. An example of such a beach is found at Gateville on the north-east coast of the Cherbourg Peninsula where the beach gradient is about 1 : 10 and the median diameter of the material varies between 3·25 mm. and 1·35 mm. from the low tide zone to the high water level respectively, the mid-tide median diameter is 1·60 mm. Another beach formed of this intermediate size material is found at Loe Bar on the south coast of Cornwall.

A more typical shingle beach which may be taken as normal is that of Chesil beach, Dorset, or Orford Ness on the coast of Suffolk. Both of these beaches are steep with gradients as steep as 1 : 2 at times. After spring tides the profile of the beach is normally a smooth curve which extends for a considerably greater distance above the high water level than on a sand beach. The reason for this will be discussed in chapter 9 (see pp. 280, 281). The form of the profile as far as the step is a curve, concave upwards. The waves break directly on to the step so that the form of the beach above this level is shaped by the swash and backwash. On a shingle beach, owing to the steep gradients and deep water off-shore, surf is rarely present. Ripples do not form on shingle beaches but beach cusps are usually much better developed on shingle beaches than they are on sand beaches, although they may be very conspicuous features on beaches which are formed of a mixture of shingle and sand.

While relatively few beaches are entirely shingle down to the lowest spring tide level there are a large number of beaches which are pre-dominantly of sand but which have a small amount of shingle which accumulates usually at about high water level; these beaches may be classified as sand beaches because the greater part of their width at low water is sandy. Most of the coasts of the British Isles have a considerable tidal range so that nearly all British beaches, which are predominantly of sand, fall into the first main category of sand beaches, that is the tidal sand beach. There is a wide difference in profile between various tidal beaches which allow further subdivision into those with a smooth profile and those with an irregular profile on the foreshore exposed at low water.

The beaches with a smooth profile vary in gradient with the coarse-ness of their sand, but in general such beaches have a smooth parabolic profile which is steeper in the upper part near high tide level and flattens out towards low tide level, where the material tends to be rather finer than it is near the high tide level. Most of the beaches exposed to the open ocean have a smooth profile; the beaches of Devon and Cornwall provide good examples of this type, such as Woolacombe beach. The beaches of the Gower Peninsula in South Wales and on the west coast of Ireland are also smooth in profile. The beach in Rhossili Bay, Gower, may be taken as an example of this type of beach. The bay is 3 miles long, and has a wide sandy beach, backed at the south end by low boulder-clay cliffs, and these provide a little shingle, forming a bank about 10 ft. high at the top of the beach. This extends from 2 ft. below high spring tide level upwards to the limit of wave action. The shingle becomes more rounded and dies out towards the north end of the bay which is backed by sand dunes. The beach is formed of fine sand of median diameter 0·23 mm. and forms a firm smooth surface, which sometimes has low ripples about 1 cm. high and about 1 ft. long. The tidal range on this beach is large, being about 26 ft. at spring tide and 12 ft. at neap tide. Owing to the large spring tide range the width of the beach at low spring tide is about 2,000 ft. Its mean gradient is 1 : 76, but the profile is concave, having a slope of 1 : 55 for 400 ft. below the steep shingle bank while seaward of this point the gradient is 1 : 88·5 ft. in an almost straight line to low water mark. Profiles surveyed in three successive years on this beach show extremely constant gradients with the exception of the zone just below the shingle bank. The profiles are shown in fig. 7–1.

In contrast to the very smooth profile of Rhossili and other beaches in this category the ridge and runnel beaches may be considered. Beaches characteristic of this type are found at Blackpool in Lancashire (see fig. 7–2); the Normandy beaches where landings were made in 1944, the beaches near Le Touquet in France and those of Brancaster and parts of the Lincolnshire coast are also similar. These beaches are characterized by ridges of sand lying more or less parallel to the coast and separated by runnels which are exposed on the beach as the tide falls. Deposits of mud are found at times in the runnels, and there may be a small amount of shingle near high tide level. The height of the ridges on the beach may vary from a few inches to a maximum of over 5 ft. between the crest of one ridge and the trough to landward of it. A further subdivision of the beaches in this category may be made according to the relationship between the general direction of the coast line and the direction of the ridges. On some beaches, such as Blackpool, the ridges lie parallel to the coast line, in others, such as on the Lincolnshire coast, the ridges run at a small angle to the general direction of the coast. All the beaches in this group, however, are situated in areas which are not exposed to the full force of the ocean waves, such as the Irish Sea and the English Channel east of the Cherbourg Peninsula, and the North Sea. They are mostly areas where the tidal range approaches 20 ft. at spring tide. The number of ridges of both types varies with the tidal range and sand grade but is usually between two and four. Often the sand of such beaches is fine, that of Blackpool is 0·22 mm., but it may be quite coarse; for example on some ridged beaches, as at Druridge Bay, Northumberland, the upper beach is composed of sand of median diameter of 0·84 mm., while the ridge nearer low tide is formed of sand having a median diameter of 0·40 mm. The details of the character, position and movement of this type of ridge will be considered in chapter 10 (see pp. 337–348).

When considering the profiles of tideless beaches the under-water profile must naturally be considered, as the water level is more or less constant. On the tidal beach the normal profile appears to be smooth, while the profile which is not in equilibrium is ridged. On a tideless coast

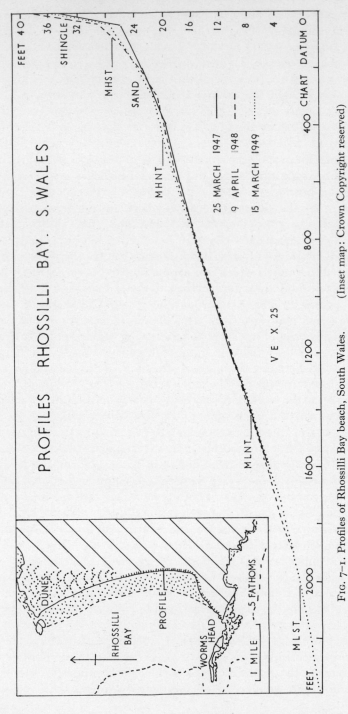

FIG. 7-1. Profiles of Rhossilli Bay beach, South Wales.   (Inset map: Crown Copyright reserved)

the reverse appears to be true; here many of the beaches appear to have submarine bars, while relatively few have smooth profiles. The exposure of the coast, again, appears to play an important part in the character of the beach. Where the exposure is limited, the normal tideless beach appears to have a profile characterized by a series of submarine bars. Examples of this type of beach are found in the Mediterranean Sea, the Baltic Sea and the Great Lakes of America, none of which are exposed to the longest ocean swells. The submarine bars typical of this beach category can be subdivided into two groups according to the form of the bars; on most open coasts the bars lie parallel to the coast, but in some

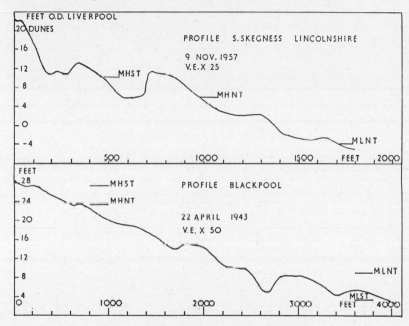

FIG. 7–2. Profiles of ridged sand beaches.

enclosed bays, such as some of those along the coast of Italy, the sub-marine bars have a crescentic form, with the points of the crescents facing inland.

On most of the beaches having submarine bars there are a series of bars, usually about three in number, whose crests are covered by in-creasing depths of water away from the shore. A beach typical of this group is that surveyed at Les Karentes, Aude, in the south of France. This beach profile, as shown in fig. 7–3, has three submarine bars on the profile extending to a depth of 20 ft. The bars are covered by 3·4 ft., 8·0 ft. and 14 ft. respectively, although profiles surveyed in other years still show three bars they are found in different positions on the beach

profile. The sand of this beach is of medium grade with a median diameter of 0·30 mm. The tidal range is very small; the spring range is 0·6 ft.
and the neap range 0·2 ft. Much greater changes in water level due to
variations in the strength and direction of the wind occur. If the bars

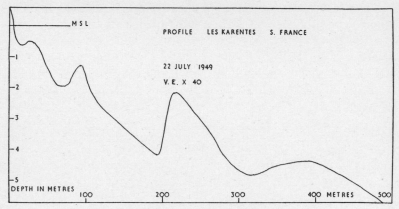

FIG. 7–3. Profile of a barred tideless beach.

are disregarded the general gradient of the beach is fairly flat; most
Mediterranean beaches are flatter than 1 : 70. The character of these
bars and the factors which govern their formation and movement will be
considered in more detail in chapter 10 (see pp. 331–337).

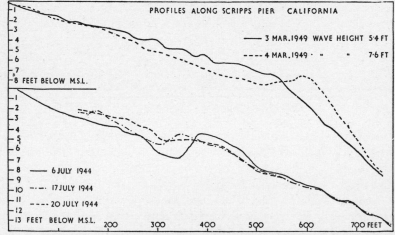

FIG. 7–4. Profiles of the Scripps beach in California to show bars and their removal.
(After Shepard, B.E.B.)

Beaches with a fairly small tidal range which are exposed to the open
ocean, such as some of the beaches of California, fall into the category

of smooth tideless beaches. The profile of Anaheim Bay, California, has a very smooth profile to a depth of 20 ft. below low water where the tidal range is of the order of 5 ft. On most Californian beaches, despite the rather small tidal range, the beaches are smooth at least at some times of the year. The mean tidal range between Ventura and Point Mugu is 3.7 ft., with an extreme range of 10.5 ft.[1] During the winter season or during storms, bars develop temporarily on the submarine profiles, but these are smoothed out by smaller waves subsequently as shown in fig. 7–4. The waves in the period 6–20 July 1944, were mostly 2 ft. high, only on one day was the maximum height of 4 ft. reached. The bars formed are probably similar to those found on tideless beaches.

Summary

Beaches may be classified firstly on the type of material into shingle and sand beaches. Further subdivision of sand beaches is based on the beach profile, which, as will be shown later (see pp. 329–353), depends to a considerable extent on the tidal régime. The tidal range is, therefore, taken as the factor on which sand beaches are subdivided. Further types are based on the form of the profile, the degree of irregularity being the criterion used.

2. CLASSIFICATION OF COASTS

No completely satisfactory classification of coasts has yet been proposed although many different ones have been put forward. There are two main groups of classification; some are purely descriptive while others are genetic. As the origin of the coastal type is of importance, a genetic form of subdivision is to be preferred, if it can be applied readily to a wide variety of coasts. Three main factors should be taken into account in devising any coastal classification; the form of the land surface against which the sea is resting is important, the movement of sea-level relative to the land is significant and the modifying effect of the marine processes must not be ignored. All three of these factors have been used by different authors in various proposed classifications.

The first of the three factors, the character of the land surface, was used by Suess (1888)[2] in his book *The face of the earth*. In this he proposed as the major groups of his classification, the well known 'Atlantic' and 'Pacific' coastal types. In the former the general trend of the land structures are supposed to run at right angles to the coastal margin, while in the Pacific type the structural lines run parallel to the coast. Such a dichotomy is clearly very generalized but it can be applied in a broad sense to most of the coasts of the Atlantic, while the general trend of the west coast of North and South America is parallel to the broad direction of the folds of the Rocky Mountains and Andes. This classification is not genetic in its approach to the problem and is too generalized to be of use for relatively small areas.

Most of the earlier classifications of coastal types were based on the relative movement of land and sea, giving the main coastal groups as those dependent on relative submergence of the land by the sea on the one hand, and emergence of the land from the sea on the other. Johnson[3] in his book on *Shore processes and shoreline development* published in 1919, used this classification and, following him, it has been much used since then. He was not, however, the first to put forward this dichotomy of coastal types. One of the first authors to recognize the effect of submergence on the coastal outline was Dana[4] in 1849. He recognized that the deeply embayed coast of Tahiti was the result of a rise of sea-level which drowned the valleys to form deep inlets. The great geomorphologist W. M. Davis[5] in 1898 and Gulliver[6] in the following year both used the distinction between submergence and emergence as the basis for their coastal classifications, although Suess (1888) and Richthofen (1886)[7] had earlier also used submergence and emergence as criteria for coastal description. Daly's (1934)[8] work on the glacial control of sea-level, in relation to the formation of coral atolls and other features, is also important because it drew attention to the oscillations of sea-level resulting from glacial advances and retreats during the recent geological past. This must clearly affect the position of sea-level relative to the land in a somewhat complex way, giving rise to considerable and relatively rapid changes.

The part played by the third major factor, the marine processes, was not recognized by Davis in his classification, so much as in his description of the cycle of marine erosion. In this, sequential stages of the various coastal types were deduced. This system of analysis had also been suggested by de Martonne[9] in 1909 in his text-book of physical geography, although he uses the terms relating to stages in the cycle rather differently from the way they are used by Davis; thus 'senility', according to de Martonne, was equivalent to the term 'maturity' as used by Davis. Some of the more important coastal classifications that have been proposed will be discussed briefly.

(a) D. W. Johnson

Perhaps the best known is that proposed by Johnson, which has already been mentioned. He enlarged the dichotomy of coastal types as put forward by the earlier workers in his classification of coasts, although he still retained, as his two major groups, coast lines of submergence and emergence. His new categories consist of neutral and compound

coasts; neutral coasts include those which are not mainly due to submergence or emergence such as delta shorelines, alluvial and outwash
plains and fault shorelines. The compound shorelines are those which
show features of two or more of the other three main categories. This
last group will include coasts which show features of both emergence and
submergence, as for example parts of the coast of eastern North America.
The coast here is characterized by a deeply embayed outline behind an
offshore barrier, which Johnson considers is a feature typical of an
emerged coast. Another example is the fjord coast of south-west New
Zealand which shows characteristics both of submerged glacial relief,
and the straightness and steepness of a typical fault coast, thus com-
bining groups one and three. Each of Johnson's main coastal type can be
further subdivided to give the following classification:

1. Submergence coasts
   i. Ria coasts
   ii. Fjord coasts

2. Emergence coasts (with barriers) coastal plain shoreline

3. Neutral coasts
   i delta coasts
   ii. alluvial plain coasts
   iii. outwash plain coasts
   iv. volcano coasts
   v. coral-reef coasts
   vi. fault coasts

4. Compound coasts—any combination of the above types. Examples
of these coastal types may be given as follows:
   1 (i) South-west Ireland—Dingle Bay
     (ii) West Norway—Sogne Fjord
   2 Baltic Sea
   3 (i) Mississippi delta coast
     (ii) North-west India
     (iii) Canterbury Plain, New Zealand
     (iv) Hawaii Islands
     (v) Great Barrier Reef, north-east Australia
     (vi) Parts of coast of North Island, New Zealand, near Wellington.

This classification has the advantage of being genetic in type but, if it
is applied strictly, it will be found that many coasts will fall into the
compound category. In the recent geological past there are very few
areas which have not been affected both by a rising and a falling sea-
level, as a result of the glacial control of sea-level. The recent date of the

major mountain building period of the Alpine orogeny has caused much crustal instability, resulting in the fairly recent uplift of considerable areas of the earth's crust. It is true that some areas show a predominance or either submergence or uplift, which will place them in one of Johnson's first two categories; the ria coast of south-west Ireland may be cited as an example, as this coast clearly shows the deep embayments which are the major criterion on which this coastal type is recognized. The fjord coasts are also often clearly recognizable but here the evidence of submergence is more doubtful, as it is theoretically possible for fjords to be eroded by glaciers below sea-level and to be drowned on the retreat of the ice without a rise of sea-level; Johnson himself recognized this possibility.

The second group of Johnson's classification is perhaps the least satisfactory; in his emergent category he recognizes only the emergence of a very flat gradient sea-floor which would give rise to a straight coast-line in plan, on which barrier beaches and islands develop as a result of the very gentle gradient of the coastal zone. The criteria by which such coasts are recognized are the barriers and dune covered low lying coast associated with coastal lagoons and salt marshes. Johnson does recognize that such features need not be restricted entirely to the type of coast of emergence which he envisaged; they may, for example, also form on a very flat coastal plain which has been slightly submerged. In this he anticipated a later criticism of this part of his classification. He did fail, however, to consider the possibility of the emergence of a steep coast; the inclusion of this type has been suggested by Putnam (1937)[10] who has discussed the development of a steep coast of emergence. In the limited interpretation of the emergent coastal type Johnson was following Davis and other earlier workers who also considered only the type of emergent coast having a very low offshore gradient. It has always been considered that emergent coasts will be straighter in outline than other coastal types, with the exception of fault coasts, but this need not necessarily be so. Where submarine canyons approach closely to the beach, an emergence of the land would lead to a more intricate coast-line in plan than the present coastal outline, this applies to part of the coast of California.

(b) F. P. Shepard

A more recent classification is proposed by Shepard [11] in 1937 which is also discussed in his book *Submarine Geology*[12] in 1948. Shepard abandons the previous dichotomy of submergence and emergence, as he considers that emergent coasts can be ignored. The basis of his classification is the distinction between coasts that have been shaped mainly by terrestrial agencies and those that have been modified by marine processes. His classification may, therefore, be considered as belonging to the third group which considers the function of marine processes as of major significance because they determine to which major group the coast under consideration will belong. The subdivisions of Shepard's classification are detailed, making the groups into which the major categories are divided numerous. This makes the classification more complex than the earlier ones which have been mentioned but it also enables a more detailed description of the coast to be given in the classification. Like that of Johnson, this newer one is genetic in type, taking into account both the terrestrial and marine processes. Before discussing the classification further it may be given in tabular form:

I. Coasts shaped primarily by non-marine agencies. Primary or youthful shoreline.

   A. Shaped by terrestrial agencies of erosion and drowned

      1. Ria coast

         i. Parallel trend between structure and coast—Dalmatian type

         ii. Transverse trend between structure and coast—South-West Ireland type

      2. Drowned glacial erosion coast

         i. Fjord coast—drowned glacial valleys

         ii. Glacial trough coast

   B. Shaped by terrestrial deposition

      1. River deposition

         i. Delta coast—convex out

         ii. Alluvial plain coast—straight

      2. Glacial deposition

         i. Partially submerged moraine

         ii. Drumlins—often partially drowned

      3. Wind deposition

         i. Dune coast—Landes

      4. Vegetation coast

         i. Mangrove coast

   C. Shaped by volcanic activity.

      1. Volcanic deposition coast—lava flow—convex out

      2. Volcanic explosion coast—concave out

   D. Shaped by diastrophism

      1. Fault coasts or fault scarp coasts

      2. Fold coasts, due to monoclinal flexures

II. Coasts shaped primarily by marine agencies. Secondary or mature coastlines.

   A. Shaped by marine erosion
      1. Coasts made more regular by marine erosion—cliffs
      2. Coasts made less regular by marine erosion—cliffs

   B. Shaped by marine deposition
      1. Coasts made more regular (straightened) by marine deposition—barriers and spits
      2. Coasts prograded by marine deposition—cuspate forelands
      3. Shorelines with barriers and spits—concavities facing ocean
      4. Organic marine deposition—coral coasts

This classification is very comprehensive and has much to recommend it, although the lack of a category for emergent coasts is deplored by Cotton (1954)[13] and is a disadvantage. The criticism of the emergent category in Johnson's classification is not a reason for entirely abandoning this coastal category, as some coasts are clearly of this type, although not many show the features which Johnson and earlier workers associate with this type of coast. Raised beaches and other direct evidence of coastal uplift, in areas which are recovering isostatically from the removal of an ice load, are present, for example, in the Baltic and parts of North America.

Another difficulty in the application of this coastal classification to actual examples of coasts, is to determine the precise moment when a coast has been sufficiently altered by marine agencies to allow it to be classified in the second major group. The classification cuts across the commonly used system of cyclic description. Coasts can be described in terms of the state of development by marine processes, from an initial form which is defined in the classification. This new classification uses what would normally be considered as the youthful stage of development as the second group of the classification, so that a coast which is put into the second group, automatically loses any reference to its initial form at the beginning of the cycle, which is running its course at the present time. This is a disadvantage as far as the description of the coast is concerned. An example of this difficulty may be considered by reference to the coast of south-east Iceland (see fig. 7–5)[14]. This coast is one which has been built out by rapid fluvio-glacial deposition of outwash from the glaciers draining the southern side of Vatnajökull. The outbuilding has been assisted by a fall in base-level, which is clearly shown by well marked raised beaches farther east along the coast. A barrier beach has been built by the waves along the greater part of this coast, which is often separated from the outwash plain or sandur, as it is called locally, by a shallow lagoon. It would appear, therefore, that this is a coast which has been straightened

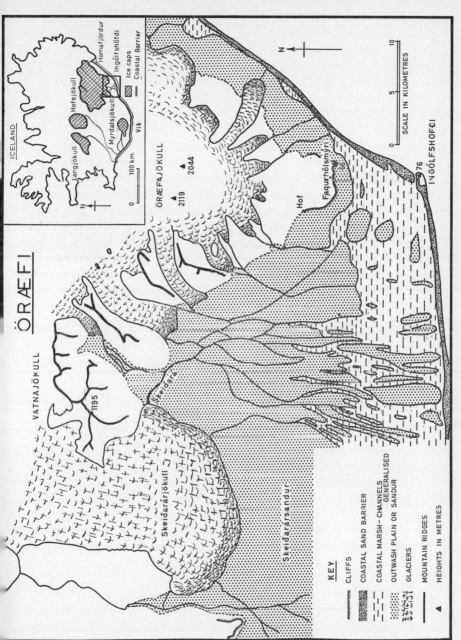

Fig. 7–5. Map of the coastal barrier of south-east Iceland.

by marine deposition in the form of an offshore barrier; it would as a result be placed in the second group of the classification under group II B 1. This does not, however, give any indication of the nature of the land surface behind the beach; in order to describe this, the coast would have to be put in the first category, in which it would appear in the subdivision B(coasts shaped by terrestrial deposition), subsection 2 i, that is, coasts shaped by glacial outwash. Whichever category this coast is placed in according to the classification of Shepard, some of its essential features must be omitted. On the other hand it would be placed in the neutral or compound group of Johnson's classification, as an outwash plain coastline; this does not describe it any more satisfactorily than Shepard's classification, unless barriers are definitely associated with the development of an outwash plain coastline, which Johnson does not state to be the case and which is probably not true.

In coastal types where the marine processes have modified the original character of the coast so much that this is difficult to recognize, then Shepard's classification has the merit that such a coast can be placed in the second group and no unwarranted assumptions concerning its original state need be made. Owing to the instability of the sea-level and mobility of the land in the present period, such coasts are likely to be rare.

(c) C. A. Cotton

A different dichotomy has been suggested by Cotton (1918)[15] which he has modified and added to at later dates. He has put forward a new classification (1952)[16] in which the two major divisions are between coasts of stable regions and those of mobile regions; although he does not feel that the type dependent on submergence and emergence should be entirely dropped, he does consider that this criterion should be relegated to second place. Many of his examples have been taken from New Zealand which has been undergoing, and still is affected by, earth movements along parts of its coasts. The main distinction between the two coastal groups is, that those areas which are stable have only been affected by oscillations of sea-level, while in the mobile areas the coast itself has been uplifted or depressed and perhaps warped, either transverse to, or parallel to, the direction of the coast. The major significance of this distinction is that all stable coasts have been affected in the recent past by the positive rise of sea-level, as a result of deglaciation, to the extent of about 300 ft. On the other hand mobile areas may have been elevated themselves to an equal or greater extent and thus show direct evidence of uplift or emergence. This does not mean, however, that all stable coasts will be coasts of submergence or that all mobile coasts will have emerged. There are other categories in both major classes which need not show any indication of changes of base-level; in coasts of stable regions, for example, there may be delta coasts or alluvial coasts. Thus a classification is arrived at having the following major groups:

A. Coasts of stable regions. These are all drowned by the recent submergence, but in reality compound.
   1. Dominated by features of the most recent submergence
   2. Dominated by some features of an earlier emergence
   3. Miscellaneous—volcanic, fjord, etc.

B. Coasts of mobile regions. These are all compound but are affected by diastrophism as well as eustatic changes of base-level.
   1. Coasts on which the most recent change has been of submergence however caused.
   2. Coasts on which recent diastrophic movements have resulted in emergence.
   3. Fault and monoclinal coasts.
   4. Miscellaneous coasts—volcanic, fjord, etc.

This classification may be considered partly as a subdivision of the all embracing compound group of Johnson, thus it is recognized that it is the last major change of base-level which is the most important in defining the coastal type, and this may be combined with other features such as faulting or flexure to give different coastal types.

The question of marginal flexure has been considered by Bourcart (1950)[17] and may have a significant bearing on coastal classification if it can be shown to have a widespread application. The result, as far as the coastal type is concerned, depends on whether the hinge-line lies seaward or inland of the present position of the coast. If it lies inland the coast will appear to be submerged, but if it lies seaward the coastline will appear as emergent. The general hypothesis suggests that the land tends to rise while the sea-floor is tending to subside. Thus the inland area may show evidence of a falling base-level in the development of terraces and other features of rejuvenation, while the coastline will show signs of submergence, such as drowned valleys, and the water of the offshore zone will deepen.

The problem of the way in which the base-level varies is very relevant to the problem of coastal classification as it is to the whole concept of a marine cycle of erosion. According to the classification of Davis and Johnson and others, which are based entirely upon the initial form of the land surface against which the sea comes to rest at the beginning of the supposed cycle, any modification of the coastline must be described by reference to stages in the cycle. To allow a cycle or even a partial cycle to run its course, however, implies that still-stands of base-level are possible, and indeed are the normal type of movement associated with a changing base-level. It is this concept of a changing base-level consisting of periods of rapid change alternating with periods of still-stand which has been questioned recently in a new classification of coasts, which has been put forward by Valentin (1952).[18]

(d) H. Valentin

The basis of the new classification of Valentin is the advance or retreat of the coast at the present time. The dichotomy on which his classification is based is that of advancing coasts in one category and retreating coasts in the other major group. The cause of the advance or retreat may be due to two possible factors so that the classification can be further subdivided on this basis. Before discussing his classification and its implications in more detail the different categories will be outlined:

I. Coasts which are advancing
   A. Coasts of emergence—coasts on newly emerged sea-floor provided the new coastline has not been eroded back to the original line.
   B. Outbuilding coasts
      1. Organic deposition
         i. Mangroves
         ii. Corals
      2. Marine deposition coasts
         i. Barrier coasts
         ii. Cuspate forelands and spits
      3. Delta and outwash coasts

(All these features can only be placed in category I if simultaneous subsidence does not counteract the effect of the outbuilding.)

II. Coasts which are retreating
   A. Coasts of submergence
      1. Drowned glacial relief
         i. Fjords
         ii. Fjards
         iii. Moraines, drumlins and outwash.
      2. Drowned river valleys
         i. Young fold
         ii. Old fold
         iii. Flat
   B. Coasts of retrogression—coasts eroded back to a continuous line of cliffs, provided a reversal of process has not caused deposition in front of the cliff.

The emphasis in this classification is on the changes which the coast is undergoing at the present time, rather than on the initial form of the coast before modification by the sea has had a marked effect on its form. An important implication of this newer approach is the recognition that marine forces are continually active and influence the coast even during the changes in base-level which should, on the basis of the older classification, initiate a new cycle of erosion on a new coastal type. According to the analysis of Valentin the possibility is left open, that changes of base-level are continually operating and that still-stands are the exception rather than the rule. A study of a large number of tide-gauge records has led Valentin to the conclusion that changes in sea-level are always taking place. This is likely to be so under the present conditions when glacier shrinkage is continuing on an almost world-wide scale, causing an eustatic rise of sea-level of about 1–2 mm. per year (Valentin 1953).[19] The same reasoning concerning the possibility of still-stand can be applied to the whole of the Pleistocene period, with the possible exception of the longer and warmer interglacial periods; during the major part of the quarternary time fluctuation of glaciers and with them the sea-level must have been taking place. There is, on the other hand, good evidence that still-stands can and have taken place, allowing such features as wave-cut benches to be eroded, some of which now form raised beaches. The erosion of these features requires a relatively constant or slowly rising sea-level over a long period of time (see pp. 292, 293). A good example of these features are the raised beaches on part of the western coast of Scotland. It has been suggested by Wright (1937)[20] that some of these raised beaches were cut during a period when both land and sea-level were rising together. Sea-level was rising eustatically due to melting ice, while the land was rising isostatically due to recovery following the removal of ice load. An apparent stability of base-level would be achieved when these two causes of base-level change were acting together in the same direction and at the same rate, thus allowing a wave-cut bench to be formed.

The rate at which coastal processes are acting in an area determines whether evidence of cyclic changes can be found in that particular region. Where the changes are rapid wave-cut benches and other features can develop rapidly; there is also the danger, however, that such features will not long survive subaerial erosion to provide evidence of the still-stand of base-level.

Valentin's classification can be expressed by means of a diagram on which each of four axes represents one of the four possibilities, coastal erosion and submergence on the negative side and coastal outbuilding and emergence on the positive side. On the diagram in fig. 7–6, *OA* represents accumulation increasing outwards from *O*, *OE* represents emergence or falling base-level, increasing in rate of fall from O; OD represents coastal erosion while OS represents submergence or a rising base-level. Thus a line ZZ' passing through O indicates the line along which the two forces balance one another and the position of the coast remains stationary. The force of erosion is balanced by the emergence of the land in the quadrant $ZEOD$, while in the opposite quadrant $OAZ'S$ the rate of accumulation is balanced by the rise of sea-level, the two factors exactly balancing along the lines OZ and OZ' respectively. In the segments EAO both the sea-level is falling, causing emergence, and the land is building out, rapid progradation will therefore result. In the opposite segment DOS the sea-level is rising, causing submergence, while erosion is taking place, thus a very rapid retrogression of the coast

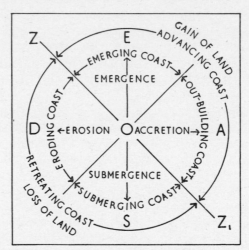

FIG. 7–6. Valentin's theory of coastal classification. (After Valentin.)

will be in progress. Lines of equal advance and retreat of the coast can be drawn parallel to ZZ', the lines indicating greater change the farther they are from ZZ'; above the line ZZ' indicates advancing coasts, while below it retreat is taking place. Valentin has attempted to apply his classification to the coasts of the whole earth in maps included in one of his publications (1952).[18]

Cotton (1954)[21] has applied Valentin's classification to the coast of New Zealand where he finds examples of many of the categories. The recent changes in sea-level due to earth-movements in this unstable zone make it an interesting area in which to test the classification. As an example of coastal type IA he cites the Motunau coast of North Canterbury where a coastal plain covered with recent shells has been uplifted and is now being cliffed by the sea and dissected by gullying. Coastal type IB is illustrated by the Eastbourne cuspate foreland in Port Nicholson, here sand coming from inland has been moved alongshore to form a low sandy plain in front of the old cliff line. In the second major group type IIA is illustrated by the fjords of the southern part of the west coast of the South Island or the drowned river valleys of the Marlborough Sounds. Cape Kidnappers on the east coast of the North Island illustrates the cliffed coasts of category IIB.

Summary and conclusions

The tables of the different classifications provide the best summary, the four discussed are found on the following pages, Johnson, p. 235, Shepard, p. 237, Cotton, p. 241, Valentin, p. 242.

In drawing conclusions concerning the problem of coastal classification it appears that none of those so far suggested is really satisfactory. Johnson's classification has the disadvantage that nearly all coasts fall into his compound class. The cyclic development of the coastal forms is implied because the major groups describe the initial form, which must then be further described by reference to the stage reached in the appropriate cycle. In some instances the sequential processes may have so greatly modified the initial form that this is unrecognizable. This coast cannot then be put into any category. It has the advantage that it is genetic, but the second major group, the coasts of emergence, is open to criticism.

Shepard, however, goes too far in the other extreme by ignoring the emergent class of coast altogether. His classification also has the disadvantage of either omitting reference to the original land surface, if a coast falls into the second major group, or the affect of marine processes, if the coast is in the first group. Its chief advantage is its comprehensiveness, so that nearly all coasts can be classified in one or other category. The classification of Cotton is an improvement on that of Johnson, which it resembles in many ways; it also has a genetic basis and implies the same cyclic development and is therefore open to the same criticism.

The newer approach to the problem by Valentin is perhaps the most satisfactory; it leaves open the problem of the way in which base-level changes, tending to emphasize the continuous change of sea-level. There are, however, specific examples, as Cotton has shown, which do not appear to be adequately described in Valentin's classification. The lack of data on the present movement of base-level in some areas where the land is mobile makes it difficult to apply everywhere. This is partly because the character of the coast does not always supply sufficient evidence to allow it to be placed in the correct group. The classification according to Valentin is descriptive rather than genetic; this is perhaps the only solution owing to the frequent and rapid changes of sea-level in the latest geological period. It applies to changes actually in progress so that if these are reversed for any reason the coast must immediately change its category. From a practical point of view it is extremely important to differentiate between coasts which are advancing and those that are retreating as these two types provide very different problems for the coastal engineer.

REFERENCES

[1]Savage, R. P., 1957, Sand bypassing at Port Hueneme, California. *B.E.B. Tech. Memo* **92.**

[2]Suess, E., 1888, *The face of the earth*, Vol. 2 (English translation 1906).

[3]Johnson, D. W., 1919, *Shore processes and shoreline development.*

[4]Dana, J. D., 1849, *Geology, U.S. Exploring Expedition—Philadelphia.*

[5]Davis, W. M., 1898, *Physical Geography.*

[6]Gulliver, F. P., 1899, Shoreline topography. *Proc. Am. Acad. Arts and Sci.* **34,** pp. 151–258.

[7]Richthofen, F. von, 1886, *Führer für Forschungsreisende*—Jänecke, Hanover.

[8]Daly, R. A., 1934, *The changing world of the ice age.* Yale Univ. Press.

[9]de Martonne, E., 1909, *Traité de géographie physique.* Paris.

[10]Putnam, W. C., 1937, The marine cycle of erosion for a steeply sloping shoreline of emergence. *Journ. Geol.* **45,** pp. 844–50.

[11]Shepard, F. P., 1937, Revised classification of marine shorelines. *Journ. Geol.* **45,** pp. 602–24.

[12]Shepard, F. P., 1948, *Submarine geology.*

[13]Cotton, C. A., 1954, Deductive morphology and the genetic classification of coasts. *Sci. Monthly* **78,** 3, pp. 163–81.

[14]King, C. A. M., 1956, The coast of south-east Iceland near Ingolfshöföi. *Geog. Journ.* **122,** pp. 241–6.

[15]Cotton, C. A., 1918, The outline of New Zealand. *Geog. Rev.* **6,** pp. 320–40.

[16]Cotton, C. A., 1952, Criteria for the classification of coasts. *17th Int. Geog. Cong. Abs. of Papers,* p. 15.

[17]Bourcart, J., 1950, La theorie de la flexure continentale. *C. R. Cong. Int. Geog.* Lisbon 1949, **2,** pp. 167–90.

[18]Valentin, H., 1952, Die Küste der Erde. *Petermanns Geog. Mitt. Ergänzsungheft* **246.**

[19]Valentin, H., 1953, Present vertical movements of the British Isles. *Geog. Journ.* **119,** pp. 299–305.

[20]Wright, W. B., 1937, *Quarternary Ice Age,* Chap. 22, pp. 404–38.

[21]Cotton, C. A., 1954, Tests of a German non-cyclic theory and classification of coasts. *Geog. Journ.* **120,** pp. 353–61.

CHAPTER 8

CONSTRUCTIVE WAVE ACTION AND COASTAL ACCRETION

IN this chapter the processes which are positive in their effect on the beach and coast will be considered; that is those forces which move beach material towards the land on the beach and cause outward building of the coast. Some of these processes have already been mentioned in discussing the characteristics of water movement in waves and in describing experimental work on sand transport in a wave tank. The positive changes of volume of material on the beaches which these processes bring about have yet to be analysed. A summary of the forces which operate on the beach to cause a building up of material will be presented. Many of these forces are not continuous in their operation and do not lead to extensive or permanent coastal accretion; the special circumstances which result in a building out of the land at the expense of the sea will be discussed in the latter part of the chapter, where changes in plan along the coast are considered.

1. *CONSTRUCTIVE ACTION IN PROFILE—THE BEACH*

(a) Effect of material

It has already been pointed out that coarser material is more mobile than fine beach material (see pp. 127, 138), it follows therefore, that accretion on a beach profile will be greater in a given period under similar conditions if the beach is composed of shingle rather than sand. The change in the form of the profile will also differ between the two main categories of material. Accretion on shingle beaches will be considered first.

SHINGLE BEACHES. Lewis (1931)[1] was one of the first authors to discuss in detail the reasons for, and the results of, constructive waves on shingle. He has drawn attention to the importance of the wave characteristics as well as noting the changes in the profile. When constructive waves are acting on shingle they tend to form a small foreshore ridge on the beach as the limit of the swash. A beach which is being built up during a period when the tides are rising from neap to spring level will, therefore, show one ridge at the limit of the last high tide; when the tide is falling from spring to neap each high tide is lower than the last and the height of each is marked by a small ridge pushed up by the waves at high water. These small ridges differ from the much larger features found on some sand beach profiles which will be considered in chapter 10, they should also not be confused with the much higher backshore ridges on shingle beaches which are built above the limit of the high spring tides; this latter type will be considered in the next chapter (see pp. 280, 281).

SAND BEACHES. Constructive action on a sandy beach may in some instances also build up a ridge. This feature, usually called a berm, is

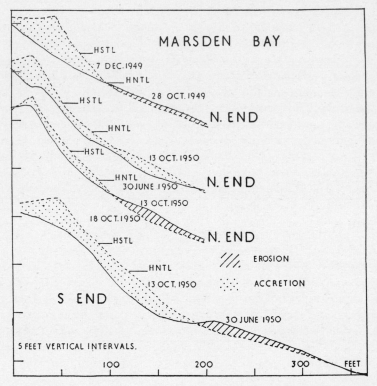

FIG. 8–1. Profiles of Marsden Bay, Co. Durham, to show the formation of berms.

rather different in dimensions from the small ridges built at each successive tide level by constructive waves on a shingle beach. The chief characteristic of a berm is the marked break of slope at the seaward edge of a nearly horizontal platform; the height of the break of slope is usually a little above the mean high water mark. The development of berms is illustrated in fig. 8–1, which shows profiles surveyed at Marsden Bay, County Durham, at different times; the later profile was surveyed after a period of constructive wave action when material was moved up the beach to its crest. The sand here is fairly coarse and has a median diameter of

0·37 mm. at the north end of the bay and 0·35 mm. at the south end. The maximum amount of accretion was about 4 ft. on one profile.

This type of constructive berm, which is the normal one, must not be confused with a similar feature resulting from destructive wave action (see pp. 294–297). A good example of this type of berm was surveyed on the Lincolnshire coast at Anderby after the 1953 storm-flood; the material of which this berm was formed was eroded from the dunes and moved seawards on to the beach (see profile 17, fig. 9–6) p.295.

The profiles which have already been mentioned were on beaches of fairly coarse sand, which show relatively large changes in level. On fine sand beaches the changes are less and, in general, the berm is not such a conspicuous feature on the profile after a period of constructive waves. On the smooth sand beach in Rhossili Bay in South Wales where daily observations of sand level were made over a period of variable weather the changes recorded rarely exceeded 1 in., and never 2 in., at any point on the profile; the constancy of the profile of this beach from year to year has already been mentioned (see pp. 138, 230 and fig. 7–1). The median diameter of the sand in this bay is 0·23 mm. Over a longer period and under more extreme conditions larger changes would be expected to occur.

On a ridged beach of fine sand, such as that at Blackpool, daily and weekly surveys also show that the rate of accretion under the action of constructive waves is slow and it is rare for large additions to take place over a short period. The growth of ridge crests has been measured at weekly intervals during the period February 1943 to August 1943, and December 1943 to October 1944; during the first period ridge accretion greater than 1 ft. only occurred on one occasion and during nearly every other week the change in level was less than 6 in. During the second period the addition of sand on the ridge crest was never greater than 1 ft. and only exceeded 6 in. on one occasion (see fig. 10–12) p.339. The reason for the greater accretion on the coarse beaches is due to the steeper gradient which allows the wave energy to be dissipated over a relatively narrow width of beach and hence renders the waves more effective as has already been explained, this applies both to constructive and destructive effects of wave action.

Some of the changes which occur on the coarse sand beach near Point Reyes, California, have been described by Trask (1956).[2] The beach is composed of sand with a median diameter ranging between 0·56 mm. and 0·77 mm. During the period from August to October 1955 a berm was built up on this beach giving an accretion of over 7 ft. of sand in a small area and between November and December over 6 ft. accumulated on the berm at the crest of the beach.

So far the accretion of material discussed has applied to the part of tidal beaches which is exposed at low water; the amount of accretion in relation to the beach material and the typical beach profile have been mentioned. Before considering accretion in the offshore zone the nature of the wave characteristics which cause accretion on the foreshore may be considered, together with the part played by wind and other forces.

(b) Effect of waves, wind and other forces

From the experiments made in the wave tank which were discussed in chapter 4 (see pp. 125–127) it was shown that the most significant wave characteristic in determining the effect of waves on the foreshore is the wave steepness; a flat wave will move material landwards and build up the profile, while a steep wave will produce the opposite effect. Lewis first drew attention to the importance of wave frequency in relation to shingle beaches when he stated that waves of low frequency were constructive while those of high frequency were destructive on the beach. A variation in length was considered as significant, but in fact it is the associated variation in steepness, assuming a constant wave height, which is the more important factor. He considered that the low frequency waves broke in such a way that the swash was more effective than the backwash, thus moving material up the beach.

The critical steepness at which the waves change in character from constructive to destructive is clearly important. It is not possible to give one value for this figure as it varies from beach to beach according to the size of the material and probably with other factors, such as the wind. Some of the different values of this critical steepness which apply to observations in the wave tank have already been given (see pp. 126, 127). The values which apply to the natural beaches seem to be lower than those found from tank experiments. There are few precise data on this point, but a short series of observations on Rhossili beach suggest that on this flat beach of fine sand the critical steepness is about 0·011; this value may have been affected, however, by the direction and strength of the wind. On a shingle beach, on the other hand, the critical steepness from a short series of surveys, was found to be about 0·017. These figures indicate a tendency for the critical steepness to increase as the beach material becomes coarser.

The dimensions of the waves are also important because their energy depends on their height and length. Lafond (1939)[3] has shown that it is the relatively long period, low waves which are constructive at La Jolla, California, on parts of the profile, but that more continuous fill occurred with low waves of shorter period. These low waves, however, did not deposit as much in seven days as was removed by high waves in one day, because of their much lower energy. The low waves, which are usually also the flat ones, require much longer to build up a beach than the big, steep storm waves require to erode it. This factor is counter-balanced by the relatively short duration of high waves along the coast in most areas.

In considering constructive wave action it is necessary to take into account the material which is moving alongshore as this may in some instances be more important than the material transported normal to the coast. The function of groynes built out at right-angles to the shore is to trap material moving alongshore, encouraging beach accretion in areas where the natural supply of sand is limited. Other obstructions may have less desirable results, by trapping too much sand on the up-wave side of the barrier, thus causing erosion the other side. Some of these problems have already been mentioned (see pp. 147–154). Accretion of material on the beach is affected, therefore, not only by the steepness of the waves but also by their direction of approach which determines the direction of movement of beach material. Shepard (1950)[4] has described a clear instance of accretion on a small beach being due to the lateral shift of beach material in a restricted bay. This beach, known as Boomer beach on the coast of California, has been built up to the extent of 8 ft. at one end during one day, while the other end of the beach was completely removed during attack by oblique waves. The changes are not normally as rapid and great as on the occasion mentioned. It is possible for accretion to take place on the beach under wave conditions which would not move material landward from deeper water if more material is moved into the area alongshore then is being moved seaward by destructive forces.

The wind is another factor which may reverse the movement to be expected from the wave characteristics; a strong onshore wind may more than counteract the effect of waves which would otherwise be constructive on the beach. The efficiency of this process has been discussed in chapter 6. In a very few areas the tidal currents might have the same effect although this is unlikely except in narrow channels where the tide is particularly strong.

Accretion on beaches with a considerable tidal range such as Marsden Bay, where the spring tidal range is 14 ft., often does not extend to low water level, a fill on the upper beach being balanced by a cut lower down the foreshore. Where the tidal range is smaller, as for example near the Scripps Institute pier in California, the change in beach level frequently continues down below the mean lower low water level. The range between M.H.H.W. and M.L.L.W. on this coast is about $5\frac{1}{2}$ ft. The seasonal changes on this beach have already been referred to (see pp. 138–140); the summer fill in this area in many years extends to a depth of about 12–14 ft. below the mean sea level, and even at this depth amounts to a maximum change of level of over 5 ft. on rare occasions although it is usually about 4 ft. During the winter period when the foreshore is being eroded the deeper water fill may amount to as much as 6 ft. in a depth of about 20 ft. of water, but usually the accretion in deep water under these conditions is nearer 3 ft. This is not accretion in the sense that it was defined in the beginning of this chapter, however, as the material was moved seaward into deeper water by destructive waves.

(c) Offshore zone

Accretion of sand can occur to considerable depths as has been considered in chapter 4 (see pp. 132–136), but it is difficult to establish whether this addition of material is the result of constructive waves because its source is often in doubt. Inman and Rusnak (1956)[5] from observations made off the coast of California south of the Scripps Institute, in depths of 30, 52 and 70 ft., suggest that there is a correlation between the changes in sand elevation at the different stations, indicating an onshore or offshore movement of sand. When the sand level fell at 70 ft. there was a rise at 30 ft., indicating a landward or constructive wave action, which probably caused accretion to begin in a depth of about 52 ft. The reverse change was also noted. There was usually a positive correlation between the changes at 70 and 52 ft., but little correlation between 30 and 52 ft. At a depth of 30 ft. the sand level tended to build up during the summer, which agrees with the summer accretion often found on the foreshore, indicating that this building up does extend to considerable depths in some areas. The amount of change in level was very small at 30 ft. depth, amounting to a total change of 0·07 ft. between the average summer and winter levels, although individual surveys showed greater changes. The maximum range at this depth was less than 0·3 ft.

(d) Summer beaches

Constructive action on the beach results from the action of waves which move material towards the shore; such waves are low relative to their length, having a low steepness ratio. Their constructive action is helped by the presence of offshore winds but may be reversed by strong onshore winds. The building up of beaches may be a seasonal process in some areas, as in parts of California, where the variation of wave type with the seasons is marked. In such areas the beach builds up during the summer to produce a profile which has a wide berm at the level of the high tide and a relatively smooth profile extending offshore. The depth to which the summer fill extends offshore may reach about 30 ft. in some areas but considerable changes of level are restricted to shallower water, about 12–20 ft. in depth. The changes are greater in volume where the beach material is coarser and the size of the material affects the depth to which the fill extends.

On ridged tidal beaches, such as Blackpool, the accretion of sand is largely achieved by additions to the ridge crests; on this beach, which has a tidal range of over 25 ft. at spring tide, a seasonal change in sand elevation has been recorded during the period 1943–5; this is shown in fig. 8–2. On this type of beach there is a tendency for the ridges to grow in height under the action of constructive waves, while the reverse is probably true of the submarine bars found in a tideless sea, such as the Mediterranean.

Other beaches do not show a seasonal change in character but build up whenever suitable wave conditions allow. Continuous accretion on a beach often follows the affects of a particularly severe storm. A good example of this type of accretion is shown in the gradual recovery of sand on the beach at Mablethorpe, Lincolnshire, after the beach material had been completely stripped off, leaving the clay base exposed, during the 1953 storm-flood. (Barnes and King, 1955)[6], see fig. 9–12.

Beach accretion is the result of the action of waves more characteristic of the summer period in many areas than the steeper storm waves common in winter, which are often accompanied by strong onshore gales.

2. *CONSTRUCTIVE ACTION IN PLAN—THE COAST*

The constructive wave action discussed in the first part of this chapter is rarely cumulative in character; the accretion of the summer season or other constructive period is removed during the winter or during periods of storm. The total amount of material on the beach over a long period usually remains more or less constant. In some areas, however, more material is added to the coast by constructive waves and other forces than is removed, the coast therefore builds outwards into the sea. The factors on which such constructive action depends and some of the resulting features will be considered in this part of the chapter.

Coastal accretion may render the outline of the coast more or less regular so that both changes will be considered; these two types of growth constitute two of the sub-groups of Shepard's coastal classification in the second major group. The place they occupy in the cycle of erosion on coasts of different types will be considered in more detail in chapter 12 (see pp. 269–278), but in this chapter the factors responsible for the formation of different types of coastal accretion will be considered. Features which straighten the coast will be considered first.

(a) Coasts straightened by marine deposition

Marine deposits which straighten the coast have a variety of different origins and forms, but there are two main features. These are both built by the waves above the high water level.

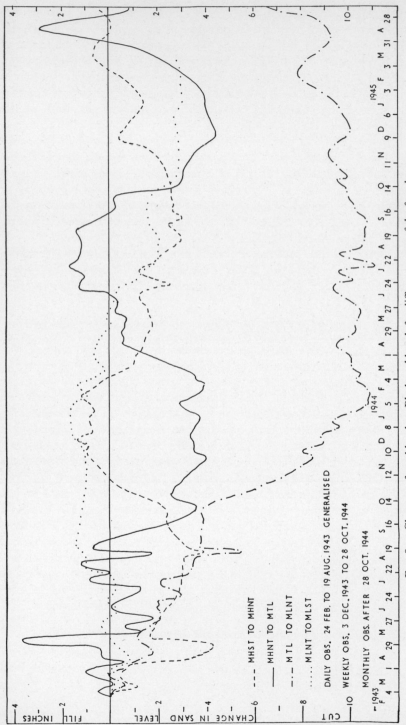

FIG. 8–2. Changes of sand level on Blackpool beach for different parts of the foreshore.

i. BARRIERS AND SPITS. Shepard (1952)[7] has proposed the term 'barrier' to describe one type of these features. A simple type of barrier consists of a beach separated from the shore by a lagoon; for more complex features of the same type he suggests the term 'barrier island' and 'barrier spit'. The difference between the two is that the barrier beach and island need not be attached to the land anywhere along their length while the barrier spits are always attached at one end. This difference is probably of some importance when the origin of these structures is examined, these terms will, therefore, be used. The term 'bar' which is frequently used to describe these features will be restricted to structures which are permanently under water.

There is evidence to suggest that barrier beaches and islands are formed by a process similar to that responsible for the development of a ridge and runnel profile on certain tidal sand beaches. A discussion of their character and origin will, therefore, be deferred till chapter 10 (see pp. 347–353). Barrier beaches and islands are found off the Baltic coasts, the Gulf of Mexico and part of the east coast of the United States. Many of these are complex structures. They are all, however, separated from the mainland by a lagoonal area, with the result that the irregular nature of the mainland coast is usually straightened by the formation of the barrier.

Other formations which are separated from the coast by a lagoon or channel are the 'barrier spits', which will be called simply 'spits'; these deposits are tied to the coast at one end only and frequently form where there is an abrupt change in direction of the coast, as for example Hurst Castle spit in the Solent off Hampshire, shown in fig. 8–3a. Spits are most common on coasts which have an irregular outline with frequent change in orientation. They often form across the mouths of estuaries either completely closing them, when they may be termed barriers, as in the case of Loe barrier in Cornwall, shown in fig. 8–3b, or almost closing them as Dawlish Warren across the mouth of the river Exe in Devonshire[8] (see fig. 8–5). A more complex formation sometimes develops at a harbour entrance, where spits extend outwards from each headland. Robinson (1955)[9] has described three examples on the south coast of England in the harbours of Poole, Christchurch and Pagham, one of these is shown in fig. 12–8, p. 376.

Many of these spits are complex recurved features which have had a long and varied history. One of the processes which is probably most significant in the development of spits is the longshore movement of beach material. This supplies the material which is built into the spit by the action of different processes which will vary with the character of the beach material; thus it is important to differentiate between sand and shingle spits. The significance of longshore movement is stressed by

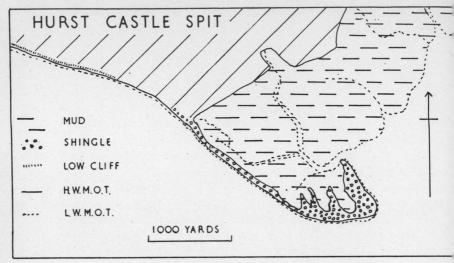

FIG. 8–3. (*a*) Map of Hurst Castle Spit.

Evans (1942)[10] who also emphasizes the importance of beach-drifting in building the spit above water level.

Before considering the difference between sand and shingle spits it may be suggested that the significant difference between barrier islands

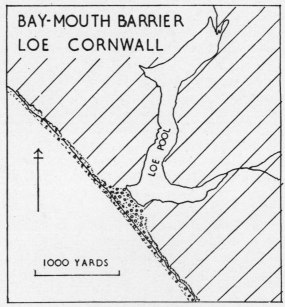

FIG. 8–3. (*b*) Map of the Loe Barrier, Cornwall.
(Crown Copyright reserved)

and spits is that the former can probably be formed without the action of longshore movement of material because they may be detached at both ends from the mainland coast. They are also more often composed of sand than shingle, which facilitates their formation by movement normal to the shore by the process which is explained in chapter 10. It is not suggested that longshore movement does not take place on barrier islands but that it is not essential for their formation as it probably is for the formation of spits.

The feature which prolongs the north-south direction of the Lincoln-shire coast provides an example of a fairly simple sand spit, with only a relatively small amount of shingle. The spit is about ½ mile in length, which has developed in its present position as a result of the outbuilding of the coast to the north by marine deposition and sand dune formation. Its growth has been measured in detail[11] from frequent surveys which give quantitative data of its gradual growth and consolidation both in volume and to a lesser degree in height. The table gives the relevant

Date		Height of highest point on spit in feet	Area above specified contour at distal end of the spit in thousands of square feet		
			10 ft.	11 ft.	12 ft.
Summer	1950	over 13·0	—	—	—
May	1951	12·80	128·5	44·3	6·7
August	1951	12·95	—	46·3	9·9
April	1952	11·9	187·9	45·8	0
August	1952	11·7	207·2	43·8	0
April	1953	12·5	202·8	78·5	8·3
November	1953	12·0	—	—	—
April	1954	11·9	—	60·7	0
June	1955	11·9	329·7	100·3	0
April	1957	12+	289·8	153·6	7·1
May	1958	11·4	298·6	153·1	0

Heights are above O.D. Liverpool.
M.H.S.T. 10·9 ft. O.D.
M.H.N.T. 5·8 ft. O.D.

figures. Its probable eventual decay may be forecast if the coast continues to build out eastwards to the north, thus cutting off its supply of sand which reaches it by longshore movement from the north. This appears to have been the fate of an earlier spit, which prolonged the line of the coast marked by a dune ridge which formed the shoreline in about 1824 at Gibraltar Point as shown in fig. 8–4. In 1951 the spit which is now forming had grown to such an extent and height that it was able to support a few plants of *Salsola kali* but subsequent high tides removed the plants which had not re-established themselves by 1958.

A larger sand spit, which has been described by Kidson (1950),[8] has formed across the mouth of the river Exe in Devon, this feature is about $1\frac{1}{4}$ miles long, extending north-east from Langstone Rock. Unlike the spit at Gibraltar Point it is a double feature, the outer or seaward part is now suffering severe erosion and is liable to disintegrate in a matter of

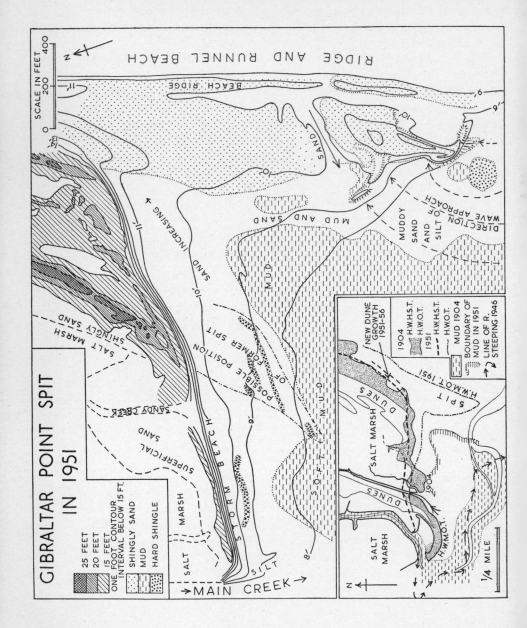

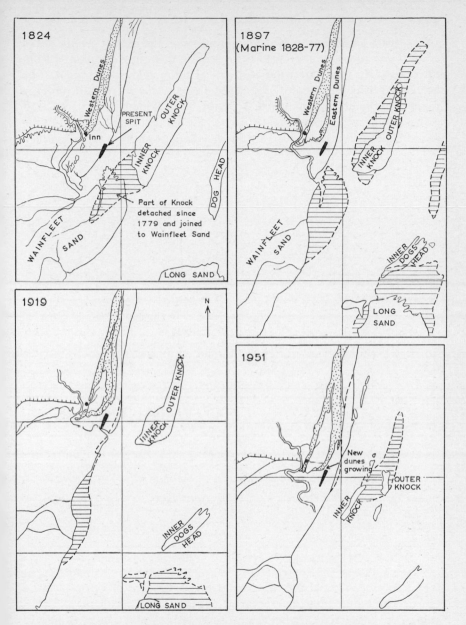

COASTAL AND INSHORE CHANGES NEAR GIBRALTAR POINT

≡ AREA LOWERED TO BELOW LOW WATER ORDINARY TIDES SINCE PREVIOUS SURVEY.

0 1 2 3 4 5 MILES

Fig. 8–4. (b) Maps to show the changes in the spit and offshore relief near Gibraltar Point, Lincolnshire.

10–15 years according to Kidson. He gives as the reason for its initial growth and subsequent erosion the variation in supply of material from the cliffs to the west. After the post-glacial submergence of this coast the headlands, which previously extended farther seaward would undergo rapid erosion. Plenty of material would be provided to form the spit across the drowned river mouth, under the influence of waves from the west. The continued erosion of these headlands would in time diminish

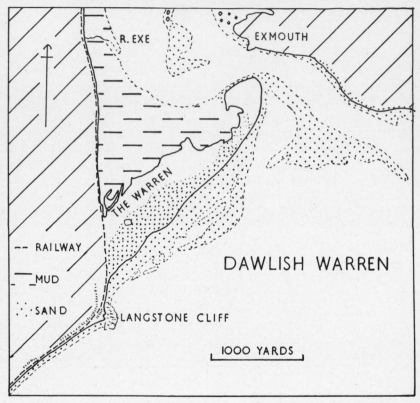

FIG. 8–5. Map of Dawlish Warren.   (Crown Copyright reserved)

the supply of material for spit formation as the rate of retreat slowed down. The building of the railway at the foot of the headland of Langstone cliff adjacent to the spit accentuated this reduction in supply of beach material (see fig. 8–5).

The recurved distal end of this spit is a feature characteristic of many spits. It is probably the result of the deflection of the waves by refraction round the end of the spit. Evans (1942)[10] gives further examples to illustrate the importance of wave refraction in the formation of recurves at the distal end of spits. The recurves typical of some shingle spits, however, probably have a different origin as exemplified by Hurst Castle spit in the Solent. This spit has frequently been described so there is no need to discuss its origin in detail; the forces responsible for its character have been discussed by Lewis (1931).[1] The recurves in this case, which are much more sharply angular in relation to the main spit, result from the operation of two sets of waves from completely different directions; the main part of the spit is formed by the waves from the south-west and west while the recurves are formed by waves from east-north-east coming down the Solent, the spit is shown in fig. 8–3a, p. 256.

ii. BEACHES AND FORELANDS. So far only those constructive features which are separated from the mainland by an estuary, lagoon or marsh have been mentioned. There are many features of marine deposition which are directly joined to the mainland but still help to render its outline straighter. Perhaps the most common of this type of coastal accretion are the bay-head beaches which are found in most indentations of an irregular coastline. The material accumulates here by lateral movement from the retaining headlands or from inland via the rivers. The longshore movement is assisted by the nature of wave refraction which concentrates wave energy on the headlands, and, by reducing wave height in the bays, causes longshore movement from the headland to the bay. Lower wave steepness values in the bays also allow the waves to be constructive in their action more often in this area.

Marine deposition is not restricted to bays in an indented coast, deposition can also render straighter a less intricate shoreline by the out-building of beach plains of considerable extent. One such feature has been described by Cotton (1951)[12] in the North Island of New Zealand, which is illustrated in fig. 8–6. The western part of the North Auckland peninsula shows straightening due to very extensive deposition of sand by the sea and dune formation by the wind. The eastern or lee coast, on the other hand, is still deeply embayed. The source of the sand is largely the volcanic material brought down to the sea by the Waikato river and moved north along the coast by wave action, it is then driven up on to the beach by the heavy surf characteristic of this coast. A shelf 30–40 miles wide has been built out here which is backed by an 8-mile wide belt of Pleistocene and recent sands. This belt of coastal sands fills in the gaps between outcrops of harder volcanic rocks on the coast, making a smooth coastline. This is in marked contrast to the deeply embayed eastern coast, with its mangrove fringed inlets; there are still, however, one or two inlets on the west coast not completely filled in, but most of these are partially closed by the development of spits. Another example cited by Cotton and illustrated in fig. 8–6 is the Paekakariki coast north of Wellington, where a wide sandy foreland fills in a broad bay in the wide northern part of Cook Strait.

A somewhat similar structure is found along much of the coast of South America between north Brazil and Venezuela; it is associated with the mouths of the Amazon and Orinoco (Armstrong Price 1954).[13] The feature, known as a chenier plain, is composed of a series of sandy barriers separated by strips of marsh and swamps with a large clay content in their deposits. A good example of this type of depositional feature

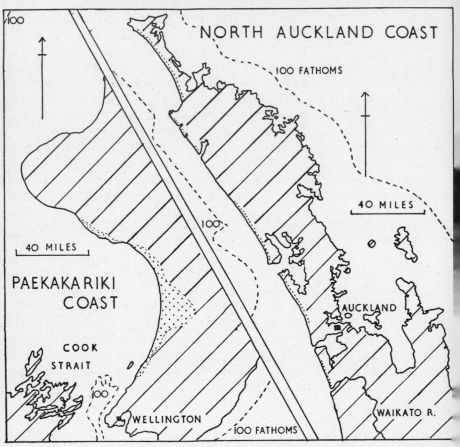

Fig. 8–6. Maps of parts of the North Island of New Zealand, to show zones of deposition.

is found on the coast of Surinam, Dutch Guiana, where the large clay content of the waters of the Amazon and Orinoco facilitate the deposition of clay on the gently sloping coast, sandy ridges are perched at intervals within and on the clay. The chenier plain of the north coast of South America is 1,400 miles long and up to 20 miles wide. The sandy ridges are usually from 3 to 9 ft. high and 250 to 300 ft. broad, the tidal range of the area is 7–9 ft. and heavy surf from the north-east occurs at times.

The waves due to the strong winds transport the sand along the shore, where it is built into the ridges by the swash of the waves, which extend above the normal level of the tide during onshore winds and spring tides.

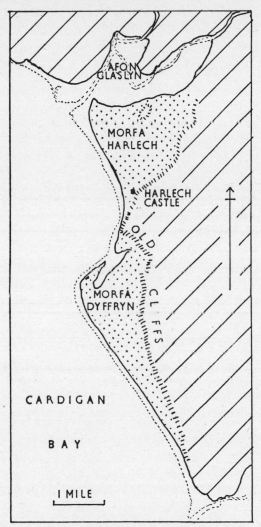

FIG. 8–7. Map of the forelands of Morfa Harlech and Morfa Dyffryn, Cardigan Bay. (Crown Copyright reserved)

These coasts are on the whole building out, but the deposition of clay ceases where the coast slopes more steeply and where the wave energy increases and the chenier plain is replaced by a barrier and lagoon coast.

On the coast of the British Isles a rather similar type of constructive feature is the foreland of Morfa Harlech (see fig. 8–7). This partially fills the estuary of the Afon Glaslyn which enters the northern part of Cardigan Bay. This foreland is largely composed of sand. The only shingle on Morfa Harlech is found in very small amounts on the beach at the southern end of the structure, apart from this it is entirely sandy, with dunes formed near the sea. From a study of aerial photographs, the inner part, as mentioned by Steers (1946),[14] is formed of sand overlying a former salt marsh, the creeks of which can be recognized. The feature started as a simple spit which allowed Harlech to be used as a port by Edward I in the fourteenth century; it has since developed and filled in all the southern part of the estuary by the northward movement of beach material along the shore and marsh formation in the sheltered waters behind the spit, while dunes have since been deposited over much of the area. It, therefore, illustrates a further stage in the process of spit development, in which the lagoon is eliminated. A feature of similar form to the south, Morfa Dyffryn, must be considered in the next section because it, unlike Morfa Harlech, makes the shoreline more irregular, as it protrudes into Cardigan Bay.

Summary

Features built by the sea which straighten the coastline are of two types; one type includes the barrier beach or island and the spit, which are both separated from the shore by a lagoon or estuary; the other type includes the cuspate foreland and beach plain. The main distinction between the barrier beach and island on the one hand and the spit on the other is that the former need not be attached to the mainland at either end, while the latter is always attached at one end and sometimes both. Barrier beaches are considered in detail in chapter 10, but both sand and shingle spits are described here. Examples of beach plains, chenier plains and forelands are mentioned.

(b) Coasts made irregular by marine deposition

It has been shown that of two very similar features one makes the coast straighter while the other makes a salient extending seaward; these are Morfa Harlech and Morfa Dyffryn respectively. Both these features, however, lie at an angle to the coast behind them. In considering the formation of coastal features which make the coast more irregular the tendency for beaches to form perpendicular to the direction of approach of the dominant waves must be fully taken into account. This tendency has been discussed by Lewis (1931),[1] (1938)[15] in some detail, elaborating the earlier work of de la Beche (1833)[16] and Harrison (1848).[17] Lewis considered that any feature of marine deposition will tend to align itself normal to the direction of approach of the dominant waves, that is the largest storm waves. These waves build shingle ridges above the reach of normal waves. If these storm waves approach a stretch of coast at an oblique angle they will tend to cause longshore movement in the opposite direction and thus will automatically tend to swing the coast round to a position normal to their direction of approach. Lewis (1938)[15] takes as one example of this process the orientation of the sandy forelands in north Cardigan Bay, which have just been mentioned, and points out that these structures are orientated to face the direction of maximum fetch, from which the largest waves may be expected to come across the Irish Sea from the Atlantic Ocean. Thus the conclusion is reached that the prevalent waves, which may be oblique to the shore, will bring the material to the beach but the dominant waves will tend to build this material into a beach orientated parallel to their crests.

Schou (1945)[18] has proposed a rather different method of establishing the alignment of the coast, or the direction of coastal simplification, by considering both the direction of maximum fetch and the resultant of winds of all directions and forces, R. This value is calculated by plotting the frequency of all winds of Beaufort Force 4 and upwards and constructing a vector diagram to establish the 'direction-resultant of wind work' R. Where the fetch coincides with the direction of R or is equal in all directions the coast will become orientated perpendicular to the direction of R. If R is in a different direction to the maximum fetch the coast should become aligned between the two directions. The examples cited in support of this theory are on the coast of Denmark, where the fetch is limited in many directions. The wind, therefore, is likely to have a greater effect on the size of the waves than in other areas where long swells, generated far from the area, form an important proportion of the wave pattern. The direction of maximum fetch from which the swells and storm waves can approach is then more likely to play the dominant role in determining the alignment of the coast.

Features which are built out from the coast in response to the dominant waves will be more common along coasts where the direction of wave approach is restricted to one or two directions, rather than a coast open to waves from many directions. These features may be expected to occur round the shores of islands, such as the British Isles, where Ireland and the Continent prevent waves coming from all directions. The position of headlands and the bottom configuration are also relevant; the latter factor influences the wave refraction pattern and thus affects the final direction of approach of the dominant waves.

Jennings (1955)[19] shows that only in areas where islands offshore prevent wave attack from all sides do irregularities in the coast build out by deposition. He describes one such outbuilt feature, Moila Point, formed in the shelter of Shortland Island on Bougainville Island in the Solomons, which is shown in fig. 8–8. This feature is a good example of a cuspate foreland, whose form as a sharp salient in the coast is the result of shelter from the south due to the presence of the island offshore. The two beaches forming the foreland are built out to face about south-west and east-south-east and extend out from the coast about 4 miles on each side. The foreland consists of a series of ridges parallel to its two sides.

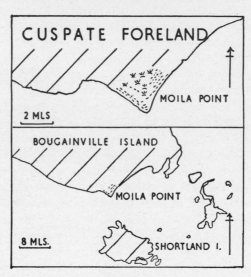

FIG. 8–8. Map to show the cuspate foreland of Moila Point, Solomon Islands. (After Jennings.)

A much larger and better known cuspate foreland is the large shingle structure of Dungeness on the south-east coast of England, with Romney Marsh lying behind the shingle ridges. Fig. 8–9 shows the form of the foreland. Much has been written concerning this feature which extends at least 10 miles outwards from the former coastline, forming a bold salient in the coast between the cliffs of Fairlight to the south and Sandgate and Folkestone to the north. Only the tip of the foreland is formed of extensive shingle storm ridges but these in their varying directions give an indication of the stages of formation of this structure as has been worked out mainly by Lewis (1932)[20] and Lewis and Balchin (1940),[21] following early work by Gulliver (1887).[22] This foreland illustrates the gradual turning of the beaches to face the dominant waves, which in this area are restricted to those coming from south-west in the English Channel and those coming from an easterly point through the Straits of Dover; the proximity of France prevents large waves approaching from the south or south-east. This accounts for the sharpness of the point of the Ness. At the present time shingle is being eroded from the

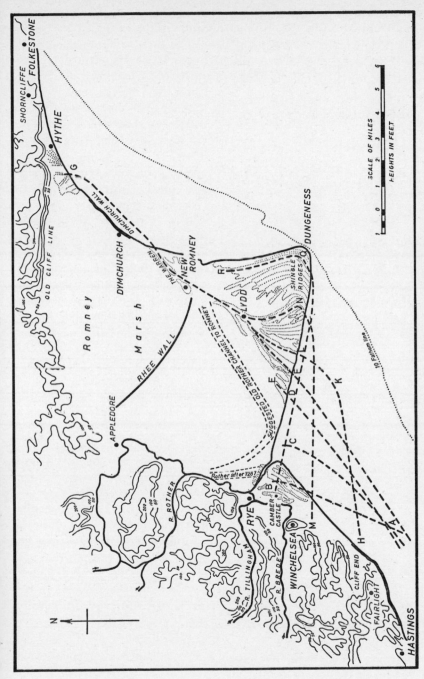

FIG. 8–9. Map of the evolution of Dungeness. (After Lewis.)

southern face of the foreland and is being built into ridges on the eastern side; this is shown by the abrupt truncation of the earlier ridges on the south side and their arrangement parallel to the east shore. It appears that the structure started as a spit across the former bay from Fairlight to Hythe, which lay in an almost south-west to north-east direction.

Since then, but particularly after the change in course of the Rother, it has swung round more and more to face the dominant waves. There is interesting historical evidence of the changes on this part of the coast from Roman times, see chapter 11.

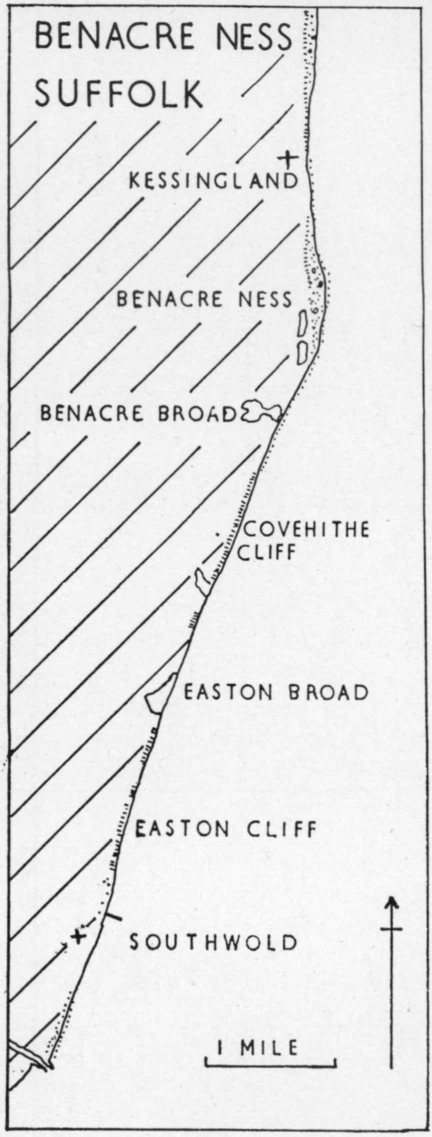

The structures built out from the coast which have so far been mentioned have been large and relatively stable in general position, although they change in form with time. Their permanency of position is due to the configuration of the neighbouring coasts which determines the nature of the wave attack upon them. An interesting feature, known as Benacre Ness, on the east coast of Suffolk is much more mobile. It has recently been studied by Williams and Fryer (1953)[23] and Williams (1956),[24] and is shown on fig. 8–10. This smooth area of accretion has been moving steadily north along the coast from a position just north of Southwold. It was shown in this position in a survey by Saxton in 1575, Bryant plotted it opposite Benacre Broad in 1826. On the Admiralty chart of 1940 it was shown over $\frac{3}{4}$ mile farther north than in 1826, and had moved another $\frac{1}{4}$ mile by 1955, so that it now lay about 1 mile south of Kes-

Fig. 8–10. Map of Benacre Ness, Suffolk. (Crown Copyright reserved) singland. The ness is formed of material derived from the soft cliffs of glacial sands and gravels, the former material being much the more plentiful. The material forming the ness, despite a superficial abundance of shingle, is largely sand. Although many surveys were carried out on the foreshore and extended offshore and current observations were made, no fully satisfactory reason for the northward movement of this zone of accretion was found, particularly as the general movement of material along this coast is to the south. It was shown that eddy currents were not responsible for the movement of the ness. The northward movement of the ness need not necessarily be due to movement of material in this direction; if sand moving from the north were deposited on its northern side and at the same time material was eroded from the southern side, the feature would move north. This particular example of coastal accretion is of interest because on either side are areas of severe erosion. It also illustrates a type of coastal deposition which is not apparently dependent on the configuration of the coast, although the offshore relief may exert an influence on its position. In this respect it is interesting to note that there is evidence of the northward movement of material in the vicinity offshore in the form of the sand waves (see pp. 204, 205).

Summary

In discussing cuspate forelands and other features which make the coast more irregular the importance of the tendency of the waves to build structures which are perpendicular to their dominant direction of approach is considered. Examples of cuspate forelands are described which illustrate this principle, including Dungeness and the more mobile feature of Benacre Ness on the coast of Suffolk. The former illustrates the importance of the configuration of the neighbouring coasts while in the latter case the offshore relief may be of importance.

(c) Salt marshes

Where coastal accretion forms features which are separated from the mainland by a lagoon or estuary, conditions suitable for the formation of salt marshes are present. There are two environments in which salt marshes will develop; firstly, in the shelter of some structure and, secondly, in areas where the force of the waves is diminished to such an extent that fine grained silt can be deposited. An essential factor in the development of a salt marsh is the part played by vegetation. The development of salt marshes varies from place to place and different characteristics have been distinguished in the marshes of the west, south and east coasts of England and Wales. In each area there is a distinct sequence of vegetation communities with changing environment as the marsh develops. Another essential factor for the growth of salt marshes is a supply of silt to build up the surface by deposition. Growth of salt marsh is accelerated by the tide which brings the silt and seeds into the marsh.

The southern part of the Lincolnshire coast illustrates well the stages in the formation of a salt marsh, growing in the shelter of marine structures to seaward (Barnes and King, 1951).[25] There are two main stages of salt marsh development which may be termed 'sloblands' and 'saltings'; both these are well shown in the Nature Reserve at Gibraltar Point, Lincolnshire. The former stage applies to areas where the tide ebbs and flows as a continuous sheet of water, while in the salting stage the tide rises and falls along a series of intricate marsh creeks. The first stage of marsh development is shown in the New Marsh, which is forming in the lee of the spit prolonging the north-south line of the coast from Gibraltar Point which has already been mentioned (see pp. 257–259). This feature is probably only about 25 years old,[11] and cannot be older than 50 years on the evidence of the 1904 6 in.–1 mile O.S. map.

Fig. 8–11a shows the extent and some of the characteristics of this marsh area. Its elevation lies between 7 and 11 ft. O.D. (Liverpool), where the M.H.S.T. level is 10·9 ft. O.D. and M.H.N.T. level is 5·8 ft. O.D., the heights of the M.L.N.T. and M.L.S.T. levels are −3·7 ft. and −7·8 ft. respectively. The new marsh is therefore covered by high spring tide but not by high neap tide. The gradient along the axis of the marsh is very gentle at 1 : 350 and the surface is generally smooth, well defined creeks having yet to form. At a level around 8 ft. O.D. the surface is composed of soft fluid mud, but above about 9 ft. O.D. the surface, particularly in the area nearer the sandy foreshore and the spit, is composed of mud layers interbedded with thin layers of sand. The sand layers can accumulate on the marsh during periods of neap tide when the mud dries and hardens; during spring tides the dominant sediment deposited is mud.

The zones of vegetation are closely related to the height of the marsh. In many marshes *Zostera* spp (eel grass) is the first colonizer, but in this area clumps and shoots of *Spartina townsendii* (rice grass) are growing in the sloppy mud and, as is characteristic of this species of marsh grass, is spreading very rapidly. This plant occurs in general at elevations below 8 ft. O.D. but may extend up to 9 ft. O.D. or more rarely even higher. Since this plant was first introduced to British coastal water around 1870 in Southampton Water it has spread very rapidly particularly along the south-coast marshes. Poole Harbour was fairly extensively colonized by this plant between 1911, when only isolated clumps were found, and 1924 when some of the bay was covered by it. The plant grows in dense clumps on mobile mud and is a very effective trapper of silt; it has been introduced into areas which require stabilization. On the other hand its rapid growth may cause problems of silting in channels in some areas.

Another marsh plant which is very important in the early stages of marsh growth is the *Salicornia herbacea* (annual glasswort), which

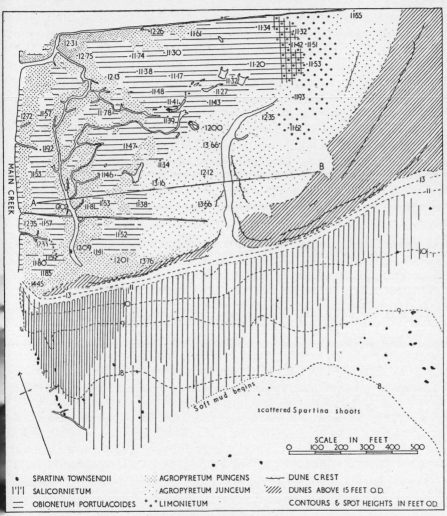

FIG. 8–11. (*a*) Map of the salt marsh at Gibraltar Point, Lincolnshire.

flourishes on the New Marsh at Gibraltar Point as well as on marshes in many other areas. This plant requires rather more stable conditions than *Spartina* and grows best at levels which are above the tide every day for a considerable period. On the New Marsh this plant is spreading outwards from the Main Creek and occurs at levels varying from 8 to 11 ft.

O.D. on muddy ground. Being an annual *Salicornia* does not trap silt so effectively as *Spartina* and it does not usually form such a complete cover on the surface. Closely associated with the Salicornietum zone is *Suaeda maritima* (annual seablite), while in other areas *Aster tripolium* (sea aster) also grows at this stage.

Over the area of the new marsh the tide ebbs and flows smoothly, but as deposition proceeds the flow of the tide will gradually become canalized into definite channels as irregularities of deposition occur around the growing vegetation. This canalization in itself leads to further variation in deposition.

At the stage where tidal creeks are well developed the marsh may be termed a salting; this is the phase reached by the mature marsh at Gibraltar Point. This marsh has developed in the shelter of the main eastern dune ridge which was forming during the middle part of the nineteenth century. In the development of marsh creeks natural levees are formed along the edge of the creek; as the rising tide overflows along the creek banks its speed is slackened and deposition takes place most rapidly along the edge of the creek. This greater height of the creek borders is well brought out by the distribution of the two major plant communities in the mature marsh. On the lower ground between the creeks the dominant plant is *Halimione portulacoides* (*Obione*) (woody sea purslane), other plants in the *Halimionetum* are *Limonium vulgare* (Sea-lavender), *Artemesia maritima* (sea-mugwort), *Glyceria maritima* (sea grass) and a variety of other plants. Spot heights surveyed in the *Halimionetum* show a very small height range from 11·2 to 11·6 ft. O.D., which indicates that this part of the marsh is only covered by the higher spring tides.

The higher borders of the creeks are covered by a dense growth of *Agropyron pungens* (sea couch grass) which lies at a height of between 11·8 and 12·7 ft. O.D. so that these creek banks are now very rarely flooded. The creeks now overflow first at their heads during periods of high spring tides (see fig. 8–11b). The heads of some of the creeks illustrate the formation of 'pans' within the area of the mature marsh. There are two types of pans; the first is the primary pan due to the original irregularity of deposition sealing off a small area with higher ground all round. It can then no longer drain freely; by evaporation of the trapped salt water the soil becomes too saline and cannot support the marsh plants, a bare patch of mud thus results. The second type of pan is the secondary pan, which is well illustrated at the heads of some of the active creeks on the mature marsh. The probable method of formation of this type is by the blocking of an active creek near its head, so that the upper part is cut off by higher ground all round and the same concentration of salt again prohibits plant growth.

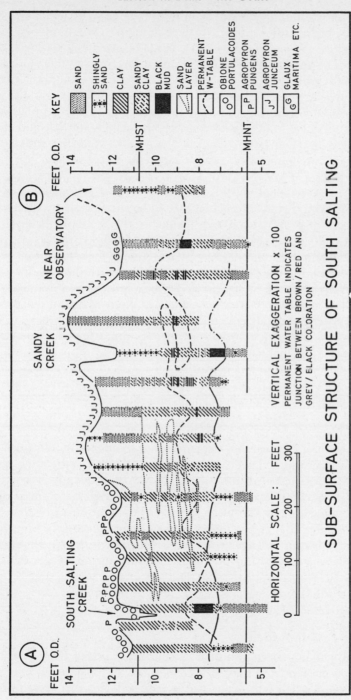

Fig. 8-11 (*b*). Profile and section across the mature salt marsh at Gibraltar Point, Lincolnshire.

Further growth in height will soon raise the mature marsh above the reach of the highest tides, when a fresh water marsh community will take the place of the salt marsh plants and eventually, providing sea-level does not rise, carr or woodland will form the vegetation climax of this sequence.

In summarizing the regional varieties in salt marshes round the coasts of England and Wales, it may be said that the east coast marshes are formed mainly of firm clay and have a sequence of vegetation phases as outlined above; the south coast marshes are mainly soft silt and their vegetation is dominated by *Spartina townsendii*, while the west coast marshes are predominantly sandy and *Glyceria maritima* is their dominant plant.

Actual measurements of the upward growth of salt marshes is of interest. Work in this field has been carried out in Norfolk by Chapman and Steers (1938)[26,27,28] on a marsh formed in the shelter of Scolt Head Inland. It was found that the rate of sedimentation varied with the environment and plant cover. The rate was usually highest on the lowest marshes and on the edges of the larger creeks, where these had a good cover of *Halimione*; the higher areas, because of the fewer inundations, grew up less rapidly. Over a period of 45 months deposition varied between 0·81 cm. and 2·67 cm. The most rapid accretion occurred in the *Asteretum* zone at the rate of 0·98 cm. per annum. Chapman calculated that to reach full maturity a marsh such as those of Norfolk would require a period of about two centuries and 4·2 ft. of silt would accumulate during this period. The sandy marshes of the west coast, such as those of the Dyfi estuary develop at a greater rate.

Summary

The growth of salt marshes depends upon the deposition of tidal silt in an area from which violent wave action is excluded. Vegetation plays an important part in salt marsh formation. Marsh development is in two stages; the slobland stage, which is characterized by *Zostera* spp, *Spartina townsendii* and *Salicornia* spp, is covered uniformly by the ebbing and flooding tide. In the higher salting stage the tide is confined to marsh creeks except at high spring tide. *Halimione* (*Obione*), *Agropyron pungens*, *Aster tripolium* and other plants dominate this stage. Pans of two types develop during the building up of the salting stage of the marsh. Growth is most rapid along the borders of the main creeks where it may reach almost 1 cm. per annum.

(d) Coastal reclamation

Coastal salt marsh environment is the most useful land as far as reclamation of land from the sea is concerned. Salt marsh silt, once the salt has been washed out, forms very fertile soil. For this reason many coastal areas where salt marsh develops have been reclaimed for farm land. One area of very extensive reclamation is around the Wash, where reclamation has been going on since Roman times. According to Borer (1939)[29] during the seventeenth century 35,000 acres in the Wash were reclaimed and in the eighteenth century 196 acres increasing again to 9,000 acres in the nineteenth century. The large amount reclaimed in the seventeenth century was made possible by taking advantage of all the natural accretion which had taken place since the Roman period. Of this land reclaimed 8,000 acres were along the Norfolk coast and 37,000 acres were in south Lincolnshire.

This type of reclamation cannot be made in large areas because the marsh must build up naturally to a certain height before successful reclamation can be achieved. When the marsh is built to such a height that only the highest tides inundate it, walls can be built on the seaward side and drains established, to enable the salt to be washed out. To facilitate this process a series of ditches is dug running across the marsh to the sea with a fall of 2 ft. per mile. The material from the ditch is placed on the side facing the flood tide so that material eroded from the pile is washed on to the marsh and can settle in the relatively quiet water. The ebbing tide is assisted by the ditches which allow the newly deposited silt time to consolidate before the next high water covers the area.

An unsuccessful reclamation scheme was started in 1839 by Sir J. Rennie and the Norfolk Estuary Company; an attempt was made to enclose a large area at one time, but by 1876 only 1,500 acres had been enclosed and reclaimed while the remainder, 30,000 acres, was bare sand. Of this area 2,381 acres were reclaimed by 1914 and 800 have been inned since then.

Successful reclamation is now being carried out in the Lincolnshire part of the Wash following unsuccessful schemes which were proposed in 1857 by the Lincolnshire Estuary Company to reclaim a strip up to nearly 3 miles in width in one operation. This failed because the width of the area prevented natural accretion taking place throughout the zone to a sufficient height. The width of active salt marsh growing in the area around Wainfleet is $\frac{1}{2}$–$\frac{3}{4}$ mile. The reclamation of 1948 in this area has taken a strip $\frac{1}{2}$ mile wide. Reclamation in Morecambe Bay has also been extensive, but because sand rather than silt is deposited in this area the reclaimed land is not of very great value and the Royal Commission on Coast Erosion[30] state in their report of 1911 that of the 1,000 acres gained about half had since been abandoned.

(e) The time factor

The rate at which marsh accretion takes place has already been mentioned but it is not always easy to estimate the rate at which other forms

of coastal accretion take place. Compared to some other geomorphological processes marine deposition is on the whole rapid. Changes in the
coastal outline can be shown by surveys over relatively short periods of
time. Precise information of the rate of growth of coastal features can, in
many areas, only be obtained for the period for which accurate surveys
are available. The Ordnance Survey maps only date back to the beginning of the nineteenth century, but in some areas fairly accurate maps
or charts give some evidence on the rate of growth before that date.
Historic evidence can in many instances give qualitative data on coastal
development long before accurate maps are available. Details of some
examples of this type of evidence will be discussed in chapter 11. One
difficulty in considering the rate of growth of coastal features is the
erratic way in which many of them grow; abnormal storms or other
unusual circumstances may make a sudden change, which causes greater
alteration in the coastal features over a short period than many years
have made previously.

Orford Ness, on the coast of Suffolk, which diverts the river Alde
southwards for 11 miles, has grown irregularly; between 1601 and 1897
it grew at an average rate of about 15 yds. per year and if estimates of
its position in 1165 are correct it must have grown $5\frac{1}{2}$ miles in a little
over 700 years till 1897. It is known that the spit lost length after the
maximum in 1897, when a great storm cut more than a mile off the distal
end of the spit. It shortened to a minimum in 1902 since this date it has
grown again. The rate of growth of the tip of Dungeness from Lydd has
also been estimated since 1617[21] or even earlier and shows great variation
from a rate of $8\frac{1}{4}$ yds. per year between 1689 and 1794 to a period of no
growth between 1794 and 1809. It is known that this whole large foreland and the Romney and Walland marshes have developed in an area
which was an embayment in Neolithic times. The rate of growth of such
shingle features as Dungeness probably depends to some extent on the
frequency of storms, which are capable of throwing shingle up to form
the beach ridges.

The growth of features largely composed of sand is probably more
regular, but may also be fairly rapid. On the Lincolnshire coast south of
Skegness the map evidence points to a rapid development of sand dunes
and marsh amounting to a total width of 900 yds. since the first quarter
of the nineteenth century, which is an average rate of 7·2 yds. per year
in the area around Gibraltar Point. It has also been shown that the large
area of dunes and sand in the Afon Glaslyn has formed since the fourteenth century into the area now known as Morfa Harlech. The building
out of features around the coast is very closely related to the variations of
sea-level which have been taking place around the coasts. During the last
few millenia in which most of the coast accretion which can now be seen

has taken place sea-level has rarely been static. During the latest period of geological time since the ice finally started to melt there has been, in general, a rising sea-level but it has not been a simple movement.

(f) Effect of sea-level changes

The details of the actual changes of sea-level which have occurred during the post-glacial period will be considered in the next chapter (see pp. 305–310). The theoretical effects of a rising and falling base-level in connexion with constructive coastal processes may be considered now. A rising base-level will probably rarely give rise directly to conditions suitable for coastal deposition, unless the land immediately behind the former coast is very low-lying so that the gradient of the new sea-floor is less than the original one. The normal conception of a rising base-level is to produce a more irregular coastline; this will tend to make the longshore movement of beach material more irregular, resulting in deposition in areas where an excess of material accumulates. Such areas are likely to be the bay-heads initially, but spits prolonging the trend of the coast will tend to form where the sharpness of headlands prevents the smooth transit of material along the coast. These are features which have long been associated with a shoreline of submergence; they are an essential positive part of the cycle of marine erosion of a steep indented coastline.

A falling base-level, by exposing part of the sea-floor, is normally considered to produce a very flat offshore gradient or what has been considered to be a typical shoreline of emergence by Johnson and others. Such a condition is liable to lead to the development of such features as barrier islands and barrier beaches. This, however, is frequently not the coastal type found in regions in which there has been a recent fall of base-level. Nevertheless such a change of base-level should, initially at at any rate, lead to a gain of land at the expense of the sea. A feature which is often characteristic of this state is the raised beach backed by an abandoned line of cliffs. This type of coastal form is very well illustrated in parts of the west coast of Scotland, where recent uplift of the land due to isostatic recovery of the land on the melting of the large Scottish ice cap is giving a falling base-level (see fig. 9–11, p. 308). The actual coastline on which the sea now breaks is, however, little different from areas which have not been affected by a falling base-level; there are no barrier islands or sand dunes often associated with an emergent coast. The clear evidence of the raised beach does, however, give proof of the fall in sea-level. The reason for this is that on the west coast of Scotland the offshore gradient and supply of beach material is not suitable for the formation of barrier islands.

REFERENCES

[1]Lewis, W. V., 1931, Effect of wave incidence on the configuration of a shingle beach. *Geog. Journ.* **78,** pp. 131–48.

[2]Trask, P. D., 1956, Changes in configuration of Point Reyes beach, California, 1955–1956. *B.E.B. Tech. Memo.* **91.**

[3]Lafond, E. C., 1939, Sand movement near the beach in relation to tides and waves. *Proc. 6th Pacific Sci. Cong.* pp. 795–9.

[4]Shepard, F. P., 1950, Beach cycles in southern California. *B.E.B. Tech. Memo.* **20.**

[5]Inman, D. L. and Rusnak, G. A., 1956. Changes in sand level on the beach and shelf at La Jolla, California, *B.E.B. Tech. Memo.* **82.**

[6]Barnes, F. A. and King, C. A. M., 1955, Beach changes in Lincolnshire since the 1953 storm surge. *East Midland Geog.* **4,** pp. 18–28.

[7]Shepard, F. P., 1952, Revised nomenclature for depositional coastal features. *Bull. Am. Assoc. Petrol. Geol.* **36,** 10. pp. 1902–12.

[8]Kidson, C., 1950, Dawlish Warren; a study of the evolution of the sand spits across the mouth of the river Exe in Devon. *Trans. and Papers Inst. Brit. Geog.* **16,** pp. 67–80.

[9]Robinson, A. H. W., 1955, The harbour entrances of Poole, Christchurch and Pagham. *Geog. Journ.* **121,** pp. 33–50.

[10]Evans, O. F. 1942, The origin of spits, bars and related structures. *Journ. Geol.* **50,** pp. 846–65.

[11]Barnes, F. A. and King, C. A. M., 1957, The spit at Gibraltar Point, Lincolnshire. *East Midland Geog.* **8,** pp. 22–31.

[12]Cotton, C. A., 1951, Accidents and interruptions in the marine cycle of erosion. *Geog. Journ.* **107,** pp. 343–9.

[13]Armstrong Price, W., 1954, Environment and formation of the chenier plain. *A. and M. Project* **63.**

[14]Steers, J. A., 1946, *The coastline of England and Wales.*

[15]Lewis, W. V., 1938, The evolution of shoreline curves. *Proc. Geol. Assoc.* **49,** pp. 107–27.

[16]de la Beche, H. T., 1833, *A geological Manual.*

[17]Harrison, J. T., 1848, Observations on causes tending to alter the outline of the English coast. *Min. Proc. Inst. Civ. Eng.* **8,** p. 344.

[18]Schou, A., 1945, Det Marine forland. *Folia Geographica Danica* **4,** pp. 1–236.

[19]Jennings, J. N., 1955, The influence of wave action on the coastal outline in plan. *The Australian Geog.* **6,** 4, pp. 36–44.

[20]Lewis, W. V., 1932, The formation of Dungeness Foreland. *Geog. Journ.* **60,** p. 310.

[21]Lewis, W. V. and Balchin, W. G. V., 1940, Past sea levels at Dungeness. *Geog. Journ.* **106,** pp. 258–85.

[22]Gulliver, F. P., 1887, Dungeness Foreland. *Geog. Journ.* **9,** p. 636.

[23]Williams, W. W. and Fryer, D. H., 1953, Benacre Ness; an east coast erosion problem. *Journ. Inst. Chart. Surveyors* **32,** pp. 772–81.

[24]Williams, W. W., 1956, An east coast survey; some recent changes in the coast of East Anglia. *Geog. Journ.* **122,** pp. 317–34.

[25]Barnes, F. A. and King, C. A. M., 1951, A preliminary survey at Gibraltar Point, Lincolnshire. *Bird Obs. and Field Res. St. Gib. Pt. Lincs. Rep.* pp. 41–59.

[26]Chapman, V. J., 1938, Marsh Development in Norfolk. *Trans. Norfolk and Norwich Nat. Soc.* **14,** p. 394.

[27]Steers, J. A., 1938, The rate of sedimentation on salt marshes on Scolt Head Island, Norfolk. *Geol. Mag.* **75,** pp. 26–39.

[28]Chapman, V. J., 1938, Studies in salt marsh ecology I, II, III. *Journ. Ecology* **26,** p. 144.

[29]Borer, O., 1939, Changes in the Wash. *Geog. Journ.* **93,** pp. 491–6.

[30]Final Report. 1911 Royal Commission on Coast Erosion.

CHAPTER 9

DESTRUCTIVE WAVE ACTION AND COASTAL EROSION

THE conditions under which destructive beach processes operate, and coastal erosion takes place, are usually much more spectacular than the slower and less noticeable changes which occur under conditions of accretion on beach or coast. It is the latter, however, which produces the greatest area change in the amount of land and sea round the coasts of the British Isles according to the report of the Royal Commission on coastal erosion published in 1911.[1] The gain takes place largely in sheltered salt marshes and estuaries while the losses occur on the open coast. Another point is worthy of note; some of the erosion now taking place is due to the effect of man-made structures. This was made clear in the discussion on longshore movement (see pp. 144–158). Before considering coastal erosion, the nature of destructive wave action on beaches will be examined, and the processes by which they attack sea cliffs and marine benches will be analysed.

1. *DESTRUCTIVE ACTION IN PROFILE—THE BEACH, CLIFF AND ROCK PLATFORM*

The characteristics of waves which cause accretion on the beach have already been discussed and it is generally true that the reverse conditions will cause erosion on the foreshore by seaward movement of material; there are some important exceptions which will be mentioned when the effect of different materials is considered.

(a) Effect of waves, wind and other forces

Flat waves are usually constructive on the beach while the steep waves are normally destructive, lowering the level of the beach surface and transporting material seaward. The larger the waves are, provided they are about the optimum steepness for destructive action, the greater will be the removal of material from the beach because of their greater energy. Destructive waves are normally associated with storms and high wind velocities; strong winds blowing near the coast generate seas which are high relative to their length and the wind itself, as has already been demonstrated in laboratory experiments and field observations (see pp. 207–216), has a marked effect on the destructive nature of the wave

279

attack. A strong onshore wind may also assist the destructive tendency of the waves by raising the water level above its normal height, thus allowing the sea to attack zones normally beyond its reach. Strong winds and the rapid changes in atmospheric pressure associated with them can generate a surge in some areas, this will be considered on pp. 283–288.

The recorded height of storm waves on the coast may be exaggerated on some occasions, but nevertheless considerable wave heights can be attained, although waves near the coast will not normally be as high as those in the open ocean (see pp. 90, 91). It has been estimated that the height of the waves in the North Sea, that caused so much damage along the east coast of England during the night of 31 January to 1 February 1953, was about 20 ft. from crest to trough. These waves were generated by winds of exceptional force; Douglas (1953)[2] calculated a geostrophic wind of 175 m.p.h. which was blowing over a long fetch for a long period, and therefore probably produced the maximum possible wave size for the North Sea. Waves of this height are more common off coasts exposed to the open ocean; Shepard (1950)[3] states that off Washington and Oregon waves of 20 ft. are fairly common, but off southern California waves are rarely higher than 10 ft. Occasional records of waves up to about 20 ft. in height have been obtained from the Atlantic coast of America, but in general waves are lower than 10 ft. there (see pp. 87–89).

(b) Destructive wave action on the beach

i. SHINGLE. The effect of destructive storm waves on the beach may be considered in relation to the type of beach material ; there is a very significant difference between the effect of storm waves on shingle and on sand beaches. Shingle may be considered first; Lewis (1931)[4] has described the action of destructive waves on a shingle beach, he noted the relative weakness of the swash compared to the backwash. The action of such destructive waves can cause very rapid removal of shingle from the upper foreshore to deeper water outside the break-point; on Chesil beach at Abbotsbury the crest of the shingle beach was cut back over a width of 5 ft. within 3 hrs. on one occasion (20.9.49). The waves were short and steep at the time with a steepness ratio of 0·019. On the following day steep waves cut away a vertical thickness of 2–3 ft. of shingle in about 1 hr. The shingle here has a median diameter of 10·3 mm. In great storms very large volumes of shingle may be removed from the foreshore into deeper water to be returned by the constructive waves following the storm.

Storm waves are not entirely destructive in their effect on a shingle beach. Although more material is removed seawards than transferred landwards some shingle is often thrown high on to the beach crest, well above the reach of normal waves. The pebbles are thrown upwards by the swash of the waves and, owing to the rapidity of percolation through the shingle, the backwash cannot remove the pebbles deposited at the upper limit of the swash (see fig. 9–1). The rate of percolation is in-

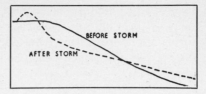

FIG. 9–1. Diagrammatic effect of storm waves on a shingle beach.

creased by the very well sorted nature of the beach shingle compared to other types of gravel as pointed out by Emery (1955).[5] Shingle can be thrown to considerable elevations above the mean sea-level by storm waves; the height of Chesil beach above high water level of normal tides illustrates this. Pebbles are still sometimes thrown over the beach crest which lies 23 ft. above normal high tide level at Abbotsbury and 43 ft. at Portland, where the beach is composed of larger shingle about 2–3 in. in diameter.

The ridges which form the bulk of the large shingle structures of Dungeness and Orford Ness have been built by storm waves. The material forming these ridges is brought to the vicinity by longshore movement of shingle under the influence of constructive waves, approaching the shore obliquely, but it is the storm waves, which are generally destructive, that build the ridges to a height well above the normal high tide level.

ii. SAND. Steep storm waves attacking a sand beach are usually entirely destructive in their effect, moving sand to deeper water off-shore. The coarser the sand the greater the amount removed under similar wave conditions. For example, during the period 2–12 December 1950, about 3 ft. depth of sand was removed from the entire width of the beach at the north end of Marsden Bay, while similar but lesser erosion occurred at the south end of the bay. In some instances a vertical scarp is left on the beach at the limit of the high tide accompanied by destructive waves, this was well shown on the profile for 28 October 1950. These profiles are shown in fig. 9–2.

In some areas the whole beach may be removed by storm waves; a good example of this was the removal of sand from some of the beaches of Lincolnshire as a result of the storm-flood of January–February 1953, leaving the clay base of the beach exposed (see fig. 9–6). Similar removal of entire beaches is reported from California by Shepard (1950);[3] in some of these examples, such as Boomer beach, which has already been mentioned, and Windansea beach, the removal was largely the result of oblique waves moving the beach material to the other end of a restricted bay. Such erosion can result in changes of beach level of over

6 ft., which sometimes takes place over periods as short as one day. On many of the Californian beaches there is marked erosion of the beach during the stormy winter period. Erosion at this season has also been observed on the ridged beach at Blackpool which is made of fine sand (see fig. 8–2).

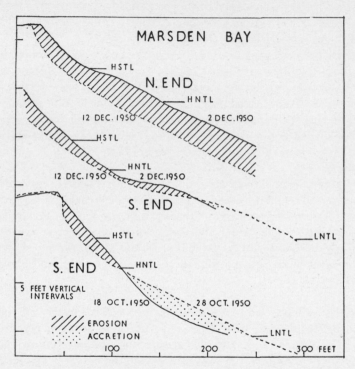

FIG. 9–2. Profiles of Marsden Bay, Co. Durham, to show the effect of destructive waves.

The most serious coastal erosion is usually associated with abnormal conditions of weather and water-level and in some localities these are associated with the development of a storm surge, which greatly raises the water-level. This is very important from the point of view of coastal defences and physiographic changes; it may, therefore, be considered in more detail.

Summary

It is the steep, storm waves, particularly when there are strong on-shore winds, that are destructive on the foreshore. On shingle beaches such waves can cause very rapid seaward removal of material, but some of it is thrown well above the ordinary high tide level by the swash of the storm waves to form high shingle ridges, which may remain as more or less permanent features of the coast. On sand beaches steep waves are entirely destructive in character, taking sand out to deeper water. The coarser the sand the greater the amount of seaward removal by storm waves.

(c) Storm surges

The North Sea is particularly susceptible to storm surges owing to its shape, while abnormal rises of sea-level are specially dangerous on part of the coasts of the North Sea, since for considerable stretches they are low-lying, requiring artificial protection in the form of sea-walls and banks. These structures often protect areas which are below the level of high tide; a breach in the defences, therefore, has very serious consequences for the coastal hinterland. This was clearly shown in the damage and loss of life caused in parts of East England[6] and Holland during the 1953 surge and storm-flood. The flooding was rendered much more serious by the very high sea-level which accompanied the extra large storm waves already mentioned. This type of surge occurs at intervals in the North Sea when suitable meteorological conditions prevail. The 1949 storm surge has been studied by Corkan (1950)[7] while Rossiter (1954)[8] has analysed the 1953 surge. Eight surges have been recorded during the present century after a very severe one in 1897.[9]

The North Sea is a shallow, more or less rectangular, basin, which opens northwards to the Atlantic Ocean, from which direction the normal tidal energy comes. The small outlet through the Straits of Dover to the south is also significant. The general tidal pattern of the North Sea has already been discussed and in some respects the behaviour of the surges resembles the normal tide (see pp. 28–30).

Surges are of two types; there are the external surges, having their origin outside the North Sea and the internal one directly due to variations of level within the area. Corkan, in his analysis of the 1949, surge, has calculated the amount of disturbance of sea-level for all places on the North Sea coasts for which data were available. This was done by eliminating the normal tidal curve from the records of sea-level changes. The time of the maximum disturbance, as shown by this analysis, occurred within one hour of the time of high water at nearly all stations on the east coast of the British Isles. At the time of this surge the tide was nearly neap so that in some places the surge only raised the level to that of a normal spring tide; the greatest rise of sea-level was about 5·5 ft. at King's Lynn; its situation in the Wash may account for this abnormality. This disturbance travelled around the North Sea in an anti-clockwise direction with the normal tide. The amplitude of the maximum disturbance was also reduced as the surge travelled round the North Sea in the same way as the normal tide.

A weather situation similar to that of 1949 in some respects caused the surge of 1953; a deep depression passed eastwards to the north of Scotland, causing the very strong south-west winds to veer suddenly northerly. Fig. 9–3 (a and b) shows the character and course of the depression. The wind and pressure affect the water level in a number of ways; firstly, the pressure acts as an inverted barometer, a very low pressure will cause a rise of sea-level at the rate of 1 ft. for a fall in pressure of 34 millibars. Secondly, there are gradients set up by the friction of the wind blowing over the sea and, thirdly, there is the inflow and outflow of water from neighbouring water bodies. It has been calculated that this third factor caused a change in the mean level of the North Sea from −0·5 ft. to +0·7 ft. in one day. When water is flowing into the North Sea from the north, owing to the rotation of the earth, the inflow takes place largely on the western side of the sea along the east coast of the British Isles, with relatively little change occurring on the coast of Denmark and Norway.

The storm surge of 1953 caused very much greater elevations in sea-

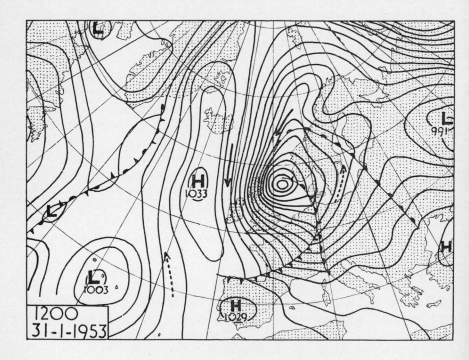

Pressure at centre of North Sea depression 967 mb.

FIG. 9–3. (a) Synoptic chart for the North Atlantic.

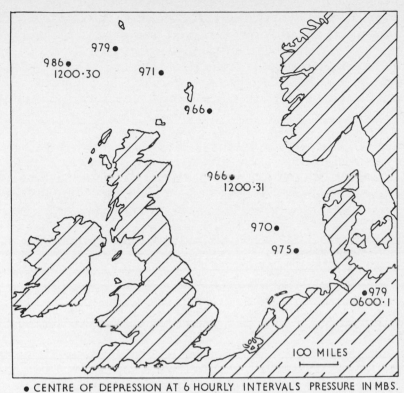

● CENTRE OF DEPRESSION AT 6 HOURLY INTERVALS PRESSURE IN MBS.

FIG. 9-3. (*b*) Track of depression centre in the North Sea from 30 Jan. to 1 Feb., 1953.

level and was more disastrous in its effect on the coast, because it occurred during a period of spring tides, when the predicted water levels
were high; had the surge occurred a fortnight later, when one of the
highest tides of the year was predicted, the maximum water-level would
have been at least 2 ft. higher in some areas. The predicted height of sea-
level was increased by 9–11 ft. in some places in the southern North Sea,
and this occurred near the time of high tide in many places.

Rossiter in his analysis of the surge uses all available data from tide
gauges round the North Sea coasts and in the eastern part of the English
Channel. In calculating the height of the surge, the normal tidal rise and
fall have been deducted, and the effect of barometric pressure variation
eliminated, enabling the effects of the wind to be studied. Before considering the changes in level, the weather situation during the period of
the surge may be outlined. A small secondary depression developed on a
trailing cold front and deepened rapidly as it passed to the north of
Scotland and turned south-east to travel across the centre of the North

Sea and into north-west Germany. The depression deepened to reach a minimum pressure of 966 millibars in its passage across the northern North Sea. When the centre of the depression passed into the North Sea a very strong north wind developed in its rear owing to the building up of a strong ridge of high pressure behind it. The geostrophic wind reached a speed of 175 m.p.h. and in itself caused much damage in Scotland.

The variation of mean-sea-level during the passage of the storm and the period of the surge have been calculated for the whole of the North Sea; this indicates the amount of water moving into or out of the sea from without. Most of this water came into the North Sea between Scotland and Norway; the other outlet through the Straits of Dover acted as a safety valve as will be mentioned. The reason for the influx of water was the action of the gale force north winds which, owing to the width of the wind belt and the presence of Scotland, did not, in fact, as it would do in the open ocean, cause a transport of water at right angles to the direction of the wind. It has been estimated that 15 billion ($\times 10^{12}$) cubic ft. of water entered the North Sea between 2100 hrs. on 31 and noon on 1 February. The increase in level averaged over the whole North Sea was in excess of 2 ft. during this period as illustrated in fig. 9-4.

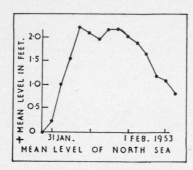

FIG. 9–4. Height of the North Sea above the mean level during 31 Jan. and 1 Feb., 1953. (After Rossiter.)

The records of tide levels for Dover, Newhaven and Dieppe show that the surge was partially transmitted through the Straits of Dover. Owing to the rotation of the earth the water was deflected to the right, giving higher elevations on the English coast than in France. Thus at Dover the surge was over 6 ft., while at Newhaven it was 4 ft. but in Dieppe it was only a little over 3 ft. The rise in level at Newhaven took place in spite of a very strong offshore northerly wind, which would usually cause a fall in level. The total volume of water escaping from the North Sea through the Straits of Dover has been estimated to be 1.7×10^{11} cubic ft., this would cause a fall in level of the southern North Sea between Orford Ness and Brouwershaven of 0.9 ft. approximately. The Straits of Dover did, therefore, act as a safety valve to a considerable degree.

To account for the nature of the surge along the coast, it is necessary to take into account both the changes in level in the North Sea mentioned above, and the progress of the surge of external origin southward down the coast of the British Isles. The arrival of this maximum dis-

turbance can be traced along the coast and differentiated from changes
due to the level of the North Sea in different areas. By 1200 hrs. on
31 January the north winds were becoming established over the north-
western North Sea and sea-level was rising owing to the traction effect of
these winds. By 1500 hrs. the general level had risen by 1 ft. and the
maximum disturbance had reached Aberdeen. At 1800 hrs. the maximum wind forces were experienced and the water level had risen by 4 ft.
in the latitude of Northumberland; the approach of the major surge,
which had now reached the Firth of Forth, was tending to cause an anti-
clockwise rotation of the co-disturbance lines. By 2100 hrs. the surge
peak reached Yorkshire and the major disturbance lay between Norfolk
and Holland, where the height of the surge was about 8 ft. The mean
level of the North Sea had now reached its maximum above undisturbed
level of 2·2 ft. By 0001 hrs. on 1 February the surge peak had passed the
coastline between the Humber and Thames and was approaching the
south coast of Holland, with maximum heights of nearly 8 ft. in the
Thames and 9–10 ft. in the Scheldt. The peak of the surge was at
Chatham and Ostend at 0100 hrs., to the south of a line joining these
places it occurred somewhat later, at 0100 hrs. at Dover and 0500 hrs. at
Newhaven and about the same time at Dieppe. By 0300 hrs. the winds
were starting to moderate and the surge was passing northwards up the
coast of Holland reaching Ijmuiden at 0400 hrs., the Friesian Islands at
about 0600 hrs. and Nordeney at 0700 hrs. A strengthening of the wind
around 0900 hrs. probably caused the second peak in the Thames when
the primary surge had reached Cuxhaven. By 1000 hrs. the surge reached
Esbjerg and by 1200 hrs. the maximum disturbance had reached the
coast of north Denmark, the extreme southern tip of Norway was reached
by 2200 hrs. The total water displaced into the North Sea remained
the same till the level started to fall at 1500 hrs. The effect of shallowing of the sea compensated the effect of friction in maintaining the
height of the surge as it progressed anticlockwise round the North Sea.

The time of the maximum disturbance was within about 2 hrs. of
predicted high tide at many places along the east coast, although the
normal high tide and the surge did not travel at exactly the same rate
round the coasts of the British Isles. Had the high water of the tide and
the surge coincided exactly, the actual level would have been considerably raised in some areas. For example along the Lincolnshire coast the
height of the water level would have been about 4 ft. higher at its maximum if the high water of the tide had coincided with the maximum
surge disturbance and the storm had occurred a fortnight later during
the period of higher spring tides. In the area near Gibraltar Point in
south Lincolnshire the water reached a height of 7·8 ft. above the predicted tide level or 17·6 ft. O.D. (Liverpool). The waves, whose swash

would reach a height greatly in excess of this figure, were not taken into account. This gives some indication of the worst that could be expected to occur in considering the height to which surges are likely to raise an abnormal sea-level. This is important in relation to the height to which coastal defences in such areas as Lincolnshire should be built.

Summary

Storm surges can occur in fairly restricted seas, such as the North Sea, when suitable meteorological conditions obtain. A deep depression moving south-east across the northern North Sea, causing a sudden veer of wind from south-west to strong northerly, is most likely to set up a surge. This travels round the sea in an anti-clockwise direction at a speed somewhat similar to that of the tide. It may raise the water level up to 10 ft. above the predicted height in extreme cases. This happened on the coast of holland during the 1953 surge, while levels of 6 to 8 ft. above predicted heights were recorded along much of the coast of the southern North Sea. During the surge the mean level of the North Sea was raised over 2 ft. above normal for about 12 hrs.

(d) Erosion of solid rocks by the sea

The sea does not only remove the loose material of the beach to deeper water when destructive conditions prevail but may, if conditions are suitable, also attack the solid rocks of the coast. In doing this cliffs are formed at the back of the foreshore and wave-cut benches, or storm wave platforms, according to the terminology of Edwards (1951),[10] are eroded in front of the cliffs. The retreat of the cliffs is intimately linked with the cutting of the platform and both depend on the ability of the waves to reach the rocks. Hence these features only develop where there is no protective beach covering the rock platform and preventing the waves from attacking the cliffs. It has already been shown that the thickness of the cover need not be great, unless it is entirely removed by destructive waves, because the depth of disturbance of sand is small (see pp. 172–176). Before considering the formation of storm-wave platforms the processes by which the sea attacks the rocks of the cliffs may be mentioned.

The four main processes are well known and need not be considered in detail; they are corrosion, corrasion, attrition and hydraulic action. The first is concerned with the chemical weathering of the rocks by contact with the sea-water; this is a process particularly effective on limestone cliffs. Corrasion implies the direct attack of the cliffs by waves laden with sand grains and pebbles; the rocks are gradually worn away and smoothed by this process. Attrition is the process of breaking up pieces of rock fallen from the cliff by undercutting or other means; they can then be more easily moved away or used as tools for corrasion. The last process, hydraulic action, is probably the most effective agent of erosion. When waves break against a cliff air in the cracks is strongly compressed and later, as the wave recedes, the pressure is suddenly released. These sudden changes of pressure can enlarge the cracks and loosen pieces of rock. This process is more effective in well jointed rocks. The forces exerted directly by the waves are also very important but these are not so frequently discussed so they will be treated in rather more detail.

The shock pressures exerted by a wave breaking against a structure in such a way that a pocket of air is enclosed as the wave breaks has already been mentioned (see pp. 16, 17, and fig. 1–5). It was shown that if the cliff descends straight into deep water or if the waves break before they reach the cliff, no shock pressures will be induced. The pressure exerted by breaking waves has been recorded by dynamometers and the values agree quite well with theoretical ones derived from a

formula of Gaillard (1904),[11] $1 \cdot 31 \ (C + V_{max})^2 \ \dfrac{\rho}{2g},$ where C is the wave velocity and V_{max} the orbital velocity at the crest of the wave. For a wave 10 ft. high and 150 ft. long the calculated pressure would be 1,241 lb./sq. ft., while the observed value was 1,210. When the waves are long, and hence have a high velocity, the pressures generated are quite sufficient to cause very extensive damage to cliffs or structures. Only a very few waves, however, produced shock pressures in experimental recording of these pressures at Dieppe. The maximum pressure recorded was 12,700 lb./sq. ft. but this pressure only attained a value above 6,000 lb./sq. ft. for 1/100 sec. The deep water wave height was nearly 6 ft. and the length 132 ft. (de Rouville, 1938).[12] These very high pressures enable waves breaking against cliffs to dislodge fragments, but as soon as the fallen debris causes the wave to break, before it reaches the cliff, the rate of erosion will slow down as shock pressures will not be generated. Where there is a large tidal range the attack of the sea at high tide will probably continue to be effective for a longer period, than in a tideless sea.

Naturally the type of rock will have a very profound effect on the cliff profile and actual mechanism of erosion; this aspect of the problem will be considered later in connexion with a discussion of the rates of coastal erosion to which it is closely related.

SHORE PLATFORMS. The process of shore platform formation has not yet been fully explained. The result of the process can be seen round many cliffed coasts, particularly near headlands where beach material is less likely to accumulate. A somewhat irregular surface of bare rock sloping gently seawards is the normal form of this feature on tidal beaches, which may terminate near low tide mark with a secondary minor cliff. Fig. 9–5 shows a profile levelled across a typical wave-cut platform at low water near Scarborough. It has an overall gradient of 1 : 90, sloping seaward with a concave upward profile. The slight irregularity is caused by the outcrop of different strata on the beach, showing that the surface does not coincide with any one bedding plane, but is cut across the dip of the relatively hard Scarborough limestone within the Upper Estuarine series of the Jurassic. The tidal range at spring tide is about 20 ft. causing a considerable width of rock to come under the influence of the swash and backwash of the waves.

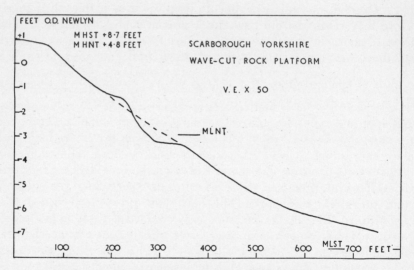

FIG. 9–5. Rock platform on the foreshore at Scarborough, Yorks.

Wentworth (1938)[13] in his study of the wave-formed benches around the coast of Oahu in the Hawaii Islands distinguished four processes as follows; 1. water-level (water-layer) weathering, 2. solution benching, 3. ramp abrasion and 4. wave quarrying. The tide here has a maximum range of only 3 ft. Some of the processes are helped by the presence of a little sand and gravel while others are hindered by it. Water-layer benching was observed to be most effective in weathered basalt with dykes and in palagonite tuff. It occurred at any level up to about 20 ft. above sea-level, in any situation where pools of quiet water can remain and can be replenished at fairly frequent intervals. At any one place a series of benches at different levels may form which do not appear to be related to variations in sea-level. The hollow which initiates the bench is gradually flattened as the parts which dry, as the water evaporates, are attacked, the margins and lip are lowered in the same way. Such benches may be 10 ft. wide and 20–30 ft. long, some are smaller but only a few larger. The bench is liable to destruction once the rampart holding in the water at its seaward edge is breached. This rampart is often very rugged, being eroded directly by the waves owing to its exposed position.

The nature of the process of water-layer benching appears to be a form of physical weathering caused by the frequent wetting of the rock, which exposes the structure very clearly. This process probably completes, and makes more perfect, the flattening of a bench, already partially formed by wave quarrying and other means. There is often a very sharp break of slope at the landward side of the bench. Wave quarrying tends to produce a broadly rounded nip under the cliff instead of the flatter slope, and sharper break, associated with water-layer weathering.

A somewhat similar form is obtained by solution weathering on calcareous rocks but this is restricted to levels about 4–5 ft. above sea-level. The two processes are, however, quite distinct. The conditions necessary for the development of the solution form are undrained hollows which are clear of debris. Much of the initial erosion on such a coast may be due to wave quarrying at a higher sea-level.

Bartrum (1938),[14] who has worked on the problem of marine benching in New Zealand, suggests that weathering is rapid down to the level of saturation but he and Turner (1928)[15] also consider that weathering can flatten platforms originally formed by other agencies. Johnson (1938)[16] suggests that weathering may roughen rather than smooth platforms.

More recent work on this problem has been published by Hills (1949).[17] Hills suggests that the term 'water-layer' weathering should be used instead of 'water-level' weathering, which Johnson had pointed out might be confused with sea-level. Hills considers that water-layer weathering can only operate on rocks susceptible to weathering by alternate wetting and drying. The platforms formed by this process are best developed where the wave attack is only moderate in intensity. The ramp at the seaward side of the platform tends to be protected from weathering by the fact that it is always wet, and therefore, below the level of saturation, but it may be eliminated when the rest of the platform is reduced to saturation level and is, therefore, also lowered at a lower rate. These features will probably not form so perfectly where the tidal range is great.

Nansen (1922)[18] has also shown that freezing is likely to prevent platform formation. On the other hand under tropical or monsoonal conditions their development will be accelerated. Hills also points out that wave action on a platform is more likely to produce a sloping surface below the cliff rather than the plane surface typical of water-layer weathering. He favours this process while minimizing the effect of wave action.

Edwards (1951)[10] has, however, put forward arguments in favour of the wave erosion theory of the development of the platform. He takes his examples from the coast of Victoria, Australia. The platforms here are best developed opposite the cliffed headlands. The level of the platforms is such that they are covered by over 1 ft. of water at high tide and are exposed at low tide; near the outer edge of the platform the level sometimes rises slightly and the surface becomes more irregular. Below the main cliff an inclined ramp forms and the platform is smoother in this zone. At low tide level another small cliff forms which can be attacked at all times. A layer of sand between $\frac{1}{2}$ and 1 ft. in thickness sometimes covers the platform, this is washed to and fro across the rocks by the waves at times, thus helping to abrade the platform. At spring tide the waves can attack the cliffs at the back of the ramp but it is mainly during the periods of storm that the main cliff is attacked and the platform abraded most strongly; the sea-level is raised by the on-shore winds and both cliffs can be attacked, although the main cliff is attacked most vigorously. Erosion is helped by the kelp which grows offshore; during storms the kelp is torn loose and is flung about by the waves, together with the rocks carried by 90 per cent of the kelp. The rocks attached to the kelp weigh up to 20 lb. and can, therefore, do considerable damage to the cliff.

The shore platform will diminish in width if the main cliff is not cut back at a greater rate than the low tide cliff; the processes, therefore, which operate to cut back the main cliff are the most important in the growth and preservation of the platform. It is the storm erosion, which concentrates the maximum energy above a certain level, that causes vigorous erosion at high water-level and causes the main cliff to retreat; this is, therefore, mainly responsible for the widening of the platform. The planation of the platform is the result of scouring by sand laden waves, water-layer weathering becomes more important as the platform becomes wider and more level.

Most authorities such as Davis, Johnson and Cotton, in what may be called the classical view of platform cutting, consider that sea-level must be stationary during its development. The main process by which the platform is widened under this view must be by submarine abrasion as the cliff is cut back and driven inland to produce the platform. The width of the platform, therefore, depends largely on the depth at which it can be cut. Bradley (1958)[19] has considered this problem in relation to observations made on the platform near Santa Cruz on the coast of California. The depth at which rocks can be abraded is less than that at which sediment can be moved; according to Rode (1930)[20] sand cannot abrade unless it is above 1 mm. in diameter. Twenhofel (1945)[21] also considers that sand grains less than 0·5 mm. can accomplish no significant erosion. Rode calculated that abrasion was theoretically possible to a depth of 150–300 ft.; this estimate reduces considerably that of Johnson (1919)[22] who set the limit of wave erosion at 600 ft. It has since been further reduced and more modern views, including that of Bradley, place it at about 30 ft.; this seems to be a much more probable depth. The evidence on which Bradley bases his estimate is related to the rounding of pyroxene grains, which takes place in the area of vigorous wave action in the surf zone. He found that in depths below 30 ft. the pyroxene grains, derived from the land, are significantly less abraded than those in shallower water.

The modern platforms off California are about 0·3 miles (1,584 ft.) wide at a depth of 30 ft., giving a gradient of about 1 : 53. This is steeper than the platform at Scarborough indicating that where the tidal range is greater the platform may be wider at that depth. Bradley considers that platforms wider than $\frac{1}{3}$ mile can only be cut during a rising sea-level. The modern platforms are in places wider than this, and their concave profile suggests cutting during slow submergence.

Summary

Solid rocks are eroded by the sea by four processes: corrosion, or chemical action, corrasion, attrition and hydraulic action. The latter is probably the most effective, particularly in well jointed rocks. Shock pressures produced by breaking waves can also exert a powerful force on the rocks.

Shore platforms are eroded by the sea to form a gently concave upward curve where the tidal range is great. In some areas of small tidal range water-layer weathering may be effective although direct wave action is still probably the dominant process. Where water-layer weathering is effective flat areas may form on a platform which has been cut largely by wave action. Where the tidal range is fairly small a cliff forms at low water, with a ramp separating the zones of water-layer weathering from the sea. Landwards of the zone of weathering a sharp break of slope forms where this process is effective, where wave scour is dominant an inclined ramp forms. Wave scour is probably the main process in the cutting of platforms, which are widened by erosion of the cliff by storm waves. Effective marine abrasion is probably restricted to a depth of 30 ft. and platforms wider than about $\frac{1}{3}$ mile can only be cut when sea-level is rising.

2. *DESTRUCTIVE MARINE ACTION IN PLAN—COASTAL EROSION*

The Royal Commission on Coast Erosion (1911)[1] gave figures which indicate the extent of erosion and accretion on the coasts and in the tidal rivers of the United Kingdom. The evidence is derived from a comparison of the various editions of the 6-in. to 1-mile Ordnance Survey maps. The results show that over an average period of 35 years in England and Wales 4,692 acres were lost while 35,444 acres were gained, giving a net gain of 30,752 acres above high tide level. For Scotland the figures are 815 acres lost, 4,704 acres gained resulting in a net gain of 3,889 acres. The interpretation of the maps was made difficult because of a change of datum from ordinary spring tide level to ordinary tide level on the maps.

The area of the foreshore lost and gained between tide levels is given as a loss of 44,629 acres, gain of 13,397 acres in England and Wales. In Scotland the loss was 12,447 acres and the gain 4,076 acres. Although part of this loss may be due to the change in tide level data on surveys, it must imply a general steepening of the foreshore. Reclamations have also reduced the area of the foreshore.

Evidence derived from the comparison of maps is not always reliable as was shown by one witness from Ireland. He pointed out that the maps of Clew Bay, Co. Mayo, show accretion between 1839 and 1898 but in fact he knew that partially submerged drumlins had been eroded during the period under consideration (27459–27569).[1] Although the figures may not be completely accurate they do show that more land is gained in the British Isles from the sea than is lost to it. Nevertheless coastal erosion remains a serious problem in many areas.

(a) Causes of coastal erosion

i. PART PLAYED BY THE BEACH. A wide beach which prevents the waves reaching the solid rock at the back of the beach or beneath it will form an effective protection to the coast and prevent coastal erosion. If, however, the beach is thin enough to be removed by storm waves it will allow the cliffs to be attacked by these waves, which are the only ones capable of effective erosion, the presence of the beach during normal conditions will prevent coastal erosion. Where there is a considerable tidal range the vertical extent of the beach must be greater to afford a protection to the coast, this applies particularly in areas where the sea-level is liable to be abnormally raised by meteorological conditions, for example the surges already discussed.

This point is very well illustrated by the effects of the 1953 storm surge on the Lincolnshire coast. As soon as possible after the floods, a series of 23 profiles were surveyed at different positions on the coast between Gibraltar Point in the south and Theddlethorpe in the north. These profiles are shown on fig. 9–6; they cover areas where the damage

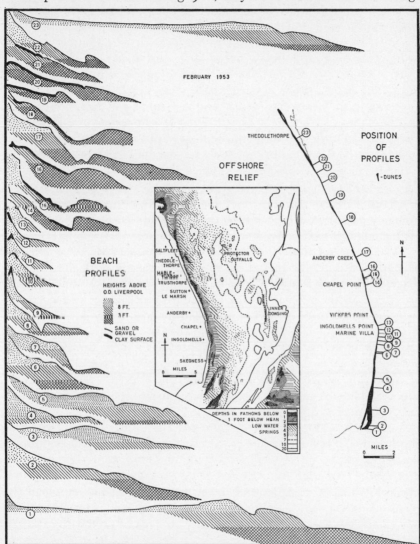

FIG. 9–6. Profiles of the Lincolnshire beaches surveyed after the surge of 1953.

ranged from minor dune cliffing to complete destruction of massive concrete defences. It can be shown that the nature and amount of damage is closely related to the character and height of the beach in the different areas. The profiles can be divided into different groups according to their beach characteristics and the nature of the damage.[6]

I. Profiles 1–4 to the south of Skegness show a wide beach, a considerable part of which is above 8 ft. O.D., protecting an area of wide, high dunes which are well vegetated. This part of the coast needs no artificial protection and damage was restricted to dune erosion resulting in sand cliffs up to 10 ft. high. There was a close correlation between the width of the beach and the amount of dune erosion.

II. The next profile, 5, was surveyed from the centre of Skegness front; this profile shows a particularly wide beach, but dunes are no longer able to form. The width and height of the beach, however, absorbed the wave energy sufficiently to prevent serious damage in the town, although the height of the pullover (18·3 ft. O.D.) was dangerously near the surge high water-level (17·6 ft. O.D.) Minor flooding of reclaimed dune slacks was the only damage.

III. Profiles 6 and 7 surveyed at the north end of Skegness are transitional in character; the beach is much narrower but still fairly high, probably partially due to combing down of sand on to the beach which prevented more serious erosion.

IV. The next series of profiles cover the area between the south end of Butlin's camp and Ingoldmells Point, these are 8–13, and in this stretch the most southerly of the major breaches of the defences occurred. All the profiles of this group are much lower and narrower than the others mentioned, the dunes at the back of the beach become attenuated and offer less resistance to the waves. At high water the waves can break close inshore and concentrate their energy on the artificial defences which were needed to protect the northern part of this stretch of coast. The concrete defences of the artificial points of Marine Villa and Ingoldmells suffered very severe damage and were completely destroyed over some distance.

V. Profiles 14, 15 and 16 cover the area near Chapel Point. This was another area of severe damage to the coast defences and houses built on the relics of the dunes behind the rather flimsy concrete wall were destroyed. This area has suffered from erosion for some time, and, owing to the lack of dune sand, no material is available on which the waves could expend their energy. The small amount of beach material was completely stripped from the beach on most of profile 16 exposing the impermeable clay base.

VI. At Anderby Creek, where profile 17 was surveyed, the beach again shows a wide berm of sand. This was formed by the storm waves of sand eroded from the dunes, which are again fairly high in this vicinity. The dunes were very severely cut back to form cliffs up to 20 ft. in height, but this sand absorbed the wave energy to a sufficient extent to prevent a complete breach and built the foreshore to a considerable height.

VII. The profiles 18–21 cover the area of most severe damage along this coast between Sandilands, Sutton-on-Sea and Mablethorpe. The beach on these four profiles is very low and narrow so that even neap high tides reach up to the sea-walls, which provide a necessary defence for this coast in the absence of effective dunes. The lack of a reserve supply of sand in the form of dunes at the back of the beach caused very extensive damage by waves; the coastal defences were completely breached over a considerable stretch of coast. The inadequate supply of beach material on the foreshore was removed by the destructive storm waves, exposing the clay base of the beach. The deep water immediately adjacent to the defences and the absence of beach material enabled all the energy of the waves to concentrate on the destruction of the sea-walls.

VIII. North of Mablethorpe profiles 22 and 23 show a return to conditions similar to those obtaining in the first 5 profiles south of Skegness. The dunes become wider and higher, making sea-defences unnecessary, and at Theddlethorpe the beach becomes very wide above 8 ft. O.D.; the wave energy, therefore, was spent over a wide area and only very minor dune cliffing resulted.

These profiles show clearly the value of a wide, high beach in protecting the coast from erosion. The reserve of sand held in dunes provides another good safeguard against erosion on a coast such as that of Lincolnshire, which has not the natural protection of cliffs of hard rock behind the beach. The presence of a thick beach absorbs the energy of the waves and prevents its dissipation against the more solid foundation and back of the beach, whether this be a natural cliff and rocky platform or artificial sea defences and a clay beach foundation.

ii. CHARACTER OF THE COAST. The liability of coasts to erosion varies greatly and depends on a number of factors which may be listed:

1. Exposure
   (a) Form of coastline in plan
   (b) Exposure to wave attack—dominant wind direction and fetch
2. Tide—range and currents
3. Coastal type
   (a) Low coast with dunes, etc.
   (b) Rocky coast, generally with cliffs
4. Rock type of 3 (b)
5. Offshore relief
6. Sea-level changes
7. The effect of man-made structures
8. Longshore movement of beach material.

The last factor is of fundamental importance in coastal erosion and will be considered separately. Sea-level changes will also be discussed in a separate section, the influence of the other factors may be mentioned briefly.

Exposure. From what has already been stated it is clear that where the coastline is irregular the attack of the sea will tend to be concentrated on the headlands; this is partly due to the concentration of wave energy on the headland, which results in the frequent failure of beaches to maintain themselves here. On the other hand headlands are frequently composed of harder rock which has already resisted erosion to a greater extent than the neighbouring areas and will tend to continue to do so. The coasts exposed to the prevailing winds would be expected to suffer more rapid erosion than the lee coasts, but this does not always happen. The east coast of Britain is probably being eroded at a greater rate than the exposed parts of the west coast, despite the fact that the prevailing wind blows offshore. In this instance the character of the coast more than compensates for the relatively smaller number of destructive storms that attack the coast. When such storms do occur their result is much more disastrous than a similar storm on many parts of the west coast which are exposed to the open ocean. This is partly due to their susceptibility to surges.

Tide. The effect of the tide is to increase the zone over which the destructive waves can operate, this facilitates the erosion of cliffs. A large tidal range also makes it more likely that the beach profile will be smooth offshore. This prevents the premature breaking of waves on submarine bars which would destroy some of their energy. As a result of the normal parabolic shape of the beach profile, the waves will be able to break closer inshore at high tide and their energy will be dissipated over a reduced width of beach, and larger amounts of material will be carried seaward when they are destructive.

Coastal type (a) low coast. From the point of view of their susceptibility to erosion, coasts may be divided broadly into low coasts and rocky coasts which are usually cliffed. The low coasts are those protected only by superficial deposits; these include sand dune coasts, which it has already been shown can stand up well to wave attack if the dunes are high and well vegetated. Some low coasts are protected by growing salt marsh if they are in very sheltered places; these are unlikely to be seriously affected by storm waves by their very nature. In other climates low coasts may be protected by the growth of mangroves or corals in warmer temperatures or ice-shelfs in very cold areas. In all these types the coasts are partially protected from erosion by features related to their marine environment and low nature. Should conditions change, such as a rise of sea-level, these coasts may be liable to rapid modification and human interference may have serious results. Not all low coasts are adequately protected by nature as can be seen in the continuous erosion along part of the Lincolnshire coast, but this may be related partly to a rising sea-level.

(*b*) *Rocky coasts*. Rocky or cliffed coasts, on the other hand, can sometimes be directly attacked by the sea if a protective beach is lacking. The susceptibility of these coasts to erosion will then depend largely on the nature of the material forming the cliff; this may range from glacial sands and gravels, as in part of the cliffs of Suffolk, to the extremely resistant rocks which form some of the cliffs of Cornwall. Exposure to wave attack and longshore movement of material will be secondary considerations; these factors will determine whether a protective beach is present or not.

Offshore relief. The offshore relief is important in a consideration of coastal erosion for several reasons; the effect of offshore relief on wave refraction was discussed in chapter 3, this may explain the concentration of wave energy and erosion at particular places with subsequent greater erosion in one area than in adjacent ones. A very wide continental shelf will render waves less effective for erosion than where water is deep immediately offshore. Changes in offshore relief near the beach may be important in determining the location of areas suffering from erosion at different periods; it may account for the variation of the areas suffering from erosion on the Lincolnshire coast from time to time. Here there are offshore sand banks which migrate slowly in position. They are exposed at low water and, therefore, provide a measure of protection to the beaches in the immediate vicinity. The gradual movement of these offshore banks may account for the change from erosion to deposition in the neighbourhood of Skegness during the last few centuries which is discussed in more detail in chapter 11 (see pp. 357–361). A similar movement of offshore shoals has been suggested as a possible cause of the northward movement of Benacre Ness on the coast of Suffolk (see pp. 268, 269), here also the areas suffering from erosion have changed for a period to accretion.[23]

Sea-Level Changes. Changes in base-level will also affect the erosion of a coast. A falling base-level, by causing a withdrawal of the sea, will probably result in reduced erosion; the depth of water offshore will be reduced and with it the efficiency of the storm waves to attack the coast. A rising base-level on the other hand will deepen the water offshore and allow waves to break closer inshore and increase their erosive capacity, hence leading to an acceleration of coast erosion in areas already affected and perhaps starting it in areas previously immune.

Man-made structure. Coastal erosion is in some areas initiated by man-made structures of several types. One of the more common types is the jetty or break-water built out from the coast. These structures, if they are built in an area where there is a strong longshore movement of material, will interfere with this transport and erosion will occur on the down-wave side of the structure; several examples of this were mentioned in chapter 4 (see pp. 147–158) when the longshore movement of material was discussed. Erosion in other instances has been caused by the artificial cutting of a passage through a coastal barrier.

A detailed study of an example of this type of artificially induced coast erosion is discussed by Bruun (1954).[24] The coast is low and in the area studied, in west Jutland near Thyboroen, consists of a series of barriers separated by bays from the mainland. This coast has been surveyed in detail since 1695 and in 1791 the coast line formed a continuous barrier across Lime Bay. In 1825 a channel was cut through the barrier. Between 1875 and 1950 twenty-two surveys of the coast have been made, at approximately 2-year intervals during the present century. The surveys extend into water between 30 and 40 ft. deep and 17 profiles extend over a 30-mile stretch of coast. The changes in the profiles show a gradual inland shift indicating retreat of the coast increasing in amount as the edge of the channel is approached. Analysis of the profiles shows that the movement of the shoreline was of three types; first, migrating waves, second, seasonal fluctuation, and third, long period changes due to erosion. The first two need not be considered here, although the second did illustrate the retreat of the coast under the action of strong onshore winds. Considering the third type of movement, the maximum annual recession since 1921 has been 5·2 yds. on the northern barrier and 3·0 yds. on the southern barrier, despite the building of groynes to help stabilize the coast, this is shown in fig. 9–7. During the retreat of the coast the beach has tended to become steeper, although the median diameter of the sand in this area, which is about 0·26 mm., has remained more or less constant.

iii. LONGSHORE MOVEMENT. The movement of material alongshore is responsible for nearly all coastal erosion, directly or indirectly. Minikin (1952)[25] stresses the importance of longshore movement of material in the protection of coasts. Destructive waves, acting normal to the shore, can only move the beach material a relatively short distance offshore from where it can be returned to the beach by constructive waves, acting during periods of normal weather. The permanent absence of a beach, however, can usually be explained, partially at least, by longshore movement, unless the water is so deep offshore that this prevents a beach forming. Coast erosion is most likely to take place, therefore, where more

material is moved alongshore out of the area, than is moving into it, from
the up-wave direction. This is likely to occur on headlands, where the
movement of material is in both directions from the headland. Selsey
Bill provides a good example of this. A coast with a smooth outline is
also liable to erosion because there is no obstruction to hold up the longshore movement of material from the beach; this will be particularly

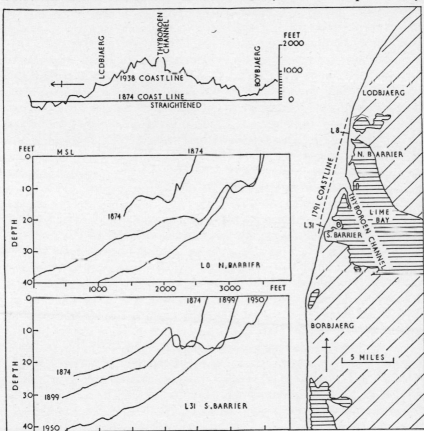

FIG. 9–7. Map and profiles of the west coast of Jutland, to illustrate the erosion since
the cutting of the Thyboroen channel. (After Bruun, B.E.B.)

effective where some outstanding feature prevents the passage of
material from the up-wave direction. Examples of coast erosion due to
this cause will be described.

Holderness. One of the best known areas of coast erosion in the
British Isles is the Holderness coast of East Yorkshire, a detailed study
of erosion along this coast has recently been made by Valentin (1954)[26]
for the period 1852–1952. Erosion has, however, been going on at least

since Roman times on this coast (Sheppard 1912).[27] The Holderness
coast forms a smooth sweeping curve between the chalk cliffs of Flamborough Head to the north and the sandy spit of Spurn Head to the
south. Flamborough Head is one of the boldest headlands on the east
coast; it is composed of the resistant upper chalk with few flints, the
amount of beach forming material is, therefore, very small and little
passes south round the headland on the foreshore to supply the beaches
in front of the Holderness cliffs. These are low cliffs, 10–30 ft. in height,
reaching a maximum of 100 ft. at Dimlington; south of Sewerby they
are composed entirely of easily eroded boulder-clay and other glacial
deposits for a distance of 38 miles (see fig. 9–8). The beach at Sewerby,
where the chalk runs inland, is composed largely of rounded chalk
pebbles, but these decrease very noticeably southwards, owing to the
relative ease with which the sea can destroy them, both by solution and
mechanical erosion. The deposits of the cliffs are not uniform in type
and the cliffs vary in height from place to place, as Valentin has shown,
but these variations are probably only of secondary importance in explaining the erosion on this coast; it will help to explain the differing
rates of erosion as will be considered on pp. 310–312. The fundamental
cause of the erosion is the inadequate protection of the coast by a beach,
because any material on the shore is transported south by the dominant
northerly waves. The sea, in its attempt to build up a gradient suitable
to the waves acting, must make good the lack of material by erosion of
the relatively soft cliffs behind the beach, to which the waves have easy
access. On the whole the rate of erosion increases towards the south-
east, probably due to the greater exposure in this area. It is interesting
to note that erosion is particularly severe immediately to the south of
the areas where coastal protection works have been built, for example,
just south of Withernsea. Here the normal supply of material eroded
from the cliffs is lacking and so must be compensated for by an increased
erosion in a down-wave direction. The actual immediate cause of the
erosion is the action of storm waves on the weakly consolidated and
inadequately protected cliffs. It is interesting to note that only 3 per cent
of the volume of material eroded from the cliffs goes to build up the
sand spit of Spurn Head; the rest must be moved into deeper water
offshore or travel south across the Humber estuary to help build out the
coast of north Lincolnshire.

   East Anglia. Another area farther south on the east coast of England
has also suffered severe erosion; this is the area around Cromer and extending south along much of the coast of Norfolk and Suffolk. The cliffs
in this area are also composed of soft glacial deposits and other unconsolidated and easily eroded strata. The main reason for the serious
erosion at Cromer is that in this vicinity the direction of beach movement

divides; to the west material moves west towards the Wash to form the complex features of Blakeney Point and Scolt Head Island, a barrier island, but to the east and south the general southerly movement of material in the North Sea is resumed. There is, therefore, no source of

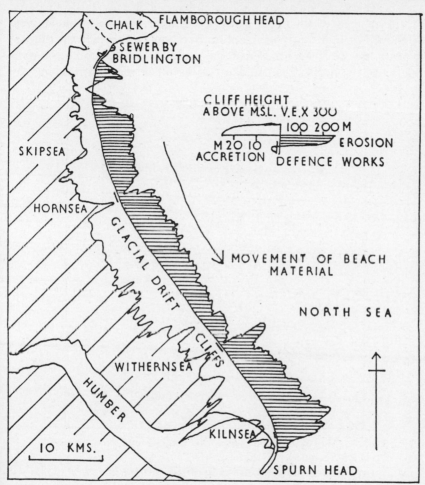

FIG. 9–8. The erosion of the Holderness coast between 1852 and 1952 showing the cliff profile. (After Valentin.)

replenishment of the beach material apart from erosion of the cliffs. The material drifted south is built into constructive shore features farther south, for example Yarmouth Spit, still farther south the shingle structure of Orford Ness shows clearly the dominant direction of beach movement. Between these two erosion still occurs when storms attack the coast.

Sumner, New Zealand. An interesting example of very local and recent erosion has been discussed by Scott (1955)[28] at Sumner near Christchurch. This beach only started to erode in 1946, but erosion has continued since then with serious results to the foreshore in the bay. This beach, whose situation is shown in fig. 9–9, lies in a fairly sheltered bay in an area which is, in general, building out. The spit at New Brighton has built out considerably, by about 160–200 ft. in the last 50 years, due to transport of material south, alongshore from the river mouths to the north. The sudden cutting off of material reaching the

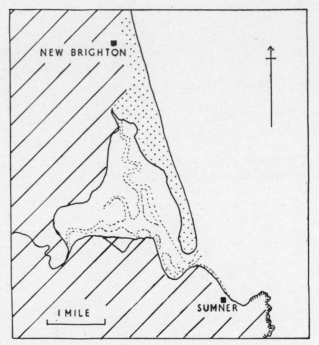

Fig. 9–9. Map of the Sumner area, near Christchurch, New Zealand.

foreshore at Sumner on the south side of the estuary has been explained by Scott as due to a change in position of the channel from the estuary. In 1940 this channel moved over to near the distal end of the New Brighton spit, causing erosion on its landward side. This resulted in the migration to the north of the submarine bar associated with the distal end of the spit. The replenishment of the foreshore at Sumner had been by longshore movement along the bar; the northward movement of the bar diverted the material away from the beach in Sumner bay. The erosion here will not cease till the channel regains its former position and the bar can move southwards again, then material moving along it will once more reach the beach in the bay. This erosion is, therefore, due to an interruption of the normal pattern of longshore movement offshore by changes in the estuary channel which cut off the normal longshore supply of material.

Longshore movement of material is a very important factor in the consideration of coastal erosion and also coastal accretion, the two movements often being complementary. In some areas, however, some of the eroded material is moved seawards to build up the offshore banks instead of replenishing the beaches down-wave. Even if a large rate of erosion occurs and it has been estimated that about 100 million cubic yds. of material has been lost from the Holderness coast in 100 years, this amount spread out over the sea-bed in an area 40 miles long and 1 mile wide would only represent a thickness of 0·34 in. per year. It would, therefore, represent only a small thickness when spread out on the sea-floor.

iv. SEA-LEVEL CHANGES. In considering the changes of sea-level there are two major factors to take into account; there is the world-wide eustatic change caused primarily by the melting and growth of ice-caps and there is the more local isostatic recovery of the areas from which ice has recently melted, other factors such as major earth movements and local upheavals are also important in some areas. The eustatic change has caused a very large positive rise of 3·0 ft. per century of sea-level during the period 14,000 to 5,500 years ago, according to radio-carbon dating from stable areas (Godwin *et al*) 1958,[29] since the ice started to retreat rapidly. Sea-level is still rising at a fairly rapid eustatic rate of 1–2 mm. per year as a result of the continued melting of ice-caps and glaciers over most of the world (Valentin 1953).[30] Warping and up-heavals due to earth-movements are also affecting the movement of sea-level in some of the less stable regions, as for example a 5-ft. uplift in Wellington Harbour, New Zealand, as a result of the earthquake in 1851.

Before considering the actual changes which are in progress at the moment a very brief summary of the main changes of sea-level since the glacial period round the coast of Great Britain will be given. At the maximum of the glacial advance sea-level was probably about 300 ft. lower than it is now, but much of the coast of Britain was then covered by ice. According to Godwin (1940)[31] in about 8000 B.C. sea-level in the English Fenland was about 180 ft. below the present level (see fig. 9–10). There was a rapid rise, known as the Flandrian transgression, during the following 3 millenia, gradually slowing down till about 3000 B.C. when the sea-level stood at about 20 ft. lower than the present level. From this time to the present day, sea-level has fluctuated with a level about 2 ft. above the present at about 1600 B.C. and about 5 ft. above at A.D. 0.

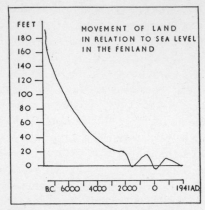

FIG. 9–10. Graph of sea-level changes in
the English Fenland. (After Godwin.)

Periods of low sea-level occurred at 700 B.C., when sea-level was nearly 15 ft. lower than now and at about A.D. 800 when sea-level was approximately 9 ft. lower than it is now. These figures only apply to the Fenland but it is likely that around the southern half of the country similar changes were taking place in the region of general land down-warping. Farther north in Scotland there is evidence, in the 25-ft. post-glacial raised beach, of continued isostatic uplift. This area was much more heavily ice covered till much later. A late glacial beach has been uplifted isostatically to about 100 ft. in some parts of western Scotland. The isostatic recovery in Scandinavia was on a very much greater scale, amounting to about 520 m. (1,710 ft.) in the north Baltic area and it is estimated that the area will still rise another 210 m. (690 ft.).

The rise of sea-level which has been in progress since about A.D. 800 has had significant results in the development of some of the lower coasts of the British Isles. The coast of Lincolnshire illustrates this point well. The new salt marshes grow to a level of about 11–12 ft. O.D. but the level of the land reclaimed several centuries ago and protected by medieval banks varies between 7 and 10 ft. O.D. (Liverpool). This difference, of the order of 3 ft., probably represents a rise of sea-level of about this amount during the last 750 years. When the coastal defences are breached the results are thus very serious as the ground is now considerably below the level of high spring tide.

The damage caused by the storm-surge in 1953 in Holland illustrated the operation of this same factor to an even more marked degree. Umbgrove (1947)[32] has considered the variation of sea-level in relation to the development of the Dutch coast, taking into account both the eustatic movement of sea-level and the change in land level. He points out that the land has been subsiding for a very long period; he gives the rate as an average of 0·4 cm. per century during the last 220 million years. However, during the last 6,000 years the subsidence has been going on at a much increased speed, varying from 12 cm. per century to 18 cm. per century during the last 1,000 years. The secular rise of sea-level since 1890 from the records of 71 tide gauges gives an amount of 12 cm. per century; this increased rate is due to the greatly accelerating glacial retreat since the beginning of the century. The 12 cm. per century added to the increasing speed of subsidence of 21 cm. per century gives the total sea-level rise of 33 cm. per century, which agrees well with estimates from tide-gauge data. The problem of defending land from a sea-level rising at this rate is clearly a very difficult one when the land surface is already considerably below high tide level.

The changes of sea-level which are now going on around the coasts of the British Isles must play their part in the development of the coast and where subsidence is in progress coastal erosion will be aggravated. Valentin (1954)[26] has suggested a correlation between the average rates of erosion and variation of sea-level during the century 1852–1952 in Holderness. High sea-level is accompanied by relatively rapid retreat. In support of his views he gives the following figures, the retreat is taken as the average for 30 stations with values in excess of 1·50 m. per annum (4·92 ft.):

1852–1889	Low sea-level	1·53 m. per year (5·02 ft.)
1889–1908	Rising sea-level	1·77 m. per year (5·81 ft.)
1908–1926	High sea-level	1·89 m. per year (6·20 ft.)
1926–1952	Slowly falling sea-level	1·71 m. per year (5·6 ft.)

It is unfortunate that sea-level is now rising along much of the coast most liable to erosion. Valentin (1953)[30], (1954)[33] has suggested that the iso-line of 1 mm. rise per annum of sea-level runs north-east to south-west from near Whitby in Yorkshire to St. David's Head in South Wales; to the south of this line sea-level is rising at a rate greater than 1 mm. per annum including the coast of Holderness and East-Anglia. South of a line from the Bristol Channel to the Thames Estuary sea-level is rising at a rate greater than 2 mm. per annum, the tide gauge at Newlyn in Cornwall shows a rise of 2·3 mm. per annum; this is supported by evidence put forward by Jolly (1939).[34] The line of no change of sea-level runs from near Aberdeen to Dunbar in east Scotland and to near Barrow-in-Furness, Lancashire, and crosses Anglesey before turning north again to Stranraer in south Scotland and round the edge of the Western Isles, across north Scotland from near Ullapool to Brora in Sutherland. Inside this area the land is still rising isostatically at a rate greater than sea-level is rising eustatically, giving a relative fall of sea-level (see fig. 9–11). It can be seen that many of the lines on Valentin's map (fig. 9–11) are probable or conjectural only. It may, however, be concluded that the northern part of the British Isles is tending to rise while the south-eastern part is certainly sinking relative to sea-level. Good evidence of the continued and steady fall of sea-level off the west coast of Scotland is given by Ting (1936),[35] who describes a series of shingle beach ridges built up by storm waves on the west coast of Jura. There are 20 ridges, grading down gradually from a height of 29 ft. to near sea-level, in which small and large quartzite shingle alternate regularly. Their arrangement and height suggest a gradual lowering of sea-level following the cutting of the 25-ft. beach in the area.

That these changes are not confined to the British Isles is made clear

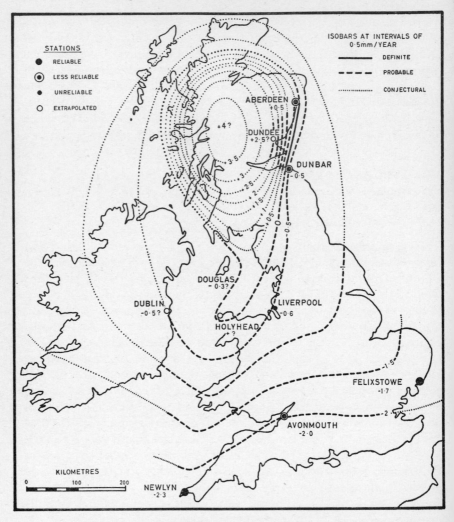

FIG. 9–11. Map to show present vertical movements in the British Isles in relation to mean sea level. + land emerging, − land submerging. (After Valentin.)

in the report on secular changes of sea-level published in 1954,[36] world wide changes of sea-level are recorded from the available data during the last few decades. The only countries which show persistently falling sea-levels are Norway, Sweden, Finland, Alaska and Canada north of

46½°; these are all areas affected by glacial-isostatic recovery. Everywhere else, with a few exceptions, sea-level is rising at varying rates. On the Atlantic coast of America at many places the rise is between 4 and 7 mm. per annum. Average values given are as follows:

U.S.A. Atlantic coast	3·9 mm. per annum
Gulf coast	5·5 mm. per annum
Pacific coast	1·5 mm. per annum
Atlantic side of canal zone	1·2 mm. per annum
Pacific side of canal zone	1·5 mm. per annum
Philippines	1·4 mm. per annum
Hawaii	2·1 mm. per annum
Formosa	2·2 mm. per annum
Japan	1·0 mm. per annum

Slight rises of sea-level of about 1 mm. per annum are recorded from Poland, Latvia and Germany; in Denmark the average value is 0·5 mm. per annum, but in Holland and Portugal it is 1·5 mm. per annum, France 1·4 mm. per annum (French North Africa 0·6 mm. per annum) and Italy 1·7 mm. per annum.

Summary

Evidence of the Royal Commission on Coast Erosion (1911) shows that more land is being gained around the British coasts than is lost by erosion. The beach plays an important part in determining the areas susceptible to erosion. The importance of a high, wide beach in preventing erosion under severe storm conditions was clearly shown by the relationship between the beach character and the nature of the coastal damage in Lincolnshire during the 1953 storm-flood. The areas lacking an adequate beach were most seriously damaged.

Wave energy will be concentrated on headlands and coasts exposed to long fetches; erosion and cliffing are, therefore, likely to be effective unless these factors are counteracted by the resistance of the rock. The nature of the rock plays an important part in determining the rate of coastal erosion, if conditions are suitable for erosion. Offshore relief may locally influence the pattern of coast erosion. Man-made structures, by impeding the normal movement of beach material, may initiate areas of erosion, as for example, the artificial cut made through the Thyboroen channel in Denmark.

Longshore movement is probably fundamental to coast erosion because it removes the beach material which alone can protect the coast naturally. Examples of erosion resulting from longshore movement are Holderness, where Flamborough Head cuts off beach material moving from the north, and east Norfolk and Suffolk. The movement need not be at the top of the beach, an example of temporary erosion at Summer N.Z. shows the effect of longshore movement on a submarine bar.

Sea-level has oscillated considerably in the last million years owing to the repeated advance and retreat of ice-sheets. Since the rapid retreat of the ice-sheets, during the period 14,000 to 5,500 years ago, a rapid rise of sea-level has taken place, amounting to 180 ft. in the Fenland of East England. Sea-level is tending to rise eustatically at about 1–2 mm. per year due to the melting ice. In the British Isles, the south and south-west of the country is sinking while the north is rising relative to sea-level.

(b) Rates of coastal erosion

The rate at which the sea can remove land depends on many factors. It is rarely a continuous process; storms will cause more damage in a few hours than has taken place over a very long period of normal weather. The presence and character of the cliffs play an important part in determining the nature and rate of erosion. This is more important than wave exposure as is clearly shown by the fact that erosion is much more serious on the east coast of Britain than on the west coast; the latter is exposed in parts to the full force of Atlantic waves and winds while the former is largely composed of much less resistant rocks.

Examples of extremely rapid erosion were reported from the coast of Suffolk as a result of the surge of 1953 by Williams (1953)[37]. He states that on the coast south of Lowestoft a cliff of glacial sand 40 ft. high was cut back 40 ft. overnight and where the cliff was only 6 ft. high it was driven back 90 ft. This is an extreme example of very destructive waves with an abnormally high water level acting on unconsolidated cliffs.

The soft cliffs of Suffolk suffer considerable erosion even under more normal circumstances as has been stated by Steers (1951)[38] from measurements made of different editions of the 6 in. to 1 mile O.S. maps. At Hopton erosion has been at the average rate of $2\frac{1}{2}$ to more than 3 ft. a year over the period 1925–50, but at Covehithe it has been much greater averaging 17 ft. per annum from 1925–50, while south of Southwold it averaged 10–11 ft. per annum. In some areas, due to shore protection works, the coast has been static, as for example at Southwold Pier and near the north end of Dunwich cliffs. There has been erosion both to the north and south of the latter place but Dunwich has escaped itself.

Valentin's work (1954)[26] in Holderness shows that here too, although erosion has been going on for a very long time, it is not at an equal rate along the coast and in fact some small areas have escaped. The average rate of erosion along this coast over the last century has been about 2 yds. per annum. The more detailed work of Valentin, illustrated in fig. 9–8, p. 303, has shown the great variation of rates of erosion along this coast between 1852 and 1952. In two areas there have been small gains, between Bridlington and Sewerby and just south of Carnaby, but elsewhere during the 100 years erosion has taken place at varying rates. It has been most rapid between Barmston and Skipsea at about 1·5 m. (4·92 ft.) per annum, while near and to the north of Easington it has been over 2·5 m. (8·2 ft.) per annum, with a maximum of 2·75 m. (9·03 ft.) per annum. The erosion has not been constant in time or place during the century. For example just north of Barmston during the whole century the coast shows a net gain in an area which had suffered severe erosion between 1941 and 1952. This change may be related to the building of coast defences. On the whole it may be said that the amount of erosion increases from north to south, this is shown by the average rates in four sections of the coast as follows:

1. Sewerby to Earl's Dyke   0·29 m. (0·95 ft.) per annum.
2. Earl's Dyke to Hornsea   1·10 m. (3·60 ft.) per annum.
3. Hornsea to Withernsea   1·12 m. (3·68 ft.) per annum.
4. Withernsea to Kilnsea Warren   1·75 m. (5·75 ft.) per annum.

There seems to be little relationship between the height of the cliff and the rate of erosion, the height being only one significant factor. Variation in the type of drift forming the cliff is another factor affecting the rate of cliff retreat. The position of coastal defences also affects the rate of erosion, with a considerable increase taking place immediately south of the defences. Much of the irregularity in the erosion along the coast is a modern phenomenon related to the building of coastal protection works. The increase of erosion southwards from Bridlington is partly due to the decreasingly effective shelter provided by Flamborough Head for waves approaching from the north. The close approach of the 10 m. (33 ft.) depth contour to within 650 yds. of the shore at Dimlington allows the wave energy to be more effectively used on the coast in this area.

The form of the whole coast is S-shaped, with Flamborough Head forming the northern promontory, the shallow bay of Bridlington to the south and the higher cliffs of Dimlington forming the southern bulge. The sea is, therefore, attempting to straighten the curve by concentrating erosion of the hard chalk headland, which yields very slowly, and the southern bulge which is much more susceptible. The whole coast is tending to swing around the hinge of Flamborough Head but has not yet been straightened completely.

In contrast to these areas of soft rocks where coastal erosion is rapid, it is interesting to consider the erosion of part of the south-west coast of the British Isles. This coast is exposed to the full force of the Atlantic waves, but erosion here has been very slow during the last 10,000 years or more. Evidence for this slow tempo of erosion is found in the nature of the cliff profile, which has been pointed out by Arber (1949)[39] and Cotton (1951).[40] The latter states that some of the features which are apparent on the cliff profiles of the Cornish coast probably date back to an earlier interglacial period about 100,000 years ago. The sea has not attacked the cliffs, however, during all this period owing to frequent lower sea-levels during the glacial periods and higher sea-levels in the interglacials, but it has probably been modifying this early cliff during the last 10,000 years. Arber points out the two-cycle nature of the cliffs and uses the term 'bevelled' cliffs to describe them, the term 'rejuvenated' proposed by Cotton is perhaps better. These cliffs have a gently sloping upper section and a more nearly vertical lower part. The vertical part is being actively freshened by the sea as it modifies what was probably a much older cliff feature. On some rejuvenated cliffs remains of raised beach deposits occur at a height of about 10 ft. above sea-level, which are attributed to an interglacial period, the sea-cliff must, therefore, have been cut before that date. The only subsequent erosion is the very small amount of freshening of the cliff profile in the short section of steeper cliff just above sea-level. The rocks of this area are extremely resistant to marine erosion, this accounts largely for the small amount of change recorded over such a long period. The cliffs of the Gower peninsula in south Wales also show an extremely slow rate of marine erosion very well. Here caves, cut at a slightly higher sea-level can still be clearly seen on the cliff face now about 10 ft. above the sea. These caves contain archaeological remains which date from an interglacial period, so that this cliff has not retreated measurably since this period.

Summary

The rate of erosion depends to a considerable extent on the nature of the coast, and the severity of the storm causing the erosion. Rates vary from 90 ft. in a cliff 6 ft. high of unconsolidated glacial sands in one night to practically no erosion in thousands of years. More local variations in the rate of erosion on the Holderness coast can be related to difference of exposure and effect of defence works as well as the character of the cliff. Raised beaches dating from an interglacial period and the nature of the cliff profile on the coast of Cornwall and the Gower peninsula illustrate the very slow retreat of these hard rock coasts, little change having been effected is several thousand years.

3. *COASTAL DEFENCE*

(a) Natural defences

In considering the defence of coasts it is only necessary to take into account those liable to erosion. Coasts in areas of hard rock do not require further protection; the resistance of the rock alone being sufficient to prevent erosion.

Where the coast is potentially erodible, as a result of either its low character or non-resistant cliff and foundation its natural defence against erosion is an adequate beach. This absorbs the energy of the waves and prevents the sea having direct access to the cliffs or wave-cut platform beneath the beach material. Where the coast is low and cliffs are lacking the best natural defence is provided by dunes built of sand derived from the beach and consolidated by the roots of suitable sand-loving plants such as marram grass. These plants also play a very important part in the initial trapping of the sand and the building of the dunes. That such protection is effective against very violent attack by the sea has been made clear in the account of the effect of the storm-flood on the low coast of Lincolnshire. The report (1954)[41] of the committee set up to investigate the coastal flooding in 1953 also stresses the importance of the beach and dunes, as a natural defence against erosion. The reserve supply of sand held in the dunes is a valuable safeguard against erosion.

The offshore relief will also play some part in determining the liability of an area to erosion as it will influence the pattern of wave attack along the coast and, as a result, affect the character of the beach. The existence of the offshore banks off the Lincolnshire coast probably plays a significant part in the relative immunity of the southern part of the coast from erosion at the present time.

(b) Artificial defences

The best natural defence of a coast is a wide, high beach so that any artificial methods of achieving this would appear to be desirable. One of the two ways in which a beach can be built up artificially is by the building of groynes; such structures, however, are not without danger on a beach. The aim of a groyne, usually built approximately at right-angles to the beach, is to trap beach material moving alongshore to build up the level of the beach. The danger of groynes, like that of break-waters and other structures, is that the area down-wave is starved of beach material and erosion may be accelerated here. The committee on coastal flooding[41] suggest that while research on the movement of beach material, offshore bank movement and other coastal problems is being carried out, groynes should be used in the meantime in areas where they are known to help to stabilize the beach. Groynes have been built or renewed along much of the badly damaged part of the Lincolnshire coast since the storm-flood. From repeated surveys of the same lines of profile, which were first surveyed soon after the 1953 floods it does appear that the very small amount of sand on the beaches after the floods has built up steadily till the beach had an almost complete cover by 1955. This is shown in the profiles in fig. 9–12.

Minikin (1952)[25] in his discussion of groynes suggests that their arrangement and character must be suited to the beach concerned, as a result generalization is not possible. In length they should be related to the amount of littoral drift; where this is small groynes should in general be shorter so that the small available supply of material is accumulated

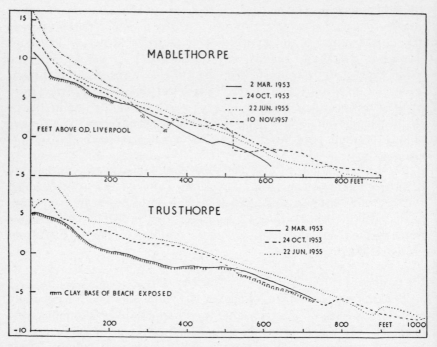

FIG. 9–12. Profiles of the beach at and near Mablethorpe, Lincolnshire, to show the recovery of the beaches since the 1953 storm-surge.

at the top of the beach where it is required. Shingle beaches should only have short groynes which end a few yards from where the beach becomes sandy.

In height Minikin considers that groynes should not exceed the maximum height to which the beach may be expected to accrete, they should dip slowly down to below beach level at their lower end and should in general conform to the slope of the beach, which will depend on the beach material. In spacing, short groynes should be put a distance apart equal to their length, while longer groynes may be spaced $1\frac{1}{2}$ lengths apart. A model study of the effect of groynes made by the Hydraulics Research Board (1958)[42] has shown that high groynes, the equivalent of

3 ft. on the prototype, and spaced at the equivalent of 180 ft. apart and having an equivalent length of 180 ft., reduced the littoral drift to $\frac{1}{8}$ of its value in the absence of groynes. However, where the groynes are high and closely spaced the beach material is often unable to build up to the top of the groyne on the up-wave side; this results in loss of beach material normal to the shore. It was concluded, therefore, that low, widely spaced groynes, which do not trap so much of the longshore moving material which can be built up to the top of the up-wave side are more beneficial to the beach. Groynes of this type did not lead to a general loss of beach material from the foreshore as occurred with the high, closely spaced groynes, under the conditions of the experiment (see pp. 45, 147).

On a low coast another safeguard against serious flooding is the existence of a strong second line of defence in the form of an inner bank. Along most of the southern part of the Lincolnshire coast the so-called 'Roman Bank', a medieval structure, lies inland from the outer dunes forming a good second line of defence. In the northern part of the coast this extra defence is lacking because earlier erosion had removed the bank. The committee on coastal flooding also drew attention to the desirability of a second line of defence in areas where the land behind the coast is below the level of high tide.

Wherever possible measures should be taken to strengthen the natural dunes which form so important a part of the defences of some low coasts. Many of the dunes of Lincolnshire, near the main holiday centres in areas where they are naturally low and thin, are severely damaged by people trampling over them; the vegetation is weakened or killed, leaving the sand unprotected and allowing its removal by the wind. This has serious consequences on a coast where the natural supply of sand has been cut off by the building of sea-walls along the coast, which prevents the small amount of sand on the beach being blown on to the dunes to help replenish the loss. A more positive approach to the problem has been attempted in some parts of this coast; brushwood fences have been erected on the dunes in areas where sand can still reach them from the beach, helping to trap sand blowing on to them. In other areas, as for example just north of Mablethorpe, marram grass has been planted artificially on the dunes. As long as fresh sand is added to the dune regularly the marram will thrive and its interlacing roots will form a very effective binding agent.

Along some coasts the only possible method of protecting land and property is to build sea-walls. Such walls can be built to protect land from erosion or to provide facilities for holiday-makers, such as promenades. In other areas walls are necessary to protect low-lying land from flooding by high tides. These defences can be earthen banks, such as those built along many tidal rivers and in areas not liable to very destructive wave action. This type of defence protected much of the coast of Essex before the 1953 flood, but the banks were overtopped and breached by the storm-flood on this occasion. On more exposed coasts more solid masonry walls are usually built. Many of those protecting the coast of Lincolnshire, where the beaches were very low and narrow, were completely destroyed. This was achieved in many areas by the undermining of the back of the wall by the water over-topping it; once the wall was undermined from the rear its complete collapse was rapid and complete. The new defences built since the floods are very much higher and have much greater strength in depth and at the rear; this method of breaching cannot happen so readily in the future. A few consequences of the presence of sea-walls on the movement of beach material, with special reference to the coast of Lincolnshire, may be mentioned.

The problem of sea-walls in connection with the maintenance of sand dunes has already been mentioned; they do provide an obstacle to the movement of sand by wind from the foreshore to the dunes. A concrete wall is a very inflexible structure which will return all the water thrown on it by the swash, the backwash will be powerful because none can be lost by percolation. This seaward movement, which will be strengthened during periods of strong onshore winds, will help to remove the beach immediately in front of the wall. No reserves of sand are available to help cushion and stabilize the upper beach. The reduction in height of the beach in front of the wall, will allow deeper water to penetrate closer inshore, and in this way, the energy of the waves becomes concentrated over a shorter distance, and their destructive effect is intensified. On the Lincolnshire coast the amount of beach material in front of many of the areas protected by sea-walls is so small, that in storms it is entirely stripped away, leaving only the clay foundation of the beach. The storm waves can then attack the clay which shows signs of erosion in places; the beach is then permanently lowered, because, even if the same amount of sand does come back to the beach after the storm, it will lie at a lower level.

It is very likely that the deterioration of the beach during periods of destructive wave activity will be transmitted in a down-wave direction. The danger of the transmission of wave energy from the areas protected by walls to adjacent areas protected by dunes was illustrated by the position of the breaches during the 1953 storm-floods; many of these occurred at points immediately south of the end of the concrete walls. Stamp (1939)[43] has drawn attention to a similar example of erosion being particularly severe at the end of a sea-wall at Hampton in Herne Bay. This erosion caused the destruction of a row of houses. This is partly accounted for by the destructive nature of the waves in front of the walls where all the sand was removed seawards and, therefore, immediately south of the end of the artificial defences in Lincolnshire no sand was available to protect the beach and dunes from attack.

An interesting example of the difficulty of maintaining a beach in the front of a sea-wall is described by Zenkovich (1958).[44] Between Tuapse and Adler, on the north-east coast of the Black Sea, the coast is backed by the Caucasus mountains and the railway is forced to run immediately behind the beach, which is narrow and shingly. An almost vertical stone wall has been built to protect the railway, this causes the backwash of the waves to remove much of the beach material, establishing a new beach profile, which is narrower and lower than before. The waves are now able to break directly on to the wall; water velocities of 8 m. per sec. have been recorded. Shingle thrown at the wall by the breaking waves, which can attack the wall continuously owing to the reduction in the level of the beach, have undercut the base of the wall to a depth of 3–4 m. (9·85–13·1 ft.) at a rate of about 1 ft. per year.

On the Lincolnshire coast artificial 'points' have been established where the main outfalls reach the sea to prevent silting up of these channels. These promontories, which may have been sited on natural headlands of boulder-clay hummocks, affect the movement of beach material in such a way that the beach, particularly on the southern side, is lowered in relation to the level of the beach on straight stretches of the coast. This may be due to the deflection of the waves round the sharp points, preventing beach material collecting immediately in their lee. The lowering of the beach in the vicinity of the points helped to weaken the area, and breaches occurred near the points in many instances. This was well shown by the destruction wrought in the vicinity of Ingoldmells Point.

There is one other method of shore protection which has yet to be mentioned; this is the artificial replacement of eroded beach material. This technique has been employed in America by a variety of methods. The sand by-passing at Port Hueneme in California is a good example. It illustrates also the danger of interfering with the natural drift of beach material which made this project necessary in the first place (Savage 1957).[45] Two jetties were built during the period 1938–40, these caused accretion on the up-wave side and serious erosion on the down-wave side of the structures. The method used to transfer the sand from the zone of accretion to the depleted beaches was new; it was done by dredging with a floating dredge which operated behind a narrow barrier and in the surf zone. The details of the amount of sand dredged is given on pp. 149, 150, in relation to the longshore movement of material. It was found that much time was lost during the dredging in the surf zone owing to the necessity of the floating dredge to retreat behind the barrier during rough weather, although the recorded wave heights during the period of dredging rarely exceeded 4 ft. and were never greater than 6 ft.

The fill used to replenish depleted beaches may be derived from the same coast up-wave of the obstruction causing the erosion, as in the example mentioned, or it may be derived from a completely different source. If the former situation applies the sand fill will have the same general character as that lost by erosion and the beach should maintain its stability. If, however, the beach fill is from a different source care must be taken that it will provide a stable beach. This problem has been discussed by Krumbein (1957).[46] He points out that an eroding beach will tend to become coarser, which must be taken into account in considering the material supplied to stabilize it. In order to assess the character of fill required careful observations and sampling of the actual beach material must be carried out, including samples from all beach zones. The results of this analysis must be correlated with the character of the material used as fill. The character of the fill should lie within the range of variation of the character of the natural beach material. For optimum results the fill should be rather coarser than the normal undisturbed material and also somewhat better sorted.

Summary

The best defence of any coast is a wide, stable beach, while sand dunes serve a valuable function in the protection of low coasts. Artificial defences should aim to stabilize or increase beaches and dunes. Where it is necessary to build sea-walls such structures, particularly during times of storm, are liable to render the destructive character of the waves more serious and are not conducive to the natural growth of beach or dunes. Groynes may in some areas serve a useful purpose in helping to build up a beach by trapping material moving alongshore, but there is always the danger that the down-wave beaches will suffer as a result. A more expensive method of combatting erosion, due largely to man-made structures, is the dumping of beach material when its absence is resulting in erosion. Care must be taken to select suitable material, which should be slightly coarser than the natural sand.

REFERENCES

[1]Report of the Royal Commission on Coast Erosion, 1911.
[2]Douglas, C. K. M., 1953, The gale of Jan. 31st, 1953. *Met. Mag.* **82**, pp. 97–100.
[3]Shepard, F. P., 1950, Longshore bars and longshore troughs. *B.E.B. Tech. Memo.* **20**.
[4]Lewis, W. V., 1931, The effect of wave incidence on the configuration of a shingle beach. *Geog. Journ.* **78**, pp. 129–48.

[5]Emery, K. O., 1955, Grain size of marine beach gravels. *Journ. Geol.* **63**, pp. 39–49.

[6]Barnes, F. A. and King, C. A. M., 1953, The Lincolnshire coastline and the 1953 storm-flood. *Geog.* **38**, pp. 141–60.

[7]Corkan, R. H., 1950, The levels in the North Sea associated with the storm disturbance of 8 Jan. 1949. *Phil. Trans. Roy. Soc. A* **242**, pp. 493–525.

[8]Rossiter, J. R., 1954, The North Sea storm surge of 31 Jan. and 1 Feb. 1953. *Phil. Trans. Roy. Soc. A* **246**, pp. 371–99.

[9]Robinson, A. H. W., 1953, The storm surge of 31 Jan.–1 Feb. 1953. *Geog.* **38**, pp. 134–41.

[10]Edwards, A. B., 1951, Wave action in shore platform formation. *Geol. Mag.* **88**, pp. 41–49.

[11]Gaillard, D. B. W., 1904, Wave action. *Corps of Eng. U.S. Army*, Washington.

[12]de Rouville, A., 1938, *Annale des Ponts et Chaussées*.

[13]Wentworth, C. K., 1938, Marine bench forming: water level weathering. *Journ. Geomorph.* **1**, pp. 6–32.

[14]Bartrum, J. A., 1938, Shore platforms (discussion of 13.) *Journ. Geomorph.* **1**, pp. 266–8.

[15]Bartrum, J. A. and Turner, F. J., 1928, Pillow lavas, peridotites and associated rocks of north-west New Zealand. *N.Z. Inst. Trans.* **59**, pp. 98–138.

[16]Johnson, D., 1938, Shore platforms (discussion of 13), *Journ. Geomorph.* **1**, pp. 268–72.

[17]Hills, E. S., 1949, Shore platforms. *Geol. Mag.* **86**, pp. 137–52.

[18]Nansen, F., 1922, *The strandflat and isostasy*.

[19]Bradley, W. C., 1958, Submarine abrasion and wave-cut platforms. *Bull. Geol. Soc. Amer.* **69**, pp. 967–74.

[20]Rode, K., 1930, Geomorphogenie des Ben Lomond (Kalifornien) eine Studie über Terrasenbildung durch Marine Abrasion. *Zeitschr. Geomorph.* **5**, pp. 16–78.

[21]Twenhofel, W. H., 1945, The rounding of sand grains. *Journ. Sed. Pet.* **15**, pp. 59–71.

[22]Johnson, D. W., 1919, *Shore processes and shoreline development*.

[23]Williams, W. W., 1956, An east coast survey (discussion). *Geog. Journ.* **122**, pp. 317–34.

[24]Bruun, P., 1954, Coast erosion and the development of beach profiles. *B.E.B. Tech. Memo.* **44**.

[25]Minikin, R. R., 1952, *Coast erosion and protection*.

[26]Valentin, H., 1954, Der Landverlust in Holderness, Ostengland von 1852 bis 1952. *Die Erde.* **3, 4**, pp. 296–315.

[27]Sheppard, T., 1912, *The lost towns of Yorkshire*.

[28]Scott, W. H., 1955, Sea erosion and coast protection at Sumner, New Zealand. *N.Z. Eng.* **10**, pp. 438–47.

[29]Godwin, H., Suggate, R. P. and Willis, E. H., 1958, Radio-carbon dating of the eustatic rise in ocean level. *Nature* **181**, pp. 1518–19.

[30]Valentin, H., 1953, Present vertical movements of the British Isles. *Geog. Journ.* **119**, pp. 299–305.

[31]Godwin, H., 1940, Studies of the post-glacial history of British vegetation III and IV. *Phil. Trans. Roy. Soc. B.* **230**, p. 239.

[32]Umbgrove, J. H. F., 1947, Origin of the Dutch coast. *Proc. Kon. Nederl. Acad. v. Wetenschappen* **50**, pp. 227–36.

[33]Valentin, H., 1954, Gegenwärtige Niveauveränderungen in Nordseeraum. *Petermanns Geog. Mitt.* pp. 103–8.

[34]Jolly, H. L. P., 1939, Supposed land subsidence in the south of England. *Geog. Journ.* **93**, pp. 408–13.

[35]Ting, S., 1936, Beach ridges in south-west Jura. *Scot. Geog. Mag.* **52**, pp. 182–7.

[36]Assoc. d'Oceanography Physique 1954, Secular variations of sea-level. *Un. Geodesique et Geophysique Inter. Pub. Sci.* **13**, p. 21.

[37]Williams, W. W., 1953, La tempête des 31 Jan. et 1 Fev. 1953. *Bull. inform.*
   C.O.E.C. **5,** pp. 206–10.
[38]Steers, J. A., 1951, Notes of the erosion along the coast of Suffolk. *Geol. Mag.*
   88, pp. 435–9.
[39]Arber, M. A., 1949, Cliff profiles in Devon and Cornwall. *Geog. Journ.* **114,**
   pp. 191–7.
[40]Cotton, C. A., 1951, Atlantic Gulfs, Estuaries and Cliffs. *Geol. Mag.* **88,** pp.
   113–28.
[41]Report of the Dept. Comm. on Coastal Flooding 1954 *Cmd.* 9165 H.M.S.O.
[42]Report of the Hydraulics Research Board 1958, *Hydraulics Research* 1957.
   D.S.I.R. H.M.S.O. pp. 52–54.
[43]Stamp, L. D., 1939, Some economic aspects of coastal loss and gain. *Geog.*
   Journ. **93,** pp. 496–503.
[44]Zenkovich, V. P., 1958, Berega Chernovo i Azovskovo morey. (Coasts of the
   Black Sea and Sea of Azov.) Moscow, *Geografgiz* p. 292.
[45]Savage, R. P., 1957, Sand bypassing at Port Hueneme, California. *B.E.B.*
   Tech. Memo. **92.**
[46]Krumbein, W. C., 1957, A method of specification of sand for beach fills
   B.E.B. Tech. Memo. **102.**

CHAPTER 10

BEACH GRADIENT AND BEACH PROFILES

1. *BEACH GRADIENT*

THE gradient of a beach in the swash zone depends mainly on three variables; these are the size of the beach material, the length of the waves and the steepness ratio of the waves. Although the effect of the first factor has been mentioned already in other connections it has not been examined in detail. These three factors affect both natural and model beaches. Each of the three variables will be considered separately.

(a) Size of material

It is well known that beaches of shingle and coarse sand are much steeper than those of fine sand. Steep beaches allow the wave energy to be absorbed over a relatively narrow zone, they are therefore more mobile. Before considering the effect of material size on natural beaches the results of model experiments will be mentioned. Bagnold (1940)[1] has recorded the gradients of beaches formed of three different sizes of material. He refers to the angle that a line joining the beach crest and the top of the step forms with the horizontal. He states that the beach angle depends only on the size of the grains composing the beach, and was independent of the wave height. For a size of 0·7 mm. the gradient was 22 deg., for 0·3 mm. it was 19·5 deg. and for a finer material of 0·05 mm. it was 14 deg. Experiments were carried out by Meyers (1933)[2] which also show that the coarser of the two sands he used formed the steeper beach slope, the sands had diameters of 0·368 mm. and 0·472 mm. and showed a consistent difference of gradient on a logarithmic scale. The different sands did, however, produce quite a variety of gradients under different wave conditions, which will be discussed later. Meyers measured the tangent of the angle of slope at the waterline.

The Beach Erosion Board in their interim report of 1933[3] show that, on natural beaches, there is an increase of gradient with increasing material size on beaches along the coast of New Jersey. There is a straight line relationship giving a gradient of tan 0·15 for a median diameter of 0·50 mm. to a tan of about 0·06 for a median diameter of 0·20 mm. More recently Bascom (1951)[4] has given further evidence of this relationship from observations on the coast of California. He takes the gradient of the beach at a reference point at mid-tide level. The

range of diameters found on the beaches he studied was from 0·17 mm.
to 0·85 mm. The following relation between the mid-tide slope and the
sand size was found to exist:

Gradient	Median diameter in mm.
1 : 90	0·17 mm.
1 : 82	0·19
1 : 70	0·22
1 : 65	0·235
1 : 50	0·235
1 : 38	0·30
1 : 13	0·35
1 : 7	0·42
1 : 5	0·85

This relationship is shown graphically in fig. 10–1, in which the minimum probable slope for any size of material is given. Half Moon Bay
(see pp. 166, 167) shows very clearly the relationship between foreshore

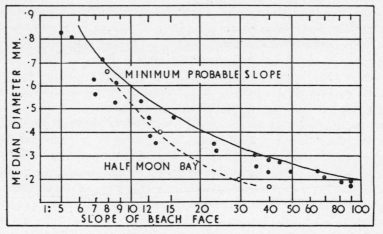

FIG. 10–1. Relationship between beach slope and sand size from observations made in
California. (After Bascom.)

slope and sand size; in the sheltered part of the bay the size is finer and
the gradient is correspondingly less. Four points in the bay are shown
in the figure illustrating this correlation.

The gradient of shingle beaches is considerably steeper than that of
sand beaches. Slopes of between 1 : 2 and 1 : 3 have been recorded on
Chesil shingle beach near Abbotsbury. This is about the maximum
beach gradient that waves can build up, and not all waves will produce
such a steep slope on this beach (see pp. 227, 228).

The cause of the decrease of slope with decreasing grain size is the variation of the percolation rate through the beach material. Coarse shingle is very permeable and a large proportion of the advancing swash sinks into the beach and the backwash is reduced correspondingly. On a fine sand beach only a relatively small amount of swash is lost by percolation owing to the much reduced permeability, the force of the swash and backwash are more nearly equal in this instance. The force of gravity, which is proportional to the slope, tends to equalize the force of the swash and backwash; when the two are very different, as they are on a shingle beach, the slope must be steep to render gravity more effective. On a fine sand beach the two opposing forces of swash and backwash are more nearly equal so that the part played by gravity need not be so large and a flatter slope results. Another point which helps to account for this relationship between swash slope gradient and material size is concerned with the relative volume of the swash and backwash and to the fact that a larger volume is associated with a flatter slope. The relatively large and effective backwash on a fine sand beach leads, therefore, to a flatter slope.

(b) Wave length

The effect of wave length on the gradient of the swash slope has been studied both in model experiments and in nature. In order to eliminate the other variables the same sand was used throughout the experiments and the waves were of constant steepness. Two series of runs were made; in the first the original gradient was 1 : 15 so that the waves, which had a steepness of 0·011, were constructive and built a swash bar. In the second series the original gradient was in 1 : 2, which was steeper than the gradient formed by these waves; in one run, therefore, the beach was built up and in the second it was combed down. The results of these experiments are shown diagrammatically in fig. 10–2 (a) and (b). The relationship between the two variables is shown to be linear, the gradient varying from 1 : 3·5 to 1 : 5·0 for wave lengths of 225–756 cm. Any one wave length produced similar gradients whether the beach was being built up or combed down. The curve of the line on the graph in fig. 10–2 (b) represents the variation of gradient with wave length. It is, therefore, concluded from these experiments that a longer wave produces a flatter swash slope gradient in the model tank.

This relationship can also be found in field observations. An interesting point is revealed by fig. 10–3; this graph combines the experimental data already discussed with full scale observations made in the Mediterranean Sea on the south French coast, which, like the model, is tideless. The model sand had a diameter of 0·41 mm. and that of the Mediterranean beach had a diameter of 0·30 mm.; the two are, therefore, broadly

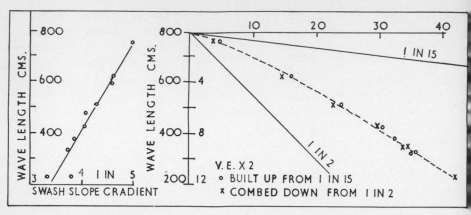

FIG. 10–2. Relationship between beach slope and wave length in model experiments.

similar. The observations, plotted on double logarithmic paper, show that there is a continuous linear relationship between gradient and wave length that covers the range of both model and full-scale observations.

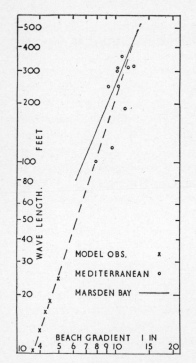

FIG. 10–3. Relationship between beach gradient and wave length on natural and model beaches.

A further series of observations to illustrate this relationship was made at Marsden Bay, County Durham (1953).[5] The observations are shown on fig. 10–4, in which beach gradient is plotted against the wave period, which is related to the wave length (see pp. 8, 13). The observations have been analysed statistically and show a significant correlation; the coefficient of correlation is 0·560. The sand in this bay has a median diameter of 0·37 mm. at the north end and 0·35 mm. at the south end of the bay. The considerable scatter of points in the graph is due to the impossibility of controlling the other significant variables during the observations. Measurements of Chesil beach confirm that this relationship applies also to shingle beaches.

The cause of the flatter gradient for longer waves cannot be explained by variations in the rate of percolation as the material size remains constant. However, if it is assumed that a larger volume of backwash leads to a flatter gradient, then it is clear that a larger wave will produce more swash and if the percolation remains constant then the proportion of backwash will increase; this increasing proportion of backwash is responsible for the flatter gradient with the longer waves.

(c) Wave steepness

A series of model experiments has been made by Rector (1954)[6] on the equilibrium profiles of model beaches. In these he has shown that the slope of different parts of the beach depends on the material size;

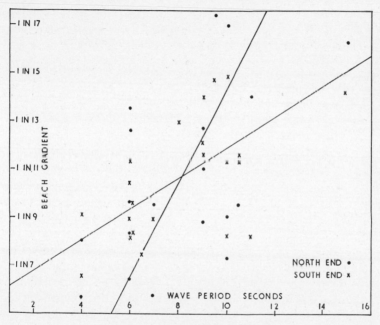

FIG. 10–4. Relationship between beach gradient and wave period in Marsden Bay, Co. Durham. Regression lines are shown.

but for any one sand size it is related to the wave steepness. He gives the following formulae to relate the wave steepness to the beach gradient; for the foreshore slope, defined as extending to the crest of the breakpoint bar for steep waves and to the foot of the swash slope for flatter waves, he gives $y_t/x_t = 0.07 (H_o/L_o)^{0.42}$ and for the foreshore slope still above still water level $y_s/x_s = 0.30 (H_o/L_o)^{-0.30}$. The figures are derived from dimensionless log. log. plots of the data. These formulae show that as the wave steepness increases so the gradient of the beach decreases. The median diameter of sand to which these results apply was 0.22 mm.

The experimental work of Meyer (1933)[2] also shows the same relationship; he finds a straight line correlation between the wave steepness and the tangent of the angle of the beach slope at the water line. The tangent of the angle varies from 0·21 with a wave steepness of 0·008 to a value of 0·111 for a wave steepness of 0·08, the sand used for the experiments has a median diameter of 0·368 mm.

Other experiments were carried out in a model tank in which the sand size and wave length were kept constant but the wave steepness was varied. The sand used had a median diameter of 0·41 mm. and the original gradient was 1 : 15. The range of gradients built up by the waves varied between 1 : 3·7 and 1 : 7·5. Fig. 10–5 shows the correlation between the tangent of the angle of slope and the wave steepness to be a straight line, the gradient flattening with increasing wave steepness. This

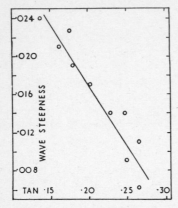

FIG. 10–5. Relationship between the wave steepness and the tangent of the angle of the beach slope in the model wave tank.

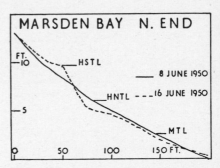

FIG. 10–6. Profile of Marsden Bay to show the increase of gradient due to the action of flatter waves.

line agrees fairly closely with that of Meyers.

The relationship between beach gradient and wave steepness has been observed also on natural beaches of both sand and shingle. The swash slope of Chesil shingle beach in Dorset has been observed to have a gradient of 1 : 4 or steeper under normal conditions of relatively flat waves in calm weather, but as the result of a storm, during which steep storm waves attacked the beach, the gradient was flattened to a slope of 1 : 9 by the removal of shingle from the beach.

The surveys made on the sand beach at Marsden Bay also illustrate this relationship. The profiles in fig. 10–6 show one instance when the gradient was steepened by the action of flat constructive waves, while other profiles illustrate the flattening of the slope by the action of steep storm waves. A cliff of sand was cut by the destructive waves, but below this the gradient, produced by the swash and backwash of the waves, was considerably flattened. Shepard (1950)[7] has published profiles of the beach at Cape Cod which also illustrate the effect of steep storm waves on the gradient of the beach very clearly. These are shown in fig. 10–7. The steep waves, by moving sand downwards from the upper beach, greatly reduce the gradient above mean sea-level.

The cause of the variation of beach gradient with wave steepness can be explained by reasoning similar to that already put forward to explain

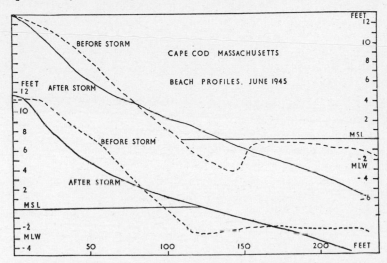

Fig. 10–7. Profiles of the beach near Cape Cod to show the decrease of gradient result- ing from the action of storm waves. The removal of the ridge near low water level by storm waves is also shown. (After Shepard, B.E.B.)

both the relationship of gradient and material size and to the wave length. In all instances the proportion of the volume of swash to back- wash will change as each variable alters. Considering the wave steepness only, the size of material remains constant, therefore the volume of percolation will remain constant. If the steepness is varied by changing the wave height as was done in the model results illustrated in fig. 10–5 the wave length will remain constant, the period of the swash and back- wash will, therefore, be the same in each run. The volume of the swash will, however, increase with increasing wave steepness and, if the per- colation volume is constant, the proportion of backwash will increase; this should result in a flatter gradient.

Summary

The beach gradient in the zone of the swash and backwash depends mainly on three variables. The slope becomes steeper as the material becomes coarser, as the wave length decreases and as the wave steepness decreases. The volume of the backwash relative to the swash is mainly responsible for these relationships; when it is large the gradient will be flatter.

(d) The equilibrium gradient

The equilibrium gradient of any beach in nature is not a static slope but one which will be continually tending to adjust itself to the changing variables on which it depends. On any one beach the material is usually more or less constant in size, although even this factor may change very greatly from time to time on some beaches as was mentioned on p. 163, particularly if there is a large proportion of the coarser grades. Even if the sand size remains constant the gradient of the swash slope is continually readjusting itself to the variations in wave length and steepness which affect it; the equilibrium is therefore a dynamic one and not a static one.

The importance of permeability in explaining the greater steepness of shingle compared with sand beaches has already been stressed. Bagnold (1940)[1] has shown that the marked difference of gradient between the two types of material is due to the effect of grain size diameter on the rate of percolation. For fine material, where the flow may be considered viscous, the velocity of percolation can be given by $v = \dfrac{A g}{v} \dfrac{H}{L} d^2$, where H is the head of water which is proportional to the wave height, d is the grain diameter and v is the kinematic viscosity, which can be taken as 0·01 for water, L, the length of the path, is proportional to the height of the beach crest which is related to the wave height, therefore $\dfrac{H}{L}$ is approximately constant, so that for fine material v is proportional to d^2. For coarse material the rate of percolation $v = B \sqrt{\dfrac{g H d}{L}}$, so that v is proportional to the square-root of d. There is, therefore, a rapid increase of permeability as the material changes from fine sand to shingle, but within the shingle grade there is much less variation.

Bagnold (1940)[1] has suggested that if the ratio of sand size to wave height is kept constant (R) the beach profiles should be comparable. In the model tank the material size is small, tending to produce a flatter slope, while the wave length is short, tending to increase the slope. In nature the equivalent material is coarser, giving a steeper gradient but the larger waves, assuming a constant steepness, compensate to give a flatter slope and to produce a similar equilibrium gradient. In connection with the relationship between wave length and beach gradient, shown on fig. 10–3, which shows both model and full-scale beaches, it is now possible to suggest why the gradients of sand beaches in the model tank more nearly resemble those of shingle beaches in nature. A similar gradient cannot be expected on a natural and model beach if the same size is used in both environments, because the very different wave dimensions will cause the equilibrium gradients to differ. The smaller model waves will produce steeper slopes which approximate more closely to the slopes of shingle beaches in nature. The experiments carried out by the Beach Erosion Board (1947)[8] in two model tanks of different sizes with the sand size also to scale showed that the larger model produced the flatter slope, proving that the effect of the wave length more than compensated for the increase in particle size.

The fact that wave length is important in determining the equilibrium gradient of a natural beach is very significant in explaining the different types of beach profiles which will be considered in the second part of the chapter. The average wave length depends partly on the exposure of the beach; where the beach is exposed to the open ocean, the average waves reaching it will be much longer than those reaching a beach in a relatively enclosed sea, in which long waves cannot be generated.

In his study of the coast of Jutland Bruun (1954)[9] has shown that the beach profiles along this coast have tended to steepen during the period since erosion started. The recession was initiated by the artificial cutting of a channel through the barrier (see pp. 300, 301). The mean gradient of the beach to a considerable depth is measured, and therefore his results are not directly comparable with those already considered which refer to the swash slope gradient mainly. To measure this increase in gradient Bruun uses the 'stc' or 'steepness characteristic' which is found by dividing the mean depth to a specified depth by the distance of this specified depth from the shoreline. The stc has increased since the barrier was first breached, its greatest value is given as stc $\times 10^3 = 13.5$. He considers that there are three types of profiles; the first is over-nourished, the second sufficiently nourished and the third is under-nourished. In the first type the profile is irregular with shoals and bars, while the last two have a smooth equilibrium form. The importance of this distinction will be discussed in the next section which deals with the formation of different types of bars and ridges on the beach profile.

2. BEACH PROFILES—SAND BARS, RIDGES AND BARRIERS AND SHINGLE BARRIERS

(a) Smooth profiles

In the classification of beaches given in chapter 7 one of the sub-divisions under the main group of tidal beaches consisted of beaches with a smooth profile. An example of such a beach in Rhossili Bay was described (see pp. 228–230). Beaches with a smooth profile may have a wide range of gradient depending on the three factors discussed. Most smooth beaches do not have a straight profile, but one which approaches a parabola in form; the example shown in fig. 10–8 illustrates this. The reason for the concave upwards or parabolic beach profile is partly related to the variation of material size perpendicular to the coast on a normal sandy beach. The coarser material tends to collect at the top of the beach and as a result the steeper slope occurs here. The form of the profile allows the waves to break closer inshore at high tide, therefore, their energy at high water would be increased per unit width of beach. It has been shown that the coarse particles will tend to accumulate at the

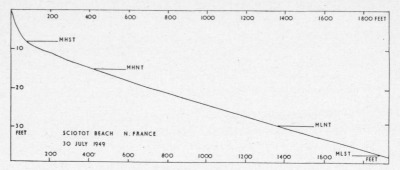

Fig. 10–8. Profiles of smooth beaches, Sciotot, North France.

points of maximum wave energy. Once this shape of beach profile has been formed considerations of wave energy show that it will be likely to be maintained.

Another point which facilitates the development of a parabolic profile on a tidal beach is the relative time during which the different parts of the beach profile come under the influence of the swash and backwash of the waves in relation to unbroken or surf waves. The upper part of the beach will only come under the influence of the swash and backwash, while farther down the proportion of time of swash will be reduced so that the waves will have less opportunity of building up the steeper part of the profile which is the swash slope.

Smooth beach slopes can have a very great variety of gradient from the steep slopes found on some shingle beaches, where gradients, under the action of short waves, have been recorded steeper than 1 : 2 on Chesil beach to a gradient of 1 : 90 recorded by Bascom (1951)[4] for a beach of very fine sand of median diameter of 0·17 mm. in Grenville Bay in California, and 1 : 82 for a median diameter of 0·19 mm.

Smooth beach profiles may be found in a wide variety of environments. A foreshore with a considerable tidal range and exposed to a long fetch, across which long waves can reach the coast, will almost always have a smooth profile. The profile should be taken as starting from the crest of the berm, if one is present, because the back slope of the berm has not been directly shaped by the waves. If the tidal range is smaller, of the order of 5 ft. for normal tides, then it is likely that, under some weather conditions at least, irregularities, in the form of submarine bars, will develop on the offshore part of the profile. These will only form if the material is fairly fine. The foreshore of a shingle beach is nearly always smooth apart from the small foreshore steps which develop during the action of constructive waves when the tide is changing from spring to neap. This is due to the fact that, owing to the steep gradient of shingle beaches, the waves break directly on to the foreshore. A step however, tends to form where the waves break and is characteristic of such beaches.

Summary

The foreshore of a tidal beach exposed to a considerable fetch normally has a smooth parabolic profile. Its equilibrium gradient, on account of the great average wave length, would be expected to be fairly flat where the beach is composed of reasonably fine sand.

(b) Submarine bars

The characteristic profile of a beach in a relatively enclosed tideless sea was briefly described in chapter 7 (see pp. 231–233). The submarine bars typical of this environment have been studied for some time; work on them was intensified during the Second World War on account of landing operations undertaken in the Mediterranean, where the bars were a problem in planning and executing the landings. Before considering the method of formation of these bars their character and distribution will be discussed.

i. CHARACTER. The term 'submarine bar' has been used to describe these features because it indicates an essential fact of their character; they are never exposed above the water level and are most perfectly developed in tideless seas where this would be impossible. The term 'longshore' bar, used by Shepard (1950),[7] also draws attention to the fact that they mostly lie parallel to the shore.

Submarine bars were mentioned by Elie de Baumont[10] in 1845 together with other types of shore bars. Several German authors including Hagen[11] in 1863, Lehmann[12] in 1884, Olsson-Seffer[13] (1910), Braun[14] in 1911, Poppen[15] in 1912, Otto[16] in 1912 and Hartnack[17] in 1926 all discuss the submarine bars of the Baltic and the coasts of Jutland. The bars of the Great Lakes of America have also been studied by

Russell in 1885,[18] Gilbert[19] in 1890 and in detail by Evans[20] in 1940 while more recent work has been done by Keulegan, (1945),[21] (1948)[22] and Shepard (1950).[7] Work has also been done in the Mediterranean by Cornaglia (1887),[23] and during the 1939–45 war by Williams and subsequently by King and Williams (1949),[24] (1951).[25]

Most of these observers find that two or three parallel bars are found along the coast; Evans (1940) for example records three bars in Lake Michigan covered at their crests by 4 ft., 8 ft. and 12 ft. of water, Poppen and Otto both show three bars on their surveyed profiles of the Baltic beaches, while surveys[25] made in the Mediterranean in three successive years (1948, 1949 and 1950) on the south coast of France all show three bars. These profiles are shown in fig. 10–9. The position of the bars

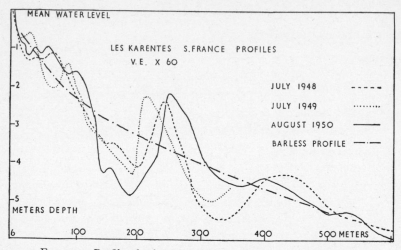

FIG. 10–9. Profile of submarine bars, Les Karentes, South France.

varies from year to year. Profiles of the North African shore of the Mediterranean show only two bars, but a third may lie beyond the limit of the profile; these two had 2 ft. of water over the inner bar crest, while the outer one had between 6 and 8 ft., this latter bar showed considerable movement over the relatively short period of about 6 days.[24]

Profiles of submarine bars surveyed by Shepard (1950) on the coast of California show that the bars here are much less regular than those of a tideless sea, in fact during the summer months the bars are frequently absent. In this region the tidal range reaches a maximum of about 8 ft. at spring tides but is only 2–3 ft. at neap tides. Shepard notes that the bars tend to be higher during the periods of small tidal range at neap tides.

Some of the earlier authors in considering the development of submarine bars suggest that these features are the forerunners of offshore bars or barriers, notably Braun (1911) and Hartnack (1926). The latter author considers that the submarine bars are transitory forms. Otto's (1912) observations revealed some of the important characteristics of these bars; he noted that there was no systematic landward movement of the bars which makes it unlikely that they would become offshore barriers above sea-level. He also noted the importance of storm waves in altering the character and position of the bars, destroying some and building others. By associating the breakers with the bar crests, he led the way to the explanation of the formation of this type of sand bar which has since been developed.

ii. DISTRIBUTION. The description of the bars shows that they are best developed in areas where the tidal range is very small, such as the Mediterranean, the Baltic, parts of the North Sea near the amphidromic point off Denmark (see pp. 28–30), and the Great Lakes of America. Where the tidal range is rather larger, for instance along the coast of California, the bars are not so well developed, nor are they permanent features of the beach profile.

This latter point cannot be related to the tidal régime which is the same during winter and summer, but is related to the different types of waves affecting the coast during the two seasons. In this difference both the climatic régime and the wave characteristics are involved, an important factor in the determination of the wave character in this instance is the available fetch. The type of waves reaching the coast during the summer months, when the bars are often absent, are long, low, constructive swells. The distribution of the well developed type of submarine bars is, therefore, partly dependent on the available fetch of the beach concerned, which is in turn related to the exposure of the coast under consideration. Thus it may be concluded that submarine bars will be found in tideless seas where the exposure to the action of long swells is restricted.

iii. FORMATION AND MOVEMENT OF SUBMARINE BARS. In considering the formation of submarine bars on natural beaches it is interesting to compare these bars with the break-point bars formed in the model wave tank, these were described in chapter 5 (see pp. 181–186). It was shown that the break-point bars in the wave tank were formed at the break-point of steep waves, which moved material seaward inside the break-point and landwards outside it. The relationship between the break-point and the position of the submarine bars of the Baltic has been pointed out by Otto (1912) and this relationship was further stressed and amplified by Evans (1940) in his work on the bars of Lake Michigan. This leads to the conclusion that the break-point bar in the model tank is the model equivalent of the natural submarine bar. It is, therefore, interesting to see how far the similarity can be followed.

In the wave tank a close correlation was found between the position of the break-point bar and the height of the wave forming it. The relationship between the wave height and the depth of water over the bar crest, which is partly a function of its position on the profile, has also been noted in some of the observations on submarine bars. It is shown by Evans (1940) and Keulegan (1945) as well as in the observations made in the Mediterranean. Shepard (1950) discusses this relationship from his observations on the coast of California, here the bars have deeper crests where the wave heights recorded are larger, but there is a considerable scatter of the points. This is probably due to the difficulty of measuring the particular waves which are responsible for the formation of the bar when the observations are not continuous.

The observations in the model tank showed that there was a constant ratio of 2 : 1 between the depth of water over the bar crest and the height of the crest above the original profile. If this relationship could be demonstrated to apply also to natural beach it would be of value. The depth of water over a bar could then be established from its distance offshore and the gradient of the smoothed profile or 'barless beach' profile. This latter profile is formed by smoothing out the bars and is the natural equivalent of the original profile of the model experiments. It is shown in fig. 10–9 that in general the same relationship between the height of the bar crest above the barless beach profile and the depth of water over the crest holds for natural beaches, with the exception of the bar in the deepest water. It appears that this bar is not fully formed, probably as a result of the extreme rarity of waves high enough to break on it.

It has been shown that there are usually two or three bars on any profile but the number varies with changing wave conditions. The tank experiments also showed that two break-point bars could be formed on one profile if small steep waves followed large steep waves. The same mechanism can account for the presence of several bars on the natural profile; the outermost bar is formed by the largest storm waves, which are large enough to break in this depth of water; the smaller bars, in shallower water inside it, are formed by the intermediate sized storm waves, while the inner bar is formed by the short, steep waves which will affect the beach much more frequently. They may be generated by the sea breezes which often blow onshore during summer afternoons. Otto (1912) has pointed out that the largest storm waves break on the outer bar, while Shepard's (1950) observations in California confirm that it is the steep storm waves which make the bars on this coast. The storm waves, in forming the outermost bar, destroy the inner bars, but these can be rebuilt quickly when the waves return to more normal dimensions.

Many observations have shown that the smaller inner bar is much more mobile than the outer bar; this is because the inner bar can come under the influence of the break-point of the waves much more often than the outer bars, which are only affected by the rare severe storms. That these outer bars are not affected by the smaller waves of normal weather was demonstrated in the periodic surveys carried out during a month in summer on the Mediterranean coast of France. Daily surveys of the inner bar in the same area, which only had about 3 ft. of water over its crest, showed it to be undisturbed by the waves, which were small during the period of observations.

When the waves were breaking on the inner bar it could be established that it moved in a similar way to the break-point bars in the wave tank. A slight increase in height caused a seaward shift of the bar crest, while a reduction in wave height caused the inner bar to move landwards as shown by the profiles in fig. 10–10. The change in wave height affects the position of the break-point of the waves and hence the position of the bar crest. A greater change of this type was recorded by Williams on the African coast of the Mediterranean at Sidi Ferruch, where, as a result of a period of high waves, the bar moved seawards 115 ft. in a period of 2 days. The crest of this bar was at a depth of about 7 ft. and was originally about 550 ft. offshore.

It was shown that the break-point bar was destroyed by a falling tide in the model experiments, this will help to account for the occurrence of well developed submarine bars in tideless seas. These features depend on the constancy of the break-point of the waves for their formation; in a tidal sea this position must clearly vary throughout the tidal cycle and bars formed at high tide would be exposed at low tide, when the break-point would have moved to deeper water offshore. The only position on a tidal beach where a submarine bar is likely to form is where the waves normally break at low spring tide. A bar in this position will be under the influence of the unbroken waves in deeper water behind the break-point when the tide is high. This is less likely to destroy the bar than the swash and backwash of the waves.

The chief characteristic of the waves forming the break-point bars in the model tank was their destructive nature and high steepness value. The relationship of the natural bars with storm conditions, particularly the formation of the bars in deeper water, shows that these bars are also the result primarily of destructive storm waves, which move material down from the foreshore and deposit some of it at the break-point of the waves. These bars, therefore, result from the action of the steeper waves and form at their break-point. The flat, constructive waves, typical of

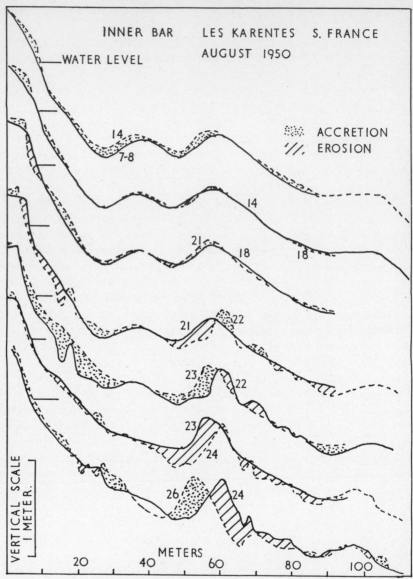

FIG. 10–10. Movement of the inner submarine bar at Les Karentes in the Mediterranean.

the Californian coast in summer, have been shown to smooth out the submarine bars on the beach profile. Bascom (1953)[26] has pointed out that there are two major types of beach profile dependent on the wave steepness; with steeper waves bars form below water, but with flatter waves a berm forms above the water level.

iv. CRESCENTIC SUBMARINE BARS. The bars which have been described normally lie parallel to the coast and extend in a continuous line for long stretches. Another type of submarine bar,[24] found in some of the more restricted bays of the northern part of the Mediterranean shoreline, has been described. The bars form a crescentic pattern in plan with the points of the crescents facing towards the land. There may be two sets of bars, the inner ones having a shorter distance between the points of the crescents than the outer one. No really satisfactory explanation of this type of submarine bar has yet been proposed but it is possible that they result from the interaction of two sets of waves approaching the shore of the bay from different directions; each set of waves would tend to form a series of bars parallel to their crests and the interaction of the two sets might account for the crescentic pattern. This is illustrated diagrammatically in fig. 10–11. Aerial photographs have shown that this pattern of submarine bars tends to move rapidly in position; this may

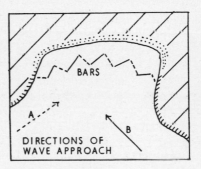

FIG. 10–11. Diagram to illustrate a possible method of formation of crescentic submarine bars.

be due to the longshore movement of the crescentic bars which would be much more apparent than similar movement of a straight bar.

Summary

The submarine sand bars, typical of tideless coasts, are the full-scale counterpart of the break-point bars formed in the model tank. The submarine bars are formed at the break-point of steep storm waves, the largest outer bar, which is often not fully developed, is formed by the very rare extreme storm conditions. This bar is not disturbed by the smaller steep waves which break nearer inshore and form the middle and inner bars. The latter bar is the most mobile and responds to varying wave heights by moving seawards with increasing wave height and landwards with slowly decreasing wave height. In some restricted bays the bars assume a crescentic form. The submarine bar cannot be built up above the water level as it is formed at the break-point of the waves and results from destructive wave action.

(c) Ridge and runnel profiles—parallel to the shore

On some tidal sand beaches the profile is interrupted by irregularities parallel to the shore or at a slight angle to it. These features have been referred to by various authors under different names, Cornish (1898)[27] and

Gresswell (1937)[28] have used the terms 'fulls' for the ridges and 'swale' for the intervening depressions. They will be called ridges and runnels here, which describes them adequately. The beach at Blackpool, where many surveys have been made, is a very good example of a ridged tidal beach. The surveys on this beach were started during the 1939–45 war as the beach is of a similar character to the Normandy beaches on which landings were being planned. These observations were necessary as no detailed theory concerning the formation and movement of these ridges was then available. The ridges, which are covered at high tide, were a danger to landing craft; these might ground on the ridge while the water in the runnels landward of the ridge crest might be several feet deeper.

i. CHARACTERISTICS. The beach at Blackpool is composed of fine sand of median diameter 0·22 mm. There is a considerable tidal range of 25 ft. at spring tide, while the width of the beach at low spring tide is 4,000 ft. The overall gradient of the foreshore, ignoring the ridges is 1 : 150. The slope of the seaward faces of the ridges is, however, considerably steeper; it ranges from 1 : 32 near the top of the beach to about 1 : 60 near the low water level although these gradients vary considerably with changing waves. The size of the ridges tend to increase towards low tide level causing a conspicuous increase in the depth of the runnels; the one near low neap tide level is often 4 ft. deep. These runnels form outlets for the falling tide which drains along them, cutting channels across the ridges at intervals at their lowest point. These cross channels change position from time to time and are conspicuous on aerial photographs; migration of a cross channel might cause a sudden apparent change in height of a ridge on any line of profile.

A series of profiles were taken daily on Blackpool beach from March to August 1943, and thereafter weekly observations were made from December 1943, to October 1944, and at less regular intervals subsequently. A study of these profiles showed that the positions of the ridges tended to remain more or less constant as shown in fig. 10–12. The most persistent positions of the ridges were at 700 ft. and about 1,000 ft., 1,800 ft., 2,800 ft. and 3,400 ft. from the high spring tide level at the top of the beach. The corresponding heights of these ridges are 6½ ft. O.D. (Newlyn) 3 ft., −3 ft., −7 ft., and −12–13 ft. O.D. The ridge at −3 ft. was least persistent. It is interesting to compare these heights with the mean tide heights; these are M.H.S.T. 12·2 ft. O.D., M.H.N.T. 5·8 ft., which is almost the same as the 700-ft. ridge, M.L.N.T. is −6·1 ft. while the 2,800-ft. ridge, which is the most persistent, is at −7 ft., M.L.S.T. is at −12·7 ft., while the lowest ridge is at about −12 to −13 ft. There appears, therefore, to be a correlation between the most persistent ridges and the positions at which the tide will stand for the longest period during the tidal cycle.

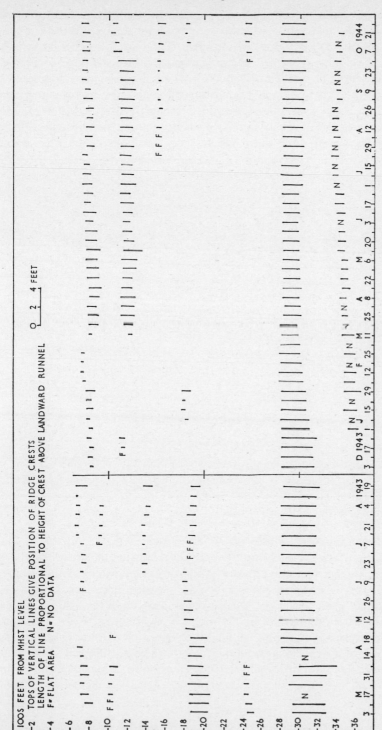

FIG. 10–12. Diagram to show the position and movement of the sand ridges on the beach at Blackpool, Lancashire.

It is quite clear from the figure that the ridges do not move systematically towards the shore, but that they maintain their positions for long periods; this is not found on all ridge and runnel beaches as will be shown (see pp. 345-347). On this particular beach it is due to the fact that the ridges lie parallel to the coast, which happens to be aligned perpendicular to the direction from which the dominant waves come from across the Irish Sea. The ridges do, however, change position slightly from time to time, but more often one ridge dies out and another reforms elsewhere, for example the 1,800 ft. ridge died out during the second

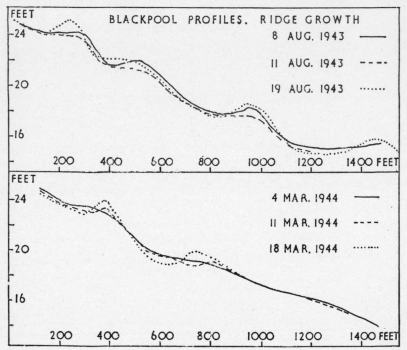

Fig. 10–13. Profiles of Blackpool beach to show the growth and removal of ridges during March 1944 and August 1943.

period of observation while a new ridge formed farther up the beach. The periods when ridge growth or removal was taking place have been studied, and the analysis shows that the ridges tend to be removed during periods of storm waves and onshore winds, while calmer weather conditions, particularly the swells which often follow a storm, cause the ridges to build up (see fig. 10–13). Gresswell (1953)[29] also notes the effect of storms in reducing the height of the ridges and moving material seawards. The profiles shown in fig. 10–13 illustrate this process.

The character of the beach surface is relevant to a consideration of the method of formation of the ridges. It was observed that nearly all the foreshore surface was rippled with the exception of the seaward faces of the ridges which were composed of very firm smooth sand, the ridge crests on the other hand were often of soft sand, which had clearly not been firmly packed by wave action.

ii. COMPARISON WITH MODEL BEACH PROFILES. A theory was put forward in 1949[24] to explain the formation and characteristics of the ridge and runnel beaches, it seems to have been followed substantially by Gresswell[29] in his book published in 1953. In considering the formation of ridge and runnel beach profiles it is relevant to consider the profiles built in the model wave tank. The correspondence of submarine bars to their model counterpart, the break-point bar, has already been pointed out. The swash bar may now be compared with ridge and runnel profiles.

This type of model bar is formed by constructive waves in front of their break-point, it is not, therefore, disturbed by a falling water level and can as a result exist above the water level in the same way as ridges are exposed at low water on a tidal beach. The two features have a similar form; both have a steep landward slope, while the seaward slope is steep compared to the overall gradient of the beach. The smooth seaward face of the ridge is clearly affected by the swash and backwash of the waves of the falling tide. This process is responsible for its smooth character and its gradient. The flattening of this seaward face during storms has been observed, which shows that the equilibrium gradient of the swash slope responds to the wave steepness as discussed in the beginning of the chapter. The ridge, therefore, has the characteristics of a model swash bar rather than a break-point bar. Ridges are smoothed by steep destructive waves but are built up by constructive waves in the same way as swash bars are in the wave tank. The main formative process in both features is the constructive action of the waves which build up the swash slope. It is, therefore, reasonable to consider that the two are counterparts of each other on a different scale. On some ridge and runnel beaches a bar may exist below the low water level, this feature clearly must have the characteristics of a submarine bar as has already been mentioned in the last section.

iii. DISTRIBUTION OF RIDGE AND RUNNEL BEACHES. Ridge and runnel beaches have a fairly wide distribution; they are found where the tidal range is considerable, for example, along the coast of parts of the Irish Sea and North Sea, parts of the Firth of Clyde. In the North Sea they are found at Druridge Bay in Northumberland, the Lincolnshire coast and parts of East Anglia. On the continental coast ridge and runnel beaches are found from north Holland to Cherbourg; they are very well developed near Le Touquet in France and occur all along the Normandy coast and extend along the east side of the Cherbourg Peninsula but they are not found on the beaches on the west side of the peninsula, nor do they occur on the foreshore of the south-west peninsula of England or south Wales, on the other side of the Channel. The ridges and runnels on the coast between Dieppe and Ostend are briefly described by Pugh (1953).[30] The runnels along some of these beaches penetrate to the clay and peat foundation of the beach as sometimes happens in Lincolnshire. In all these areas the tide is considerable, and reaches a very great range in parts of the Irish Sea and in certain localities on the north French coast. The main point about this distribution is that the ridges are found on coasts which are not exposed to the open ocean and which cannot, therefore, be influenced by the very long swells characteristic of really exposed coasts. The fact that the west coast of the Cherbourg Peninsula has smooth beaches while the east coast is ridged illustrates the significance of this factor.

The importance of the exposure on the development of ridges is related to the equilibrium gradient which the waves will attempt to establish on the beach. It has been shown that long waves will produce flatter gradients than short waves, thus a beach which is exposed to long swells will have a flatter equilibrium gradient than one which is only worked on by waves generated in the restricted fetch of a small sea like the Irish Sea, North Sea and English Channel.

Not all the beaches in the relatively restricted Irish Sea or North Sea have ridged profiles, there must be an additional factor, therefore, which will also encourage the waves to form ridges on the beach. The ridged beaches develop where the overall gradient of the foreshore, without taking the ridges into consideration, is much flatter than the gradient of the swash slope of the seaward side of the ridge. A surfeit of sand on the foreshore, resulting in the formation of a ridged profile, appears to be one factor in accounting for the distribution of the ridge and runnel beaches as this will help to produce a flat overall gradient. In many areas the extra beach material can be associated with the deposition of much glacial or fluvio-glacial sand and other material in the areas which now form the shallow waters of the offshore zone, as a result of the postglacial rise of sea-level. The work of Van Veen (1936)[31] in the southern North Sea shows that there is a super-abundance of material in this area which has a glacial origin (see pp. 6, 203). The sand forming the beaches with ridge and runnel profiles in the northern part of the Irish Sea is also probably mainly derived from the glacial deposits, which are sandy in this area. It was deposited on the floor of the Sea by the Irish Sea ice sheet, which completely filled the northern part of this sea.

Where there is not a surplus of sand on the foreshore the waves can maintain their equilibrium gradient throughout the beach; this will be more easily achieved in areas where the equilibrium gradient is flat. These areas will be where the exposure allows very long waves to reach the beach, because it has already been shown that long waves will produce a flatter beach than short waves on the same-sized material. Thus it may be concluded that ridges and runnels on a sandy beach are the result of an attempt by the waves to produce a swash slope gradient suitable to their dimensions on a beach whose overall gradient is flatter than this equilibrium gradient. Even where the sand supply is not excessive, if the overall gradient of the foundation of the beach is flat, the sand available will be built into ridges. Pugh (1953)[30] points out that the overall gradient of some of the north French beaches is very flat, for example, at Walde, just north of Calais, the upper beach has a gradient of 1 : 400 and is soft and muddy. On the lower part of the foreshore sand ridges and runnels have formed, but the supply of sand is reduced here and the clay foundation of this flat beach is exposed in the runnels. This beach is suffering erosion at the present time. Pugh states that there is relatively little sand on the bottom of the Channel coast in the vicinity of Calais as it has been moved back into the southern North Sea, which is in the direction of the dominant movement of beach material along this coast (see pp. 204, 205).

iv. FORMATION OF RIDGE AND RUNNEL BEACHES. Having suggested a possible reason why ridge and runnel beaches should develop in certain areas, the method of formation will now be considered. Where waves are trying to adjust the gradient of the swash slope to suit their dimensions this process will continue most effectively where the waves are at one level for the longest period on a tidal beach. These levels will be the positions of the mean low spring tide and neap tides and the corresponding high tide levels. It is at these positions, therefore, that ridges may be expected to be most permanent and best developed, where the ridges are parallel to the shore. That this does in fact take place has been shown in the description of the ridges on the beach at Blackpool, another example is illustrated in the profile of the beach at Druridge Bay, Northumberland, shown in fig. 10–14. This beach shows two ridges below a

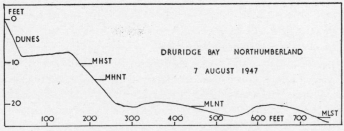

FIG. 10–14. Profile of Druridge Bay, Northumberland, to show sand ridge formation.

berm at high water level; these ridges are clearly related to the positions in which the swash zone would lie at low neap and low spring tides respectively. On this beach the sand is much coarser than at Blackpool, having a median diameter of 0·4 mm. on the two lower ridges, but it is even coarser on the berm where the median diameter is 0·84 mm. The tidal range here is 14 ft. at spring tide so there is only room for two ridges to form; the coarse nature of the sand necessitates the formation of ridges owing to the steep equilibrium gradient which is required in this size of sand. Fig. 10–7 (p. 327) illustrates an example from the east coast of America, where the level of the ridge is associated with the mean lower low water level. This figure also gives a very good example of the elimination of a ridge by destructive storm waves.

In considering the initiation of the ridges it may be assumed that the initial profile is smooth throughout the width of the foreshore. At low water the waves will expend their energy over a wide zone owing to the flat gradient and, if they are constructive, they will deposit some of the sand they carry at the limit of the swash. This deposition will increase the gradient of this area and render the wave energy more effective by concentrating it. The energy can now be used in building up the equilibrium gradient in the swash zone in the same way as illustrated in the model experiments. The growing ridge will first be apparent as a flat area with a steeper seaward slope. This was frequently observed in a study of the daily profiles of Blackpool beach, where a new ridge was nearly always preceded by the development of a flat area. The flat area will reduce the efficiency of the drainage of water from the beach as the tide falls, and as soon as a slight runnel is formed, the water draining from the beach as the tide ebbs will cause erosion and deepening of the runnel. These stages in growth are illustrated in fig. 10–13, taken from an example on Blackpool beach. A ridge is formed in this way at low tide level and as the tide rises it quietly fills the runnel behind the ridge, eliminating the action of the swash from the runnels, hence its rippled character. As the tide continues to rise the waves can now break inland of the low tide ridge and a new ridge will tend to form where the swash again becomes active, but if this is the mid-tide zone the tide will be rising fast here and the ridge formed will not be so fully developed as the ridge near low tide level. Near the level of high neap tide the process can again continue more effectively.

The smaller size of the upper ridges can be explained by the parabolic or concave shape of the overall beach gradient on Blackpool beach. The steeper overall gradient in the upper part requires a smaller ridge to produce the necessary steepening to provide the equilibrium gradient; the difference between the overall and equilibrium gradient is less at the top of the beach than it is in the lower part, where a larger ridge must be formed to produce the required steepening of slope. The increase in gradient of the seaward faces of the ridges towards high water level is the result of the coarser sand accumulating at the top of the beach.

V. RIDGE AND RUNNEL BEACHES WHERE THE RIDGES AND RUNNELS ARE NOT PARALLEL TO THE SHORE. It has been shown that on a ridge and runnel beach, where the ridges are parallel to the shore, they do not move systematically in either direction, but tend to remain at about the mean tide positions. On some beaches the ridges are not parallel to the shore. This depends on the direction of approach of the ridge-building waves; where these approach the beach with their crests parallel to the shore the ridges will lie parallel to the shore, but where the waves approach with their crest at an angle to the shore the ridges have a tendency to turn to face the direction from which the waves come. This is apparent in the orientation of the ridges on the Lincoln-shire coast (Barnes and King, 1951).[32] Gresswell (1953)[29] has also drawn attention to this pattern of ridges on the coast between Liverpool and Southport, in Lancashire, here the direction of the ridges tend to turn to lie at right angles to the direction from which the dominant waves come. Thus at Ainsdale, where the coast trends at 32 deg from north, the ridges diverge from the coast to the north, while at Formby Point the ridges lie parallel to the coast, south of the Point they diverge from the coast southwards, as the trend of the coast here is to the south-east. The dominant waves come from a little north of west.

On the north-south coast of Lincolnshire the ridges trend away from the coast southwards because the dominant waves come from the direction of maximum fetch to the north. The ridges are well developed on the southern part of the coast, which is an area of active accretion with a wide overall beach gradient. South of Skegness they sometimes reach considerable heights above the runnels to landward, for example a beach profile surveyed in November 1957, at the southern end of Skegness showed a ridge $5\frac{1}{2}$ ft. high, with a very steep slope to the runnel. Very soft mud frequently collects in these deep runnels, up to a foot in depth; this shows that the runnels do not come under the influence of violent wave action. The seaward slopes of the ridges on the other hand are of firm smooth sand, indicating the part played by the swash in shaping them. Surveys of the beach profiles in Lincolnshire have been repeated several times a year since 1951; these surveys show that the ridges on each profile move gradually landwards. This movement is very steady and continuous. It is illustrated in fig. 10–15 which shows the landward movement of the swash slope of the ridges in front of the spit at Gibraltar Point plotted against the time. This movement is, therefore, unlikely to be seasonal in character and is most easily explained by the movement of the whole ridge southwards. Clearly, as the ridges diverge from the coast southwards, if they move in this direction it will appear that the ridges are moving inland on any one profile. This southerly movement

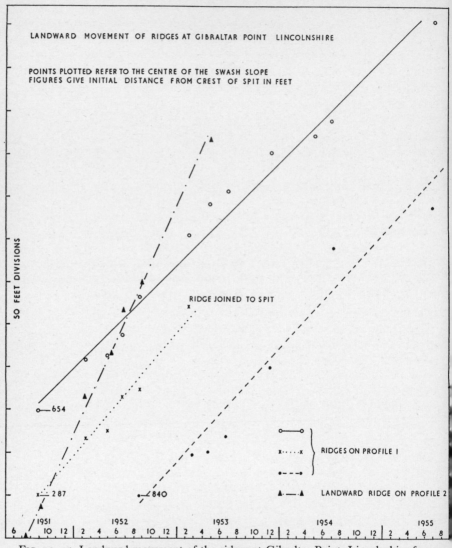

FIG. 10–15. Landward movement of the ridges at Gibraltar Point, Lincolnshire from 1951 to 1955.

of beach material is confirmed in other ways; the shingle which occurs in small quantities at the top of the beach is of very mixed origin; its most likely source is the boulder-clay which is frequently exposed on the beaches to the north. This explains why the ridges remain in the same positions for prolonged periods on some beaches, while on apparently similar beaches in other areas the ridges appear to move steadily towards the shore. The reason for and method of formation of the ridges is probably the same in both areas.

Summary

Ridge and runnel sand beaches, developed in a tidal sea, are the full-scale counterpart of the model swash bar. The ridges are formed in front of the break-point by the swash of the waves and owe their growth to constructive wave action; the ridges tend to be destroyed and the profile smoothed by destructive waves. They form as a result of an attempt by the waves to build up a gradient suitable to their dimensions on an over-all beach gradient which is flatter than the equilibrium gradient. Thus they occur more readily in relatively enclosed seas where the equilibrium gradient will be steeper, owing to the restricted fetch limiting the wave length. The ridges will lie parallel to or diverge from the shore where the waves approach parallel to or at an angle to the shore respectively. In the former area the ridges will form most readily at the mean high and low tide levels and will be more or less constant in position. Where they diverge from the coast they will appear to move landward on a fixed line of profile as a result of the movement of the whole ridge alongshore in areas where there is a considerable longshore movement of material.

(d) Barrier beach or island (offshore bar)

The features which are to be considered in this section are on a different scale from those just discussed. Their nomenclature was discussed in chapter 8 (see pp. 255, 257) where coastal accretion was considered; it was suggested that the term 'barrier', as used by Shepard, describes one important respect in which these features differ from those just described. They are features which are built permanently above the high tide level, unlike the sand ridges of some tidal beach profiles, and are separated from the mainland shore by a lagoon. These barrier beaches are also much more stable than the bars and ridges described, in that their position remains more or less constant for long periods, although geologically they are ephemeral features of a developing coastline. Another important characteristic of these barriers, implicit in the term 'island', which Shepard suggests should be used to describe the more complex barriers, is the fact that they need not be attached to the land at either end. Very often, however, they are joined to the land at one or both ends, although they are frequently broken by inlets.

One of the early authors to describe these barriers was Elie de Beaumont[10] in 1845. He considered that the barriers were built up by the landward movement of material from offshore. Johnson (1919)[33] argued that as a result of this onshore movement of material the offshore profile seaward of the barrier should become flatter. A line continuing this offshore gradient should, therefore, cut the coast inland from the inner margin of the lagoon, unless the offshore gradient is very flat, in which case the lagoon would be exceptionally wide. Another theory which Johnson tested was that of Gilbert (1890),[19] who considered that the bar was entirely constructive, the material being derived from alongshore and leaving the offshore zone uneroded, a line continuing the offshore gradient would cut the coastline either at the inner edge of the lagoon or within the lagoon. Johnson found that 15 out of 18 profiles supported Elie de Beaumont's theory; this result might not be significant, however, as it is unlikely that the original slope would be quite uniform. If it were the normal concave curve, a continuation of the flatter offshore slope would in any case cut the original coast inland from the inner lagoon margin. Despite this the theory put forward by Elie de Beaumont over 100 years ago is probably essentially correct, although the details of the wave processes were not known at that time.

i. SHINGLE BARRIERS. Barrier beaches may be composed of either sand or shingle but as they are characteristic of low sandy shores the true barriers are normally mainly built of sand. The method of formation will differ considerably between the two materials. A beach ridge formed of shingle will be built up above the limit of normal wave action by the effect of storm waves which throw the shingle to the limit of their swash; thus waves which are permanently constructive on shingle, forming barrier features, are the opposite of the wave type which can make positive additions to a sandy coast. Here the flat waves will produce the constructive effect that builds barriers.

Owing to the fact that it is the waves which are on the whole destructive that build the shingle barriers, these waves are not capable in themselves of providing the material to form the barrier. The material of which shingle barriers are formed must be brought into the area either by constructive waves or by longshore movement; the latter is much the most important method as constructive waves on shingle are not able to move the pebbles onshore from great depths to which, in any case, they rarely extend. A shingle barrier entirely separated from the mainland at both ends is very rare because of the importance of longshore movement, which is mainly by beach drifting in shingle. Shingle barriers are often tied to the mainland at both ends, for example Chesil beach, which is strictly a tombolo as it ties the island of Portland to the mainland; Loe barrier in Cornwall is a shingle ridge of this type joining two headlands across the intervening bay. The Boulder Bank off Nelson, on the north coast of the South Island of New Zealand, is a good example of a shingle barrier, which is only tied to the mainland at one end. Because shingle barriers of this type are probably formed by a very different mechanism from the true sandy barriers, it is convenient to refer to them by a different term, they may, therefore, be called 'shingle beach ridges'. These features can be built to a much greater height above sea-level than sandy formations by wave action alone; the great height of Chesil beach which extends up to 43 ft. above high water level illustrates this point.

ii. SAND BARRIERS. Most of the true barrier beaches and islands are largely composed of sand, although some shingle may occur and be built into ridges by the storm waves. These barriers are, according to Elie de Beaumont, very widespread; he states that they are found round one-third of the coasts of the world. The coastlines along which they are found are usually fairly straight; if they were not so initially, they are straightened as a result of the formation of the barriers. They are well developed on the coast of eastern North America, extending most of the way from the southern end of Florida to the coast of New Jersey and Long Island north-east of New York. They also occur very widely round the Gulf of Mexico, the Baltic, parts of the Mediterranean, the coasts of Ceylon and parts of Australia.

The chenier plain (see pp. 262, 263) already described is a somewhat similar feature which lacks the open lagoon, its place is taken by strips of marshland and swamp; these structures are widespread on the coast between the Amazon and Orinoco in South America.

A good example of a relatively simple barrier beach is the one which extends along the south coast of Iceland for 134 miles from Vik in the west to Hornafjordur in the east. The barrier has been surveyed in the neighbourhood of the island of Ingolfshöfði, which forms one of the major hinge-points of the barrier along this coast. The island is separated from the mainland by a shallow lagoon nearly 4 miles wide but only about 1–2 ft. deep. Its sandy bottom gradually rises above the water level to the foot of a recently abandoned cliff about 5 miles from the island. Fig. 7–5 (see p. 239), illustrates the character of the coast. The lagoon is everywhere floored with basaltic sand of a very dark colour, which becomes finer towards the open sea. This coast is being rapidly built out by the deposition of a large amount of fluvio-glacial material which is brought down by the glaciers on to the outwash plain, which gradually slopes down to become the lagoon at its seaward edge. Across the outwash plain the melt–water rivers follow very variable and braided channels which gradually merge into the waters of the lagoon. In some areas the lagoon becomes very narrow and the outwash continues at places right to the barrier forming the coastline. The easily weathered nature of the volcanic rocks of the area, and the active glaciers ensure a superfluity of beach material, which is very considerably augmented by the occasional sudden emptying of lakes under and on the ice cap of Vatnajökull, giving rise to 'Jökulhlaup' or glacier bursts. These outbursts of large volumes of water from the glacier snouts bring down very large amounts of material of all grades to the coast, of which the sand sizes are the most important in the building up of the barrier beach along this part of the coast. This excess of sand is an important factor in the development of the barrier.

To the west of the island of Ingolfshöfði there are two barriers, the inner or more northerly one is much the most conspicuous feature, as it is much higher than the more continuous but lower feature seaward of it, which extends much farther along the shore. Fig. 10–16 illustrates the character of the two features. Both features are formed of sand, the inner high one is built of sand of median diameter 0·39 mm., while the median diameter of the sand of the outer barrier is 0·42 mm. The inner feature, which reaches a height of nearly 80 ft. above mean sea-level, is a wind-formed bar, which is clearly related to the island in whose shelter it has developed. It has a length of nearly 4,000 ft., gradually tapering downwards away from the island.

The structure seaward of the wind-formed bar is a true barrier beach, being a wave-formed feature. It is not very high but it extends a long way along the coast, although there are occasional breaks in it through which the distributaries of the large melt-water rivers escape to the sea and the tide ebbs and flows. The tidal flow of water is not very important as the tidal range is small. There are no very precise measurements of tidal range on this coast, but the evidence available suggests that the mean range is only 4 ft., with a mean spring range of $5\frac{1}{2}$ ft. This small tidal range is important in explaining the presence and character of the barrier beach. The surveyed profile across the barrier shows that it extends only about 5 ft. above the high water level. At high tide the swash of the larger waves could reach the crest of the beach and wash over it towards the lagoon lying between it and the wind bar. The low height of the barrier is explained by the sand grade of the material of which it is composed. Destructive waves on this beach will, therefore, be entirely destructive in their effect and the barrier would be built by the smaller, constructive waves.

The characteristics of a barrier beach provide evidence on which the method of development of this and similar features can be based. From the description of the lagoon it is clear that it must have a very low gradient. The sand of the lagoon floor and beach is fairly coarse, it should, therefore, have a reasonably steep equilibrium gradient. According to the work of Bascom (1951)[4] the minimum slope to be expected on a beach formed of material of this grade would be 1 : 21, from his

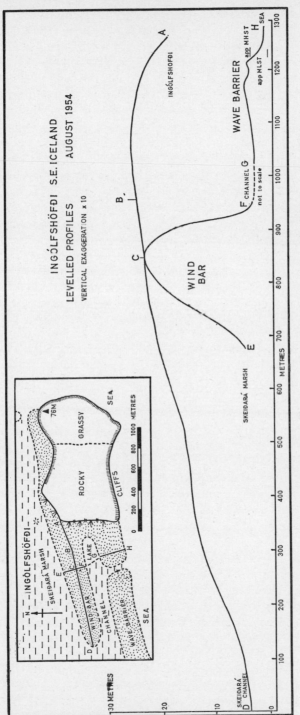

FIG. 10-16. Profiles across the wind and wave barrier on the south-east coast of Iceland, near Ingolfshofdi.

analysis of many beaches on the coast of California. The surveyed gradient of the barrier beach in Iceland was 1 : 18·5, which agrees reasonably closely with the value given by Bascom. This gradient will vary with changing wave conditions, but whatever the wave dimensions the gradient of the lagoon, which would form the coastline in the absence of the barrier beach, is very much flatter than the equilibrium gradient of the barrier beach. It is, therefore, probable that this type of barrier beach is related to the swash bar in the wave tank in a somewhat similar way as the ridges on a tidal beach. The main difference between the two types of profile is the tidal range; whereas on a beach with a large tidal range the waves cannot concentrate their activity for a prolonged period, where the tide is small, as it is on the south coast of Iceland, the waves can act on almost the same part of the beach for long periods. As a result they can build up a barrier which is always above the mean sea-level in the same way as the swash bar in the wave tank is built up above the still water level.

The building up of a barrier by this means requires the activity of constructive waves, the régime of waves and winds are therefore relevant. Because the sand of the barrier in Iceland is fairly coarse, it is likely that the wave steepness which will produce a constructive effect on this beach will be rather greater than it would on a fine sand beach. This suggests that the Atlantic swells which must often reach this coast will be more likely to be constructive in their effect on the beach. The wind régime on this coast is such that winds more often blow offshore or alongshore which would help to render the waves constructive, as has already been shown.[34]

The suggested method of formation of the Icelandic barrier beach may be more widely applicable; in many of the areas where barrier islands or beaches are found the tidal range is also small, and these coasts tend to have low offshore gradients. This is true of the Gulf of Mexico, where the Mississippi delta has a tidal range of 2–3 ft., the Baltic and Mediterranean are tideless, the coast of Surinam, South America, has a low range, most of the Atlantic coast of U.S.A. also has a fairly small tidal range; for example at Sandy Hook, New Jersey,[35] the tide has a mean range of 4·6 ft., while at Atlantic City and Delaware Breakwater, farther south, it is 4·1 and 4·2 ft. respectively. In these environments constructive action in the swash zone could build a feature permanently above the water line which would in time become a barrier beach. The subsequent development of the barrier beach to become the more complex feature Shepard calls the barrier island is often achieved by the growth of wind blown dunes on the crests of the barrier beaches, when these grow wide and high enough to be able to support vegetation.

Some of the earlier authors suggested that the submarine bars, which have already been considered, and are also found in seas of small tidal range, are an early form of the barrier beach and that one feature develops into the other. Braun (1911)[14] put forward this view; he considered that the submarine bar is the early form of the barrier beach, the intermediate stage he calls the 'zuwachsriff', he was followed by Hartnack,[17] in 1926; later, in 1935, Timmermans[36] put forward the same hypothesis, but he considered that the 'zuwachsriff' was formed in front of the breaker by the swash of the waves.

The part played by longshore movement in the development of shingle barriers has been stressed; because longshore movement of shingle plays an important part in their formation they are, perhaps, in many instances better described as spits rather than barriers. The part played by longshore movement in the formation of sand barriers is more doubtful; some authors, notably Gilbert, would suggest that longshore movement is essential in the formation of sandy barrier beaches, but Elie de Beaumont, followed by Johnson, did not consider that longshore movement was essential to their growth. The discontinuous nature of many of these barriers is a point in favour of the second theory, and the probability that they are the result of constructive waves. These move material towards the shore, and the very flat gradient would enable them to transport sand from some distance offshore because the waves would break far from the water-line.

Summary

Barrier beaches are similar to ridge and runnel beaches in that they are the result of constructive waves building up the beach to form their equilibrium gradient on a slope which is flatter than their equilibrium gradient. Where the tidal range is small this process can build up a barrier beach which will be permanently above the mean sea-level. A feature built by this process is more likely to be formed of sand, because shingle will not form a sufficiently flat slope to allow this process to operate. Shingle ridges built above the water-level are normally the product of steep storm waves which are mainly destructive in their effect. Such waves can throw some shingle well above the reach of normal waves to form shingle ridges. These are higher than sand barriers unless the latter are raised by the development of wind-blown dunes. In some areas a composite feature may form if sand and shingle are mixed on the beach. It seems likely that longshore movement plays an essential part in the formation of a pure shingle ridge, but that this factor is not essential to the development of a barrier beach of pure sand. Shingle structures are nearly always tied to the land at one end at least, while sand barriers may be unattached at one or both ends, and they are frequently broken by inlets.

REFERENCES

[1]Bagnold, R. A., 1940, Beach formation by waves; some model experiments in a wave tank. *Journ. Inst. Civ. Eng.* **15,** pp. 27–52.

[2]Meyers, R. D., 1933, A model of wave action on beaches. Unpub. thesis for M.Sc. Univ. of California.

[3]*B.E.B. Interim Report* 1933, Washington.

[4]Bascom, W. N., 1951, The relationship between sand size and beach face slope. *Trans. Am. Geoph. Un.* **32,** 6, pp. 866–74.

[5]King, C. A. M., 1953, The relationship between wave incidence, wind direction and beach changes at Marsden Bay, Co. Durham. *Inst. Brit. Geog. Trans. and Papers* **19,** pp. 13–23.

[6]Rector, R. L., 1954, Laboratory study of the equilibrium profiles of beaches. *B.E.B. Tech. Memo.* **41.**

[7]Shepard, F. P., 1950, Longshore bars and longshore troughs. *B.E.B. Tech. Memo.* **15.**

[8]Beach Erosion Board, 1947, A comparative study of waves on model beaches of different scale. *Bull.* **1,** 2, p. 8.

[9]Bruun, P., 1954, Coast erosion and the development of beach profiles. *B.E.B. Tech. Memo.* **44.**

[10]Elie de Beaumont, L., 1845, *Leçons de Geologie pratique, 7me Leçon—Levées de sables et galet.*

[11]Hagen, 1863, *Handbuch der Wasserbaukunst.*

[12]Lehmann, F. P. W., 1884, Das Kustengebiet Hinterpommerns. *Zeitschr. Gesell. Erdkunde zu Berlin* **19,** p. 391.

[13]Olson-Seffer, P., 1910, Genesis and development of sand formations on marine coasts. *Augustana Lib. Pub.* **7.**

[14]Braun, G., 1911, Entwickelungsgeschichtliche Studien an Europaischen Flachlandsküsten und irhe Dunen. *Inst. Meereskunde Geog. Inst.* **15,** pp. 1–174.

[15]Poppen, H., 1912, Die Sandbänke an der Küster der Deutschen Bucht. *Ann. für Hydrographie etc.* **6** Berlin, pp. 393–403.

[16]Otto, T., 1911–12, Der Darss und Zingst. *Jber. Geog. Ges. Greifswald* **13,** pp. 235–485.

[17]Hartnack, W., 1926, *Die Küste Hinterpommerns und besonderer Berücksichtigung der Morphologie.* Stolpmünde.

[18]Russell, I. C., 1885, Geological history of Lake Lahontan. *U.S. Geol. Surv. Mono.* **11,** pp. 92–93.

[19]Gilbert, G. K., 1890, Lake Bonneville. *Monogr. U.S. Geol. Surv.*

[20]Evans, O. F., 1940, The low and ball of the east shore of Lake Michigan. *Journ. Geol.* **48,** pp. 476–511.

[21]Keulegan, G. H., 1945, Depths of offshore bars. *B.E.B. Tech. Memo.* **8.**

[22]Keulegan, G. H., 1948, An experimental study of submarine sand bars. *B.E.B. Tech. Rep.* **3.**

[23]Cornaglia, P., 1887, *On beaches* (trans. from Italian).

[24]King, C. A. M. and Williams, W. W., 1949, The formation and movement of sand bars by wave action. *Geog. Journ.* **113,** pp. 70–85.

[25]Williams, W. W. and King, C. A. M., 1951, Observations faites sur la plage des Karentes en Août, 1950. *Bull. Inform. du Com. Cent. d'Ocean. et d'Etudes des Côtes* 2 *pt. Notes. Tech.* pp. 363–8.

[26]Bascom, W. N., 1953, Characteristics of natural beaches. Chap. 10 *Proc. 4th Conf. on Coastal Eng.* pp. 163–80.

[27]Cornish, V., 1898, On sea beaches and sand banks. *Geog. Journ.* **11,** pp.628–51.

[28]Gresswell, R. K., 1937, The geomorphology of the south-west Lancashire Coastline. *Geog. Journ.* **90.** pp. 335–48.

[29]Gresswell, R. K., 1953, Sandy shore of south Lancashire. *Liverpool Studies in Geography.*

[30]Pugh, D. C., 1953, Etudes mineralogique des plages Picardes et Flamandes. *Bull. d'Inf. Com. Cent. d'Oceangr. et d'Etudes des Côtes* **5,** 6.

[31]Van Veen, J., 1936, *Onderzockingen in de Hoofden.*

[32]Barnes, F. A. and King, C. A. M., 1951, A preliminary survey at Gibraltar Point, Lincolnshire. *Bird Obs. and Field Res. St. Gib. Pt. Lincs.* Rep. 1951, pp. 41–59.

[33]Johnson, D. W., 1919, *Shore processes and shoreline development.*

[34]King, C. A. M., 1956, The coast of south-east Iceland near Ingolfhöföi. *Geog. Journ.* **122,** pp. 241–6.

[35]Wicker, C. F., 1951, History of the New Jersey coastline. Chap. 33 *Proc. 1st Conf. on Coastal Eng.* pp. 299–319.

[36]Timmermans, P. D., 1935, Proeven over den invloed van golven op een strand. *Leidische Geol. Med.* **6,** pp. 231–386.

Chapter 11

HISTORICAL DATA ON COASTAL CHANGE

1. *EVIDENCE OF MAPS*

PERHAPS the most useful evidence of coastal change can be obtained from maps although these have their drawbacks when accurate values of change are required. One major difficulty is the possible inaccuracy of the map. Few maps can be relied on to give accurate changes of the coast before the Ordnance Survey maps were published at the beginning of the nineteenth century; even these maps, on the scale of 1 in. to 1 mile, are of limited value unless the coastal changes are large in amount. The 6-in. to 1 mile maps can be used to give an accurate measure in cliff recession, and where the coasts are low, the tide lines often provide useful evidence, but frequently the exact state of the tide shown on the map is not made sufficiently clear for comparison with modern maps. One example of the possible error this method involves is mentioned on p. 294. Maps can only give evidence of the state of the coast at the date of survey; they cannot give a continuous picture of coastal development, it is possible that several important steps will be omitted in the cartographic evidence of coastal change, if the dates of survey are far apart, as is usually the case.

It must not be assumed that all cartographic evidence before the Ordnance Survey is useless, but it is always as well to treat early maps with caution. During the seventeenth and eighteenth centuries many very excellent county surveys were made by such well known surveyors as Saxton and Speed, but these maps can be misleading. Some of the early work of Norden, which was specifically surveyed to give an accurate map of some coastal areas such as Orford, is of considerable value. The hydrographic surveys of the coastline also provide valuable evidence of coastal and offshore changes.

The analysis of the development of the spits across the harbour mouths of Poole, Christchurch and Pagham on the south coast of England by Robinson (1955)[1] illustrated well the use to which information from surveys of different kinds can be put in the elucidation of coastal change. The maps and charts used for the study of Poole harbour area include an early undated and unsigned map, which, from comparison with others, probably dates from about 1585–6. It is on a scale of 0·78 in. to 1 mile. The second map is dated 1597 and it is drawn by Robert Adams and covers all Poole Harbour. About 100 years later in 1698 naval commanders produced a chart of the ports of the south coast, including Poole. A small scale map was produced of the area in 1720, while a 6-in. to 1 mile map of Poole Harbour, surveyed by Lieutenant Mackenzie, is dated 1785. Further hydrographic surveys were produced in the years 1849, 1878, 1891, 1910, 1924, and 1934. The Ordnance Survey maps of the area include the first edition 1 in. to 1 mile; a 25 in. to 1 mile plan was produced in 1886 and revised in 1900 and 1924, while the Ordnance Survey produced an air photo mosaic of the area, flown in 1947. This area has, therefore, been surveyed at least 16 times since the end of the sixteenth century at increasingly frequent intervals.

A similar number of surveys of the other two harbours studied by Robinson are also available, it was possible, therefore, to trace with fair accuracy the evolution of the spits from the beginning of the eighteenth century to the present day. It must be remembered that these areas include entrances to harbours important to navigation which are subject to fairly rapid changes in the position of channels, accurate information of the coastal area was, therefore, essential. It is not likely that such a complete cartographic record of coastal change would be available for more open coasts.

2. OTHER EVIDENCE OF COASTAL CHANGE

Sources other than maps may provide evidence of coastal change. The nature of the evidence will vary with the type of coast; on a coast where erosion is dominant records of the loss of land and buildings may be available and give information concerning the time and place of erosion. On coasts which are building out by accretion evidence may refer to silting up of ports and similar events. An example of the type of evidence available will be considered for each of these major groups, taking Lincolnshire as an example of an erosion coast and the Dungeness area as one of accretion.

(a) Erosion coast—Lincolnshire

The loss of land on the Lincolnshire coast is not as well known or conspicuous as that of the Holderness area; it is nevertheless quite extensive and the type of coast renders the erosion more dangerous to life and property as it is often associated with coastal flooding. Much of the relevant information has been assembled by Owen (1952).[2] The earlier history of the coast in Lincolnshire during the post-glacial period before the erosion started in the fourteenth century has been worked out by Swinnerton (1931)[3] and (1936)[4] and is illustrated in fig. 11–1. During the post-glacial period silt and salt marsh clay with layers of peat, the latter deposited at times of low sea-level, accumulated on the boulder-clay which formed the shore in immediate post-glacial times. Submerged forests are incorporated in the lower of the two peat layers; the trees grew on the boulder-clay exposed during the period of low sea-level as the ice retreated in late and post-glacial times. These stumps are now exposed at extreme low tide on the beach. The upper layer of peat occurs at about 1 ft. O.D. and is of late bronze and iron age as Hallstadt pottery has been found incorporated within the peat. Between the two peat layers are thick deposits of tidal salt-marsh clay, which were deposited with a rising sea-level behind some barrier to seaward which cut off direct wave action from the area. Since the deposition of the upper peat, sea-level must have risen about 9 ft. in this area. During the period of the late bronze-early iron age, the evidence points to the use of the

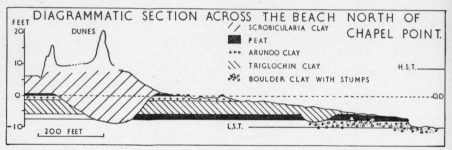

FIG. 11–1. Diagrammatic section through the post-glacial deposits of the Lincolnshire coast. (After Swinnerton.)

coastal zone for salt extraction from the sea. This industry had ceased before the area was occupied by the Romans but it seems likely, from the position of the Roman remains, that the sea-level started to rise before the end of the period of Roman occupation. After the Roman period sea-level continued to rise and deposited a layer of salt-water clay on the upper peat. The gradually rising sea-level, and the stormy years of the thirteenth century, probably caused the break up of the coastal barrier behind which the salt-marsh deposits had been accumulating, as frequent inundations are recorded in the area after the opening of the fourteenth century.

Since the end of the thirteenth century erosion by the sea has been serious on the Lincolnshire coast and Owen states that five parishes have been lost to the sea. During the last four centuries the sea has advanced between ¼ and ½ mile in the Mablethorpe, Trusthorpe and Sutton-on-Sea areas (see fig. 11–2). Some of the earliest evidence of loss of land and buildings in the Mablethorpe area, given by Owen, refers to the stormy thirteenth century; in the year 1287 the Louth Park Chronicle records that St. Peter's church in Mablethorpe was 'rent asunder by the waves of the sea'. In 1335, according to records, the waves breached

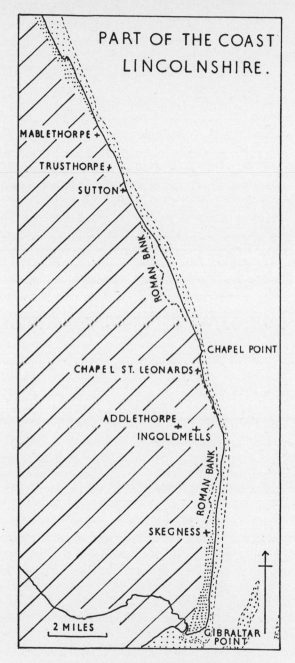

Fig. 11-2. Map of the Lincolnshire coast.
(Crown Copyright reserved.)

the sea-banks and flooded land behind, causing loss of stock and crops. By 1430 the sea-walls again needed repair; a statement records that the parson of St. Mary's, Mablethorpe, was required to furnish an account of the use of money and goods received for the repair of the sea-walls, which were necessary for the protection of the parish. The lord of Mablethorpe manor in 1443 was exempted from certain duties, which would have entailed expense, on account of loss of revenue resulting from inroads by the sea and cost of repairs to sea defences. The duties included appointment to various public offices and acceptance of the honour of knighthood. A survey of 1503 states that Mablethorpe was 'in very great danger of the sea'. Evidence of erosion is found in the Alford and Spilsby Courts of Sewers records which begin in the middle of the sixteenth century and provide useful information on the problem of erosion. In 1540 or thereabouts the church of St. Peter's was finally destroyed and an account of 1602 tells that 'both church and chancel were swallowed up with the sea above 50 or 60 years past'. The number of communicants of the parish dwindled from sixty-seven in 1603 to only four families in 1722, while in 1745 the parish was joined to that of Theddlethorpe St. Helen. The tax imposed by parliament in 1645 on on Linconshire for defence of the county was demanded from Mablethorpe, amongst other places, on account of the severe losses recently sustained by sea erosion; this was partly due to the bad state of repair of the sea-banks, necessary to the safety of the coast then as now.

There are also interesting records of damage and danger from the sea at Sutton, just south of Mablethorpe. The records of the Commissioners of Sewers show that in 1631 the sea-banks at Sutton were in a very bad state of repair, with the sea coming over the old bank at every high spring tide, while a new one was being built landward of it. In 1637 the inhabitants of Sutton sent a petition to the Privy Council; in this they complained of the failure of the Commissioners to provide a new bank, stating that: 'the town hath been divers years and yet is in great danger to be destroyed by the rage and violence of the sea', and pointing out that 'our ancient parish church, some houses inhabited, and very much of the best grounds in our said town was destroyed by the sea and now is sea'. Sutton is still very much in danger of the sea, as the serious flooding here in 1953 showed, but this recent disaster can be seen in its historical perspective as only one event of a long continued process of incursion by the sea.

In areas farther south along the coast there is further evidence of the inroads of the sea. For example as early as 1272 it was a customary service for tenants to do sea-walling at Ingoldmells, and during the fifteenth century there are plenty of records of inundation of land by the sea. A particularly interesting account is quoted by Owen from an earlier source (Oldfield, 1829)[5] which is worth giving as it illustrates the occurrence of a disaster very similar to that of 1953 about 200 years earlier, when serious flooding occurred on 16 February 1735. 'From five to eight in the morning, the day after the full moon and a boisterous wind blowing north-west the sea for some hours before and after the time of high water overflowed Ingoldmells Bank for above a mile together, and laid the greatest part of the lands on this side of Dydick Bank in this parish and in Addlethorpe under water. There was so much salt water in the Parishes that it was near three weeks in running off. So great a tide has not been known in the memory of man.' This flood was clearly the result of a North Sea surge resulting from strong northerly winds and coinciding with a period of spring tides.

These few examples show that this low-lying coast has been suffering from erosion for at least 400 years; the fact that the land behind the thin line of natural dunes has been increasingly lowered below the level of high tide by the rise of sea-level means that breaching of the banks and dunes leads to increasingly serious flooding of the land behind. This naturally leads to public demands for security, and other evidence of the encroaching of the sea.

(b) Coast of accretion—Dungeness area

During the early stages of development of the large shingle structure of Dungeness, and the Romney and other marshes formed in its shelter, the shingle probably formed a fairly simple spit across the mouth of a wide shallow bay whose shores ran from Hythe in the north via Appledore to Rye and Winchelsea in the south (see fig. 11–3). The development of this coastal area is bound up with such problems as the draining of the marsh, the changing of the courses of rivers across the area and the silting up of former ports due to the retreat of the sea.

The reclaiming of Romney Marsh may have been achieved in the Roman period. This would have been facilitated by the relatively low sea-level at this time. Evidence for this is given by Lewis and Balchin (1940)[6] who state that the sea-level was probably 5 or 6 ft. lower during the Roman period than it is now. This result was obtained from an accurate survey of the heights of the shingle ridges of Dungeness foreland. It supports the historical evidence of draining of the Romney Marsh area during the Roman period, when the relatively low sea-level would assist this operation, according to the deduction of Rice-Holmes (1907)[7] who supports a Roman date for this wall.

This date for the Rhee wall is not accepted by Ward (1933).[8] In discussing Lewis and Balchin's work he raises several historical arguments against the Roman date of the Rhee wall. He points out that if the wall were Roman in date the marsh to the south would be expected to differ from that to the north; it would probably be flooded by the high tide whereas good arable land would be expected to the north. The Roman date of the wall is now, however, generally accepted and is supported by the evidence of the Saxon charters; these mention no difference at all between the area to the north and south of the wall, in fact a wall is never mentioned in them. The place names do not differ on either side of the wall; the oldest ones which end in -ham are found equally on either side of the wall. There is also positive evidence in the

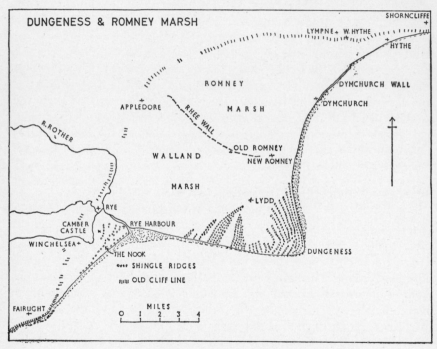

FIG. 11–3. Map of Dungeness and Romney Marsh area.
(Crown Copyright reserved.)

possible reference to the building of the wall during the fourteenth century in the form of banks on either side of a channel. In 1324 the king appointed a commission to inquire into damage caused by a trench cut across the marsh, which may refer to the Rhee wall channel. This cut was for drainage and periodic deepening to keep it clear would lead to an increase in the height of the banks.

This controversy over the date of the Rhee wall is related to the former course of the Rother, or Limen as some think it was called. Ward considers that the Rother flowed to the sea at or near Hythe, but most other authorities suggest that it reached the sea nearer to Appledore. This contradiction may have arisen over confusing the Portus Lemanis, where Caesar landed near Hythe with the river Limen or Rother, which was probably not in the same place (Lewin, 1862).[9] These doubts illustrate the possible danger of relying too much on the interpretation of rather vague historical material.

There is, however, definite historical evidence of the growth of the shingle ridges and the development of marsh strips between them in the eighth century. There are two charters, Eadbriht's of 741 and Offa's of 774 which make grants of land in the marsh near Lydd to the Church of Christ at Canterbury. This indicates the growth of Dungeness towards the east, but at the same time there is evidence of sea to the east and north of Lydd as in 893 Danes sailed past Lydd to Appledore with a fleet of 250 vessels. The outgrowth of Dungeness to the east held up shingle travelling from the south-west and prevented it from reaching the area to the north near Dymchurch; this necessitated the building of the Dymchurch wall by Rennie in 1803–4, where the lack of shingle was causing danger of erosion (Elliott, 1847).[10]

Another major change had a marked effect on the development of the coast, for which there is also historical evidence (Lewis, 1932);[11] this is the diversion of the Rother in the thirteenth century from its old outlet near New Romney to Rye. This change was accompanied by the destruction of Old Winchelsea and Promehill. The probable site of Old Winchelsea was about 6 miles north-east of Fairlight Cliff and 2 miles south-south-east of the present site of Rye. These settlements were probably situated on a shingle spit which formed a link across the bay, allowing communication between Winchelsea and a part of its parish which is now on the Rye side of the estuary. The gradual erosion of this spit, which culminated in the break-through of the Rother in 1287, is shown by references to the half-ruined state of the town of Old Winchelsea from 1236 to 1276 when the king himself visited the town and planned its removal, it was almost entirely swept away in the catastrophe of 1287. The early chroniclers, quoted by Homan (1938),[12] give evidence of these facts. New Winchelsea was built by Edward I to be used as the headquarters of the Cinque Ports and in 1292 the inhabitants moved to the new town. Before long, however, another change in the marine processes defeated the king's purpose. The old Winchelsea was destroyed by the destructive action of the sea, but the new one was ruined by its constructive action. It was not long before deposition isolated the new Winchelsea from the open coast and its days as a port were over. This growth of the coast outwards in the region of Rye and Winchelsea may also be connected with the break-through of the river, which completed the destruction of Old Winchelsea, as this reduced the speed of longshore movement of material along the developing southern side of Dungeness, which was now beginning to turn farther and farther to face the dominant waves from the south-south-west. The increasing eastward projection of the ness will have helped to trap beach material in this angle, thus cutting these places off from the sea.

Winchelsea had become useless for defence from the sea during the sixteenth century. Henry VIII, therefore, built Camber Castle to take its place. This fortification was sited near enough to the sea to act as a substitute for Winchelsea, but the sea again spoilt the plans; the continued withdrawal of the sea, as shingle ridges were built out from the shore, soon isolated Camber Castle from the sea and it now stands as a ruin, an historical monument of coastal change. The alignment of the Camber Castle shingle ridges and the date at which they were built has been analysed recently by Lovegrove (1953).[13] The earliest ridges that he mentions are related to the destruction in 1287 of an old sea-wall extending north-north-east to protect the marshes east of Winchelsea. Between this date and 1594 a complex series of ridges were formed which extended the coast northwards to beyond Camber Castle; the fortification was at this time about 800 ft. from the sea. The evidence for the position of the coastline at this date is derived from Philip Symonson's map which agrees very well with the evidence provided by the alignment of the shingle ridges. An undated and unsigned map, which Lovegrove considers to date from about 1695, illustrates the rapid growth of the coast outwards during the seventeenth century. This growth included the development of salt marshes, which were sheltered behind the ridges which now form Nook beach. In the neighbourhood of Camber Castle the coast built out over 2,000 ft. during this century, and also extended farther north to within 1,250 ft. of the present position of the river Rother. A map by Yeakell and Gardner of 1778 shows the continued rapid outward growth, particularly in the north where the coast built out to the position of Rye harbour and reached to within 300 ft. of the river Rother. Two miles to the south-east the outward growth was only about 200 ft.

Surveys during the nineteenth century showed the development of the ridges to the south-east of the Nook, which first formed as a salt marsh in their shelter and was reclaimed by 1845. This series of surveys, with supporting historical evidence, gives a fairly complete picture of the outward growth of this part of the coast; this evidence can be confirmed and supported by a physiographic study of the distribution of the shingle ridges and strips of salt marsh on the ground.

Summary

Historical evidence gives a consistent picture of the incursion of the sea along the Lincolnshire coast, by reference to loss of land and damage to sea-banks, which have been a necessary defence since the thirteenth century, which was particularly stormy. Description of flooding clearly indicate the result of a surge in 1735, similar to that of 1953.

The Dungeness area has built-out mainly since Neolithic times; the evidence for this process is found in records of land reclamation, or inning, dating from the eighth century onwards, as well as earlier evidence of Roman activity in the marsh areas, as the Rhee wall is generally acknowledged to be Roman in date. Erosion has also taken place locally and records give evidence of the loss of Winchelsea in 1287, but the gradual cutting off from the sea of New Winchelsea, built to replace the old town, from this time onward is illustrated by cartographic evidence as well as evidence of buildings, of which Camber Castle, dating from the sixteenth century is the most conspicuous.

REFERENCES

[1]Robinson, A. H. W., 1955, The harbour entrances of Poole, Christchurch and Pagham. *Geog. Journ.* **121**, pp. 33–50.
[2]Owen, A. E. B., 1952, Coast erosion in east Lincolnshire. *Linc. Hist.* **9**, pp. 330–9.
[3]Swinnerton, H. H., 1931, The post-glacial deposits of the Lincolnshire coast. *Quart. Journ. Geol. Soc.* **87**, pp. 360–75.
[4]Swinnerton, H. H., 1936, The physical history of east Lincolnshire. *Trans. Lincs. Nat. Trust. Pres. Add.* pp. 91–100.
[5]Oldfield, E., 1829, *History of Wainfleet and the Wapentake of Candleshore*, p. 366.
[6]Lewis, W. V. and Balchin, W. G. V., 1940, Past sea-levels at Dungeness. *Geog. Journ.* **96**, pp. 258–85.
[7]Rice-Holmes, T., 1907, *Ancient Britain and the Invasions of Julius Caesar*.
[8]Ward, G., 1933, The river Limen at Ruckinge. *Arch. Cant.* **45**, p. 129.
[9]Lewin, T., 1862, *The Invasion of Britain by Julius Caesar*. 2nd Ed.
[10]Elliott, J., 1847, Account of the Dymchurch Wall. *Mins. Proc. Inst. Civ. Eng.* **6**, p. 466.
[11]Lewis, W. V., 1932, The formation of Dungeness foreland. *Geog. Journ.* **80**, pp. 309–24.
[12]Homan, W. MacL., 1938, The Marshes between Hythe and Pett. *Sussex Arch. Coll.* **79**.
[13]Lovegrove, H., 1953, Old shorelines near Camber Castle. *Geog. Journ.* **119**, pp. 200–7.

CHAPTER 12

COASTAL TYPES AND THEIR DEVELOPMENT. THE
MARINE CYCLE

THE great variety of coastal forms renders a discussion of coastal development difficult because each area should be treated individually, as each is unique. Nevertheless it is possible to generalize with sufficient accuracy to suggest a normal pattern of development for coasts of differing types. In this connexion the elements of major importance are the general gradient of the shore region and the outline of the coast. Four major groups result which provide a basis for discussion of coastal development through a marine cycle. These groups are as follows:

1. Steep indented coast
2. Steep straight coast
3. Flat indented coast
4. Flat straight coast

It is not necessary for this purpose to inquire into the origin of the coastal type which is considered in the problem of classification, dealt with in chapter 7. The second category, the steep straight coasts, occur relatively infrequently except in areas of faulting or steep monoclinal folding parallel to the sea, as in the northern part of the west coast of the South Island, New Zealand; for the purposes of this discussion, therefore, only the first type of steep coast will be considered. After the initial stage on the flat coasts, a similar cycle may be expected to run its course on both straight and indented types so that the last two groups may be combined. The development of shore forms on these two contrasting coastlines will be considered.

1. *SHORE FEATURES AND DEVELOPMENT OF STEEP INDENTED COASTS*

(a) **The initial form and modifying processes**

The initial form is theoretically one which has not been altered at all by marine agencies where sea-level comes to rest against an area of diverse relief with fairly steep slopes. This form is well shown in the north-east part of the South Island of New Zealand in the Marlborough Sound area as shown by Cotton (1954).[1] This is a recently submerged mountainous area, which does not even show cliffing on the headlands.

This coastal type is most often formed as the result of submergence, but it need not necessarily be initiated in this way; it is what Johnson (1919)[2] considered to be the typical shoreline of submergence.

The most important modifying process on such a coast is the wave action. The effect of the outline of the coast on the pattern of wave attack is also significant. Wave attack will be very uneven in intensity on an indented coast; refraction will cause concentration of energy of the longer waves on the headlands and dissipation in the bays. The oblique approach of waves, particularly the shorter ones, along an intricate coastline, is also very important as it affects the direction of movement of beach material, which will probably be towards the bays. Under these conditions the direction of movement of beach material will not necessarily be in a uniform direction along great stretches of coastline but will be directed away from the headlands, which will, in any case, hamper the free movement of material alongshore.

On an indented coast of this type it is likely that the tidal range will vary from place to place and tidal currents are likely to be strong locally, particularly where there are narrow straights through which the tide flows. These currents may in some instances be of importance to local movement of material, but on the whole the direction of wave approach is the fundamental factor on which the direction of movement, and hence the character of the coast in detail, depends in the early stage.

The influence of the wind in the early youthful stage of the development of the shoreline of this type is very small. There is little loose beach material available and the steep slopes of the land discourages deposition of wind-blown sand. The wind is only important in its effect on the waves and their constructive or destructive influence on the beach, but as the beach material is in short supply at first the wind factor is of least importance at this early stage.

The beach material is mainly of importance by its absence in the initial stages on a steep indended coast. This allows the waves unhampered access to the rocks of the headlands and allows these to become cliffed. This process, however, provides the material which can initiate the formation of beaches; but in the bays the rivers will provide the bulk of the material which is built into the bay-head beaches. The character of the cliffs and the type of material brought down by the rivers will determine the size of the beach material, while the resultant shore forms will vary according to whether sand or shingle predominates in the beach material.

The modification of a coast of this type is likely to be delayed if the base-level is rising because any beach material which is eroded from the cliffs, or brought down by the rivers, will tend to be drowned. A static base-level will allow the cycle to run its course most effectively at first;

in the later stages, when the offshore zone has been shallowed, a rising base-level will help to prolong the stage of active erosion.

(b) Modification produced

i. BY EROSION. The absence of beaches allows the waves to attack the coast, their attack is most effective where the energy of the sea is concentrated on the headlands. In general this has the effect of straightening the coastline, which is the ultimate aim of the marine forces. In detail, however, the initial result may be the reverse because if the rocks are of

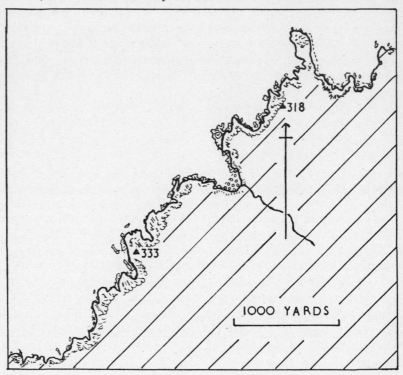

FIG. 12-1. Map of the crenulate coast of Cornwall. (Crown Copyright reserved.)

uneven resistance to marine erosion the softer ones will be worn away more quickly and the resultant coast will be more irregular than at first. This initial increase in the detailed complexity of the coastal outline produces a 'crenulate' coastline. It is well illustrated on the coasts of south-west Wales and parts of the south-west peninsula of Devon and Cornwall and is illustrated in fig. 12-1. Coastal irregularity, due to differences of rock resistance, is very clearly shown on the part of the coast of Dorset where the strike of the rocks trends parallel to the coast. The resistant Portland and Purbeck rocks have been narrowly breached in Lulworth Cove while a wide bay has been scooped out in the soft Wealden clay inland of the limestone. Stair Hole just to the west of the cove illustrates an earlier stage in such a development where the hard rock has only just been breached by a tunnel, while the sea is starting to remove the softer rock from behind, in which work it is assisted by much slumping and mudflow activity in the clays.[3] The various stages including the more open Worbarrow Bay to the east are shown in fig. 12–2.

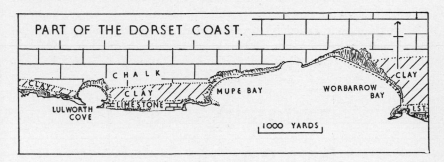

FIG. 12–2. Map of part of the coast of Dorset to show Lulworth Cove in relation to the rock type. (Crown Copyright reserved.)

ii. BY DEPOSITION. During the early stage of modification of a steep indented coast the features formed by deposition are many and varied; their form depending mainly on the type of material available and on the relationship between the coastal outline and the incidence of wave forces. In considering the form of the depositional features there are two tendencies to be taken into account. Firstly, the movement of material along the shore tends to prolong the direction of the solid coastline at points where there is an abrupt change in direction of the rocky shore. Secondly, there is the tendency for wave built structures to turn to face the direction from which the dominant waves are approaching. The former process depends on the movement of beach material alongshore either under the influence of short, therefore less refracted, waves with an oblique approach or under the influence of longshore movement resulting from the convergence or divergence of long, and therefore greatly refracted, waves. The second process may be expected to operate under the influence of the dominant storm waves; it will apply, therefore, particularly to shingle structures as it is only on shingle that storm waves can produce a constructive effect, in the form of beach ridges thrown up to the limit of the swash. These are relatively permanent features of the shore. The importance of the material in the reaction of shore features to storm waves is mentioned by Ting (1937),[4] who considers that storm waves are responsible for the formation of shingle features at great heights above sea-level, but that such features as Brodrick Bar (barrier) which is a bay-head barrier, composed entirely of fine sand, is formed by the action of normal waves. The first process will operate equally well on sand or shingle, the spit at Gibraltar Point is predominantly sand and prolongs the north-south coast of Lincolnshire where this turns west (see pp. 257–259), while Spurn Head, Yorkshire, prolonging the Holderness coast is another example of a simple sand spit shown in fig. 12–3; a similar type of shingle spit is found in Orford Ness on the Suffolk coast, which is about 11 miles long. Examples of shingle structures facing the dominant waves are found in Chesil beach and the eastern side of Dungeness where the shingle ridges are parallel to the shore. The southern shore of Dungeness cannot be con-

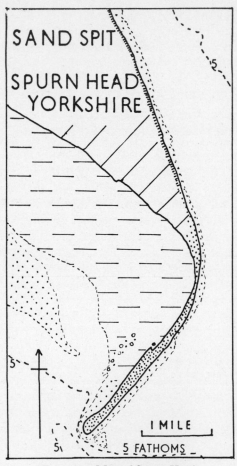

FIG. 12–3. Map of Spurn Head.
(Crown Copyright reserved.)

sidered similar as the ridges are truncated by the present coastline along this shore; it is, therefore, a feature of erosion and has not been built in its present form by storm beach ridges (see pp. 266–268).

It was pointed out in chapter 8, dealing with coastal deposition, that the longshore movement of material in forming spits was tending to straighten the coastline, whereas the tendency of structures to face the dominant waves was producing greater irregularity of outline. The two processes are linked by the fact that the longshore movement of material must, in the first place, allow the structures to turn towards the direction from which the dominant waves come, by moving material towards the down-wave side of the coast in relation to the dominant waves. This may be achieved entirely by deposition, or by erosion or a combination of the two processes. The former state is seen in the outbuilding of False Cape on the east coast of Florida, while the south side of Dungeness represents the latter process. The diagrams in fig. 12–4a show the different forms. In fig. 12–4b a foreland, or more precisely a cuspate barrier, owing to the presence of a lagoon, formed by the meeting of two spits from different directions in Guadalcanal is shown; Pool reef allows the point to remain sharp, by preventing waves approaching from the south. Other examples of somewhat similar types are illustrated and discussed by Schou (1945)[5] from the coast of Denmark. The development of a cuspate foreland will be facilitated where the offshore relief is favourable for the

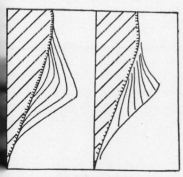

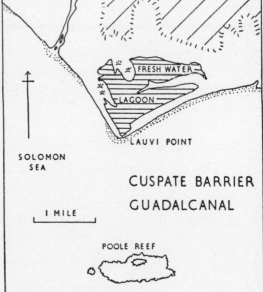

FIG. 12–4. (*a*) Diagrammatic map to show different types of cuspate foreland. The lines indicate the shingle ridges.

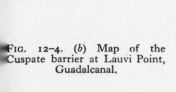

FIG. 12–4. (*b*) Map of the Cuspate barrier at Lauvi Point, Guadalcanal.

outbuilding of a large feature; this will be where the offshore gradient is gentle to enable deposition to take place. The sharpness of the point of a cuspate foreland depends on the presence of land to prevent waves approaching from a direction between the two from which the dominant waves come; Dungeness and Moila Point, Solomon Islands, provide examples and were mentioned in chapter 8 (see pp. 265, 266).

In considering the processes which tend to build out the coast and to prolong the direction of the hard rock coast by spit formation, the direction of the prevalent onshore wind, in relation to the dominant wind is important; another factor of significance is the availability of material moving alongshore. If the prevalent and dominant waves come from the same direction both factors will tend to favour the development of the shoreline perpendicular to the approach of the dominant waves as was pointed out by Lewis (1938).[6] If the supply of beach material is restricted by headlands then the dominant waves will the more readily be able to turn the coastline to face their direction of approach by moving the material to the down-wave end of the bay, until longshore movement is almost stopped, because the beach faces the direction from which the waves come. If this is in a fairly restricted bay the shore will tend to form an almost circular arc, lines drawn normal to the shore will meet near the centre of the bay (Lewis, 1938).[4] On a more open coast the shoreline will become fairly straight facing the direction of greatest fetch from which the dominant waves would come. Examples are given by Lewis; Poole Bay and Christchurch Bay on the Hampshire coast, illustrating the first point, (see fig. 12–5), while Chesil beach in Dorset illustrates the second type (see fig. 4–20 and pp. 167-170) where the coast is straighter. The sorting of shingle on this beach, already referred to, points to the small amount of longshore movement which now takes place here.

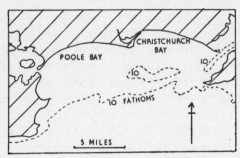

FIG. 12–5. Map of Poole and Christchurch Bays on the south coast of England. (Crown Copyright reserved.)

Where the direction of approach of the waves is very oblique to the shore, as along parts of the east coast of England, longshore movement will be the predominant process and as a result spits may be expected to form, particularly where the coastline is open in nature as in East Yorkshire, Lincolnshire and east Norfolk and Suffolk. Even here there is a tendency for wave action to turn shore features to face the dominant waves as is indicated in the trend of the sand ridges on the Lincolnshire coast (see pp. 345–347). Examples of these features are the spits of Spurn Head, Gibraltar Point spit, Yarmouth spit and the rather more complex feature of Orford Ness in Suffolk.

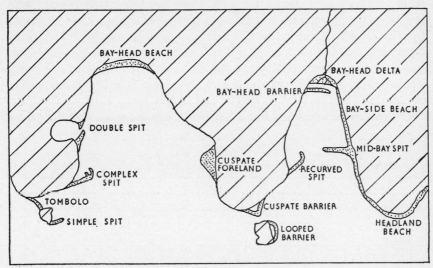

FIG. 12–6. Diagrammatic map to show the different types of depositional features on a youthful steep indented coast.

The features formed during the early stage of modification of a steep indented shoreline are very varied in character. The main types of features are illustrated diagrammatially in fig. 12–6 and may be listed as follows:

> Bay-head beach
> Bay-head delta
> Bay-head barrier
> Bay-side beach
> Mid-bay spit
> Headland beach
> Spit—simple sand
>> shingle
>> mixed sand and shingle
>> recurved
>> complex
>> two direction—double spit
> Looped barrier
> Tombolo
> Cuspate barrier
> Cuspate foreland

Some of these features have already been discussed but examples of some of the others may be considered. The bay-head beach is probably the most common type and occurs in nearly all bays on an indented coastline; in the much smaller bays of a crenulate coastline, small areas of deposition, often known as pocket beaches, are often found. The rapidity with which material can move in these small bays was discussed from examples on the coast of California, see pp. 249, 281. Bay-head deltas are characteristic of relatively tideless areas where rivers bring large volumes of material down to the sea. They are perhaps more characteristic of lakes than the sea. An example of a bay-head barrier is given by Johnson in the western bay of Lake Superior near Duluth. It is a feature near the head of a bay but separated from the shore by a

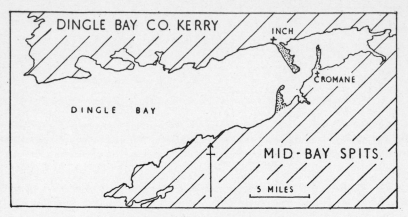

FIG. 12–7. Map of the mid-bay spits of Dingle Bay, Co. Kerry, Eire.
(Crown Copyright reserved.)

lagoon. Mid-bay spits are interesting features which are very well shown in Dingle Bay on the coast of Kerry, Eire. There are three spits in this bay which leave the coast at an abrupt angle and face the open water down the bay; they are shown in fig. 12–7. Two of these spits leave the southern shore of the bay and trend south-west to north-east, while the largest spit trends south-east from the north shore at Inch for a distance of about 3 miles. This spit directly faces the waves coming up the bay from the open Atlantic ocean at its mouth. The material forming the Inch and Glenbeigh spits is almost entirely fine sand, a very little shingle occurs near the landward end of the spits, both these spits have beaches of fine sand, which have very smooth flat profiles; they are backed by extensive and high sand dunes which form a belt almost a mile wide behind the beaches. The inner spit near Cromane is composed mostly of shingle, its beach is flatter than a normal shingle beach because it is protected from wave action by the other spits to seaward of it. The details of the formation of these spits have yet to be worked out. It is possible that they are related to shallower areas in the bay resulting from the deposition of glacial or fluvio-glacial material.

Somewhat similar features are found in the Moray Firth in Scotland. Here Chanonry Point extends south-east from the northern shore of the Firth; this feature, according to Lewis (1938)[6], is rather more in the nature of a cuspate foreland, which is shaped on its north-eastern side by waves coming down the axis of the Firth while the inner side is shaped by waves coming across the Firth from the south-west. Ogilvie (1914),[7] on the other hand, suggests that part of this feature is related to a higher sea-level, although he also notes the importance of the approach of waves from two directions. Bay-side and headland beaches do not require any further explanation; the latter feature is unlikely to be much in evidence in the early stages of development of this type of coast.

Various types of spits have already been mentioned and briefly discussed. It is difficult to generalize concerning the formation of spits; many of them are complex in form, being a mixture of sand and shingle and having an involved pattern of recurves towards the distal end. Evans (1942)[8] emphasized the importance of wave refraction round the end of the spit in accounting for the recurved nature of many relatively simple spits. It is usually possible to find clues from which the development of the spit can be deduced in considering the pattern of the recurves and other ridges which form the complex spit. One feature of this type which has been very intensively studied and described in detail is the barrier island of Scolt Head Island and Blakeney Point spit on the north coast of Norfolk. Much of this work has been published by Steers (1934),[9] (1946),[10] there is no need, therefore, to discuss these features in detail here.

The two direction spits to which Robinson (1955)[11] drew attention are of interest and have been briefly mentioned before (see pp. 255, 373). Robinson has produced cartographic evidence to suggest the method by which two spits trending in opposite directions almost close a wide bay. The examples he illustrates are all on the south coast of England at Poole, Christchurch and Pagham. The latter harbour, shown in fig. 12–8, is almost closed by two spits; one trends north-east from the southern headland of Selsey Bill, continuing the line of the coast, while the other trends south-west from the opposite shore near the Pagham beach estate. The cartographic evidence points to this pattern being due to the breaking through of a spit which had grown from south-west to north-east in the normal direction of movement of beach material along this coast. This earlier spit is shown on a map dated 1909 as extending right across the harbour entrance. The material of which the spits are formed is derived from the rapid erosion which is taking place in the weak deposits forming Selsey Bill to the south-west. During 1910 the continuous spit was breached by storm waves at a point about half way along its length; this left two spits apparently trending in opposite directions, giving the double spit feature. Periodic changes in the position of the harbour outlet make the spits of different lengths at different times. The double spit form is, therefore, the result of breaching by storm waves or flood waters of a shingle bank. This hypothesis, put

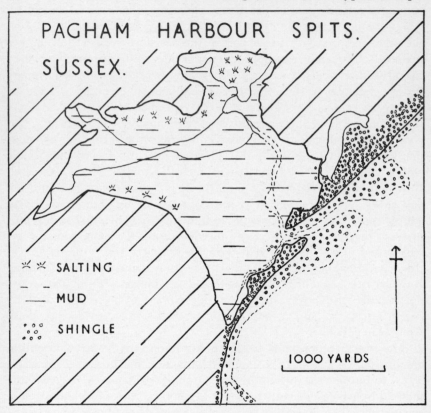

FIG. 12–8. Map of the double spits of Pagham Harbour, Sussex.
(Crown Copyright reserved.)

forward by Robinson, seems more satisfactory than other theories which suggest that this type of double spit is due to local counter-drift resulting from irregularities along the shore. It allows the drift of beach material to be continuously in one direction which agrees with observations and is supported by cartographic evidence.

Looped barriers and tombolos are associated with islands. The former feature, which is rather rare, consists of a barrier which forms on the lee side of an island in such a way that a lagoon is enclosed. This type of feature requires shelter to be permanently available on one side of the island, where the barrier forms and material must be available to form the deposit. The second feature, the tombolo, is a structure of sand or shingle tying an island to the mainland. The name is Italian in origin, from the very fine examples of these features found on the Italian coast; the well known double tombolo at Orbetello is the classic example. The tideless character of the Mediterranean is probably a factor which aids the development of these features, particularly where they are formed of sand. The cause of the formation of this type of feature is related to the shallower water connecting the island to the mainland which facilitates the building up of the area above sea-level by deposition and also affects the wave refraction in such a way that the orthogonals diverge

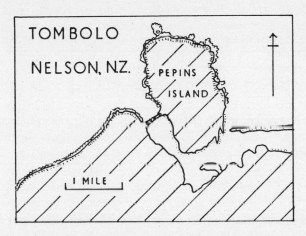

Fig. 12–9. Map of the tombolo near Nelson, South Island, New Zealand.

towards the straights between the island and the mainland. There is, therefore, a reduction of wave energy here and longshore movement will tend to be directed towards these areas from the adjacent areas. Longshore movement along the shores of the mainland may in some instances help to build the tombolo, where the orientation of the coastline is suitable.

There is an interesting example of a tombolo near Nelson in the South Island of New Zealand. This feature, illustrated in fig. 12–9, is built of large shingle and is set back from the angle of the coast where it might be expected to form. This may be because the depth of water is too great at the entrance of Cable Bay, causing the shingle ridge forming the tombolo to develop, facing the open sea, at a point where the water is shallow enough for the waves to break. The other side of the tombolo is shallow and is being silted up by deposits brought into the bay by the river as marine action is excluded by a spit which almost closes the bay, indicating that the direction of movement alongshore to the east of Pepin's Island is to the west.

The final features mentioned, the cuspate barrier and foreland have already been mentioned in considering the building out of the coast and need not be mentioned further here, except to point out that Johnson recognized three types of cuspate foreland, a simple type like the False Cape, already referred to (see pp. 371, 372), truncated cuspate foreland such as the Darss foreland in the Baltic, and finally the complex cuspate foreland such as Dungeness in south-east England which has already been discussed (see pp. 266–268).

These many types of depositional features all play their part in the cycle of marine erosion on a steep indented coast; their function is, on the whole, to straighten the coastline. This process is carried further during the period when the coast is approaching the mature state, which may now be considered.

(c) Maturity

As maturity is reached the coastline becomes much straighter, the headlands are worn back and the bays filled; maturity may be said to have been reached when the coast-line consists of smooth sweeping curves along which material can travel for considerable distances without interruption. The complex features, characteristic of the indented stage of youth, are eliminated and simplified as the outline of the coast becomes smoother. The formation of bay-mouth barriers facilitates this process by eliminating the bays, from the point of view of wave action. Examples of this type of barrier have already been mentioned (see pp. 255, 256). The speed with which the shoreline may develop these characteristics depends very much upon the nature of the rocks; this determines the speed with which the cliffs can recede. The softer rocks of the east coast of England already show the smooth outline associated with a mature coastline, while the hard rocks of the south-west of the British Isles are still in the crenulate stage of early youth in many areas.

Full maturity is theoretically reached when the coastline has been worn back to the original bay heads, the whole coastline is then in solid rock. This process will naturally be very slow where the rocks are resistant and it seems unlikely that sea-level will stay constant long enough to allow this stage to be reached in the hard rocks under present conditions, while in soft rocks, such as those of East Anglia, it may be reached very quickly. The chalk cliffs of the south coast between Newhaven and Beachy Head are sometimes cited as an example of a mature coastline, but it is doubtful how indented the initial coast was in this area, and changes in sea-level further complicate the development.

Marine erosion is, however, rapid here, compared to subaerial erosion and the small valleys, which are often dry, are left hanging as the cliffs retreat.

The existence along the whole coastline of a beach of loose material is another important feature of a mature coastline; even the headland cliffs should be protected by beaches at this stage, except perhaps during severe storms when destructive waves can still remove the beach material to expose the solid rock behind and beneath the beach to the waves.

Summary

The initial stage of a steep indented coast is soon modified by the waves to become crenulate in outline. Waves are the dominant modifying influence and the concentration of energy on the headlands by refraction is an important process; it assists the ultimate aim of the sea to straighten the coastline. In the early stages of the modification of such a coast depositional features assume many forms. Their growth depends on two important factors; first, longshore movement of material tends to prolong the direction of the coast, where this takes an abrupt bend. Second, wave built structures tend to form facing the direction from which the dominant waves come. The latter process tends to cause outbuilding or greater irregularity of outline and is most effectively accomplished in areas where the supply of beach material is not excessive. Some of the many features characteristic of the coast in this stage of development are described.

In maturity the coastal outline becomes much simpler in plan, this stage is reached in very different periods of time according to the character of the rock and to the exposure, the former factor being the more important. Continuous beaches are characteristic of a mature coastline.

2. *FLAT COASTS*

(a) Method of formation

Flat coasts which have a very low gradient both inland and offshore may be formed by three methods; the classical type of flat coast is Johnson's coast of emergence, this results from a fall of sea-level, but clearly, a flat coast will only result if the offshore gradient is small. This is likely to be the case if marine deposition has built up a wide shallow shelf, such as that found round part of the coast of the British Isles. In other areas the offshore gradient is steep and intricate and a fall of sea-level would not lead to a flat smooth offshore gradient, specially in areas where submarine canyons approach close inshore as they do along part of the Californian coast (see fig. 4–12 inset, p. 151). The weak material of a coast formed of recently elevated marine sediments will assist the development of the typical flat coastline.

In suitable areas subsidence can also produce a flat coast. If subaerial denudation has reduced the area adjacent to the coast to the very low gradient typical of a peneplane, a rise of sea-level will partially submerge this almost flat plain. The resultant coastline will be of a very low gradient but may at first be highly intricate in outline. The same processes will be able to alter such a coastline as the former type, because a peneplane of this type will probably be thickly covered in fine deposits, which will come under the influence of the sea as the base-level rises. The low coast of Lincolnshire was initiated by a rising base-level, which drowned a low-lying plain formed of glacial deposits resting on an older marine-cut bench.

A low coast may also be initiated by rapid outbuilding of fine material from the land to form a low-lying plain of considerable extent. The coast of south-east Iceland, which has been described in chapter 10 (see pp. 349–352, and fig. 7–5), illustrates this type of low coast; in this instance it results from outbuilding of fluvio-glacial deposits. The Canterbury Plains of New Zealand illustrate the same form, but the material is coarser here, and only in some parts of the coast is a typical low shoreline formed. The outbuilt coastal plains of large river, such as the Ganges, provide other conditions giving rise to a low coast without the necessity for a change in base-level.

(b) Modifying processes

The waves are again the chief modifying process on the coast. The flat offshore gradient will cause the larger ones to break some distance offshore, but the greater smoothness of the coastal outline will render the attack of the waves more uniform along the shore with the result that forms will not be so complex in plan as on an indented shoreline.

The tide is of importance on such a flat coast; the tidal range is significant in the formation of barrier beaches and islands as discussed in chapter 10 (see pp. 347–353), where the tidal range is small the development of barriers is facilitated. Johnson draws attention to the relationship between the number of channels through the barrier and the tidal range. He points out that on the coast of New Jersey, where the tidal range is 4–5 ft., the inlets are more numerous than on the Texas coast, where the tidal range is only 1–2 ft., here barriers may run unbroken for up to 100 miles.

Many of the barrier beaches are formed of sand, the wind, therefore, plays an important part in stabilizing and increasing the height of the barrier once it has been built by the waves above the high tide level.

Dune formation is an important process in the development and final
stages on a low flat coast of this type.

Because of the low gradient sand is much more likely to form the
predominant material on a flat coast. Shingle requires steep slopes on
the beach and is not likely to be the dominant material when the different
methods, already mentioned, of producing a flat coast are considered.
Some glacial outwash plains provide an exception and on parts of the
coast of the Canterbury Plains shingle is the dominant beach material.
One of the barriers on this coast, Ellesmere spit, at the southern side of
Banks' Peninsula, has many of the features of a flat coast (see fig.
12–10).[12] It is separated from the shore by the lagoon of Lake Ellesmere

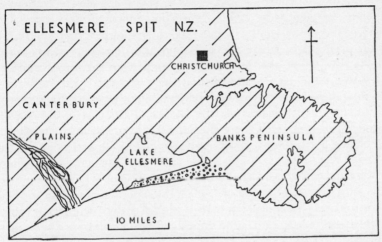

FIG. 12–10. Map of Lake Ellesmere spit, near Christchurch, New Zealand.

and is composed of a mixture of sand and shingle. The latter material,
which forms the north-eastern distal end of the spit, rises to a maximum
height of 30–35 ft. above sea-level in ridges built by storm waves.
Farther south-west, however, sand forms the beach and dunes have
grown to a height of 50 ft. above sea-level.

In areas near large rivers clay may be plentiful and chenier plains may
develop; in these sand barriers are separated by clay strips up to a width
of 10 miles with a longitudinal extent of hundreds of miles along the
coast. The Surinam coast (see pp. 262–263) is a good example of this
type, which is also found in other low-lying river plains.

(c) Modification of the initial coast—youth

The main factor about the initial coast is its low offshore gradient, it
may or may not be straight in outline. The gentle slopes will initiate the
formation of barrier beaches as has been discussed in chapter 10. The

barrier beaches will usually form broad sweeping curves and will eliminate any irregularity of the original coastline in plan. The formation of the barrier, by waves building up their own equilibrium gradient, establishes a coastline, which will be similar, whatever process originally led to the formation of the flat offshore slope. During the stage of youth the barrier beach or island will be separated from the mainland by a lagoon, which will gradually be filled with finer sediment and where conditions are suitable salt marsh will form.

The development of the barrier deepens the water offshore by movement of material landwards, this allows more effective wave action which will tend to drive the barrier towards the shore. This process will be considerably speeded up if the base level is rising slowly as the waves will more frequently be able to wash material over the crest of the barrier. Wind blown sand will also help the landwards movement of the barrier, particularly where the prevalent and dominant winds are onshore. A slow fall of base-level will tend to dry out the lagoon and delay the transfer of the barrier landwards.

In time the sand of the barrier is driven inland over the finer deposits, accumulating in its shelter, in the lagoon. The coast of Lincolnshire illustrates this stage well; here the inland movement of the barrier has been helped by the slow rise of sea-level. The beach and dune sand can be seen to rest on the salt marsh clay and freshwater peat which originally were deposited behind the barrier beach, but which now outcrop on the seaward face of the barrier when the sand is stripped off the beach by storm waves. This development is discussed by Swinnerton (1931)[13] and illustrated in fig. 11–1. The dunes and beach sand have been driven landwards over the lagoonal deposits. The coast of Normandy and Picardy also show this stage of development (Pugh 1953);[14] here peat and clay of earlier marshes form the beach platform which is backed by dunes, this coast is also still retreating.

(d) Maturity

The mature stage of the development of a flat coast is reached when the barrier has been driven inland over the lagoon deposits so far that the lagoon is entirely eliminated and its deposits removed by the waves. At this stage a line of sand dunes, in about the position of the original coast, is likely to be bordered by a beach which is in equilibrium with the waves. These can now approach right to the shore on account of the deepening of the water offshore. As further erosion takes place small cliffs are likely to form, which will gradually increase in height unless the rate of subaerial erosion can keep pace with the retreat of the coast; this is likely to be fairly slow on account of the original flat gradient, which will have been modified near the shore, but fairly shallow water may still extend for some distance offshore if the initial flat slope was an extensive one. This will reduce the energy of the waves reaching the coast and give what Armstrong Price (1954)[15] calls a 'low energy' coast. The formation of barriers and the general smoothing of the coastal outline he considers to be the production of a 'high energy' shore. In the mature stage the outline of the coast will be one of very smooth wide curves.

Summary

The characteristic feature of the early stages of the development of a low coast is the formation of a barrier beach or island. Owing to the low gradient typical of such a beach the true barrier is more often composed of sand. A low coast may be formed in three ways, only one of which is associated with emergence. Waves are the most important modifying process, but the tide is important, in that a small range facilitates the formation of barriers. Wind is important in the development of dunes on the barrier beaches in that it helps to raise their level above the limit of the swash. In maturity the barrier is pushed inland over the marsh deposits, formed in the lagoon behind it, a process which is accelerated by a slowly rising sea-level. A good example of this process is seen on the coast of Lincolnshire. The mature stage of development is characterized by the formation of a line of dunes on the original solid coast and the elimination of the lagoonal area.

3. *THE PENULTIMATE AND ULTIMATE STAGES OF THE CYCLE OF MARINE EROSION*

The problem of the final stage of the cycle of marine erosion is not one that can be answered by reference to any examples from the present-day coastline, because nowhere has sea-level remained stationary for a sufficient length of time for the cycle to run its full course. Johnson (1919)[2] considers that the ultimate stage of the marine cycle has been attained when the land surface is reduced to the level of wave-base or the base-level of wave action. This term was introduced first by Gulliver (1899)[16] and according to Johnson it probably extends to a depth of 600 ft. below sea-level. This view cannot be accepted now, as it seems likely that marine abrasion is limited to a depth of the order of 30 ft. below sea-level (see pp. 292, 293). The ultimate stage is a very long way removed in time and condition from the mature stage already considered, the intermediate stage may be termed the old age or penultimate stage. It is not necessary to consider this stage in plan, as it has been shown that by the time maturity is reached the outline of the coast should be one of simple curves and relative straightness, whatever the initial form of the coast.

During the old age stage of the cycle, according to Johnson, the coastal abrasion platform increases greatly in width and is extended seaward by a wide continental terrace, while on its landward side a low degraded cliff may be found; this feature will become imperceptible in time as the wave energy is almost completely expended in crossing the wide shelf and at the same time subaerial denudation reduces the height of the land to very small proportions. As the land is reduced in height the supply of material to the sea is also reduced to very small amounts of fine debris and the shelf may be almost bare rock in its landward part as the fine material can more easily be carried to the offshore zone in suspension. This will not, however, significantly speed up the erosion of the platform as it has been shown (see p. 293) that material must be larger than about 0·5 mm. diameter before it can cause appreciable erosion.

As examples of very wide wave-cut platforms Johnson suggests the standflat off the west coast of Norway and part of the east coast of India. Neither of these areas, however, show features which correspond with Johnson's theoretical old age stage, when degraded cliffs should be very low inconspicuous features. Cotton (1955)[17] points out that both these cases can be more reasonably explained as the result of quite different denudational processes. The Norwegian strandflat has been discussed in detail by Nansen (1922)[18] and others, the former considers it to be the result of glacial sapping by ice-foot glaciers. The feature is about 30–40 miles wide but it is not smooth and is backed by steeply rising ground, in an area which can be shown to have undergone very considerable vertical movements in the relatively recent geological past. The example from India, which consists of a low lying plain up to 50 miles wide in places, with steep-sided residuals on it, is backed by steep cliffs. Cotton explains this feature as an example of subaerial weathering and erosion under climatic conditions conducive to the formation of inselbergs separated by flat areas. Cotton (1955) discusses part of the Cantabrian coast of Spain as a possible example of the old age stage of the cycle of erosion; this coast has been discussed by Hernandez-Pacheco who considers it to be a one-cycle coast showing a very wide abrasion platform. He assumes that changes of base-level have not been of vital importance in the development of this coast. Cotton points out that there are other possible interpretations, and evidence in favour of variations in sea-level is available.

Cotton reaches the conclusion, which appears quite justified, that the theoretical concept of Johnson (1933)[19] regarding marine planation is not proven. He considers, however, that it remains as a highly probable theory but is not a demonstrated fact. The whole problem of marine planation, in the way that Johnson envisaged, is the problem of the constancy of sea-level. He considered that the ultimate stage could be reached without subsidence of the land, while other workers have suggested that a slowly rising sea-level will greatly assist the completion of the cycle, among these are Davis (1896)[20] and Richthofen (1886),[21] the latter considers a rising base-level essential for planation. Considering the relatively small depth to which waves can abrade rock surfaces, this conclusion seems to be justified. The view that sea-level could remain constant for periods long enough to effect complete marine planation of an area of considerable extent, is difficult to appreciate owing to the fact that the present is still strongly affected by the considerable fluctuations of sea-level resulting from the ice ages of the Pleistocene period. In all the 500 million years since the pre-Cambrian only two relatively short periods of glaciation occurred.

The speed with which land masses may be reduced to peneplanes has been discussed recently by Linton (1957),[22] who suggests that 20–40 million years will allow peneplanation of a continental margin according to the range of initial relief. This erosion will mainly be carried out by subaerial agencies, while the sea is cutting a bench round the edge. An important point to bear in mind is the effect of changing base-level on marine and subaerial denudation respectively; a slight change of base-level of about 10–20 ft. will not have a marked result for a long time on the denudation of the inland area, but a similar fall of base-level on the coast will cause the sea to start afresh on its work of altering the coast-line. This is clearly shown on parts of the west coast of Scotland, where the 25-ft. raised beach is left stranded above the level of the waves which have started anew to cliff the rocks at a lower level. A similar fall in base-level would accelerate the subaerial erosion, except in the rather unusual case when the gradient across the newly exposed land is flatter than that of the lower reaches of the pre-existing river.

The evidence of the great geological transgressions of the past indicate that very extensive areas had been reduced to an almost plane surface and that these are covered by marine sediments. It is likely that the main work of reducing the surface to a peneplane was largely the result of subaerial processes. The fact that the overlying strata are marine in type is not proof that the surface on which they rest is the result of marine planation, but it seems likely that the final trimming of the surface before the deposition of the marine sediments was done by the waves. Evidence for this is shown by the fact that the marine sediments normally rest on the eroded edges of the older rocks, without any sign of subaerial weathering or any intervening subaerial deposits.

The Cretaceous period, as seen in Europe, is one of the great transgressions with marine deposits gradually spreading on to old worn down land masses. That it took many millions of years to complete this transgression is shown by the way the gradually expanding sea spread more and more widely as time went on. It was only the later strata which reached to the maximum extent. The transgression, which spread from restricted Jurassic basins, finally covered nearly all Europe north of the Alpine geosyncline. It would appear that during this long period sea-level must have been rising steadily throughout the time; this would have assisted the waves to trim the underlying rocks over such a wide area.

Erosion along a coast has been shown to depend chiefly on the removal of the eroded material, primarily by longshore movement; when the deposits reach such a thickness that the reduced energy of the waves, coming in over an ever greater width of shallow water, is such that destructive waves can no longer remove all the material, they can then no longer reach the cliffs and erosion will cease. The thickness of material on the abrasion platform need not be very great before the waves fail to disturb it to its base, as was discussed in chapter 4 (see pp. 172–176). The wide abrasion platform and shallow zone offshore also affect the waves in such a way that their height will be reduced to a greater extent as the water becomes shallower; they will become flatter in steepness and will, as a result, tend to become more constructive in character, moving material towards the land and further strengthening the natural coastal defence of a wide high beach.

The work of Valentin (1952)[23] has thrown some doubt on the validity of the concept of the marine cycle of erosion by his emphasis on the variability of sea-level. However, to discard the cyclic idea of coastal development is to loose a valuable tool in the elucidation of coastal change. Even though the latter part of the cycle must remain theoretical and doubtful of possible accomplishment, the earlier stages do provide a frame-work in which coastal studies may be set, on shores of different types, and for which examples may be found on the very varied coasts of the world. The speed with which coastal forms develop in favourable circumstances can illustrate the progress of a marine cycle over a relatively short span of time; measureable changes can be studied over a period of years, while historical and cartographic evidence can extend the study backwards in time to an earlier stage of development. A physiographic study of the features themselves can also provide clues by which their formation can be worked out. This applies to both coastal erosion in areas of fairly non-resistant rock and to features of coastal deposition.

Summary

No old age or ultimate stage of the cycle of marine erosion is in existence on any coast now, owing to the recent large changes of sea-level. The examples cited are not true plains of marine denudation. The great unconformities which underlie some marine transgressions may illustrate the ultimate stage of the cycle; but such features have been largely formed by subaerial erosion, only the final trimming of the surface may be the work of the waves. Extensive plains of marine denudation or even marine trimming cannot be achieved unless sea-level is rising slowly.

REFERENCES

[1]Cotton, C. A., 1954, Deductive morphology and the genetic classification of coasts. *Sci. Month.* **78,** pp. 163–81.

[2]Johnson, D. W., 1919, *Shore processes and shoreline development.*

[3]Davies, G. M., 1935, *The Dorset Coast.*

[4]Ting, S., 1937, Shore forms in south-west Scotland. *Geol. Mag.* **74,** pp. 132–41.

[5]Schou, A., 1945, Det Marine Forland. *Folia Geog. Danica* **4,** pp. 1–236.

[6]Lewis, W. V., 1938, The evolution of shoreline curves. *Proc. Geol. Assoc.* **49,** pp. 107–27.

[7]Ogilvie, A. G., 1914, The physical geography of the entrance to Inverness Firth. *Scot. Geog. Mag.* **30,** pp. 21–35.

[8]Evans, O. F., 1942, The origins of spits, bars and related structures. *Journ. Geol.* **50,** pp. 846–65.

[9]Steers, J. A., 1934, Scolt Head Island. (Ed.)

[10]Steers, J. A., 1946, *The coastline of England and Wales.* Cambridge.

[11]Robinson, A. H. W., 1955, The harbour entrances of Poole, Christchurch and Pagham. *Geog. Journ.* **121,** pp. 33–50.

[12]Speight, R., 1930, Lake Ellesmere Spit. *Trans. N.Z. Roy. Soc.* **61,** pp. 147–69.

[13]Swinnerton, H. H., 1931, The post-glacial deposits of the Lincolnshire coast. *Quart Journ. Geol. Soc.* **87,** pp. 360–75.

[14]Pugh, D. C., 1953, Etudes mineralogiques des plages Picardes et Flamandes. *Bull. d'Inf. Co. Cen. d'Ocean. et d'Etudes des Côtes* **5,** 6.

[15]Armstrong-Price, W., 1954, Dynamic environments. *Trans. Gulf. Coast Assoc. of Geol. Soc.* **4,** pp. 75–107.

[16]Gulliver, F. P., 1899, Shoreline topography. *Proc. Amer. Acad. Arts and Sci.* **34,** p. 189.

[17]Cotton, C. A., 1955, The theory of secular marine planation. *Am. Journ. Sci.* **253,** pp. 580–9.

[18]Nansen, F., 1922, Strandflat and isostasy. *Vidensk Skr. M.N. kl.* **11.**

[19]Johnson, D. W., 1933, Role of analysis in scientific investigations. *Geol. Soc. Am. Bull.* **44,** pp. 461–94.

[20]Davis, W. M., 1896, Plains of marine and subaerial denudation. *Geol. Soc. Amer. Bull.* **7,** pp. 377–98 (also *Geog. Essays*)

[21]Richthofen, F. von, 1886, *Führer für Forschungsreisende.* Hanover.

[22]Linton, D. L., 1957, The everlasting hills. *Adv. of Sci.* **14,** pp. 58–67.

[23]Valentin, H., 1952, Die Küste der Erde. *Petermanns Geog. Mitt. Ergänzungsheft* **246.**

INDEX

All place-names and entries relating to specific places are arranged under the appropriate county in England and elsewhere under the state or country concerned. Authors names are printed in italic.

A

Adams, Robert, 356
Admiralty charts, 268, 357
— Manual of Tides, 24–33
Air-sea temperature, affect on wave height, 85
Airy, G. B., 54, 106, ref 118, 131
Alaska, 308
Alignment of structures, 265
Allen, J., 43, ref 53
Alluvial plain coast, 235, 237
Alpine orogeny, crustal instability, 236
Amphidromic system, 25, 28, 32, 333
Arber, M. A., 310, ref 320
Arlman, J. J., Santema, P., and Svâsek, J. N., ref 177
Armstrong-Price, W., 262, ref 278, 383, ref 387
Arthur, R. S., 95, ref 120
— and Isaacs, 95, 97, ref 120
Association d'Oceanography Physique, ref 319
Atlantic coastal type, 233
Atlantic Ocean, 283
— Bay of Fundy tides, 28
—, North, synoptic chart, 284
— Tides, 28
—, Waves in, 79, 86, 90, 91, 93, 265
Attrition, 288
Australia
— Barriers, 349
— Coastal dunes, 219
— Great Barrier Reef, 235
— New South Wales, rip currents, 114–15
— Victoria, shore platforms, 292
— Western Australia, Bunbury Harbour, 3

B

Baak, J. A., 6, ref 36, 154
Bagnold, R. A., 39, 47, ref 53, 101, 102, 103, ref 120, 128, 130, 137, 163, 171, ref 176, ref 177, 179, ref 206, 221, 222, ref 226, 321, 328, ref 354
Balchin, W. G. V., 361, ref 365
Baltic, 235, 238
— Barriers, 255, 349
— Beach type, 231
— Darss foreland, 378
— Submarine bars, 331, 333
— Tideless character, 333, 352
Barber, N. F., 60, 62, 63, 64, 93, ref 119, ref 120
Barnes, F. A., ref 206, ref 226, 270, ref 278, ref 319, 345, ref 355
Barriers, 50, 236, 238, 239, 242, 255, 256, 277, 347–53, 381, 382, 383
—, Baymouth, 378
—, Looped, 376
Bartrum, J. A., 291, ref 319
— and Turner, F. J., 291, ref 319
Bascom, W. N., 166, 167, ref 178, 321, 322, 330, 336, 350, ref 354
Bay-head barrier, 373
— beach, 261, 373
— delta, 373
Bay-side beach, 373
Beach cycle, 52, 140, 252
Beach definition, 1
Beach drifting, 144, 145, 256
Beach Erosion Board, Washington, 40, ref 53, 141, 142, ref 177, 321, 329, ref 354
Beach material 3–7, 51
— Capillarity, 4
— Cohesion, 4, 7

389